Lecture Notes in Computer Science 13037

More information about this subseries at https://link.springer.com/bookseries/7407

Yo-Sub Han · Sang-Ki Ko (Eds.)

Descriptional Complexity of Formal Systems

23rd IFIP WG 1.02 International Conference, DCFS 2021
Virtual Event, September 5, 2021
Proceedings

Editors
Yo-Sub Han 🆔
Yonsei University
Seoul, Korea (Republic of)

Sang-Ki Ko 🆔
Kangwon National University
Chuncheon, Korea (Republic of)

ISSN 0302-9743 ISSN 1611-3349 (electronic)
Lecture Notes in Computer Science
ISBN 978-3-030-93488-0 ISBN 978-3-030-93489-7 (eBook)
https://doi.org/10.1007/978-3-030-93489-7

LNCS Sublibrary: SL1 – Theoretical Computer Science and General Issues

This Springer imprint is published by the registered company Springer Nature Switzerland AG
The registered company address is: Gewerbestrasse 11, 6330 Cham, Switzerland

Preface

This volume contains the papers accepted to DCFS 2021: 23rd International Conference on Descriptional Complexity of Formal Systems. DCFS 2021 was planned to be held in June 2021 in Seoul, South Korea. Unfortunately, due to the ongoing crisis caused by COVID-19, the DCFS steering committee decided to cancel DCFS 2021 as an in-person meeting and switched to proceedings only.

The DCFS conference series is an international venue for disseminating new results related to all aspects of descriptional complexity—the costs of description of objects in various computational models such as Turing machines, pushdown automata, finite automata, or grammars. The topics of DCFS include, but are not limited to:

- Automata, grammars, languages and other formal systems; various modes of operations and complexity measures.
- Succinctness of description of objects, including state-explosion-like phenomena.
- Circuit complexity of Boolean functions and related measures.
- Size complexity of formal systems.
- Structural complexity of formal systems.
- Trade-offs between computational models and mode of operation.
- Applications of formal systems—for instance in software and hardware testing, in dialogue systems, in systems modeling, or in modeling natural languages—and their complexity constraints.
- Co-operating formal systems.
- Size or structural complexity of formal systems for modeling natural languages.
- Complexity aspects related to the combinatorics of words.
- Descriptional complexity in resource-bounded or structure-bounded environments.
- Structural complexity as related to descriptional complexity.
- Frontiers between decidability and undecidability.
- Universality and reversibility.
- Nature-motivated (bio-inspired) architectures and unconventional models of computing.
- Blum Static (Kolmogorov/Chaitin) complexity and algorithmic information.

DCFS became an IFIP working conference in 2016, continuing the former Workshop on Descriptional Complexity of Formal Systems, which was a merger in 2002 of two other workshops: Formal Descriptions and Software Reliability (FDSR) and Descriptional Complexity of Automata, Grammars and Related Structures (DCAGRS). DCAGRS was previously held in Magdeburg, Germany (1999), London, UK (2000), and Vienna, Austria (2001). FDSR was previously held in Paderborn, Germany (1998), Boca Raton, USA (1999), and San Jose, USA (2000). Since 2002, DCFS has been successively held in London, Ontario, Canada (2002), Budapest, Hungary (2003), London, Ontario, Canada (2004), Como, Italy (2005), Las Cruces, New Mexico, USA (2006), Nový Smokovec, High Tatras, Slovakia (2007), Charlottetown, Prince Edward Island,

Canada (2008), Magdeburg, Germany (2009), Saskatoon, Canada (2010), Gießen, Germany (2011), Braga, Portugal (2012), London, Ontario, Canada (2013), Turku, Finland (2014), Waterloo, Ontario, Canada (2015), Bucharest, Romania (2016), Milan, Italy (2017), Halifax, Nova Scotia, Canada (2018), and Košice, Slovakia (2019).

This year we received a lot of excellent submissions. After strict evaluation and careful discussion, the Program Committee (PC) finally selected 16 papers out of 21 submissions. Each submission was reviewed by at least three PC members, except for one submission which had only two reviews. We thank all authors who submitted their works for consideration in this volume. We also thank the PC members and external reviewers for their help in selecting the papers.

We would furthermore like to thank the editorial staff at Springer for their guidance and help during the process of publishing this volume.

Unfortunately, we could not meet face-to-face this year. Nevertheless we hope that this volume helps the DCFS community and inspires new research and collaborations. We are all looking forward to DCFS 2022 in Debrecen, Hungary!

September 2021   Yo-Sub Han
                                                                   Sang-Ki Ko

Organization

Program Committee

Johanna Björklund	University of Umeå, Sweden
Da-Jung Cho	Ajou University, South Korea
Cezar Câmpeanu	University of Prince Edward Island, Canada
Zoltán Fülöp	University of Szeged, Hungary
Pawel Gawrychowski	University of Wroclaw, Poland
Dora Giammarresi	University of Rome Tor Vergata, Italy
Yo-Sub Han (Chair)	Yonsei University, South Korea
Galina Jirásková	Slovak Academy of Sciences, Slovakia
Christos Kapoutsis	Carnegie Mellon University in Qatar, Qatar
Sang-Ki Ko (Chair)	Kangwon National University, South Korea
Stavros Konstantinidis	Saint Mary's University, Canada
Martin Kutrib	Justus Liebig University, Germany
Ian McQuillan	University of Saskatchewan, Canada
Timothy Ng	University of Chicago, USA
Alexander Okhotin	St. Petersburg State University, Russia
Giovanni Pighizzini	University of Milan, Italy
Daniel Průša	Czech Technical University, Czech Republic
Andrei Păun	University of Bucharest, Romania
Narad Rampersad	University of Winnipeg, Canada
Rogério Reis	University of Porto, Portugal
Michel Rigo	University of Liège, Belgium
Kai Salomaa	Queen's University, Canada
György Vaszil	University of Debrecen, Hungary
Juraj Šebej	Pavol Jozef Šafárik University, Slovakia

Additional Reviewers

Hertling, Peter
Holub, Stepan
Holzer, Markus
Ivan, Szabolcs
Jirasek, Jozef
Kószó, Dávid
Malcher, Andreas
Mereghetti, Carlo
Moreira, Nelma

Moutot, Etienne
Nakanishi, Masaki
Prigioniero, Luca
Rubtsov, Alexander
Shemetova, Ekaterina
Smith, Taylor
Szykuła, Marek
Young, Joshua

Contents

Complexity Issues for the Iterated h-Preorders

Pavel Alaev[1] and Victor Selivanov[2]

[1] S.L. Sobolev Institute of Mathematics SB RAS, Novosibirsk, Russia
alaev@math.nsc.ru
[2] A.P. Ershov Institute of Informatics Systems SB RAS and S.L. Sobolev Institute
of Mathematics SB RAS, Novosibirsk, Russia
vseliv@iis.nsk.su

Abstract. We show that many natural structures related to the so called homomorphic preorder (or h-preorder) on the iterated labeled forests have isomorphic copies computable in polynomial time. Moreover, the polynomials in the upper bounds are of low degree which makes the computational content of the whole theory feasible. We apply these results to relevant questions of automata and computability theory.

Keywords: Preorder · Labeled forest · Iterated h-preorder · Structure · Polynomial-time presentation

1 Introduction

The h-preorder $(\mathcal{F}_k; \leq_h)$ on the finite k-labeled forests (where $2 \leq k \leq \omega$) was introduced in [5] (where notation $\leq_0$ is used instead of $\leq_h$) to characterize a small initial segment of the Wadge degrees of k-partitions of Baire space. Motivated by some applications, the second author of the present paper developed this study in several directions, including the study of arbitrary preorders Q in place of the antichain with k-elements implicitly used in [5], the study of iterated versions of the construction $Q \mapsto \mathcal{F}_Q$, introduction and study of natural operations and relations on the resulting structures, the study of countable well founded forests instead of the finite ones. See recent preprints [8,9] for a systematic account of relevant notions and references to the source papers.

Since applications of the corresponding theory (say, to automata, computability, and fine hierarchies) have a strong algorithmic flavour, the problem of finding feasible presentations of structures arising from the aforementioned study seems natural and even instructive. In [6] it was shown (among other results) that the structure $(\mathcal{F}_k; \leq_h)$ is presentable in polynomial time (P-presentable, for short), and some natural operations on this structure are P-computable.

The work is supported by Mathematical Center in Akademgorodok under agreement No. 075-15-2019-1613 with the Ministry of Science and Higher Education of the Russian Federation.

Y.-S. Han and S.-K. Ko (Eds.): DCFS 2021, LNCS 13037, pp. 1–12, 2021.
https://doi.org/10.1007/978-3-030-93489-7_1

In this paper we develop the technique and extend the results from [6] concerning $\leq_0$ to most of the aforementioned generalizations of the h-preorder. Surprisingly, the upper complexity bounds remain the same (up to multiplicative constants) as in [6]. This concerns, in particular, the iterated h-preorder itself which remains computable in cubic time due to a high uniformity of our algorithms with respect to the chosen coding of trees and forests. Similar low upper bounds are also established for other operations and relations which makes the computational content of the whole theory feasible. We apply these results to some questions of automata and computability theory recently discussed in [8,9]. Some technical details and proofs are omitted because of the space bound.

2   Preliminaries

Here and below we subsequently recall basic notions on trees and forests from [8,9] and describe their codings which develop the coding in [6].

Let ω^* denote the set of words over the alphabet ω, including the empty word ε. A number $i \in \omega$ is identified with the corresponding word from ω^* of length 1. If $x, y \in \omega^*$, then xy denotes the concatenation of x and y, and $x \preccurlyeq y$ denotes that x is a prefix of y. By a *tree* we mean any non-empty initial segment of $(\omega^*, \preccurlyeq)$. If A is a tree and $x \in A$, let $A(x)$ denote the tree $\{y \in \omega^* \mid xy \in A\}$. A tree A is *normal* if, for any $x \in \omega^*$ and $i \in \omega$, $x(i+1) \in A$ implies that $xi \in A$. In this paper we consider only finite normal trees, the set of which is denoted by Tr. If $A \in$ Tr and $x \in A$, then $A(x) \in$ Tr. The *rank* of $A \in$ Tr is the number $h + 1$ where h is the length of a longest word in A.

Let $(Q, \leq)$ be a preorder (usually denoted just by Q). A *Q-labeled tree*, or just a *Q-tree*, is a pair $\mathcal{A} = (A, t)$ where $A \in$ Tr and $t : A \to Q$. Denote by Tr(Q) the set of all Q-trees. If $\mathcal{A} = (A, t)$ is a Q-tree and $x \in A$, let $\mathcal{A}(x)$ denote the Q-tree $(A(x), t_x)$ where $t_x(y) = t(xy)$. The *cardinality* $|\mathcal{A}|$ of a Q-tree $\mathcal{A}$ is the cardinality $|A|$ of A.

We introduce the relation $\leq_h$ on Tr(Q) as follows: $(A, t) \leq_h (B, v)$, if there is a monotone function $f : (A, \preccurlyeq) \to (B, \preccurlyeq)$ such that $t(x) \leq v(f(x))$ for every $x \in A$. This is clearly a preorder on Tr(Q), which is called the *h-preorder*. By $\mathcal{A} \equiv_h \mathcal{B}$ we denote the induced equivalence relation $\mathcal{A} \leq_h \mathcal{B} \wedge \mathcal{B} \leq_h \mathcal{A}$.

A *forest* is an initial segment D of $(\omega^* \setminus \{\varepsilon\}, \preccurlyeq)$, including the empty segment. Clearly, $D \subseteq \omega^* \setminus \{\varepsilon\}$ is a forest iff $D \cup \{\varepsilon\}$ is a tree. The notion of a *normal forest* is similar to that of a normal tree. Let Fr denote the set of all finite normal forests. If D is a forest and $x \in D$ then $D(x) = \{y \in \omega^* \mid xy \in D\}$ is a tree. If $D \in$ Fr and $x \in D$ then $D(x) \in$ Tr. If $D \cap \omega = [0, k-1] = \{i \in \omega \mid 0 \leq i \leq k-1\}$ then we say that the forest D *consists of the trees* $D(0), D(1), \ldots, D(k-1)$.

Similarly we can define the notion of a *Q-forest*: this is a pair $\mathcal{D} = (D, t)$ where $D \in$ Fr and $t : D \to Q$. By Fr(Q) we denote the set of normal Q-forests. The notation $\mathcal{D}(x) = (D(x), t_x)$ is defined just as above. Repeating the definition of $\leq_h$ for trees, we obtain the h-preorder $\leq_h$ on Fr(Q). We again set $|\mathcal{D}| = |D|$.

Let us now define a coding of Q-trees by words. Let Σ be a finite alphabet containing the left bracket (and the right bracket), and let $\Sigma_0 = \Sigma \setminus \{(,)\}$. Let

Σ^* be the set of words over Σ. In this context, we denote the empty word as $\varnothing$. A word a is a *subword* of a word b, if $b = b_1 a b_2$ for some words b_1, b_2. We call a word $a \in \Sigma^*$ *connected*, if $a \neq \varnothing$, the number of entries of the left bracket in a is equal to that of the right bracket, and for any nonempty proper prefix $b \prec a$ the number of left brackets is strictly larger than the number of right brackets.

Lemma 1. a) *Any connected word has the form $a = (b)$, for some $b \in \Sigma^*$;*

b) *every nonempty proper suffix of a connected word has more right brackets than left brackets;*

c) *if a, b are connected words and $a \preccurlyeq b$ then $a = b$;*

d) *any entry of the left bracket in a connected word is the beginning of a connected subword;*

e) *if b_1, b_2 are connected subwords of a connected word b and the first letter of b_1 occurs in b_2, then b_1 is a subword of b_2.*

Suppose that for the preorder Q some injective coding $c : Q \to \Sigma^* \setminus \{\varnothing\}$ is given such that if $q \in Q$ then $c(q) \in \Sigma_0^*$ or $c(q)$ is a connected word. We denote by the same symbol a new coding $c : \mathrm{Tr}(Q) \to \Sigma^*$ defined as follows: if $\mathcal{A} = (A, t) \in \mathrm{Tr}(Q)$ and $A \cap \omega = [0, k-1]$, where $k \geqslant 0$, then $c(\mathcal{A}) = (v u_0 u_1 \dots u_k \,)$, where $v = c(t(\varepsilon))$ and $u_i = c(\mathcal{A}(i))$ for $i < k$. In particular, if $A = \{\varepsilon\}$ then $c(\mathcal{A}) = (v)$. It can be proved that this new coding is injective.

Lemma 2. *Let $\mathcal{A} \in \mathrm{Tr}(Q)$ be a tree with n nodes. Then $c(\mathcal{A})$ is a connected word, and $|c(\mathcal{A})| = 2n + \sum\{|c(t(x))| \mid x \in A\}$.*

The coding of Q-trees is naturally extended to a coding $c' : \mathrm{Fr}(Q) \to \Sigma^*$. Let $\mathcal{D} = (D, t) \in \mathrm{Fr}(Q)$. If D is the empty forest then we set $c'(\mathcal{D}) = \varnothing$ where $\varnothing$ is a special new symbol. Let $D \neq \varnothing$, $D \cap \omega = [0, k-1]$ where $k \geqslant 1$ and the forest $\mathcal{D}$ consists of the trees $\mathcal{D}(0), \dots, \mathcal{D}(k-1)$. We set $c'(\mathcal{D}) = u_0 u_1 \dots u_{k-1}$ where $u_i = c(\mathcal{D}(i))$ for $i < k$. If $\mathcal{D}$ consists of only one tree $\mathcal{D}(0)$ then $c'(\mathcal{D}) = c(\mathcal{D}(0))$.

Let $p \in \omega$, $p \geqslant 2$. We define a function $t_p : \omega^2 \to \omega$ by $t_p(x, y) = x^p y + x y^p$. For $p = 2$ the next lemma was proved in [6].

Lemma 3. *Let $p \geqslant 2$ and $x = x_1 + x_2 + \dots + x_k$ where $k \geqslant 2$ and $x_i \geqslant 1$ for $i \leqslant k$, and $y \geqslant 1$. Then $t_p(x, y) \geqslant t_p(x_1, y) + t_p(x_2, y) + \dots + t_p(x_k, y) + \frac{2}{3}(x + y)$. Since $t_p(x, y) = t_p(y, x)$, a similar inequality holds for the second argument.*

Our basic computational model is a standard multi-tape Turing machine described e.g. in Section 1.6 of [1]. The machine has an input tape for every argument, the output tape for the result, and may have several working tapes. Each tape has a leftmost cell and is infinite to the right.

3 Presenting Q-Trees and Forests

The next theorem was proved in [6] for the particular case when Q is an at most countable antichain and $p = 2$. Although our proof uses a simple recursion on trees, we write it down very carefully because some of its parts are also used in more involved proofs below.

Theorem 1. *Suppose we have a Turing machine T_0 which, starting with input words $c(q)$ and $c(r)$, where $q, r \in Q$, outputs 1 if $q \leqslant r$, and outputs 0 otherwise, and let it make this work in time $O(x^p y + xy^p)$ where $x = |c(q)|$, $y = |c(r)|$, and $p \geqslant 2$. Then there is a Turing machine T which, starting with input words $c(\mathcal{D})$ and $c(\mathcal{E})$, where $\mathcal{D}, \mathcal{E} \in \mathrm{Fr}(Q)$, outputs 1 if $\mathcal{D} \leqslant_h \mathcal{E}$, and outputs 0 otherwise. Furthermore, it makes this work in time $O(x^p y + xy^p)$ where $x = |c(\mathcal{D})|$ and $y = |c(\mathcal{E})|$.*

Proof. Suppose that words $c(\mathcal{D})$ and $c(\mathcal{E})$ are given as input. First we recall an informal algorithm (see e.g. p. 5 of [9]) to check the relation $\mathcal{D} \leqslant_h \mathcal{E}$. If $\mathcal{D} = \varnothing$ then $\mathcal{D} \leqslant_h \mathcal{E}$. If $\mathcal{E} = \varnothing$ then $\mathcal{D} \leqslant_h \mathcal{E} \Leftrightarrow \mathcal{D} = \varnothing$. Further we assume that $\mathcal{D}, \mathcal{E} \neq \varnothing$, $\mathcal{D}$ consists of trees $\mathcal{D}(0), \ldots, \mathcal{D}(k-1)$ and $\mathcal{E}$ consists of trees $\mathcal{E}(0), \ldots, \mathcal{E}(n-1)$ where $k, n \geqslant 1$. Consider the possible cases.

1) $k \geqslant 2$. Then $\mathcal{D} \leqslant_h \mathcal{E} \Leftrightarrow \mathcal{D}' \leqslant_h \mathcal{E}$ and $\mathcal{D}(k-1) \leqslant_h \mathcal{E}$ where $\mathcal{D}'$ consists of the trees $\mathcal{D}(0), \ldots, \mathcal{D}(k-2)$ and $\mathcal{D}(k-1)$ consists of the unique tree $\mathcal{D}(k-1)$.
2) $k = 1$, $n \geqslant 2$. Then $\mathcal{D} \leqslant_h \mathcal{E} \Leftrightarrow \mathcal{D} \leqslant_h \mathcal{E}'$ or $\mathcal{D} \leqslant_h \mathcal{E}(n-1)$ where $\mathcal{E}'$ consists of the trees $\mathcal{E}(0), \ldots, \mathcal{E}(n-2)$.
3) $k = n = 1$. Denote the tree $\mathcal{D}(0)$ by $\mathcal{A} = (A, t)$ and the tree $\mathcal{E}(0)$ by $\mathcal{B} = (B, v)$. Let $A \cap \omega = [0, k^* - 1]$ and $B \cap \omega = [0, n^* - 1]$ where $k^*, n^* \geqslant 0$. Let $\mathcal{A}^*$ denote the forest consisting of trees $\mathcal{A}(0), \ldots, \mathcal{A}(k^* - 1)$ and $\mathcal{B}^*$ denote the forest consisting of trees $\mathcal{B}(0), \ldots, \mathcal{B}(n^* - 1)$. If $t(\varepsilon) \leqslant v(\varepsilon)$ then $\mathcal{D} \leqslant_h \mathcal{E} \Leftrightarrow \mathcal{A}^* \leqslant_h \mathcal{E}$. If $t(\varepsilon) \not\leqslant v(\varepsilon)$, then $\mathcal{D} \leqslant_h \mathcal{E} \Leftrightarrow \mathcal{D} \leqslant_h \mathcal{B}^*$.

To realize this algorithm on a Turing machine with finitely many tapes, we use a stack and assume that the machine T_0 concludes its work with deleting all traces of the auxiliary computations. This may be achieved with multiplying its working time by a fixed constant. The machine T will have three main working tapes and a number of auxiliary ones. The content of any tape is a word $R\mathrm{p}R'$ where RR' are the tape symbols starting from the leftmost cell and p is the tape head observing the first letter of the word R'. The word $R\mathrm{p}$ means that the head observes the first blank cell after R. The three main tapes will be described as a configuration $[R_1\mathrm{p}R_1', R_2\mathrm{p}R_2', R_3\mathrm{p}R_3']$. We add to the alphabet of T_0 and Σ three new separating symbols $\perp, \&, \vee$, and also symbols $0, 1$.

We will use a machine T_1 which is responsible for the main cycle of the informal algorithm. The work of T is simple: starting with input words $c(\mathcal{D})$ and $c(\mathcal{E})$, it creates the initial configuration $[\perp\perp c(\mathcal{D})\mathrm{p}, \perp\perp c(\mathcal{E})\mathrm{p}, \perp\mathrm{p}]$ and starts the machine T_1. After some cycle repetitions, T_1 should stop at configuration of the form $[\perp\mathrm{p}, \perp\mathrm{p}, \perp\beta\mathrm{p}]$ where $\beta \in \{0, 1\}$ and $\beta = 1 \Leftrightarrow \mathcal{D} \leqslant_h \mathcal{E}$. The following four cases may happen during the work of T_1.

    Case 1. T_1 starts with a configuration $[R_1 \perp c(\mathcal{D})\mathrm{p}, R_2 \perp c(\mathcal{E})\mathrm{p}, R_3\mathrm{p}]$, where R_1, R_2, R_3 are arbitrary words. Its goal is to compute $\beta \in \{0, 1\}$ such that $\beta = 1 \Leftrightarrow \mathcal{D} \leqslant_h \mathcal{E}$, arrive at $[R_1\mathrm{p}, R_2\mathrm{p}, R_3\beta\mathrm{p}]$, and restart T_1.

    Case 2. T_1 starts with $[R_1 \perp \mathrm{p}, R_2 \perp \mathrm{p}, R_3 \& \beta_1 \beta_2 \mathrm{p}]$, where $\beta_i \in \{0, 1\}$ for $i \leqslant 2$. It finds $\beta = \beta_1 \& \beta_2$, arrives at $[R_1\mathrm{p}, R_2\mathrm{p}, R_3\beta\mathrm{p}]$, and restarts T_1.

    Case 3. T_1 starts with $[R_1 \perp \mathrm{p}, R_2 \perp \mathrm{p}, R_3 \vee \beta_1 \beta_2 \mathrm{p}]$, where $\beta_i \in \{0, 1\}$ for $i \leqslant 2$. It finds $\beta = \beta_1 \vee \beta_2$, arrives at $[R_1\mathrm{p}, R_2\mathrm{p}, R_3\beta\mathrm{p}]$, and restarts T_1.

Case 4. T_1 starts with $[R_1\perp p, R_2\perp p, R_3\perp\beta p]$, where $\beta \in \{0,1\}$. It arrives at $[R_1 p, R_2 p, R_3 p]$, outputs β as the result of the algorithm, and stops.

The machine's work in cases 2–4 is clear. The heads on the first two tapes move to the left and determine that one of the three cases holds, while the third head moves to the left to determine precisely which of the three cases holds.

Now we describe the work of T_1 in case 1. Let its starting configuration be $[R_1\perp c(\mathcal{D})p, R_2\perp c(\mathcal{E})p, R_3 p]$. Moving the heads to the left, the machine comes to $[R_1 p\perp c(\mathcal{D}), R_2 p\perp c(\mathcal{E}), R_3 p]$ and simultaneously determines whether $\mathcal{D}$ or $\mathcal{E}$ consists of only one tree, or is empty. How to do this, is explained below. Let, as in cases 1)–3) of the informal algorithm, $\mathcal{D}$ consist of k trees and $\mathcal{E}$ consist of n trees. If $\mathcal{D} = \varnothing$ or $\mathcal{E} = \varnothing$, we can immediately go to $[R_1 p, R_2 p, R_3\beta p]$ where β is the correct answer, and start T_1. Let $\mathcal{D}, \mathcal{E} \neq \varnothing$ and consider variants 1)–3).

1) $k \geqslant 2$. T_1 goes to $[R_1\perp\perp c(\mathcal{D}')\perp c(\mathcal{D}(k-1))p, R_2\perp\perp c(\mathcal{E})\perp c(\mathcal{E})p, R_3\ \&\ p]$ and restarts T_1. The forest $\mathcal{D}'$ is described in case 1) of the informal algorithm.
2) $k = 1, n \geqslant 2$. T_1 goes to $[R_1\perp\perp c(\mathcal{D}) \perp c(\mathcal{D})p, R_2\perp\perp c(\mathcal{E}')\perp c(\mathcal{E}(n-1))p, R_3\vee p]$ and restarts T_1.
3) $k = n = 1$. Let $\mathcal{D}(0) = \mathcal{A} = (A, t)$ and $\mathcal{E}(0) = \mathcal{B} = (B, v)$, $q = t(c)$ and $r = v(\varepsilon)$. The machine extracts from $c(\mathcal{D})$ and $c(\mathcal{E})$ the words $c(q)$ and $c(r)$, copies them to the input tapes of T_0 and starts it, thus obtaining $\beta_0 \in \{0,1\}$ such that $\beta_0 = 1 \Leftrightarrow q \leqslant r$. If $\beta_0 = 1$ then the machine goes to the configuration $[R_1\perp c(\mathcal{A}^*)p, R_2\perp c(\mathcal{E})p, R_3 p]$. If $\beta_0 = 0$ then it goes to the configuration $[R_1\perp c(\mathcal{D})p, R_2\perp c(\mathcal{B}^*)p, R_3 p]$. After that it restarts T_1.

Now we describe how to decompose $c(\mathcal{D})$ to its components. The word $c(\mathcal{D})$ has the form $c_1 c_2 \ldots c_k$ where c_i are connected words for $i \leqslant k$. On a separate tape, we organize a counter of the form $10^t p 0^s$ where $t + 1$ is the difference of the numbers of left and right brackets. Moving along c_1, we move the counter tape head to the right on the left bracket and to the left on the right bracket. When it finds 1, the word c_1 is read. Thus, in one run along $c(\mathcal{D})$ we will find the beginnings of all words $c_1, \ldots, c_k$ and the word $c(\mathcal{D}')$ equal to $c_1 c_2 \ldots c_{k-1}$. Note that the connected words may also be recognized by reading them from right to left, because their definition is symmetric. The word $c(\mathcal{A})$ is of the form $(c_1 c_2 \ldots c_{k^*+1})$ where c_1 is a connected word or $c_1 \in \Sigma_0^*$, and c_i are connected words for $2 \leqslant i \leqslant k^* + 1$. Furthermore, $c(\mathcal{A}^*)$ equals $c_2 \ldots c_{k^*+1}$.

Let $t_p(x, y) = x^p y + x y^p$ and let T_0 check the relation $q \leqslant r$ in time $C_0 t_p(x, y)$ where $x = |c(q)|$ and $y = |c(r)|$ and C_0 is a constant not depending on x and y. By induction on $|\mathcal{D}| + |\mathcal{E}|$ we can prove the following.

Lemma 4. *Let T_1 start with a configuration of case 1. Then it really fulfils the prescribed job in time $C_1 t_p(x, y)$ where $x = |c(\mathcal{D})|$, $y = |c(\mathcal{E})|$, and C_1 is a constant not depending on x and y.*

4 Iterated Q-Trees and Forests

Let again $(Q, \leqslant)$ be a fixed preorder and c its injective coding but now we additionally assume that $c : Q \to \Sigma_0^* \setminus \{\varnothing\}$, i.e. $c(q)$ does not contain brackets for every $q \in Q$. Since $(\mathrm{Tr}(Q), \leqslant_h)$ is again a preorder, we may consider the sets $\mathrm{Tr}(\mathrm{Tr}(Q))$, $\mathrm{Tr}(\mathrm{Tr}(\mathrm{Tr}(Q)))$, and so on. Let $\mathrm{Tr}_0(Q) = Q$ and $\mathrm{Tr}_{n+1}(Q) = \mathrm{Tr}(\mathrm{Tr}_n(Q))$ for $n \in \omega$. If the preorder $\leqslant_h$ is already defined on $\mathrm{Tr}_n(Q)$ then we can define $\leqslant_h$ on $\mathrm{Tr}_{n+1}(Q)$ according with the definition from Sect. 2. We will think that $\leqslant_h$ is also defined on $\mathrm{Tr}_0(Q) = Q$ (by identifying it with $\leqslant$).

Now we define a coding $c : \mathrm{Tr}_n(Q) \to \Sigma^*$ by induction on n where for $n = 0$ the coding $c : \mathrm{Tr}_0(Q) \to \Sigma_0^*$ is given above. If $c : \mathrm{Tr}_n(Q) \to \Sigma^*$ is already defined then we define $c : \mathrm{Tr}_{n+1}(Q) \to \Sigma^*$ precisely as it was done in the definition of $c : \mathrm{Tr}(Q) \to \Sigma^*$ in Sect. 2. By induction we easily check the following:

Lemma 5. *If $\mathcal{A} \in \mathrm{Tr}_n(Q)$, $n \in \omega$ then $(^n p$ is a prefix of $c(\mathcal{A})$ where $p \in \Sigma_0$. Thus, n is determined uniquely from $c(\mathcal{A})$.*

For $n \geqslant 1$ let $\mathrm{Fr}_n(Q)$ denote $\mathrm{Fr}(\mathrm{Tr}_{n-1}(Q))$, i.e., the set of finite normal forests the nodes of which are labeled by elements of $\mathrm{Tr}_{n-1}(Q)$. In particular, $\mathrm{Fr}_1(Q) = \mathrm{Fr}(Q)$. The coding above is extended to such forests according to the scheme of Sect. 2. Let $\mathcal{D} = (D, t) \in \mathrm{Fr}_n(Q)$. If D is the empty forest then $c(\mathcal{D}) = \varnothing$. If $D \neq \varnothing$ then $D \cap \omega = [0, k-1]$ where $k \geqslant 1$. The forest $\mathcal{D}$ consists of the trees $\mathcal{D}(0), \ldots, \mathcal{D}(k-1)$, and we set $c(\mathcal{D}) = u_0 u_1 \ldots u_{k-1}$ where $u_i = c(\mathcal{D}(i))$ for $i < k$. In a series of papers (see e.g. [9]) the second author considered this construction for $Q = \{0, 1, \ldots, k-1\}$ or $Q = \omega$. In the first case we set $\Sigma_0 = Q$ and $c(q) = q$ for $q \in Q$. In the second case we set $\Sigma_0 = \{0, 1\}$, and let $c(q)$ be the binary expansion of $q \in \omega$. In both cases, the preorder $q \leqslant r$ on Q is the equality relation $q = r$. Clearly, in both cases the relation $q \leqslant r$ is checked in linear time from given codes $c(q), c(r)$. By Theorem 1, for any $n \geqslant 1$ the relation $\mathcal{D} \leqslant_h \mathcal{E}$ on $\mathrm{Fr}_n(Q)$ may be checked from given $c(\mathcal{D}), c(\mathcal{E})$ in time $Ct_2(x, y)$ where $x = |c(\mathcal{D})|$ and $y = |c(\mathcal{E})|$. However, the constant C may increase if n increases. Also, the number of tapes of the recognizing Turing machines increases.

In this section we show that there is a polynomial time algorithm which computes $\leqslant_h$ simultaneously for all n. The algorithm is based on the fact that for distinct n the relation $\leqslant_h$ and the codings on $\mathrm{Fr}_n(Q)$ are defined in the same way, hence we can use a uniform recursion.

Theorem 2. *Suppose that there is a Turing machine T_0 which, for given inputs $c(q)$ and $c(r)$ where $q, r \in Q$, outputs 1 if $q \leqslant r$, and outputs 0 otherwise. Let this take time $O(x^p y + xy^p)$ where $x = |c(q)|$, $y = |c(r)|$, and $p \geqslant 2$. Then there is a Turing machine T which, for given inputs $c(\mathcal{D})$ and $c(\mathcal{E})$ such that $\mathcal{D}, \mathcal{E} \in \mathrm{Fr}_m(Q)$ for some $m \geqslant 1$, outputs 1 if $\mathcal{D} \leqslant_h \mathcal{E}$, and outputs 0 otherwise. Its working time is also estimated as $C(x^p y + xy^p)$ where $x = |c(\mathcal{D})|$ and $y = |c(\mathcal{E})|$ and the constant C does not depend on m, x and y.*

Proof. We use the machines T and T_1 from the proof of Theorem 1 and discuss modifications for the case 1. If $k \geqslant 2$ or $n \geqslant 2$, the scheme remains unchanged. Let $k = n = 1$, $\mathcal{A} = (A, t)$, $\mathcal{B} = (B, v)$, $q = t(\varepsilon)$, and $r = v(\varepsilon)$. If $q, r \in Q$, i.e. $m = 1$, then the relation $q \leqslant r$ is checked using the machine T_0. If $m > 1$ and $q, r \in \mathrm{Tr}_{m-1}(Q)$ then we make a recursive call of the same machine T_1 on words

$c(q)$ and $c(r)$. Now two kinds of recursion appear (on the number of nodes in the forests, and on m) which complicate stack manipulations. We modify the work of T_1 by adding a new case $1'$ to the case 1, a new separator symbol $*$ to the alphabet, and a new case 5.

Case $1'$. T_1 starts with $[R_1 \perp c(\mathcal{A})p, R_2 \perp c(\mathcal{B})p, R_3 p \beta_0]$, where $\beta_0 \in \{0,1\}$, $\mathcal{A} = (A,t)$, $\mathcal{B} = (B,v) \in \mathrm{Tr}_m(Q)$, $m \geqslant 1$. Let $q = t(\varepsilon)$ and $r = v(\varepsilon)$. T_1 assumes that β_0 satisfies $\beta_0 = 1 \Leftrightarrow q \leqslant_h r$. Based on this, it determines $\beta \in \{0,1\}$ such that $\beta = 1 \Leftrightarrow \mathcal{A} \leqslant_h \mathcal{B}$, goes to $[R_1 p, R_2 p, R_3 \beta p]$, and restarts T_1.

Case 5. T_1 starts with $[R_1 * p, R_2 * p, R_3 \beta p]$ where $\beta \in \{0,1\}$. It goes to the configuration $[R_1 p, R_2 p, R_3 p \beta]$ and restarts T_1.

Case 5 needs no comment, so we only describe modifications for the case 1. The algorithms for variants 1) and 2) remain unchanged. Consider the variant 3). Let $\mathcal{D}(0) = \mathcal{A} = (A,t)$, $\mathcal{E}(0) = \mathcal{B} = (B,v)$, and $q = t(\varepsilon)$, $r = v(\varepsilon)$. We extract from the input data the words $c(q)$ and $c(r)$. If they are in Σ_0^*, i.e. $m = 1$, then T_1 works just as in Theorem 1: it starts T_0, finds β_0 such that $\beta_0 = 1 \Leftrightarrow q \leqslant r$, and proceeds as in Theorem 1.

Let $c(q), c(r) \notin \Sigma_0^*$, i.e. $m > 1$. Then T_1 goes to $[R_1 \perp c(\mathcal{A}) * \perp c(q)p, R_2 \perp c(\mathcal{B}) * \perp c(r)p, R_3 p]$ and restarts T_1. Further steps lead to case $1'$.

The work of T_1 in case $1'$ is the same as the work of T_1 in the proof of Theorem 1 in case 1 and variant 3), with the only exception that now there is no need to bother about computing β_0, which is given as parameter; we only have to delete it from the third tape. As in the proof of Theorem 1, T_1 starts with $[\perp\perp c(\mathcal{D})p, \perp\perp c(\mathcal{E})p, \perp p]$. Let $t_p(x,y) = x^p y + xy^p$. By induction on $|c(\mathcal{D})| + |c(\mathcal{E})|$ we prove a lemma which completes the proof of the theorem:

Lemma 6. *Let $\mathcal{D}, \mathcal{E} \in \mathrm{Fr}_m(Q)$ where $m \geqslant 1$, and let T_1 start working from the configuration specified in case 1. Then it really behaves as described in this case, and its working time is bounded by $C_1 t_p(x,y)$, where $x = |c(\mathcal{D})|$, $y = |c(\mathcal{E})|$, and C_1 is a constant not depending on m, x, and y.*

In particular, the theorem tells us that for simple preorders Q (like the countable antichains) the testing of $\mathcal{D} \leqslant_h \mathcal{E}$ is doable in cubic time.

Lemma 7. *Let $n \geqslant 1$. A word $u \in \Sigma^*$ equals to $c(\mathcal{A})$ for some $\mathcal{A} \in \mathrm{Tr}_n(Q)$ iff it starts with a prefix $(^n p$ where $p \in \Sigma_0$, and the following conditions hold:*

a) u is a connected word;

b) if u' is a connected subword of u with prefix $(^k p$, where $k \geqslant 1$ and $p \in \Sigma_0$, then it has the form $u' = (v_0 u_1 u_2 \ldots u_s)$ where v_0 is either a connected word or $v_0 = c(q)$, $q \in Q$, $s \geqslant 0$, and every u_i, $i \leqslant s$ is a connected word starting with $(^k p_i$, where $p_i \in \Sigma_0$.

By induction one can also show that a word $c(\mathcal{A})$, where $\mathcal{A} \in \mathrm{Tr}_n(Q)$, does not contain subwords $(^k$ for $k > n$. We denote $\{c(q) \mid q \in Q\}$ by $c(Q)$, $\{c(\mathcal{A}) \mid \mathcal{A} \in \bigcup_{n \geqslant 1} \mathrm{Tr}_n(Q)\}$ by T_ω, and $\{c(\mathcal{D}) \mid \mathcal{D} \in \bigcup_{n \geqslant 1} \mathrm{Fr}_n(Q)\}$ by F_ω.

Proposition 1. *If the set $c(Q)$ is computable in time $O(x^p)$, where x is the length of a non-empty input word and $p \geqslant 2$, then the sets T_ω and F_ω are also computable in time $O(x^p)$.*

5   Operations on Trees and Forests

Here we discuss some operations on trees and forests from [8,9]. The simplest operation is disjoint union of two forests $\mathcal{D} \sqcup \mathcal{E}$. If $\mathcal{D} \in \mathrm{Fr}_m(Q)$ consists of trees $\mathcal{D}(0), \ldots, \mathcal{D}(k-1)$, and $\mathcal{E} \in \mathrm{Fr}_m(Q)$ consists of trees $\mathcal{E}(0), \ldots, \mathcal{E}(n-1)$ then the forest $\mathcal{D} \sqcup \mathcal{E}$ consists of trees $\mathcal{D}(0), \ldots, \mathcal{D}(k-1), \mathcal{E}(0), \ldots, \mathcal{E}(n-1)$. Consequently, $c(\mathcal{D} \sqcup \mathcal{E}) = uv$, where $u = c(\mathcal{D})$ and $v = c(\mathcal{E})$. If $\mathcal{D} = \varnothing$ then $\mathcal{D} \sqcup \mathcal{E} = \mathcal{E}$, and if $\mathcal{E} = \varnothing$ then $\mathcal{D} \sqcup \mathcal{E} = \mathcal{D}$.

A more complex operation is multiplication of two forests. A *leaf* of a forest D is a node $x \in D$ such that $xi \notin D$ for $i \in \omega$. Let $\mathcal{D}, \mathcal{E} \in \mathrm{Fr}_m(Q)$. Then $\mathcal{D} \cdot \mathcal{E}$ is the forest obtained by adjoining a copy of $\mathcal{E}$ to every leaf of $\mathcal{D}$. More formal definition may be given by induction on the number of trees in $\mathcal{D}$, and for a forest with only one tree, by induction on the number of nodes.

Proposition 2. *There is a Turing machine which, starting with input words* $c(\mathcal{D})$ *and* $c(\mathcal{E})$*, where* $\mathcal{D}, \mathcal{E} \in \mathrm{Fr}_m(Q)$ *for some* $m \geqslant 1$*, outputs the word* $c(\mathcal{D} \cdot \mathcal{E})$ *in time* Cxy*, where* $x = |c(\mathcal{D})|$*,* $y = |c(\mathcal{E})|$*, and the constant* C *does not depend on* $m, x,$ *and* y*.*

Another useful operation is the operation $s : \mathrm{Tr}_n(Q) \to \mathrm{Tr}_{n+1}(Q)$ for every $n \geqslant 0$. It sends any $q \in Q$ or $\mathcal{A} \in \mathrm{Tr}_n(Q)$ to the singleton tree $(\{\varepsilon\}, t)$, where $t(\varepsilon) = q$ or $t(\varepsilon) = \mathcal{A}$. In terms of codes this means the conversion of a word $u = c(\mathcal{A})$ to the word (u). Clearly, $\mathcal{A} \leqslant_h \mathcal{B} \Leftrightarrow s(\mathcal{A}) \leqslant_h s(\mathcal{B})$, i.e. s is an isomorphic embedding of $(\mathrm{Tr}_n(Q), \leqslant_h)$ into $(\mathrm{Tr}_{n+1}(Q), \leqslant_h)$. This operation may be extended to the operation $s : \mathrm{Fr}_n(Q) \to \mathrm{Fr}_{n+1}(Q)$ for $n \geqslant 1$: if a forest $\mathcal{D}$ consists of trees $\mathcal{A}_1, \ldots, \mathcal{A}_k$, then $s(\mathcal{D})$ consists of trees $s(\mathcal{A}_1), \ldots, s(\mathcal{A}_k)$. If $c(\mathcal{D}) = u_1 u_2 \ldots u_k$, where u_i are connected words for $i \leqslant k$, then $c(s(\mathcal{D})) = (u_1)(u_2) \ldots (u_k)$. This operation is computed in linear time.

We also recall the operation $r : \mathrm{Fr}_{n+1}(Q) \to \mathrm{Fr}_n(Q)$, $n \geqslant 1$, which is in a sense converse to s: if $\mathcal{D} = (D, t) \in \mathrm{Fr}_{n+1}(Q)$ then $r(\mathcal{D}) \in \mathrm{Fr}_n(Q)$ is a forest consisting of the trees in $\{t(x) \mid x \in D\}$. To get also an order of these trees, we define $r(\mathcal{D})$ inductively. First define $r(\mathcal{A})$ for a tree $\mathcal{A} \in \mathrm{Tr}_{n+1}(Q)$ as follows:

1) if $\mathcal{A} = (\{\varepsilon\}, t)$ then $r(\mathcal{A})$ is the forest consisting of only one tree $t(\varepsilon)$;

2) if $\mathcal{A} = (A, t)$ and $A \cap \omega = [0, k-1]$, where $k \geqslant 1$, then $r(\mathcal{A})$ equals $\{t(\varepsilon)\} \sqcup r(\mathcal{A}(0)) \sqcup \ldots \sqcup r(\mathcal{A}(k-1))$.

If a forest $\mathcal{D} \in \mathrm{Fr}_{n+1}(Q)$ consists of trees $\mathcal{A}_0, \ldots, \mathcal{A}_{s-1}$, we define $r(\mathcal{D}) = r(\mathcal{A}_0) \sqcup r(\mathcal{A}_1) \sqcup \ldots \sqcup r(\mathcal{A}_{s-1})$.

Proposition 3. *There is a Turing machine which, starting with an input word* $c(\mathcal{D})$*, where* $\mathcal{D} \in \mathrm{Fr}_{m+1}(Q)$ *for some* $m \geqslant 1$*, outputs the word* $c(r(\mathcal{D}))$ *in time* Cx*, where* $x = |c(\mathcal{D})|$ *and* C *is a constant not depending on* m *and* x*.*

We can similarly extend the proof of Theorem 11 in [6] to show that with the same complexity one can compute a forest of minimal cardinality h-equivalent to a given forest from $\mathrm{Fr}_m(Q)$ (see Proposition 2 in [9] for details.)

Proposition 4. *There is a Turing machine which, starting with an input word* $c(\mathcal{D})$*, where* $\mathcal{D} \in \mathrm{Fr}_m(Q)$ *for some* $m \geqslant 1$*, outputs a word* $c(\mathcal{E})$ *in time* Cx^3*,* *where $x = |c(\mathcal{D})|$, C is a constant not depending on m and x, and $\mathcal{E} \in \mathrm{Fr}_m(Q)$ is a forest of minimal cardinality h-equivalent to $\mathcal{D}$.*

6   The Union of Iterated Trees and Forests

Let again $(Q, \leqslant)$ be a fixed preorder. Above we have defined the sequence of pre-orders $\{(\mathrm{Tr}_n(Q), \leqslant_h)\}_{n \in \omega}$. Now we define embeddings $g_n : \mathrm{Tr}_n(Q) \to \mathrm{Tr}_{n+1}(Q)$. If $n = 0$ and $q \in \mathrm{Tr}_0(Q) = Q$ then $g_0(q) = s(q) = (\{\varepsilon\}, t)$, where $t(\varepsilon) = q$. Suppose that g_n is already defined and $\mathcal{A} \in \mathrm{Tr}_{n+1}(Q)$. If $\mathcal{A} = (A, t)$, let $g_{n+1}(\mathcal{A}) = (A, g_n \circ t)$. By induction on $n \geqslant 0$ it is easy to show that $g_n : \mathrm{Tr}_n(Q) \to \mathrm{Tr}_{n+1}(Q)$ is injective and $\mathcal{A} \leqslant_h \mathcal{B} \Leftrightarrow g_n(\mathcal{A}) \leqslant_h g_n(\mathcal{B})$ for all $\mathcal{A}, \mathcal{B} \in \mathrm{Tr}_n(Q)$. This means that g_n is an isomorphic embedding of $(\mathrm{Tr}_n(Q), \leqslant_h)$ into $(\mathrm{Tr}_{n+1}(Q), \leqslant_h)$. Denote by $(\mathrm{Tr}_\omega(Q), \leqslant_h)$ the colimit (known also as direct limit) of the sequence $\{\mathrm{Tr}_n(Q), g_n\}_{n \in \omega}$ described in [9]. There are standard embeddings $g'_n : \mathrm{Tr}_n(Q) \to \mathrm{Tr}_\omega(Q)$ such that $g'_{n+1} = g_n \circ g'_n$ and $\bigcup_{n \geqslant 0} \mathrm{ran}(g'_n) = \mathrm{Tr}_\omega(Q)$. In the same way we can define embeddings $g_n : \mathrm{Fr}_n(Q) \to \mathrm{Fr}_{n+1}(Q)$ for $n \geqslant 1$, using the formula $g_{n+1}(\mathcal{D}) = (D, g_n \circ t)$, where $\mathcal{D} = (D, t)$. We get that g_n is an embedding of $(\mathrm{Fr}_n(Q), \leqslant_h)$ into $(\mathrm{Fr}_{n+1}(Q), \leqslant_h)$, and we can define $(\mathrm{Fr}_\omega(Q), \leqslant_h)$ as the colimit of the sequence $\{\mathrm{Fr}_n(Q), g_n\}_{n \geqslant 1}$. Again, there are standard embeddings $g'_n : \mathrm{Fr}_n(Q) \to \mathrm{Fr}_\omega(Q)$ such that $g'_{n+1} = g_n \circ g'_n$ and $\bigcup_{n \geqslant 1} \mathrm{ran}(g'_n) = \mathrm{Fr}_\omega(Q)$.

We now define codings for the colimit structures. Since elements of $\mathrm{Tr}_0(Q)$ are not trees and our codings above are adjusted to trees, we exclude these elements from our considerations since $\mathrm{Tr}_\omega(Q)$ may be defined without them. Recall that for the construction of $\mathrm{Tr}_\omega(Q)$ we introduce on $\bigcup_{n \geqslant 1} \mathrm{Tr}_n(Q)$ the following equivalence relation: if $\mathcal{A} \in \mathrm{Tr}_k(Q)$ and $\mathcal{B} \in \mathrm{Tr}_n(Q)$, where $k \leqslant n$, then $\mathcal{A} \equiv \mathcal{B} \Leftrightarrow g_{k,n}(\mathcal{A}) = \mathcal{B}$, where $g_{k,n} = g_{n-1} \circ \ldots \circ g_{k+1} \circ g_k$, and $g_{k,k} = \mathrm{id}_{\mathrm{Tr}_k(Q)}$. The equivalence classes are the elements of the colimit. Note that in any equivalence class we can choose a canonical representative. Call a tree $\mathcal{A} \in \mathrm{Tr}_n(Q)$ *basic*, if $n = 1$ or $n \geqslant 2$ and $\mathcal{A}$ cannot be represented as $g_{n-1}(\mathcal{A}_0)$ for some $\mathcal{A}_0 \in \mathrm{Tr}_{n-1}(Q)$. Then the elements of $\mathrm{Tr}_\omega(Q)$ may be identified with the basic trees, so we think that $\mathrm{Tr}_\omega(Q) = \{\mathcal{A} \in \bigcup_{n \geqslant 1} \mathrm{Tr}_n(Q) \mid \mathcal{A} \text{ is a basic tree}\}$.

If $\mathcal{A} \in \mathrm{Tr}_n(Q)$ then there is a unique pair $(\mathcal{A}_0, k)$ such that $k \leqslant n$, $\mathcal{A}_0 \in \mathrm{Tr}_k(Q)$ is a basic tree, and $g_{k,n}(\mathcal{A}_0) = \mathcal{A}$. We denote $\mathcal{A}_0$ as $\lambda(\mathcal{A})$. Similarly we define the notion of a *basic forest* $\mathcal{D} \in \mathrm{Fr}_n(Q)$: $n = 1$ or $n \geqslant 2$ and $\mathcal{D}$ cannot be represented as $g_{n-1}(\mathcal{D}_0)$ for some $\mathcal{D}_0 \in \mathrm{Fr}_{n-1}(Q)$. The elements of $\mathrm{Fr}_\omega(Q)$ may be identified with the basic forests and we can think that $\mathrm{Fr}_\omega(Q) = \{\mathcal{D} \in \bigcup_{n \geqslant 1} \mathrm{Fr}_n(Q) \mid \mathcal{D} \text{ is a basic forest}\}$. The forest $\lambda(\mathcal{D}) \in \mathrm{Fr}_\omega(Q)$ is defined similarly.

Lemma 8. a) *There is a Turing machine which, starting with input words $c(\mathcal{A})$ and 1^y, where $\mathcal{A} \in \mathrm{Tr}_n(Q)$ and $y \geqslant 0$, outputs the word $c(g_{n,n+y}(\mathcal{A}))$ in time Cxy, where $x = |c(\mathcal{A})|$ and C is a constant not depending on n and x; furthermore, $|c(g_{n,n+y}(\mathcal{A}))| \leqslant 2xy$;*

b) *The same holds, if we replace $\mathcal{A} \in \mathrm{Tr}_n(Q)$ by $\mathcal{A} \in \mathrm{Fr}_n(Q)$.*

Let $c(\mathrm{Tr}_\omega(Q)) = \{c(\mathcal{A}) \mid \mathcal{A} \in \mathrm{Tr}_\omega(Q)\}$ and $c(\mathrm{Fr}_\omega(Q)) = \{c(\mathcal{D}) \mid \mathcal{D} \in \mathrm{Fr}_\omega(Q)\}$.

Proposition 5. a) *Suppose that the set* $c(Q)$ *is computable in time* $O(x^p)$, *where* $p \geqslant 2$. *Then the sets* $c(\mathrm{Tr}_\omega(Q))$ *and* $c(\mathrm{Fr}_\omega(Q))$ *are also computable in time* $O(x^p)$;

b) *The functions* $c(\mathcal{A}) \mapsto c(\lambda(\mathcal{A}))$, $\mathcal{A} \in \bigcup_{n \geqslant 1} \mathrm{Tr}_n(Q)$, *and* $c(\mathcal{D}) \mapsto c(\lambda(\mathcal{D}))$, $\mathcal{D} \in \bigcup_{n \geqslant 1} \mathrm{Fr}_n(Q)$, *are computable in time* $O(x)$, *where* $x = |c(\mathcal{A})|$ *or* $x = |c(\mathcal{D})|$, *respectively.*

Since every $(\mathrm{Fr}_n(Q), \leqslant_h)$ embeds in the colimit $(\mathrm{Fr}_\omega(Q), \leqslant_h)$, we can define the relation $\leqslant_h$ on the whole $\bigcup_{n \geqslant 1} \mathrm{Fr}_n(Q)$: if $\mathcal{D} \in \mathrm{Fr}_n(Q)$ and $\mathcal{E} \in \mathrm{Fr}_k(Q)$ then $\mathcal{D} \leqslant_h \mathcal{E} \Leftrightarrow g_{n,k}(\mathcal{D}) \leqslant_h \mathcal{E}$ for $n \leqslant k$, and $\mathcal{D} \leqslant_h \mathcal{E} \Leftrightarrow \mathcal{D} \leqslant_h g_{k,n}(\mathcal{E})$ for $n \geqslant k$. The same applies to other operations introduced above on $\mathrm{Fr}_n(Q)$: they "commute" with the embedding g_n and hence may naturally be transferred to $\mathrm{Fr}_\omega(Q)$. For instance, if $\mathcal{D}, \mathcal{E} \in \mathrm{Fr}_n(Q)$, $n \geqslant 1$ then $g_n(\mathcal{D} \cdot \mathcal{E}) = g_n(\mathcal{D}) \cdot g_n(\mathcal{E})$. This enables to define the operation $\cdot$ on $\mathrm{Fr}_\omega(Q)$ by the following formula: if $\mathcal{D} \in \mathrm{Fr}_n(Q)$ and $\mathcal{E} \in \mathrm{Fr}_k(Q)$, then $\mathcal{D} \cdot \mathcal{E} = \lambda(g_{n,m}(\mathcal{D}) \cdot g_{k,m}(\mathcal{E}))$, where $m = \max\{n, k\}$. This precisely corresponds to the definition of the colimit of the sequence $\{(\mathrm{Fr}_n(Q), \cdot), g_n\}_{n \in \omega}$. Observe that we can remove λ from the formula because if $\mathcal{D}, \mathcal{E}$ are basic forests, then the forest $g_{n,m}(\mathcal{D}) \cdot g_{k,m}(\mathcal{E})$ is also basic.

If $\mathcal{D}, \mathcal{E} \in \mathrm{Fr}_n(Q)$, $n \geqslant 1$ then $g_n(\mathcal{D} \sqcup \mathcal{E}) = g_n(\mathcal{D}) \sqcup g_n(\mathcal{E})$. The operation $\sqcup$ is transferred to $\mathrm{Fr}_\omega(Q)$ just as above.

Denote the operation s on $\mathrm{Fr}_n(Q)$ by $s_n : \mathrm{Fr}_n(Q) \to \mathrm{Fr}_{n+1}(Q)$. If $\mathcal{A} \in \mathrm{Tr}_n(Q)$, $n \geqslant 1$ then $s_{n+1}(g_n(\mathcal{A})) = g_{n+1}(s_n(\mathcal{A}))$. Thus, if $\mathcal{D} \in \mathrm{Fr}_n(Q)$, then $s_{n+1}(g_n(\mathcal{D})) = g_{n+1}(s_n(\mathcal{D}))$. This enables to define the operation s on $\mathrm{Fr}_\omega(Q)$ by the formula: if $\mathcal{D} \in \mathrm{Fr}_n(Q)$ then $s(\mathcal{D}) = \lambda(s_n(\mathcal{D}))$.

Denote the operation r on $\mathrm{Fr}_n(Q)$ as $r_n : \mathrm{Fr}_n(Q) \to \mathrm{Fr}_{n-1}(Q)$ for $n \geqslant 2$. If $\mathcal{D} \in \mathrm{Fr}_n(Q)$, $n \geqslant 2$ then $g_{n-1}(r_n(\mathcal{D})) = r_{n+1}(g_n(\mathcal{D}))$. It enables to define the operation r on $\mathrm{Fr}_\omega(Q)$ by the formula: if $\mathcal{D} \in \mathrm{Fr}_n(Q)$, $n \geqslant 2$ then $r(\mathcal{D}) = \lambda(r_n(\mathcal{D}))$. It is not hard to check that if $\mathcal{D}$ is a basic forest then so is also $r_n(\mathcal{D})$. Thus, the formula may be simplified to $r(\mathcal{D}) = r_n(\mathcal{D})$.

Suppose that $\mathcal{D} = (D, t) \in \mathrm{Fr}_1(Q)$. To preserve the consistency with the embeddings g_n, we set $r(\mathcal{D}) = r_2(g_1(\mathcal{D}))$, i.e., $r(\mathcal{D}) = \bigsqcup_{x \in D}\{s(t(x))\}$.

As a result, we obtain the structure $\mathcal{F}_\omega(Q) = (\mathrm{Fr}_\omega(Q), \leqslant_h, \sqcup, \cdot, s, r)$. The coding $c : \mathrm{Fr}_\omega(Q) \to \Sigma^*$ is a bijection between $\mathrm{Fr}_\omega(Q)$ and $c(\mathrm{Fr}_\omega(Q))$. Transferring the relations and operations from $\mathcal{F}_\omega(Q)$ to $c(\mathrm{Fr}_\omega(Q))$, we obtain the structure $c(\mathcal{F}_\omega(Q))$ with the universe $c(\mathrm{Fr}_\omega(Q))$ and the isomorphism $c : \mathcal{F}_\omega(Q) \to c(\mathcal{F}_\omega(Q))$. We are interested in the algorithmic properties of the latter structure.

Let $\mathcal{S} = (S, L^\mathcal{S})$ be an arbitrary structure of a finite signature L, where $S \subseteq \Sigma^* \setminus \{\varnothing\}$. We say that $\mathcal{S}$ is a structure *computable in time* $O(x^p)$, where $p \in \omega$, if the universe S and all operations and relations from $L^\mathcal{S}$ are computable on some Turing machines in time $O(x^p)$, where x is the maximum length of the arguments of an operation or relation. We say that $\mathcal{S}$ is *P-computable* [4] if it is computable in time $O(x^p)$ for some $p \in \omega$.

Several facts on the computation complexity in $c(\mathcal{F}_\omega(Q))$ were already established above. Let $\mathcal{D} \in \mathrm{Fr}_k(Q)$, $\mathcal{E} \in \mathrm{Fr}_n(Q)$ be basic forests, $k < n$, $\bar{\mathcal{D}} = g_{k,n}(\mathcal{D})$, $x = |c(\mathcal{D})|$, and $y = |c(\mathcal{E})|$. Then $n - k \leqslant n \leqslant y$ and, by Lemma 8 $|c(\bar{\mathcal{D}})| \leqslant 2xy$. Using Theorem 2, we obtain that, for a sufficiently simple preorder Q, the relation $\mathcal{D} \leqslant_h \mathcal{E}$ may be computed in time $O(x^2 y^3)$, i.e. in time $O(\max\{x, y\}^5)$. This estimate may be improved by modifying the proof of Theorem 1.

Corollary 1. *Suppose that there is a Turing machine T_0 which, starting with input words $c(q)$ and $c(r)$, where $q, r \in Q$, outputs 1 if $q \leqslant r$, and outputs 0 otherwise. Let it does this in time $O(x^p y + x y^p)$ where $x = |c(q)|$, $y = |c(r)|$, and $p \geqslant 2$. Then there is a Turing machine T, which, starting with input words $c(\mathcal{D})$ and $c(\mathcal{E})$, where $\mathcal{D} \in \mathrm{Fr}_m(Q)$ and $\mathcal{E} \in \mathrm{Fr}_l(Q)$ for some $m, l \geqslant 1$, outputs 1 if $\mathcal{D} \leqslant_h \mathcal{E}$, and outputs 0 otherwise. It also works in time $C(x^p y + x y^p)$, where $x = |c(\mathcal{D})|$, $y = |c(\mathcal{E})|$, and C is a constant not depending on m, l, x, y.*

Since $c : Q \to c(Q)$ is a bijection, we can transfer the preorder $\leqslant$ from Q to $c(Q)$ and get a structure $(c(Q), \leqslant)$ isomorphic to $(Q, \leqslant)$.

Theorem 3. *Suppose that the structure $(c(Q), \leqslant)$ is computable in time $O(x^p)$ where $p \geqslant 2$. Then the structure $c(\mathcal{F}_\omega(Q)) = (c(\mathrm{Fr}_\omega(Q)), \leqslant_h, \sqcup, \cdot, s, r)$ is computable in time $O(x^{p+1})$.*

7 Two Applications

Here we deduce two corollaries of the results above for automata theory and computability theory.

For any integer $k \geq 2$, let $\mathcal{R}_k$ (resp. $\mathcal{A}_k$) be the set of regular (regular aperiodic) k-partitions of the set X^ω of infinite words over a finite alphabet X with at least two symbols. A partition is regular (regular aperiodic) if every its component is a regular (regular aperiodic) ω-language. For k-partitions $A, B : X^\omega \to \{0, \ldots, k-1\} = \bar{k}$, let $A \leq_W B$ mean that $A = B \circ f$ for some continuous function f on X^ω. Continuing a series of previous results, the second author characterized the quotient-posets of $(\mathcal{R}_k; \leq_W)$ and of $(\mathcal{A}_k; \leq_W)$ by showing them to be isomorphic to the quotient-poset of $(\mathrm{Fr}_2(\bar{k}); \leq_h)$ [7,8]. Moreover, the following extension was proved. Let $\mathbb{R}_k$ be the quotient-structure of $(\mathcal{R}_k; \leq_W, I, \oplus, \cdot, q_0, \ldots, q_{k-1})$ under $\equiv_W$ where I is the unary relation true precisely on the join-irreducible elements, $\oplus$ is the binary operation of disjoint union, and $\cdot, q_0, \ldots, q_{k-1}$ are some natural operations coming from the Wadge theory. Let the structure $\mathbb{A}_k$ be defined similarly but on the universe $\mathcal{A}_k$. Let $\mathbb{F}_2(\bar{k})$ be the quotient-structure of $(\mathrm{Fr}_2(\bar{k}); \leq_h, I, \sqcup, \cdot, q_0, \ldots, q_{k-1})$ under $\equiv_h$ where I is defined similarly, and $q_i(F) = s(i \cdot r(F))$ for every $F \in \mathrm{Fr}_2(\bar{k})$ and $i < k$. By Proposition 9 in [8], the structures $\mathbb{R}_k$, $\mathbb{A}_k$, and $\mathbb{F}_2(\bar{k})$ are isomorphic. By Theorem 3 and Proposition 4, the structure $(\mathrm{Fr}_2(\bar{k}); \leq_h, I, \sqcup, \cdot, q_0, \ldots, q_{k-1})$ is P-presentable. Since the structure $\mathbb{F}_2(\bar{k})$ is finitely generated, from Theorem 2 in [3] we obtain the following.

Theorem 4. *The structures $\mathbb{R}_k$ and $\mathbb{A}_k$ are P-presentable.*

Fix k satisfying $2 \leq k \leq \omega$. Let $\oplus$ be the binary operation of disjoint union on $\bar{k}^\omega$ where $\bar{k} = \{i \mid i < k\}$. We say that a function f on ω reduces $A \in \bar{k}^\omega$ to $B \in \bar{k}^\omega$ if $A = B \circ f$. For any $n < \omega$, let $\leq^n$ be the binary relation on

$\bar{k}^\omega$ where $A \leq^n B$ means that some function f computable in the n-th Turing jump $\varnothing^{(n)}$ of the empty set reduces A to B. These relations are popular in computability theory (in particular, the relation $\leq^0$ on $\bar{2}^\omega$ coincides with the many-one reducibility).

For any $n < \omega$, let u^n be the universal partial function on ω computable in $\varnothing^{(n)}$. We define the binary operation $\cdot^n$ on $\bar{k}^\omega$ as follows: if $u^n(y)$ is defined then $(A \cdot^n B)\langle x, y \rangle$ equals $A(u^n(y))$, otherwise it equals $B(x)$. Here $\langle\ \rangle$ is the usual pairing function on ω. See Section 5 in [9] for arguments why these operations are natural objects of computability theory. Let A_k be the subset of $\bar{k}^\omega$ generated by these operations from the constant functions. For any $n < \omega$, let I_n be the unary relation on A_k true precisely on the elements which induce join-irreducible elements in the quotient semilattice of $(A_k; \oplus, \leq^n)$.

In Section 2.3 of [9], binary relations $\leq^n$ and binary operations $\cdot^n$ on $\mathrm{Fr}_\omega(Q)$ where defined by induction on n as follows: $\leq^0 = \leq_h$ and $F \leq^{n+1} G$ iff $r(F) \leq^n r(G)$; $F \cdot^0 G = F \cdot G$ and $F \cdot^{p+1} G = s(r(F) \cdot^p r(G))$. Let also I_n be the unary relation on $\mathrm{Fr}_\omega(Q)$ true precisely on the elements which induce join-irreducible elements in the quotient semilattice of $(\mathrm{Fr}_\omega(Q); \sqcup, \leq^n)$. By the results in Sect. 6 of [9], the quotient-structure of $(A_k; \oplus, \cdot^0, \cdot^1, \ldots, I_0, I_1, \ldots, \leq^0, \leq^1, \ldots)$ under $\equiv^0$ is isomorphic to the quotient-structure of $(\mathrm{Fr}_\omega(\bar{k}); \sqcup, \cdot^0, \cdot^1, \ldots, I_0, I_1, \ldots, \leq^0, \leq^1, \ldots)$ under $\equiv^0$, and the quotient semilattice of $(A_k; \oplus, \leq^n)$ for every n is isomorphic to the quotient semilattice of $(\mathrm{Fr}_\omega(\bar{k}); \sqcup, \leq^n)$ and to the quotient semilattice of $(\mathrm{Fr}_\omega(\bar{k}); \sqcup, \leq^0)$. These results, Proposition 4, and Theorem 3 imply:

Theorem 5. *The structure $(A_k; \oplus, I_0, \leq^0)$ has a P-presentation in which the relations $I_n, \leq^n$ and the operations $\cdot^n$ are P-computable for every n.*

References

1. Aho, A., Hopcroft, J.V., Ullman, J.E.: The Design and Analysis of Computer Algorithms. Addison Wesley, Massachusetts (1969)
2. Alaev, P.E.: Structures computable in polynomial time. I. Algebra Logic **55**(6), 421–435 (2016)
3. Alaev, P.E.: Polynomially computable structures with finitely many generators. Algebra Logic **59**(3), 266–272 (2020)
4. Cenzer, D., Remmel, J.: Polynomial time versus recursive models. Ann. Pure Appl. Logic **54**(1), 17–58 (1991)
5. Hertling P.: Topologische Komplexitätsgrade von Funktionen mit endlichem Bild. Informatik-Berichte, vol. 152, 34 pages. Fernuniversität Hagen, December 1993
6. Hertling P., Selivanov V.L.: Complexity issues for preorders on finite labeled forests. In: Brattka, V., Diener, H., Spreen, D. (eds.) Logic, Computation, Hierarchies, pp. 165–190. Ontos Publishing, de Gruiter, Boston-Berlin (2014)
7. Selivanov, V.: Classifying ω-regular aperiodic k-partitions. In: Jirásková, G., Pighizzini, G. (eds.) DCFS 2020. LNCS, vol. 12442, pp. 193–205. Springer, Cham (2020). https://doi.org/10.1007/978-3-030-62536-8_16
8. Selivanov V.: Wadge degrees of classes of ω-regular k-partitions. Submitted, Arxiv:2104.10358
9. Selivanov, V.: Non-collapse of the effective Wadge hierarchy. In: De Mol, L., Weiermann, A., Manea, F., Fernández-Duque, D. (eds.) CiE 2021. LNCS, vol. 12813, pp. 407–416. Springer, Cham (2021). https://doi.org/10.1007/978-3-030-80049-9_40

On the Uniform Distribution of Regular Expressions

Sabine Broda, António Machiavelo, Nelma Moreira, and Rogério Reis[✉]

CMUP & DM-DCC, Faculdade de Ciências da Universidade do Porto, Rua do
Campo Alegre, 4169-007 Porto, Portugal
{sabine.broda,antonio.machiavelo,nelma.moreira,rogerio.reis}@fc.up.pt

Abstract. Although regular expressions do not correspond univocally
to regular languages, it is still worthwhile to study their properties and
algorithms. For the average case analysis one often relies on the uniform
random generation using a specific grammar for regular expressions, that
can represent regular languages with more or less redundancy. Generators
that are uniform on the set of expressions are not necessarily uniform on
the set of regular languages. Nevertheless, it is not straightforward that
asymptotic estimates obtained by considering the whole set of regular
expressions are different from those obtained using a more refined set that
avoids some large class of equivalent expressions. In this paper we study
a set of expressions that avoid a given absorbing pattern. It is shown
that, although this set is significantly smaller than the standard one, the
asymptotic average estimates for the size of the Glushkov automaton for
these expressions does not differ from the standard case.

1 Introduction

Average-case studies often rely on uniform random generation of inputs. In general, those inputs correspond to trees, and generators are uniform on the set of
these trees, but not on the set that those inputs represent (such as languages
or boolean functions). Koechlin et al. [7,8] studied expressions that have subexpressions which are (semantically) absorbing for a given operator, calling them
absorbing patterns. For instance, $(a + b)^\star$ is absorbing for the union of regular
expressions over the alphabet $\{a, b\}$, since $\alpha + (a+b)^\star$, or $(a+b)^\star + \alpha$, is equivalent
to $(a + b)^\star$ for any expression α. After repeatedly applying the induced simplification, in the example above replacing $\alpha + (a + b)^\star$ by $(a + b)^\star$, the resulting
expression can be significantly smaller. For uniformly random generated expressions of a given size, Koechlin et al. showed that the expression resulting from
this simplification has constant expected size. That result led the authors to the
conclusion that uniform random generated regular expressions lack expressiveness, and in particular that uniform distribution should not be used to study the
average case complexity in the context of regular languages. This conclusion is

This work was partially supported by CMUP, through FCT - Fundação para a Ciência
e a Tecnologia, I.P., under the project with reference UIDB/00144/2020.

Y.-S. Han and S.-K. Ko (Eds.): DCFS 2021, LNCS 13037, pp. 13–25, 2021.
https://doi.org/10.1007/978-3-030-93489-7_2

misleading in at least two aspects. First, as pointed out above, one is considering regular expressions and not regular languages themselves. For instance, if one wants to estimate the size of automata obtained from regular expressions, one disregards whether they represent the same language or not. What is implied by the results of Koechlin et al. is that, if one uniformly random generates regular expressions, one cannot expect to obtain, with a reasonable probability, regular languages outside a constant set of languages. This means that a core set of regular languages have so many regular expression representatives that the remaining languages very scarcely appear. While neither regular expressions (RE) nor nondeterministic finite automata (NFA) behave uniformly when representing regular languages, it is known that deterministic automata (DFA) are a better choice, in the uniform model, as they are asymptotically minimal [10]. In this sense, minimal DFAs are a perfect model for regular languages. However, in practice, regular expressions are usually preferred as a representation of regular languages, and are used in a non-necessarily simplified form. Moreover, all of these objects (REs, NFAs, and DFAs) are combinatorial objects *per se* that can have their behaviour, as well as of the algorithms having them as input, studied on average and asymptotically. One should not confuse regular expressions by themselves with the languages that they represent. Second, the results of Koechlin et al. do not imply that asymptotic estimates obtained by considering the whole set of regular expressions are different from those obtained by using a more refined set with less equivalent expressions. For instance, some results obtained for expressions in strong star normal form coincide with the ones for standard regular expressions [2]. In order to further sustain the above claim, in this paper we consider the set R of regular expressions avoiding an absorbing pattern which extends the pattern in the example above and was the one considered by Koechlin et al. It is shown that, although the set R is significantly smaller than the set RE, the asymptotic estimates for the size of the Glushkov automaton on these sets is the same. Given the complexity of the grammars expressing the classes here studied, we had to deal with algebraic curves and polynomials of degree depending on the size of the alphabet, k, which brought up challenges that are new, as far as we know. Not only we had to use the techniques developed in our previous work [3], but also some non-trivial estimates using Stirling approximation, and some asymptotic equivalence reductions in order to obtain the asymptotic estimates, and their limits with k.

2   The Analytic Tools

Given some measure of the objects of a combinatorial class, $\mathcal{A}$, for each non-negative integer $n \in \mathbb{N}_0$, let a_n be the sum of the values of this measure for all objects of size n. Now, let $A(z) = \sum_n a_n z^n$ be the corresponding generating function (*cf.* [5]). We will use the notation $[z^n]A(z)$ for a_n. The generating function $A(z)$ can be seen as a complex analytic function. When this function has a unique dominant singularity ρ, the study of the behaviour of $A(z)$ around it gives us access to the asymptotic form of its coefficients. In particular, if $A(z)$ is analytic in some indented disc neighbourhood of ρ, then one has the following [5, Corol. VI.1, p. 392]:

Theorem 1. *The coefficients of the series expansion of the complex function* $f(z) \underset{z \to \rho}{\sim} \lambda \left(1 - \frac{z}{\rho}\right)^{\nu}$, *where* $\nu \in \mathbb{C} \setminus \mathbb{N}_0$, $\lambda \in \mathbb{C}$, *have the asymptotic approximation* $[z^n]f(z) = \frac{\lambda}{\Gamma(-\nu)} n^{-\nu-1} \rho^{-n} + o\left(n^{-\nu-1} \rho^{-n}\right)$. *Here* Γ *is, as usual, the Euler's gamma function and the notation* $f(z) \underset{z \to z_0}{\sim} g(z)$ *means that* $\lim_{z \to z_0} \frac{f(z)}{g(z)} = 1$.

2.1   Regular Expressions

Given an alphabet $\Sigma = \{\sigma_1, \ldots, \sigma_k\}$, the set RE of (standard) *regular expressions*, β, over Σ contains $\emptyset$ and the expressions defined by the following grammar:

$$\beta := \varepsilon \mid \sigma \in \Sigma \mid (\beta + \beta) \mid (\beta \cdot \beta) \mid (\beta^\star). \tag{1}$$

The *language* associated with β is denoted by $\mathcal{L}(\beta)$ and defined as usual (with ε representing the empty word). Two expressions β_1 and β_2 are *equivalent*, $\beta_1 = \beta_2$, if $\mathcal{L}(\beta_1) = \mathcal{L}(\beta_2)$. The *(tree-)size* $|\beta|$ of $\beta \in$ RE is the number of symbols in β (disregarding parentheses). The *alphabetic size* $|\beta|_\Sigma$ is the number of letters occurring in β. The generating function of RE is $B_k(z) = \sum_{\beta \in \text{RE}} z^{|\beta|} = \sum_{n > 0} b_n z^n$, where b_n is the number of expressions of size n, cf. [1,9]. From grammar (1) one gets $B_k(z) = (k+1)z + 2zB_k(z)^2 + zB_k(z)$. Considering the quadratic equation this yields $B_k(z) = \frac{1 - z - \sqrt{1 - 2z - (7+8k)z^2}}{4z}$. To use Theorem 1 one needs to obtain the singularity, ρ, as well as the constants ν and λ. Following Broda et al. [1,3], we have $B_k(z) \underset{z \to \rho_k}{\sim} - \frac{\sqrt{2 - 2\rho_k}}{4\rho_k} \left(1 - \frac{z}{\rho_k}\right)^{\frac{1}{2}}$, where the singularity $\rho_k = \frac{1}{1 + \sqrt{8 + 8k}}$ is the positive root of $p_k(z) = 1 - 2z - (7 + 8k)z^2$. Thus, applying Theorem 1 and noting that $\Gamma(-\frac{1}{2}) = \sqrt{\pi}$, the number of expressions of size n is asymptotically given by

$$[z^n]B_k(z) \underset{n}{\sim} \frac{\sqrt{2 - 2\rho_k}}{8\rho_k \sqrt{\pi}} n^{-\frac{3}{2}} \rho_k^{-n}, \tag{2}$$

where we use the notation $\underset{n}{\sim}$ instead of $\underset{n \to \infty}{\sim}$.

3   Regular Expressions Without $\Sigma^\star$ in Unions

We consider the set R of all regular expressions α such that $\Sigma^\star$ does not occur in an union. Here $\Sigma^\star$ denotes any expression $(\sigma_{i_1} + \cdots + \sigma_{i_k})^\star$ where $\sigma_{i_1}, \ldots, \sigma_{i_k}$ is a permutation of Σ. Note that $\Sigma^\star$ represents an absorbing pattern in the sense of [7], i.e. $(\alpha + \Sigma^\star) = (\Sigma^\star + \alpha) = \Sigma^\star$, and that R still generates all regular languages over Σ. We first consider $\Sigma = \{a, b\}$, for which we have the following grammar $\mathcal{G}_2$ for R.

$$\alpha := \varepsilon \mid a \mid b \mid (\alpha \cdot \alpha) \mid (\alpha^\star) \mid (\alpha_P + \alpha_P) \tag{3}$$
$$\alpha_P := \varepsilon \mid a \mid b \mid (\alpha \cdot \alpha) \mid (\alpha_\Sigma^\star) \mid (\alpha_P + \alpha_P)$$
$$\alpha_\Sigma := \varepsilon \mid a \mid b \mid (\alpha \cdot \alpha) \mid (\alpha^\star) \mid \gamma$$
$$\gamma := (\alpha_{ab} + \alpha_{ab}) \mid (\alpha_{ab} + a) \mid (\alpha_{ab} + b) \mid (a + \alpha_{ab}) \mid (b + \alpha_{ab}) \mid (a + a) \mid (b + b)$$
$$\alpha_{ab} := \varepsilon \mid (\alpha \cdot \alpha) \mid (\alpha_\Sigma^\star) \mid (\alpha_P + \alpha_P).$$

The set of expressions generated by the nonterminals of $\mathcal{G}_2$, are, respectively,

$$\llbracket \alpha \rrbracket = \mathsf{R},$$
$$\llbracket \alpha_P \rrbracket = \{ \alpha \in \mathsf{R} \mid \alpha \neq (a+b)^\star \wedge \alpha \neq (b+a)^\star \},$$
$$\llbracket \alpha_\Sigma \rrbracket = \{ \alpha \in \mathsf{R} \mid \alpha \neq (a+b) \wedge \alpha \neq (b+a) \},$$
$$\llbracket \gamma \rrbracket = \{ (\alpha_1 + \alpha_2) \in \mathsf{R} \mid \{\alpha_1, \alpha_2\} \neq \{a, b\} \},$$
$$\llbracket \alpha_{ab} \rrbracket = \{ \alpha \in \llbracket \alpha_P \rrbracket \mid \alpha \neq a \wedge \alpha \neq b \}.$$

Let $R_2(z)$ denote the generating function for the class R when $|\Sigma| = 2$. It follows from (3) that $R_2(z) = 3z + zR_2(z)^2 + zR_2(z) + zR_P(z)^2$, where $R_P(z)$ is the generating function for the class of expressions generated by α_P. Comparing $\llbracket \alpha \rrbracket$ and $\llbracket \alpha_P \rrbracket$, one observes that the only expressions not generated by α_P are $(a+b)^\star$ and $(b+a)^\star$, which are both of size 4. Thus, $R_P(z) = R_2(z) - 2z^4$. In general, for an arbitrary alphabet $\Sigma = \{\sigma_1, \ldots, \sigma_k\}$, the expressions $\alpha \in \mathsf{R}$ satisfy the following grammar $\mathcal{G}_k$

$$\alpha := \varepsilon \mid \sigma_1 \mid \cdots \mid \sigma_k \mid (\alpha \cdot \alpha) \mid (\alpha^\star) \mid (\alpha_P + \alpha_P), \tag{4}$$

where $\llbracket \alpha_P \rrbracket = \{ \alpha \in \mathsf{R} \mid \alpha \neq (\sigma_{i_1} + \cdots + \sigma_{i_k})^\star \wedge \{\sigma_{i_1}, \ldots, \sigma_{i_k}\} = \Sigma \}$. As before, we obtain the following two equations for the corresponding generating functions, where $(k-1)!\binom{2k-2}{k-1}$ denotes the number of expression $(\sigma_{i_1} + \cdots + \sigma_{i_k})^\star$ with $\{\sigma_{i_1}, \ldots, \sigma_{i_k}\} = \Sigma$, each of which has size $2k$,

$$R_k(z) = (k+1)z + zR_k(z)^2 + zR_k(z) + zR_{P,k}(z)^2, \tag{5}$$

$$R_{P,k}(z) = R_k(z) - (k-1)! \binom{2k-2}{k-1} z^{2k}. \tag{6}$$

In the next section, the asymptotic estimates of $[z^n]R_k(z)$ are computed.

3.1   Asymptotic Estimates for the Number of Expressions in R

The generating function $R_k = R_k(z)$ satisfies the following equation:

$$2zR_k^2 - r_k R_k + zs_k = 0, \tag{7}$$

where

$$r_k = r_k(z) = 1 - z + 2z^{2k+1}C_k,$$
$$s_k = s_k(z) = 1 + k + z^{4k}C_k^2,$$
$$C_k = \binom{2k-2}{k-1}(k-1)! = \frac{(2k-2)!}{(k-1)!}.$$

The discriminant of Eq. (7) is $\Delta_k = \Delta_k(z) = p_k(z) + 4z^{2k+1}C_k h_k(z)$, where $p_k = p_k(z) = 1 - 2z - (7 + 8k)z^2$ and $h_k = h_k(z) = 1 - z - C_k z^{2k+1}$. Thus,

$$R_k = R_k(z) = \frac{r_k - \sqrt{\Delta_k}}{4z}, \tag{8}$$

where the choice of the sign is determined by noticing that $r_k(0) = \Delta_k(0) = 1$. Let us now show that $R_k(z)$ has a unique determinant singularity in the interval $]0,1[$, for all k. The ideia is to use the fact that the polynomial $p_k(z)$ has only one positive zero, namely ρ_k, use Rouché's Theorem to show that, in the disk $|z| < \frac{1}{\sqrt{8+8k}}$, the polynomial $\Delta_k(z)$ has exactly one root in that disk, and finally show that unique root is real. We recall that Rouché's Theorem states that, in particular, for polynomials $f(z)$ and $g(z)$ such that $|f(z) - g(z)| < |f(z)| + |g(z)|$ holds for all $|z| = R$, in the complex plane, then $f(z)$ and $g(z)$ have the same number of roots, taking into account multiplicities, in the disk $|z| < R$ [11, Thm 3.3.4]. In order to estimate $|\Delta_k(z) - p_k(z)|$, we start by noticing that from Stirling approximation, $\sqrt{2\pi}\, n^{n+\frac{1}{2}} e^{-n} \le n! \le n^{n+\frac{1}{2}} e^{1-n}$, valid for all $n \in \mathbb{N}$, one gets that, for all $k \ge 2$,

$$\frac{\sqrt{2\pi}\,(2k-2)^{2k-\frac{3}{2}} c^{2-2k}}{(k-1)^{k-\frac{1}{2}} e^{2-k}} \le C_k = \frac{(2k-2)!}{(k-1)!} \le \frac{(2k-2)^{2k-\frac{3}{2}} c^{3-2k}}{\sqrt{2\pi}\,(k-1)^{k-\frac{1}{2}} e^{1-k}},$$

i.e.,

$$\frac{\sqrt{2\pi}\, 2^{2k-\frac{3}{2}}(k-1)^{k-1}}{e^k} \le C_k \le \frac{2^{2k-\frac{3}{2}}(k-1)^{k-1}}{\sqrt{2\pi}\, c^{k-2}}. \tag{9}$$

Therefore, for $|z| = \frac{1}{\sqrt{8+8k}}$,

$$|\Delta_k(z) - p_k(z)| \le 4C_k \frac{1}{(8+8k)^{k+\frac{1}{2}}} |h_k(z)|$$

$$\le \frac{(k-1)^{k-1}}{\sqrt{2\pi}\, e^{k-2}\, 2^{k+1}(k+1)^{k+\frac{1}{2}}} \left(1 - \frac{1}{\sqrt{8+8k}} - \frac{C_k}{(8+8k)^{k+\frac{1}{2}}}\right)$$

$$\le \frac{1.48}{(2e)^k (k-1)\sqrt{k+1}} \left(1 - \frac{1}{\sqrt{8+8k}} - \frac{C_k}{(8+8k)^{k+\frac{1}{2}}}\right).$$

Noticing that, from (9), one has

$$\frac{\sqrt{2\pi}\,(k-1)^{k-1}}{e^k 2^{k+3}(k+1)^{k+\frac{1}{2}}} \le \frac{C_k}{(8+8k)^{k+\frac{1}{2}}} \le \frac{(k-1)^{k-1}}{\sqrt{2\pi}\, e^{k-2} 2^{k+3}(k+1)^{k+\frac{1}{2}}},$$

one concludes that $\lim_{k\to\infty} |\Delta_k(z) - p_k(z)| = 0$.

Let us now find the minimum of $|p_k(z)|$ on the circumference $|z| = \frac{1}{\sqrt{8+8k}} = R$. Put $z = Re^{i\theta}$. One has

$$|p_k(z)|^2 = |1 - 2Re^{i\theta} - (7 + 8k)R^2 e^{2i\theta}|^2$$
$$= (1 - 2R\cos\theta - (7 + 8k)R^2\cos 2\theta)^2 + (1 - 2R\sin\theta - (7 + 8k)R^2\sin 2\theta)^2$$
$$= 2 + 4R^2 + (7 + 8k)^2 R^4 - 4R(\cos\theta + \sin\theta) - 2(7 + 8k)R^2(\cos 2\theta + \sin 2\theta)$$
$$+ 4R^3(7 + 8k)(\cos\theta\cos 2\theta + \sin\theta\sin 2\theta)$$
$$= 2 + \frac{1}{2 + 2k} + \left(\frac{7 + 8k}{8 + 8k}\right)^2 - \frac{2(\cos\theta + \sin\theta)}{\sqrt{2 + 2k}} - \frac{(7 + 8k)(\cos 2\theta + \sin 2\theta)}{4 + 4k}$$
$$+ \frac{(7 + 8k)(\cos\theta\cos 2\theta + \sin\theta\sin 2\theta)}{4(k + 1)\sqrt{2 + 2k}}.$$

It follows that $\lim_{k\to\infty} |p_k(z)|^2 = 3 - 2(\cos 2\theta + \sin 2\theta)$. Since $\max_\theta(\cos\theta + \sin\theta) = \sqrt{2}$, one concludes that $\lim_{k\to\infty} |p_k(z)|^2 \geq 3 - 2\sqrt{2} > 0$. From all this, one concludes that $|\Delta_k(z) - p_k(z)| < |p_k(z)|$ for large enough values of k, and so Rouché's Theorem applies to show that the polynomial $\Delta_k(z)$ has exactly one root in the open disk $|z| < \frac{1}{\sqrt{8+8k}}$.[1] Since $\Delta_k(0) = 1$, in order to show that root must be real it suffices to show that one has $\Delta_k\left(\frac{1}{\sqrt{8+8k}}\right) < 0$. This can be shown as follows. Since

$$\Delta_k\left(\frac{1}{\sqrt{8 + 8k}}\right) = 2^{-6k-\frac{7}{2}}(k + 1)^{-2k-1}\left(2^{3k+2}\left(4\sqrt{k + 1} - \sqrt{2}\right)(k + 1)^k C_k\right.$$
$$\left. - 4\sqrt{2}\,C_k^2 - 64^k\left(8\sqrt{k + 1} - \sqrt{2}\right)(k + 1)^{2k}\right),$$

we want to show that

$$2^{3k}\left(\sqrt{8k + 8} - 1\right)(k + 1)^k C_k < C_k^2 + 2^{6k-2}\left(2\sqrt{8k + 8} - 1\right)(k + 1)^{2k}.$$

Using (9), it is enough to show that

$$\frac{2^k e^{k+2}\left(\sqrt{8k + 8} - 1\right)}{\sqrt{\pi}} < 2^{2k}\left(2\sqrt{8k + 8} - 1\right)\frac{(k + 1)^k}{(k - 1)^{k-1}}e^{2k} + \pi\frac{(k - 1)^{k-1}}{(k + 1)^k},$$

that follows from this trivially true inequality

$$\frac{\sqrt{8k + 8} - 1}{\sqrt{\pi}} < 2^k\left(2\sqrt{8k + 8} - 1\right)\frac{(k + 1)^k}{(k - 1)^{k-1}}e^{k-2}.$$

The singularity of $R_k(z)$ is therefore given by the unique root of $\Delta_k(z)$ in the interval $\left]0, \frac{1}{\sqrt{8k+8}}\right[$, which will henceforth denote by η_k. It also follows from Rouché's Theorem that this root has multiplicity one. Now, $\Delta_k(z) = \left(1 - \frac{z}{\eta_k}\right)\psi_k(z)$, for some $\psi_k(z) \in \mathbb{R}[z]$. Using L'Hôpital's Rule, one has

$$\psi_k(\eta_k) = -\eta_k \Delta'_k(\eta_k). \tag{10}$$

Then, one has $R_k(z) \underset{z\to\eta_k}{\sim} \dfrac{-r_k(\eta_k) - \sqrt{\psi_k(\eta_k)}\left(1 - \frac{z}{\eta_k}\right)^{\frac{1}{2}}}{4\eta_k}$. By Theorem 1, one gets the following asymptotic approximation for the number of regular expressions

---

[1] It is actually true that $|\Delta_k(z) - p_k(z)| < |p_k(z)|$ for all $|z| = \frac{1}{\sqrt{8+8k}}$ and $k \geq 2$.

Theorem 2. *With the notation above, one has*

$$[z^n]R_k(z) \underset{n}{\sim} \frac{\sqrt{\psi_k(\eta_k)}}{8\eta_k\sqrt{\pi}} n^{-\frac{3}{2}}\eta_k^{-n}.$$

Using (2), we have

Theorem 3. *The asymptotic ratio of the number of expressions in* R *and the number of expressions in* RE *is given by,*

$$\frac{[z^n]R_k(z)}{[z^n]B_k(z)} \underset{n}{\sim} \frac{\frac{\sqrt{\psi_k(\eta_k)}}{8\eta_k\sqrt{\pi}} n^{-\frac{3}{2}}\eta_k^{-n}}{\frac{\sqrt{2-2\rho_k}}{8\rho_k\sqrt{\pi}} n^{-\frac{3}{2}}\rho_k^{-n}} = \frac{\sqrt{\psi_k(\eta_k)}}{\sqrt{2-2\rho_k}}\left(\frac{\rho_k}{\eta_k}\right)^{n+1}.$$

Since, as seen before, $\eta_k > \rho_k$, for all k, this yields that, for every k, this ratio tends to 0 as $n \to \infty$. As such, considering R instead of RE, actually avoids a significant set of redundant expressions. Such an improvement, in the sense of [7], might influence the results obtained by asymptotic studies. In the following section we show that is not the case for the average asymptotic size of the Glushkov automaton in terms of states and transitions [1,9].

4   Asymptotic Average Size of the Glushkov Automaton

The Glushkov automaton [6] is constructed from an equivalent regular expression β using the set $\mathsf{Pos}(\beta)$ of positions of the letters in β, as the set of states (plus one initial state). Let $\mathsf{Pos}(\beta) = \{1, 2, \ldots, |\beta|_\Sigma\}$, $\mathsf{Pos}_0(\beta) = \mathsf{Pos}(\beta) \cup \{0\}$ and $\overline{\beta}$ denote the expression obtained from β by marking each letter with its position in β. The construction is based on the position sets $\mathsf{First}(\beta) = \{i \mid (\exists w)\ \sigma_i w \in \mathcal{L}(\overline{\beta})\}$, $\mathsf{Last}(\beta) = \{i \mid (\exists w)\ w\sigma_i \in \mathcal{L}(\overline{\beta})\}$, and $\mathsf{Follow}(\beta) = \{(i, j) \mid (\exists u, v)\ u\sigma_i\sigma_j v \in \mathcal{L}(\overline{\beta})\}$. The *Glushkov automaton* for β is $\mathcal{A}_{\mathrm{POS}}(\beta) = \langle \mathsf{Pos}_0(\beta), \Sigma, \delta_{\mathrm{POS}}, 0, F\rangle$ with the set of transitions $\delta_{\mathrm{POS}} = \{(0, \overline{\sigma_j}, j) \mid j \in \mathsf{First}(\overline{\beta})\} \cup \{(i, \overline{\sigma_j}, j) \mid (i, j) \in \mathsf{Follow}(\overline{\beta})\}$ and the set of final states $F = \mathsf{Last}(\overline{\beta}) \cup \{0\}$ if $\varepsilon \in \mathcal{L}(\beta)$, and $F = \mathsf{Last}(\overline{\beta})$, otherwise.

4.1   Estimates for the Number of Letters

The average number of letters in uniform random generated regular expressions of a given size have been estimated for different kinds of expressions [3,9]. For standard regular expressions that value is half the size of the expressions as the size of the alphabet goes to ∞. In the following we obtain the same value for expressions in R. To count the number of letters in all expressions of a given size we use the bivariate generating function $\mathcal{L}_k(u, z) = \sum_{n,i\geq 1} c_{n,i} u^i z^n$, where $c_{n,i}$ is the number of regular expressions of size n with i letters. Therefore, the total number of letters in all the regular expressions of size n is given by the coefficients of the sum of the two series

$$L_k(z) = \left.\frac{\partial \mathcal{L}_k(u, z)}{\partial u}\right|_{u=1} = \sum_{n,i\geq 1} i\, c_{n,i}\, z^n.$$

From grammar (4) the generating function $L_k(z)$ satisfies the following.

$$L_k(z) = kz + 2zL_k(z)R_k(z) + zL_k(z) + 2zP_k(z)R_P(z), \tag{11}$$

$$P_k(z) = L_k(z) - k!\binom{2k-2}{k-1}z^{2k}. \tag{12}$$

Using Eqs. (5), (6), (16), (12) and Buchberger's algorithm [4] one obtains the following equation, which is satisfied by the generating function $L_k = L_k(z)$:

$$\Delta_k L_k^2 + \bar{r}_k L_k - \bar{s}_k = 0, \tag{13}$$

where

$$\bar{r}_k = kz^{2k}C_k \Delta_k,$$
$$\bar{s}_k = kz^2 + k^2 z^{2k+1} C_k \left((z-1)(1+2z^{4k+1}C_k^2) + 2C_k(2+k) + 2z^{6k+1}C_k^3\right).$$

The discriminant of Eq. (13) can be shown to be

$$\bar{\Delta}_k(z) = z^2 k^2 \Delta_k(z) g_k(z)^2, \tag{14}$$

where

$$g_k(z) = 2 - C_k z^{2k-1}\left(h_k(z) - C_k z^{2k-1}\right). \tag{15}$$

Therefore,

$$L_k(z) = \frac{kz^{2k}C_k \Delta_k(z) \pm \sqrt{\bar{\Delta}_k(z)}}{2\Delta_k(z)} = \frac{kz^{2k}C_k}{2} \pm \frac{kzg_k(z)}{2\sqrt{\Delta_k(z)}}.$$

Using the fact that we know $L_k'(0) = k$, one deduces that

$$L_k(z) = \frac{kz^{2k}C_k}{2} + \frac{kzg_k(z)}{2\sqrt{\Delta_k(z)}}. \tag{16}$$

Now, applying the procedure described in *Broda et al.* [3] one obtains:

Theorem 4. *With the same notation as above, where η_k is as defined in page 6,*

$$[z^n]L_k(z) \underset{n}{\sim} \frac{k\,\eta_k\,g_k(\eta_k)}{2\sqrt{\pi}\sqrt{\psi_k(\eta_k)}}n^{-\frac{1}{2}}\eta_k^{-n}.$$

Therefore, from Theorems 2 and 4, one deduces:

Theorem 5. *The asymptotic ratio of letters in the expressions in* R *is given by*

$$\frac{[z^n]L_k(z)}{n[z^n]R_k(z)} \underset{n}{\sim} \frac{4k\,\eta_k^2\,g_k(\eta_k)}{\psi_k(\eta_k)}.$$

Let us now see that

$$\lim_{k\to\infty} k\,\eta_k^2 = \frac{1}{8}. \tag{17}$$

Since we know that $\Delta_k(0) = 1$, and $\Delta_k(x)$ has exactly one real root in the interval $\left[0, \frac{1}{\sqrt{8+8k}}\right]$, in order to show that $\eta_k > \rho_k$ for all k, it is enough to show that:

$$\Delta_k(\rho_k) = p_k(\rho_k) + 4\rho_k^{2k+1}C_k h_k(\rho_k) > 0, \text{ i.e. } h_k(\rho_k) > 0.$$

Now, $h_k(\rho_k) > 0 \iff 1 > \rho_k + C_k\rho_k^{2k+1} \iff \sqrt{8+8k} > \frac{C_k}{(1+\sqrt{8+8k})^{2k}}$. From (9) it follows that

$$\frac{C_k}{(1+\sqrt{8+8k})^{2k}} < \frac{2^{2k-\frac{3}{2}}(k-1)^{k-1}}{\sqrt{2\pi}\,e^{k-2}(1+\sqrt{8+8k})^{2k}}.$$

It is therefore enough to show:

$$\frac{2^{2k-\frac{3}{2}}(k-1)^{k-1}}{\sqrt{2\pi}\,e^{k-2}(1+\sqrt{8+8k})^{2k}} < \sqrt{8+8k},$$

which is equivalent to $2^{2k-\frac{3}{2}}(k-1)^{k-1} < \sqrt{2\pi}\,e^{k-2}(1+\sqrt{8+8k})^{2k}\sqrt{8+8k}$. This is the same as $\left(\frac{4}{e}\right)^k (k-1)^{k-1} < \frac{2^{\frac{3}{2}}\sqrt{2\pi}}{e^2}(1+\sqrt{8+8k})^{2k}\sqrt{8+8k}$, which follows from: $\left(\frac{4}{e}\right)^k (k-1)^k < \frac{2^{\frac{3}{2}}\sqrt{2\pi}}{e^2}2^{2k+1}(2+2k)^{k+\frac{1}{2}}$. That is obvious when rewritten as $\left(\frac{4}{e}\right)^k (k-1)^k < \left(\frac{2^{\frac{3}{2}}\sqrt{2\pi}}{e^2}2\right)4^k(2+2k)^{k+\frac{1}{2}}$. Thus, we conclude that

$$\rho_k = \frac{1}{1+\sqrt{8+8k}} < \eta_k < \frac{1}{\sqrt{8+8k}}. \tag{18}$$

From this it immediately follows that $\lim_{k\to\infty} k\,\eta_k^2 = \frac{1}{8}$, and then $\lim_{k\to\infty} p_k(\eta_k) = 0$. Using the right hand inequality in (9) together with (18), it is not hard to show the following result.

Lemma 1. *For all $t, s \in \mathbb{R}$, one has $\lim_{k\to\infty} C_k k^t \eta_k^{2k+s} = 0$.*

From all this, and from (15) and (10), one easily gets $\lim_{k\to\infty} g_k(\eta_k) = \lim_{k\to\infty} \psi_k(\eta_k) = 2$, and thus:

$$\lim_{k\to\infty} \frac{4k\,\eta_k^2\,g_k(\eta_k)}{\psi_k(\eta_k)} = \frac{1}{2}. \tag{19}$$

Theorem 6. *In regular expressions without Σ^* in unions, the asymptotic ratio of letters goes to $\frac{1}{2}$ as k goes to ∞.*

4.2   Estimates for the Number of Transitions

The transitions of the Glushkov automaton are defined using the sets First, Last and Follow. These sets can be inductively define for $\alpha \in \mathsf{R}$, as it is usually done [1]. Let $\alpha_\varepsilon \in \mathsf{R}$ be the set of expressions such that $\varepsilon \in \mathcal{L}(\alpha_\varepsilon)$ and let $\alpha_{\overline{\varepsilon}}$ represent the set of expressions such that $\varepsilon \notin \mathcal{L}(\alpha_{\overline{\varepsilon}})$. We have

$$
\begin{aligned}
&\mathsf{First}(\varepsilon) &&= \emptyset, &&\mathsf{First}(\alpha_P + \alpha'_P) = \mathsf{First}(\alpha_P) \cup \mathsf{First}(\alpha'_P), \\
&\mathsf{First}(\sigma_i) &&= \{i\}, &&\mathsf{First}(\alpha_\varepsilon \cdot \alpha) \;\; = \mathsf{First}(\alpha_\varepsilon) \cup \mathsf{First}(\alpha), \\
&\mathsf{First}(\alpha^\star) &&= \mathsf{First}(\alpha), &&\mathsf{First}(\alpha_{\overline{\varepsilon}} \cdot \alpha) \;\; = \mathsf{First}(\alpha_{\overline{\varepsilon}}).
\end{aligned}
$$

The definition of Last is almost identical and differs only for the case of concatenation, which is $\mathsf{Last}(\alpha \cdot \alpha_\varepsilon) = \mathsf{Last}(\alpha) \cup \mathsf{Last}(\alpha_\varepsilon)$ and $\mathsf{Last}(\alpha \cdot \alpha_{\overline{\varepsilon}}) = \mathsf{Last}(\alpha_{\overline{\varepsilon}})$. Following Broda et al. [1] the set Follow satisfies

$$
\mathsf{Follow}(\varepsilon) = \mathsf{Follow}(\sigma_i) = \emptyset,
$$
$$
\mathsf{Follow}(\alpha_P + \alpha'_P) = \mathsf{Follow}(\alpha_P) \cup \mathsf{Follow}(\alpha'_P),
$$
$$
\mathsf{Follow}(\alpha \cdot \alpha') = \mathsf{Follow}(\alpha) \cup \mathsf{Follow}(\alpha') \cup \mathsf{Last}(\alpha) \times \mathsf{First}(\alpha'),
$$
$$
\mathsf{Follow}(\alpha^\star) = \mathsf{E}^\star(\alpha), \text{ where}
$$
$$
\mathsf{E}^\star(\varepsilon) = \emptyset, \;\; \mathsf{E}^\star(\sigma_i) = \{(i,i)\}, \;\; \mathsf{E}^\star(\alpha^\star) = \mathsf{E}^\star(\alpha),
$$
$$
\mathsf{E}^\star(\alpha_P + \alpha'_P) = \mathsf{E}^\star(\alpha_P) \cup \mathsf{E}^\star(\alpha'_P) \cup \mathsf{Cross}(\alpha_P, \alpha'_P),
$$
$$
\mathsf{E}^\star(\alpha_\varepsilon \cdot \alpha'_\varepsilon) = \mathsf{E}^\star(\alpha_\varepsilon) \cup \mathsf{E}^\star(\alpha'_\varepsilon) \cup \mathsf{Cross}(\alpha_\varepsilon, \alpha'_\varepsilon),
$$
$$
\mathsf{E}^\star(\alpha_\varepsilon \cdot \alpha'_{\overline{\varepsilon}}) = \mathsf{Follow}(\alpha_\varepsilon) \cup \mathsf{Follow}^\star(\alpha'_{\overline{\varepsilon}}) \cup \mathsf{Cross}(\alpha_\varepsilon, \alpha'_{\overline{\varepsilon}}),
$$
$$
\mathsf{E}^\star(\alpha_{\overline{\varepsilon}} \cdot \alpha'_\varepsilon) = \mathsf{Follow}^\star(\alpha_{\overline{\varepsilon}}) \cup \mathsf{Follow}(\alpha'_\varepsilon) \cup \mathsf{Cross}(\alpha_{\overline{\varepsilon}}, \alpha'_\varepsilon),
$$
$$
\mathsf{E}^\star(\alpha_{\overline{\varepsilon}} \cdot \alpha'_{\overline{\varepsilon}}) = \mathsf{Follow}(\alpha_{\overline{\varepsilon}}) \cup \mathsf{Follow}(\alpha'_{\overline{\varepsilon}}) \cup \mathsf{Cross}(\alpha_{\overline{\varepsilon}}, \alpha'_{\overline{\varepsilon}}),
$$

with $\mathsf{Cross}(\alpha, \alpha') = \mathsf{Last}(\alpha) \times \mathsf{First}(\alpha') \cup \mathsf{Last}(\alpha') \times \mathsf{First}(\alpha)$. The function that counts the cardinality of $\mathsf{First}(\alpha)$ is $\mathsf{f}(\alpha)$ and is defined as follows: $\mathsf{f}(\sigma_i) = 1$, $\mathsf{f}(\alpha_P + \alpha'_P) = \mathsf{f}(\alpha_P) + \mathsf{f}(\alpha'_P)$, $\mathsf{f}(\alpha_\varepsilon \cdot \alpha') = \mathsf{f}(\alpha_\varepsilon) + \mathsf{f}(\alpha')$, $\mathsf{f}(\alpha_{\overline{\varepsilon}} \cdot \alpha') = \mathsf{f}(\alpha_{\overline{\varepsilon}})$ and $\mathsf{f}(\alpha^\star) = \mathsf{f}(\alpha)$. Note that $\mathsf{f}((\sigma_{i_1} + \cdots + \sigma_{i_k})^\star) = k$ for any permutation $\sigma_{i_1}, \ldots, \sigma_{i_k}$ of $\Sigma = \{\sigma_1, \ldots, \sigma_k\}$. The correspondent generating function $F_k(z) = \sum_\alpha \mathsf{f}(\alpha) z^{|\alpha|} = F_k$ satisfies

$$
F_k = kz + zF_k + 2zF_{P,k}R_{P,k} + zF_k R_{\varepsilon,k} + zF_k R_k,
$$
$$
F_{P,k} = F_k - kC_k z^{2k},
$$
$$
R_{\varepsilon,k} = z + zR_k + 2zR_{\varepsilon,k}R_k + zC_k^2 z^{4k} - 2zR_k C_k z^{2k},
$$

where $R_{\varepsilon,k} = R_{\varepsilon,k}(z)$ is the generating function for expressions $\alpha_\varepsilon \in \mathsf{R}$. Let $\mathsf{s}(\alpha)$ be the function that counts the cardinality of $\mathsf{Last}(\alpha)$ and $S_k(z)$ the correspondent generating function. By symmetry we have that $S_k(z) = F_k(z)$. The functions counting the cardinalities of $\mathsf{Follow}(\alpha)$ and $\mathsf{E}^\star(\alpha)$ are $\mathsf{e}(\alpha)$ and $\mathsf{e}^\star(\alpha)$, respectively. Those functions are defined as follows: $\mathsf{e}(\sigma) = \mathsf{e}(\varepsilon) = 0$, $\mathsf{e}(\alpha_P + \alpha'_P) = \mathsf{e}(\alpha_P) + \mathsf{e}(\alpha'_P)$, $\mathsf{e}(\alpha \cdot \alpha') = \mathsf{e}(\alpha) + \mathsf{e}(\alpha') + \mathsf{s}(\alpha)\mathsf{f}(\alpha')$, $\mathsf{e}(\alpha^\star) = \mathsf{e}^\star(\alpha)$; $\mathsf{e}^\star(\varepsilon) = 0$, $\mathsf{e}^\star(\sigma) = 1$, $\mathsf{e}^\star(\alpha^\star) = \mathsf{e}^\star(\alpha)$, $\mathsf{e}^\star(\alpha_P + \alpha'_P) = \mathsf{e}^\star(\alpha_P) + \mathsf{e}^\star(\alpha'_P) + \mathsf{c}(\alpha_P, \alpha'_P)$, $\mathsf{e}^\star(\alpha_\varepsilon \cdot \alpha'_\varepsilon) = \mathsf{e}^\star(\alpha_\varepsilon) + \mathsf{e}^\star(\alpha'_\varepsilon) + \mathsf{c}(\alpha_\varepsilon, \alpha'_\varepsilon)$, $\mathsf{e}^\star(\alpha_{\overline{\varepsilon}} \cdot \alpha'_\varepsilon) = \mathsf{e}^\star(\alpha_{\overline{\varepsilon}}) + \mathsf{e}(\alpha'_\varepsilon) + \mathsf{c}(\alpha_{\overline{\varepsilon}}, \alpha'_\varepsilon)$,

$e^\star(\alpha_\varepsilon \cdot \alpha'_{\overline{\varepsilon}}) = e(\alpha_\varepsilon) + e^\star(\alpha'_{\overline{\varepsilon}}) + c(\alpha_\varepsilon, \alpha'_{\overline{\varepsilon}})$, and $e^\star(\alpha_{\overline{\varepsilon}} \cdot \alpha'_{\overline{\varepsilon}}) = e(\alpha_{\overline{\varepsilon}}) + e(\alpha'_{\overline{\varepsilon}}) + c(\alpha_{\overline{\varepsilon}}, \alpha'_{\overline{\varepsilon}})$, with $c(\alpha, \alpha') = s(\alpha) f(\alpha') + s(\alpha') f(\alpha)$. From the above the corresponding generating functions $E_k(z) = \sum_\alpha e(\alpha) z^{|\alpha|} = E_k$ and $E_k^\star(z) = \sum_\alpha e^\star(\alpha) z^{|\alpha|} = E_k^\star$, respectively, satisfy the following equations.

$$E_k = 2zE_{P,k}R_{P,k} + 2zE_kR_k + zF_k^2 + zE_k^\star,$$

$$E_k^\star = kz + 2zE_{P,k}^\star R_{P,k} + 2zF_{P,k}^2 + 2zE_{\varepsilon,k}^\star R_{\varepsilon,k} + 2zF_{\varepsilon,k}F_{\varepsilon,k}$$
$$+ zE_{\overline{\varepsilon},k}^\star R_{\varepsilon,k} + zE_{\varepsilon,k}R_{\overline{\varepsilon},k} + 2zF_{\varepsilon,k}F_{\overline{\varepsilon},k} + zE_{\varepsilon,k}R_{\overline{\varepsilon},k}$$
$$+ zE_{\overline{\varepsilon},k}^\star R_{\varepsilon,k} + 2zF_{\varepsilon,k}F_{\overline{\varepsilon},k} + 2zE_{\overline{\varepsilon},k}R_{\overline{\varepsilon},k} + 2zF_{\overline{\varepsilon},k}F_{\overline{\varepsilon},k} + zE_k^\star$$

$$= kz + 2zE_{P,k}^\star R_{P,k} + 2zE_k^\star R_{\varepsilon,k} + 2zE_k(R_k - R_{\varepsilon,k})$$
$$+ 2zF_{P,k}^2 + 2zF_k^2 + zE_k^\star,$$

$$E_{P,k} = E_k - k^2 C_k z^{2k},$$

$$E_{P,k}^\star = E_k^\star - k^2 C_k z^{2k}.$$

The last two equations follow from the fact that $e((\sigma_{i_1} + \cdots + \sigma_{i_k})^\star) = e^\star((\sigma_{i_1} + \cdots + \sigma_{i_k})^\star) = k^2$, for any permutation $\sigma_{i_1}, \ldots, \sigma_{i_k}$ of Σ. The cost function $t(\alpha) = f(\alpha) + e(\alpha)$ computes the number of transitions in the Glushkov automaton of α. The generating function associated to t is given by $T_k(z) = F_k(z) + E_k(z)$. Setting $w = T_k(z)$, one has

$$c_2 w^2 + c_1 w + c_0 = 0,$$

where the $c_i = c_i(k, z)$. Therefore,

$$w = \frac{-c_1 \pm \sqrt{c_1^2 - 4c_0 c_2}}{2c_2}.$$

Now, one can see that $c_1 = \Delta_k s_k$, $c_2 = \Delta_k a_k b_k^2$ and $c_1^2 - 4c_0 c_2 = k^2 \Delta_k q_k^2$, from which it follows that

$$w = -\frac{s_k}{2a_k b_k^2} \pm \frac{kq_k}{2a_k b_k^2 \sqrt{\Delta_k}}.$$

With η_k as defined in p. 6, one can now deduce, as above, that

$$T_k(z) \underset{z \to \eta_k}{\sim} \frac{kq_k(\eta_k)}{2a_k(\eta_k)b_k(\eta_k)^2 \sqrt{\psi_k(\eta_k)}} \left(1 - \frac{z}{\eta_k}\right)^{\frac{1}{2}},$$

and therefore

$$[z^n]T_k(z) \underset{n}{\sim} \frac{kq_k(\eta_k)}{2\sqrt{\pi}a_k(\eta_k)b_k(\eta_k)^2 \sqrt{\psi_k(\eta_k)}} \eta_k^{-n} n^{-\frac{1}{2}}.$$

From all this, one gets:

$$\frac{[z^n]T_k(z)}{[z^n]R_k(z)} \underset{n}{\sim} \frac{4k\eta_k q_k(\eta_k)}{a_k(\eta_k)b_k(\eta_k)^2 \psi_k(\eta_k)} n.$$

With the help of a symbolic and numeric computing system one can explicitly find out the polynomials[2] a_k, b_k, q_k, and then reducing them modulo Δ_k (which has η_k as a root), and then using Lemma 1 and (17), one obtains:

$$a_k(\eta_k) \underset{k}{\sim} \frac{1}{2}k\eta_k \quad ; \quad b_k(\eta_k) \underset{k}{\sim} \frac{1}{8}k\eta_k \quad ; \quad q_k(\eta_k) \underset{k}{\sim} \frac{1}{2048}k.$$

This yields

$$\lim_{k\to\infty} \frac{4k\eta_k q_k(\eta_k)}{a_k(\eta_k)b_k(\eta_k)^2\psi_k(\eta_k)} = 1.$$

We have thus obtained the following result.

Theorem 7. *For expressions of size n over an alphabet of size k, the number of transitions in the Glushkov automaton for regular expressions, without $\Sigma^\star$ in unions, is asymptotically, with respect to n, given by $\lambda_k n$, where $\lim_{k\to\infty} \lambda_k = 1$.*

To grasp the progression of λ_k, observe that $\lambda_2 = 4.03$, $\lambda_5 = 2.91$, $\lambda_{10} = 2.30$, $\lambda_{10} = 1.89$, $\lambda_{50} = 1.54$, $\lambda_{100} = 1.38$, $\lambda_{10000} = 1.03$. Theorems 6 and 7 show that the size of the Glushkov automaton, both in states and transitions, is, on average and asymptotically, independent of whether we consider all regular expressions or the restricted set R mentioned by Koechlin et al.

References

1. Broda, S., Machiavelo, A., Moreira, N., Reis, R.: On the average size of Glushkov and partial derivative automata. Int. J. Found. Comput. Sci. **23**(5), 969–984 (2012)
2. Broda, S., Machiavelo, A., Moreira, N., Reis, R.: On average behaviour of regular expressions in strong star normal form. Int. J. Found. Comput. Sci. **30**(6–7), 899–920 (2019)
3. Broda, S., Machiavelo, A., Moreira, N., Reis, R.: Analytic combinatorics and descriptional complexity of regular languages on average. ACM SIGACT News **51**(1), 38–56 (2020)
4. Buchberger, B.: Gröbner bases: a short introduction for systems theorists. In: Moreno-Díaz, R., Buchberger, B., Luis Freire, J. (eds.) EUROCAST 2001. LNCS, vol. 2178, pp. 1–19. Springer, Heidelberg (2001). https://doi.org/10.1007/3-540-45654-6_1
5. Flajolet, P., Sedgewick, R.: Analytic Combinatorics. CUP (2008)
6. Glushkov, V.M.: The abstract theory of automata. Russ. Math. Surv. **16**(5), 1–53 (1961)
7. Koechlin, F., Nicaud, C., Rotondo, P.: Uniform random expressions lack expressivity. In: Rossmanith, P., Heggernes, P., Katoen, J. (eds.) 44th MFCS 2019, vol. 138, pp. 51:1–51:14. LIPIcs (2019)
8. Koechlin, F., Nicaud, C., Rotondo, P.: On the degeneracy of random expressions specified by systems of combinatorial equations. In: Jonoska, N., Savchuk, D. (eds.) DLT 2020. LNCS, vol. 12086, pp. 164–177. Springer, Cham (2020). https://doi.org/10.1007/978-3-030-48516-0_13

---

[2] These polynomials are quite large, *e.g.* q_k has 437 monomials and degree $10 + 28k$.

9. Nicaud, C.: On the average size of Glushkov's automata. In: Dediu, A.H., Ionescu, A.M., Martín-Vide, C. (eds.) LATA 2009. LNCS, vol. 5457, pp. 626–637. Springer, Heidelberg (2009). https://doi.org/10.1007/978-3-642-00982-2_53

10. Nicaud, C.: Random deterministic automata. In: Csuhaj-Varjú, E., Dietzfelbinger, M., Ésik, Z. (eds.) MFCS 2014. LNCS, vol. 8634, pp. 5–23. Springer, Heidelberg (2014). https://doi.org/10.1007/978-3-662-44522-8_2

11. Simon, B.: Basic Complex Analysis, vol. 2A. American Mathematical Society, Providence (2015)

Deterministic One-Way Simulation of Two-Way Deterministic Finite Automata over Small Alphabets

Viliam Geffert[1]([⊠]) and Alexander Okhotin[2]([⊠])

[1] Department of Computer Science, P. J. Šafárik University,
Jesenná 5, 04154 Košice, Slovakia
viliam.geffert@upjs.sk
[2] Department of Mathematics and Computer Science, St. Petersburg
State University, 7/9 Universitetskaya nab., Saint Petersburg 199034, Russia
alexander.okhotin@spbu.ru

Abstract. It is shown that a two-way deterministic finite automaton (2DFA) with n states over an alphabet Σ can be transformed to an equivalent one-way automaton (1DFA) with $|\Sigma| \cdot \mathcal{F}(n) + 1$ states, where $\mathcal{F}(n) = \max_{k=0}^{n} k^{n-k+1} \leq (n+1)^{n+1}/(\ln(n+1) \cdot e^{1-o(1)})^{n+1}$.

This reflects the fact that, by keeping the last processed symbol in memory, the simulating 1DFA needs to remember only the state from which the 2DFA leaves the prefix read so far for the first time to the right together with a function that maps some $n - k$ states moving to the left from the last processed symbol to some other k states moving to the right from this symbol. This reduces the number of functions describing the behaviour of the 2DFA on the prefix read so far.

A close lower bound of $\mathcal{F}(n)$ states is established using a 5-symbol alphabet. The complexity of transforming a sweeping or a direction-determinate 2DFA to a 1DFA is shown to be exactly $\mathcal{F}(n)$.

Keywords: Finite automata · Two-way automata · State complexity

1 Introduction

The state complexity of transforming two-way finite automata to one-way automata has received much attention in the literature. For deterministic (2DFA) and nondeterministic (2NFA) automata, the exact complexity of transforming them to deterministic and nondeterministic one-way automata (1DFA, 1NFA) was determined by Kapoutsis [5]. Similar problems for related models were investigated as well, and the state complexity of transformations involving sweeping automata [14], complements of deterministic two-way automata [15], alternating automata [4], unambiguous automata [11] was estimated. For the basic transformations of 2DFA/2NFA to 1DFA/1NFA, the case of a unary alphabet has

Supported by the Slovak grant contract VEGA 1/0177/21.

Y.-S. Han and S.-K. Ko (Eds.): DCFS 2021, LNCS 13037, pp. 26–37, 2021.
https://doi.org/10.1007/978-3-030-93489-7_3

received special attention [2,7,9], and its complexity was shown to be much less than in the general case studied by Kapoutsis [5].

Even though all four bounds by Kapoutsis [5] are precise, his lower bound arguments rely on using alphabets of exponential size, and this leaves open the state complexity of this transformation for small alphabets. As previously shown by the authors [3], the 2DFA-to-1NFA transformation can in fact be improved from $\binom{2n}{n+1}$ to $|\Sigma| \cdot \binom{n}{\lfloor n+1 \rfloor} + 1$ states, and a close lower bound of $\binom{n}{\lfloor n+1 \rfloor}$ states holds already for a 2-symbol alphabet. The purpose of this paper is to improve the 2DFA-to-1DFA transformation in a similar way.

A transformation of 2DFA to 1DFA was known since the introduction of two-way automata by Rabin and Scott [12]. Shepherdson [13] presented a transformation of an n-state 2DFA to a 1DFA with ca. $(n + 1)^{n+1}$ states. The lower bound was given by Moore [10], who constructed an n-state 2DFA over a fixed alphabet, for which the every 1DFA must have at least $(\frac{n-5}{2})^{\frac{n-5}{2}}$ states. Much later, the precise succinctness tradeoff between 2DFA and 1DFA was determined by Kapoutsis [5], who showed that $\mathcal{K}(n) = n(n^n - (n-1)^n) + 1$ states are sufficient and in the worst case necessary, with the lower bound established over a growing alphabet with around n^n symbols.

This paper investigates the transformation of 2DFA to 1DFA for small alphabets. Classical transformations, which are recalled in Sect. 3, compute the outcomes of all computations of the 2DFA on the prefix read by the 1DFA. According to the new method, presented in Sect. 4, the constructed 1DFA additionally remembers *the last symbol read*, and this allows it to store less information on the computations: the resulting number of states is $|\Sigma| \cdot \mathcal{F}(n) + 1$, where $\mathcal{F}(n) = \max_{k=0}^{n} k^{n-k+1}$. Then, provided that the alphabet is small, the overall number of states is reduced.

As a side note, if the original 2DFAs are sweeping or direction-determinate, the complexity of transforming them to 1DFAs is shown to be exactly $\mathcal{F}(n)$, regardless of the size of the input alphabet.

The proposed construction for small alphabets is actually fairly close to optimal. As shown in Sect. 5, already for a fixed 5-symbol alphabet, there exist n-state 2DFA that require 1DFA with at least $\mathcal{F}(n)$ states.

The growth rate of the function $\mathcal{F}(n)$ is estimated in Sect. 6, and it is shown that $\mathcal{F}(n) \leq (n+1)^{n+1}/(\ln(n+1) \cdot e^{1-o(1)})^{n+1}$. Therefore, for every alphabet of size subexponential in n, with $|\Sigma| \leq \frac{e-1}{e^2} \cdot (\ln(n+1) \cdot e^{1-o(1)})^{n+1}$, the proposed transformation yields fewer states than the exact bound by Kapoutsis [5].

2   Two-Way Automata

Definition 1. *A two-way deterministic finite automaton (2DFA) is a quintuple $\mathcal{A} = (\Sigma, Q, q_0, \delta, F)$, in which Σ is a finite alphabet, which does not contain two special symbols: the left endmarker ($\vdash$) and the right endmarker ($\dashv$); Q is a finite set of states; $q_0 \in Q$ is the initial state; $\delta : Q \times (\Sigma \times \{\vdash, \dashv\}) \to Q \times \{-1, +1\}$ is a partially defined transition function; and $F \subseteq Q$ is the set of accepting states, effective at the right endmarker $\dashv$.*

Given an input string $w \in \Sigma^*$, a 2DFA operates on a read-only tape containing the string $\vdash w \dashv$. It begins its computation in the state q_0, with the head observing the left endmarker $\vdash$. At every step of the computation, when $\mathcal{A}$ is in a state $q \in Q$ and observes a square of the tape containing a symbol $a \in \Sigma \cup \{\vdash, \dashv\}$, the value $\delta(q, a)$ defines the next state and the direction of motion. The computation of $\mathcal{A}$ on w is defined uniquely; if $\mathcal{A}$ eventually reaches an accepting state in F while at the right endmarker $\dashv$, this computation is accepting; otherwise, it either encounters an undefined transition or gets into an infinite loop. The set of strings, on which the computation is accepting, is the language recognized by the 2DFA, denoted by $L(\mathcal{A})$.

Two-way automata of a special kind, which remember the direction of their motion and can turn only on the endmarkers, are known as sweeping [14]. There is also a larger class of direction-determinate automata [8] that remember the direction in which they came to the current state, but may turn at any point.

Definition 2. *A 2DFA is said to be* direction-determinate, *if there is a partition* $Q = Q_{-1} \uplus Q_{+1}$, *so that every transition* $\delta(p, a) = (q, d)$ *must satisfy* $q \in Q_d$. *The states in* Q_{-1} *are called* left-bound, *those in* Q_{+1} right-bound.

A direction-determinate 2DFA is called sweeping, *if* $\delta(p, a) = (q, d)$ *implies* $p, q \in Q_d$, *as long as* $a \in \Sigma$ *(that is, the symbol* a *is not an endmarker).*

One-way automata (1DFA) are a special case of 2DFA, which move to the right after every transition. This makes the endmarkers unnecessary.

3   The Known Simulation of 2DFA by 1DFA

The new transformation of 2DFA to 1DFA presented in this paper is based on the classical transformation by Shepherdson [13], with the refinements by Kapoutsis [6] that made it optimal.

Theorem 1 (Kapoutsis [5,6]). *For every n-state 2DFA, there exists a partial 1DFA with $\mathcal{K}(n) = n \cdot (n^n - (n-1)^n)$ states recognizing the same language.*

Proof (a sketch). The idea is to precompute all computations of the 2DFA on the processed prefix of the input string, and to remember their outcomes in the state of the constructed 1DFA. These precomputed computations can later be joined together into longer computations, and eventually the 1DFA can determine the outcome of the single computation beginning in the initial configuration.

Let $(Q, \Sigma, \delta, q_0, F)$ be a 2DFA. The 1DFA has states of the form $(\hat{q}, f)$, where $\hat{q} \in Q$ is a state of the 2DFA and $f : Q \to Q$ is a function mapping states to states. On an input string $w \in \Sigma^*$, the 1DFA reaches a state $(\hat{q}, f)$, for which

- in the computation of the 2DFA on $\vdash w$, the first time it leaves the rightmost symbol of $\vdash w$ to the right, it does so in the state $\hat{q}$;
- if the 2DFA begins its computation at the rightmost symbol of $\vdash w$ in a state q, then it eventually moves to the right of this rightmost symbol in the state $f(q)$, and if this computation of a 2DFA rejects or loops, then $f(q)$ is defined as $\hat{q}$: this represents the *behaviour* of the 2DFA on this prefix.

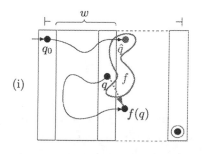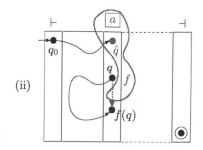

(i)   (ii)

Fig. 1. The data collected by a 1DFA simulating a 2DFA: (i) in the construction by Kapoutsis using states $(\hat{q}, f)$, with $f : Q \to Q$; (ii) in the new construction using states $(a, \hat{q}, f)$, with $f : \overleftarrow{Q}_a \to \overrightarrow{Q}_a$.

These conditions defining a state $(\hat{q}, f)$ are illustrated in Fig. 1(i). The image of f must contain $\hat{q}$, because this state must be reached from some state at the previous position; this accounts for the term $-(n-1)^n$ in the expression for the number of states in the resulting 1DFA for L. The number of such pairs $(\hat{q}, f)$ is exactly $\mathcal{K}(n) = n \cdot (n^n - (n-1)^n)$.   □

It is interesting to note that the construction in Theorem 1 yields fewer states on any direction-determinate 2DFA (hence, on any sweeping 2DFA).

Corollary 1. *For every n-state direction-determinate 2DFA with $|Q_{+1}| = k$, there exists a partial 1DFA with k^{n-k+1} states recognizing the same language.*

Proof. The idea is simple: in the automaton in Theorem 1, in a pair $(\hat{q}, f)$, the function f needs to be defined only on arguments in Q_{-1} (its values on Q_{+1} are irrelevant for the construction), and all its values are in Q_{+1} by definition. Furthermore, the state $\hat{q}$ is also in Q_{+1} by definition. Then there are exactly $k^{n-k} \cdot k = k^{n-k+1}$ such pairs $(\hat{q}, f)$, where $k = |Q_{+1}|$.   □

The number of states thus depends on the value of k, and the maximum number is $\mathcal{F}(n) = \max_{k=0}^{n} k^{n-k+1}$. It will be shown later in Sect. 6 that the maximum is reached for $k = (1 + o(1)) \cdot \frac{n+1}{\ln(n+1)}$, and that the number $\mathcal{F}(n)$ is of the order $(n + 1)^{n+1}/(\ln(n + 1) \cdot e^{1-o(1)})^{n+1}$.

This improvement over Theorem 1 is obtained by reducing the domain and the range of functions f. The new transformation for 2DFA of the general form presented in the next section achieves a similar reduction by additionally remembering one input symbol.

4   Efficient Transformation for Small Alphabets

The behaviour function $f : Q \to Q$ used in Theorem 1 maps states at the last symbol read to states in the next position. The new construction is different from the classical one in two respects. First, the 1DFA shall remember a different behaviour function, which traces *computations beginning and ending at the last symbol read*, and $\hat{q}$ shall also be *positioned on the last symbol read*. Second, the 1DFA additionally remembers *the last symbol read*. Let a be this symbol. Knowing it, the 1DFA also knows the transitions by a, and in particular, in which direction they move the head. Let $\overleftarrow{Q}_a$ be the set of all states q with left-moving transitions $\delta(q, a) = (q', -1)$, and let $\overrightarrow{Q}_a$ consist of all states with right-moving transitions $\delta(q, a) = (q', +1)$. Then, the new behaviour function can map states in $\overleftarrow{Q}_a$ to states in $\overrightarrow{Q}_a$, as illustrated in Fig. 1(ii). And there are fewer such functions than functions $f : Q \to Q$, used in Theorem 1.

Let $\mathcal{A} = (\Sigma, Q, q_0, \delta, F)$ be a 2DFA. For each symbol $a \in \Sigma$, let $\overleftarrow{Q}_a = \{q : \delta(q, a) \in Q \times \{-1\}\}$ be the set of states in which $\mathcal{A}$ moves to the left on a, and similarly define $\overrightarrow{Q}_a = \{q : \delta(q, a) \in Q \times \{+1\}\}$.

Theorem 2. *For every 2DFA $\mathcal{A} = (\Sigma, Q, q_0, \delta, F)$, there exists a partial 1DFA $\mathcal{B} = (\Sigma, Q', q_0', \delta', F')$ that recognizes the same language and uses the following set of states.*

$$Q' = \{(a, \hat{q}, f) : a \in \Sigma, \hat{q} \in \overrightarrow{Q}_a, f : \overleftarrow{Q}_a \to \overrightarrow{Q}_a\} \cup \{(\vdash, q_0, f_0)\},$$

where f_0 is a trivial function with an empty domain, that is, $f_0 : \varnothing \to \varnothing$.

Proof. Each state $(a, \hat{q}, f)$ of $\mathcal{B}$ consists of three components: the last read input symbol $a \in \Sigma$; the state $\hat{q} \in \overrightarrow{Q}_a$, from which $\mathcal{A}$ first leaves the prefix read so far to the right; and the function $f : \overleftarrow{Q}_a \to \overrightarrow{Q}_a$, describing the behaviour of $\mathcal{A}$ on the prefix read so far, which maps states at the last symbol read to states at the last symbol read, as in Fig. 1(ii).

Note that $\overleftarrow{Q}_\vdash = \varnothing$, as $\mathcal{A}$ cannot move beyond the left endmarker. For this reason, there is only one function mapping $\overleftarrow{Q}_\vdash$ to $\overrightarrow{Q}_\vdash$, namely, $f_0 : \varnothing \to \varnothing$, which is a trivial function with an empty domain. This leads to the following initial state of $\mathcal{B}$:

$$q_0' = (\vdash, q_0, f_0).$$

This is the only state of $\mathcal{B}$ with an endmarker in the first component.

The transition in a state $(a, \hat{q}, f)$ by a symbol $b \in \Sigma$ leads to a triple $(b, \hat{r}, g)$, defined as follows. For every state $q \in \overleftarrow{Q}_b$, consider the uniquely defined sequence of states $s_0, \ldots, s_\ell, s_{\ell+1} \in Q$ entered by the automaton at the symbol b, where $s_0 = q$, $\ell \geq 0$, $s_0, \ldots, s_\ell \in \overleftarrow{Q}_b$, $s_{\ell+1} \in \overrightarrow{Q}_b$, and every two consecutive states s_i, s_{i+1} in this sequence are connected in one of the following two ways. Let $\delta(s_i, b) = (t, -1)$. Then,

- either $t \in \overrightarrow{Q}_a$, and then $\delta(t, a) = (s_{i+1}, +1)$,
- or $t \in \overleftarrow{Q}_a$, in which case $\delta(f(t), a) = (s_{i+1}, +1)$.

This exchange between a and b is illustrated in Fig. 2. Define $g(q) := s_{\ell+1}$. However, if the construction of the above sequence reaches an undefined transition, if the sequence is infinite, or if it reaches $\hat{q}$, then let the value $g(q)$ be temporarily undefined—to be specified later.

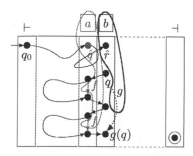

Fig. 2. New simulation of a 2DFA by a 1DFA: transition from a state $(a, \hat{q}, f)$ by a symbol b to a state $(b, \hat{r}, g)$.

The state $\hat{r}$ is set by first considering the transition $\delta(\hat{q}, a) = (q', +1)$: if $q' \in \overrightarrow{Q}_b$, then $\hat{r} := q'$, and if $q' \in \overleftarrow{Q}_b$, then $\hat{r} := g(q')$, provided that the value $g(q')$ has been defined already. With $\hat{r}$ specified, all values of g not defined yet can be set equal to $\hat{r}$.

Finally, let

$$\delta'((a, \hat{q}, f), b) := (b, \hat{r}, g).$$

However, if the above construction has left $\hat{r}$ undefined, then let the whole transition $\delta'((a, \hat{q}, f), b)$ be undefined.

The set F' of accepting states of $\mathcal{B}$ is defined similarly to transitions. A state $(a, \hat{q}, f)$ is marked as accepting, if the following condition holds. Consider the uniquely defined sequence of states $s_0, \ldots, s_\ell, \ldots \in Q$, finite or infinite, where $\delta(\hat{q}, a) = (s_0, +1)$, and every two consecutive states s_i, s_{i+1} in this sequence are connected in one of the following two ways. Let $\delta(s_i, \dashv) = (t, -1)$. Then,

- either $t \in \overrightarrow{Q}_a$, and then $\delta(t, a) = (s_{i+1}, +1)$,
- or $t \in \overleftarrow{Q}_a$, in which case $\delta(f(t), a) = (s_{i+1}, +1)$.

If this sequence eventually reaches an accepting state $s_\ell \in F$ at the right endmarker, then let the state $(a, \hat{q}, f)$ be accepting for $\mathcal{B}$. In all other cases, i.e., if the above sequence reaches an undefined transition or it is infinite, $(a, \hat{q}, f) \notin F'$.

The correctness statement for the construction reads as follows.

Claim 1. Let $(a, \hat{q}, f)$ be the state reached by $\mathcal{B}$ after reading $w \in \Sigma^*$. Then:

- *the last symbol of w is a (if $w = \varepsilon$, then $a = \vdash$);*
- *the automaton $\mathcal{A}$, having begun its computation on the tape $\vdash w$ at the left endmarker in the state q_0, eventually reaches the last symbol of w in the state $\hat{q}$;*
- *for each state $q \in \overleftarrow{Q}_a$, the automaton $\mathcal{A}$, having begun its computation on the tape $\vdash w$ at the last symbol of w in the state q, eventually reaches the last symbol of w in the state $f(q) \in \overrightarrow{Q}_a$; and if the latter computation rejects or loops, then $f(q) = \hat{q}$.*

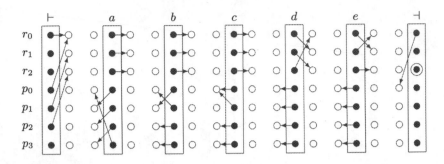

Fig. 3. Transitions of the 2DFA $\mathcal{A}$, defined in Lemma 1, for $k = 3$ and $\ell = 4$.

This can be proved by induction on the length of w; the proof is omitted due to space constraints.   □

How many states are there in such automaton? For each symbol a, the construction produces $|\overrightarrow{Q}_a|^{|\overleftarrow{Q}_a|+1}$ states, which is at most $\mathcal{F}(n) = \max_{k=0}^{n} k^{n-k+1}$, and Theorem 2 produces a 1DFA with at most $|\Sigma| \cdot \mathcal{F}(n)$ states.

5 Lower Bound

The first lower bounds on the 2DFA to 1DFA transformation were given by Barnes [1] and by Moore [10], the latter uses a sweeping 2DFA with half of the states right-bound and the other half left-bound, so that the simulating 1DFA has to store an arbitrary function from right-bound states to left-bound states, and therefore must have at least $(\frac{n-5}{2})^{\frac{n-5}{2}}$ states. This paper establishes a stronger lower bound by using an optimal distribution between left-bound and right-bound states. First, the lower bound is presented for a sweeping 2DFA with k right-bound states and ℓ left-bound states.

Lemma 1. *For all $\ell \geq k \geq 3$, there exists a sweeping 2DFA with $k + \ell$ states over the alphabet $\Sigma = \{a, b, c, d, e\}$, such that every 1DFA recognizing the same language must use at least $k^{\ell+1}$ states.*

Proof. Define a 2DFA $\mathcal{A} = (\Sigma, Q, r_0, \delta, F)$ with $\Sigma = \{a, b, c, d, e\}$ and with the set of states $Q = \{r_0, \ldots, r_{k-1}, p_0, \ldots, p_{\ell-1}\}$. In the states $r_0, \ldots, r_{k-1}$, the automaton moves to the right until it reaches the right endmarker, and the states $p_0, \ldots, p_{\ell-1}$ are used for moving to the left without changing the direction.

The automaton begins its computation by the transition (see also Fig. 3)

$$\delta(r_0, \vdash) = (r_0, +1),$$

and then changes its direction of motion only at the endmarkers, using the following transitions:

$$\delta(p_i, \vdash) = (r_i, +1), \quad \text{for } i \in \{0, \ldots, k - 1\},$$
$$\delta(r_0, \dashv) = (p_0, +1).$$

At the right endmarker $\dashv$, the automaton accepts in the state r_{k-1}, that is, $F = \{r_{k-1}\}$. The transitions at the left endmarker $\vdash$ in the states p_k, p_{k+1}, ..., $p_{\ell-1}$, as well as at the right endmarker $\dashv$ in the states $r_1, r_2, \ldots, r_{k-2}$ are undefined, and some inputs are rejected in these configurations. The remaining transitions at the endmarkers are undefined as well, but the automaton shall never get into the corresponding configurations.

The symbols a and b do not affect the computation on the way from left to right, and apply permutations to the states $p_0, \ldots, p_{\ell-1}$ on the way back. Specifically, a implements a circular permutation.

$$\delta(r_i, a) = (r_i, +1), \qquad \text{for } i \in \{0, \ldots, k-1\},$$
$$\delta(p_i, a) = (p_{(i+1) \bmod \ell}, +1), \quad \text{for } i \in \{0, \ldots, \ell-1\}.$$

The symbol b swaps p_0 with p_1.

$$\delta(r_i, b) = (r_i, +1), \quad \text{for } i \in \{0, \ldots, k-1\},$$
$$\delta(p_0, b) = (p_1, -1),$$
$$\delta(p_1, b) = (p_0, -1),$$
$$\delta(p_i, b) = (p_i, -1), \quad \text{for } i \in \{2, \ldots, \ell-1\}.$$

Using a and b, one can generate an arbitrary permutation of the states $p_0, \ldots, p_{\ell-1}$. The next symbol c merges both states p_0 and p_1 into p_0.

$$\delta(r_i, c) = (r_i, +1), \quad \text{for } i \in \{0, \ldots, k-1\},$$
$$\delta(p_0, c) = (p_0, -1),$$
$$\delta(p_1, c) = (p_0, -1),$$
$$\delta(p_i, c) = (p_i, -1), \quad \text{for } i \in \{2, \ldots, \ell-1\}.$$

This allows to implement all completely defined functions from $\{p_0, \ldots, p_{\ell-1}\}$ to $\{p_0, \ldots, p_{\ell-1}\}$, injective and non-injective.

The last two symbols d and e are used to permute the states $r_0, \ldots, r_{k-1}$, in the same way as a and b permute the second group of states. The symbol d defines a circular permutation, and e exchanges the first two states:

$$\delta(r_i, d) = (r_{(i+1) \bmod k}, +1), \quad \text{for } i \in \{0, \ldots, k-1\},$$
$$\delta(p_i, d) = (p_i, -1), \qquad \text{for } i \in \{0, \ldots, \ell-1\},$$
$$\delta(r_0, e) = (r_1, +1),$$
$$\delta(r_1, e) = (r_0, +1),$$
$$\delta(r_i, e) = (r_i, +1), \qquad \text{for } i \in \{2, \ldots, k-1\},$$
$$\delta(p_i, e) = (p_i, -1), \qquad \text{for } i \in \{0, \ldots, \ell-1\}.$$

Claim 2. For every complete function $g : \{p_0, \ldots, p_{\ell-1}\} \to \{p_0, \ldots, p_{\ell-1}\}$, there exists a string $w_g \in \{a, b, c\}^*$, on which the automaton, having begun its computation at the last symbol of w_g in a state p_i, eventually exits the string to the left of its leftmost symbol in the state $g(p_i)$.

It is well-known that every complete function can be expressed as a composition of three generators: circular permutation g_a, swapping of two elements g_b, and merging of two elements g_c. Let $g = g_{\sigma_1} \circ \ldots \circ g_{\sigma_m}$, where $\sigma_1, \ldots, \sigma_m \in \{a, b, c\}$. Then $w_g := \sigma_1 \ldots \sigma_m$ is the desired string.

Claim 3. For every state $r_{i_0} \in \{r_0, \ldots, r_{k-1}\}$ and for every complete function $f : \{p_0, \ldots, p_{\ell-1}\} \to \{r_0, \ldots, r_{k-1}\}$, there exists a string $u_{r_{i_0}, f} \in \{a, b, c, d\}^*$, such that the automaton, operating on the tape $\vdash u_{r_{i_0}, f}$,

- *having begun its computation at the left endmarker $\vdash$ in the state r_0, eventually exits the string to the right of its rightmost symbol in the state r_{i_0};*
- *having begun its computation at the last symbol of $u_{r_{i_0}, f}$ in a state p_j, eventually reaches the left endmarker $\vdash$, and then moves from there to the right in the state $f(p_j)$.*

Consider the function $g : \{p_0, \ldots, p_{\ell-1}\} \to \{p_0, \ldots, p_{k-1}\}$ defined as follows: for every state p_j, first take $f(p_j) = r_i$. Then define $g(p_j) := p_{(i-i_0) \bmod k}$. Now, let w_g be the string defined for g in Claim 2, and define the string $u_{r_{i_0}, f}$ as

$$u_{r_{i_0}, f} := w_g d^{i_0}.$$

Then, having started on $\vdash w_g d^{i_0}$ in the initial configuration, the automaton moves all the way to the right: it remains in the state r_0 while reading w_g, and then finishes reading d^{i_0} in the state r_{i_0}, as desired. If the automaton begins its computation at the last symbol of $\vdash w_g d^{i_0}$ in a state p_j, then it first moves all the way to the left, arriving to the left endmarker in the state $g(p_j) = p_{(i-i_0) \bmod k}$. After that, it leaves this endmarker in the state $r_{(i-i_0) \bmod k}$ and starts sweeping back to the right. It remains in $r_{(i-i_0) \bmod k}$ while reading w_g, and then leaves d^{i_0} in the state $r_i = f(p_j)$. This proves Claim 3.

Claim 4. For every permutation $\pi : \{r_0, \ldots, r_{k-1}\} \to \{r_0, \ldots, r_{k-1}\}$, there exists a string $x_\pi \in \{d, e\}^*$, on which the automaton, beginning its computation at the first symbol of x_π in a state r_i, eventually exits the string to the right of its rightmost symbol in the state $\pi(r_i)$.

This is a standard generation of a permutation using two generators.

Claim 5. For every two distinct states $r_i, r_j \in \{r_0, \ldots, r_{k-1}\}$ and for every two complete functions $f, g : \{p_0, \ldots, p_{\ell-1}\} \to \{r_0, \ldots, r_{k-1}\}$ (not necessarily distinct), there exists a string $v \in \{d, e\}^*$, for which the string $u_{r_i, f} v$ is accepted but the string $u_{r_j, g} v$ is rejected.

Define a permutation $\pi : \{r_0, \ldots, r_{k-1}\} \to \{r_0, \ldots, r_{k-1}\}$ by setting $\pi(r_i) = r_{k-1}$ and $\pi(r_j) = r_1$, while the rest of the values can be set arbitrarily. Set $v := x_\pi$, where $x_\pi \in \{d, e\}^*$ is the string defined for π in Claim 4. On the input $u_{r_i, f} x_\pi$, the automaton accepts the string in one left-to-right traversal, entering the state r_i after reading $u_{r_i, f}$, and then reaching the state $\pi(r_i) = r_{k-1}$ upon reading x_π. On the other hand, on the input $u_{r_j, g} x_\pi$, the automaton is in the state r_j after $u_{r_j, g}$, and then it enters the state $\pi(r_j) = r_1$ by x_π, in which the transition by the right endmarker is undefined, and thus the string is rejected.

Claim 6. For every state $r_i \in \{r_0, \ldots, r_{k-1}\}$ and for every two distinct complete functions $f, g : \{p_0, \ldots, p_{\ell-1}\} \to \{r_0, \ldots, r_{k-1}\}$, there exists a string $v \in \{a, d, e\}^*$, for which exactly one of the strings $u_{r_i, f} v$ and $u_{r_i, g} v$ is accepted by the automaton.

Let p_j be any argument on which f and g assume different values. Then at least one of $f(p_j)$ and $g(p_j)$ is different from r_i; assume, without loss of generality, that $f(p_j) = r_t \neq r_i$, and $g(p_j) \neq r_t$. Define a permutation $\pi : \{r_0, \ldots, r_{k-1}\} \to \{r_0, \ldots, r_{k-1}\}$ by $\pi(r_i) = r_0$ and $\pi(r_t) = r_{k-1}$, the rest of the values can be anything. Let $x_\pi \in \{d, e\}^*$ be the string defined for π in Claim 4. Then the promised string is defined by

$$v := x_\pi a^j.$$

The 2DFA accepts the string $u_{r_i, f} x_\pi a^j$ in two stages. In the first left-to-right sweep, it enters the state r_i after $u_{r_i, f}$, then comes to the state $r_0 = \pi(r_i)$ after x_π, and stays in this state until it reaches the right endmarker $\dashv$. Then it makes a right-to-left sweep, first coming to the state p_j after reading a^j, then maintaining this state while reading x_π, so that it enters the prefix $\vdash u_{r_i, f}$ from the right in the state p_j. By Claim 3, the automaton eventually moves from the last symbol of this prefix to the right in the state $f(p_j) = r_t$. The automaton continues by moving to the right through the substring x_π, and finishes reading it in the state $\pi(r_t) = r_{k-1}$. In this state, the automaton passes through a^j and reaches the right endmarker for the second time, accepting this time.

The computation on the string $u_{r_i, g} x_\pi a^j$ begins in the same way. Eventually, the automaton enters the prefix $\vdash u_{r_i, g}$ from the right in the state p_j, and later emerges from this prefix to the right in the state $g(p_j) \neq r_t$. Next, the automaton reads the substring x_π from left to right, and finishes reading it in a state that is *not* r_{k-1}. If the state is r_0, then the automaton loops, and if it is neither r_0 nor r_{k-1}, it rejects at the right endmarker.

Now Lemma 1 is proved as follows. Assume that $\mathcal{B}$ is a 1DFA recognizing the same language as the 2DFA $\mathcal{A}$. Then, the states reached by $\mathcal{B}$ upon reading different strings of the form $u_{r_i, f}$ must be pairwise distinct, for otherwise it would not be able to accept one of them and reject the other upon reading a string constructed in Claims 5 and 6. □

Theorem 3. *For every $n \geq 6$, there exists a language over a 5-symbol alphabet recognized by an n-state sweeping 2DFA, such that every 1DFA recognizing that language needs to have at least $\mathcal{F}(n) = \max_{k=0}^{n} k^{n-k+1}$ states.*

Therefore, the state complexity of transforming a sweeping or a direction-determinate 2DFA to a 1DFA is exactly $\mathcal{F}(n)$, whereas for 2DFA of the general form it is between $\mathcal{F}(n)$ and $|\Sigma| \cdot \mathcal{F}(n)$.

6   Estimation

Both the upper bound and the lower bound on the 2DFA to 1DFA tradeoff have been expressed in terms of the function $\mathcal{F}(n) = \max_{k=0}^{n} k^{n-k+1}$. We are now going to estimate the growth rate of this function.

Lemma 2. *For each $a \geq 16$, the maximum of the real function $\mathcal{G}_a(x) = x^{a-x}$ is reached for $x_a = (1 + o(1)) \cdot \frac{a}{\ln a}$, and this maximum accordingly is of order $\mathcal{G}_a(x_a) \leq \frac{a^a}{(\ln a)^a \cdot (e^{1 - o(1)})^a}$.*

Proof. First, it is quite easy to derive the following inequality, for $a \geq 3$:

$$a \leq \left(\tfrac{a}{\ln a}\right)^{1+r_1(a)}, \quad \text{where } r_1(a) = \tfrac{\ln\ln a}{\ln a - \ln\ln a}. \tag{1}$$

This follows from $\tfrac{\ln\ln a}{\ln a - \ln\ln a} \leq r_1(a)$. It should also be easily seen that $r_1(a) > 0$ for $a \geq 3$, and that $\lim_{a\to\infty} r_1(a) = 0$.

Our next task is to find the maximum for $\mathcal{G}_a(x) = x^{a-x} = e^{\ln x \cdot (a-x)}$. By differentiating $\mathcal{G}_a(x)$, we get $\mathcal{G}_a'(x) = e^{\ln x \cdot (a-x)} \cdot \left(\tfrac{a-x}{x} - \ln x\right)$ and, by setting $\mathcal{G}_a'(x_a) = 0$, we see that $\tfrac{a-x_a}{x_a} - \ln x_a = 0$, which gives

$$x_a \cdot \ln x_a = a - x_a. \tag{2}$$

To evaluate x_a, we first derive the following inequalities, using (2) and (1), under assumption that $a \geq 16$:

$$\tfrac{a}{\ln a} \cdot \ln \tfrac{a}{\ln a} + \tfrac{a}{\ln a} = \tfrac{a}{\ln a} \cdot (\ln \tfrac{a}{\ln a} + 1) < \tfrac{a}{\ln a} \cdot (\ln \tfrac{a}{\ln a} + \ln\ln a)$$
$$= \tfrac{a}{\ln a} \cdot \ln(\tfrac{a}{\ln a} \cdot \ln a) = \tfrac{a}{\ln a} \cdot \ln a = a = x_a \cdot \ln x_a + x_a,$$
$$x_a \cdot \ln x_a = a - x_a < a = \tfrac{a}{\ln a} \cdot \ln a \leq \tfrac{a}{\ln a} \cdot \ln\left(\tfrac{a}{\ln a}\right)^{1+r_1(a)}$$
$$= (1+r_1(a)) \cdot \tfrac{a}{\ln a} \cdot \ln \tfrac{a}{\ln a} \leq (1+r_1(a)) \cdot \tfrac{a}{\ln a} \cdot \ln\left((1+r_1(a)) \cdot \tfrac{a}{\ln a}\right).$$

Now, since both $t \cdot \ln t + t$ and $t \cdot \ln t$ are real functions monotone increasing in t, we see that $\tfrac{a}{\ln a} < x_a$ and $x_a < (1+r_1(a)) \cdot \tfrac{a}{\ln a}$. Thus, the exact value x_a can be expressed in the form

$$x_a = (1+r_2(a)) \cdot \tfrac{a}{\ln a}, \quad \text{with } 0 < r_2(a) < r_1(a). \tag{3}$$

Since $\lim_{a\to\infty} r_1(a) = 0$ by (1), we see that $\lim_{a\to\infty} r_2(a) = 0$ as well.

It only remains to evaluate $\mathcal{G}_a(x_a)$. Using (2) and (3), we get:

$$\mathcal{G}_a(x_a) = x_a^{a-x_a} = e^{\ln x_a \cdot (a - x_a)} = e^{a \cdot \ln x_a - x_a \cdot \ln x_a} = e^{a \cdot \ln x_a - a + x_a}$$
$$= e^{a \cdot (\ln(1+r_2(a)) + \ln a - \ln\ln a) - a + (1+r_2(a)) \cdot a / \ln a}$$
$$= e^{a \cdot \ln(1+r_2(a)) + a \cdot \ln a - a \cdot \ln\ln a - a + a / \ln a + r_2(a) \cdot a / \ln a}$$
$$= e^{a \cdot \ln a - a \cdot \ln\ln a - a} \cdot e^{a \cdot (\ln(1+r_2(a)) + 1 / \ln a + r_2(a) / \ln a)}$$
$$= \tfrac{a^a}{(\ln a)^a \cdot e^a} \cdot e^{a \cdot r_3(a)} = \tfrac{a^a}{(\ln a)^a \cdot (e^{1 - r_3(a)})^a}, \quad \text{where}$$
$$r_3(a) = \ln(1+r_2(a)) + \tfrac{1}{\ln a} + \tfrac{r_2(a)}{\ln a}.$$

Since $r_2(a) > 0$ and $\lim_{a\to\infty} r_2(a) = 0$, also $r_3(a) > 0$ for $a > 1$ and, moreover, $\lim_{a\to\infty} r_3(a) = 0$. ☐

Using this lemma, the following estimation of $\mathcal{F}(n)$ can be obtained:

Theorem 4. $\mathcal{F}(n) = \max_{k=0}^{n} k^{n-k+1} \leq \tfrac{(n+1)^{n+1}}{(\ln(n+1))^{n+1} \cdot (e^{1-o(1)})^{n+1}}.$

Proof. $\mathcal{F}(n) = \max_{k=0}^{n} k^{n-k+1} = \max_{k=0}^{n} k^{a-k} \leq \mathcal{G}_a(x_a) = \tfrac{a^a}{(\ln a)^a \cdot (e^{1-o(1)})^a}$
$= \tfrac{(n+1)^{n+1}}{(\ln(n+1))^{n+1} \cdot (e^{1-o(1)})^{n+1}}$, using substitution $a = n+1$. ☐

We are now ready to compare $\mathcal{F}(n)$ with $\mathcal{K}(n) = n \cdot (n^n - (n-1)^n)$, the standard tradeoff for 2DFA to 1DFA transformation, derived by Kapoutsis [5]:

Theorem 5. $\sup_{n\to\infty} \frac{\mathcal{F}(n)}{\mathcal{K}(n)} \cdot \frac{e-1}{e^2} \cdot (\ln(n+1) \cdot e^{1-o(1)})^{n+1} \leq 1.$

This is based on the fact that $\lim_{n\to\infty} \frac{(n+1)^{n+1}}{n\cdot(n^n-(n-1)^n)} = \frac{e^2}{e-1}$ (omitted due to space constraints). Accordingly, the proposed 2DFA to 1DFA transformation given in Theorem 2 improves over the construction by Kapoutsis [5] as long as $|\Sigma| < \frac{e-1}{e^2} \cdot (\ln(n+1) \cdot e^{1-o(1)})^{n+1}$.

References

1. Barnes, B.: A two-way automaton with fewer states than any equivalent one-way automaton. IEEE Trans. Comput. **C-20**, 474–475 (1971)
2. Geffert, V., Mereghetti, C., Pighizzini, G.: Converting two-way nondeterministic unary automata into simpler automata. Theoret. Comput. Sci. **295**, 189–203 (2003)
3. Geffert, V., Okhotin, A.: One-way simulation of two-way finite automata over small alphabets. In: Proceedings of Non-Classical Models of Automata & Application, pp. 151–162. Österreichische Comput. Gesellschaft (2013)
4. Geffert, V., Okhotin, A.: Transforming two-way alternating finite automata to one-way nondeterministic automata. In: Csuhaj-Varjú, E., Dietzfelbinger, M., Ésik, Z. (eds.) MFCS 2014. LNCS, vol. 8634, pp. 291–302. Springer, Heidelberg (2014). https://doi.org/10.1007/978-3-662-44522-8_25
5. Kapoutsis, C.: Removing bidirectionality from nondeterministic finite automata. In: Jędrzejowicz, J., Szepietowski, A. (eds.) MFCS 2005. LNCS, vol. 3618, pp. 544–555. Springer, Heidelberg (2005). https://doi.org/10.1007/11549345_47
6. Kapoutsis, C.: Algorithms and lower bounds in finite automata size complexity. Ph.D. thesis, Massachusetts Institute of Technology (2006)
7. Kunc, M., Okhotin, A.: Describing periodicity in two-way deterministic finite automata using transformation semigroups. In: Mauri, G., Leporati, A. (eds.) DLT 2011. LNCS, vol. 6795, pp. 324–336. Springer, Heidelberg (2011). https://doi.org/10.1007/978-3-642-22321-1_28
8. Kunc, M., Okhotin, A.: Reversibility of computations in graph-walking automata. Inform. Comput. **275** (2020). Art. 104631
9. Mereghetti, C., Pighizzini, G.: Optimal simulations between unary automata. SIAM J. Comput. **30**, 1976–1992 (2001)
10. Moore, F.: On the bounds for state-set size in the proofs of equivalence between deterministic, nondeterministic, and two-way finite automata by deterministic automata. IEEE Trans. Comput. **C-20**, 1211–1214 (1971)
11. Petrov, S., Okhotin, A.: On the transformation of two-way deterministic finite automata to unambiguous finite automata. In: Leporati, A., Martín-Vide, C., Shapira, D., Zandron, C. (eds.) LATA 2021. LNCS, vol. 12638, pp. 81–93. Springer, Cham (2021). https://doi.org/10.1007/978-3-030-68195-1_7
12. Rabin, M., Scott, D.: Finite automata and their decision problems. IBM J. Res. Develop. **3**, 114–125 (1959)
13. Shepherdson, J.: The reduction of two-way automata to one-way automata. IBM J. Res. Develop. **3**, 198–200 (1959)
14. Sipser, M.: Lower bounds on the size of sweeping automata. In: Proceedings of the ACM Symposium on Theory of Computing, pp. 360–364 (1979)
15. Vardi, M.: A note on the reduction of two-way automata to one-way automata. Inform. Process. Lett. **30**, 261–264 (1989)

Sync-Maximal Permutation Groups Equal Primitive Permutation Groups

Stefan Hoffmann$^{(\boxtimes)}$ (iD)

Informatikwissenschaften, FB IV, Universität Trier, Universitätsring 15,
54296 Trier, Germany
hoffmanns@informatik.uni-trier.de

Abstract. The set of synchronizing words of a given n-state automaton forms a regular language recognizable by an automaton with $2^n - n$ states. The size of a recognizing automaton for the set of synchronizing words is linked to computational problems related to synchronization and to the length of synchronizing words. Hence, it is natural to investigate synchronizing automata extremal with this property, i.e., such that the minimal deterministic automaton for the set of synchronizing words has $2^n - n$ states. The sync-maximal permutation groups have been introduced in [S. HOFFMANN, Completely Reachable Automata, Primitive Groups and the State Complexity of the Set of Synchronizing Words, LATA 2021] by stipulating that an associated automaton to the group and a non-permutation has this extremal property. The definition is in analogy with the synchronizing groups and analog to a characterization of primitivity obtained in the mentioned work. The precise relation to other classes of groups was mentioned as an open problem. Here, we solve this open problem by showing that the sync-maximal groups are precisely the primitive groups. Our result gives a new characterization of the primitive groups. Lastly, we explore an alternative and stronger definition than sync-maximality.

Keywords: Finite automata · Synchronization · Set of synchronizing words · Primitive permutation groups · Sync-Maximal groups

1 Introduction

An automaton is synchronizing if it admits a word that drives every state into a single definite state. Synchronizing automata have a range of applications in software testing, circuit synthesis, communication engineering and the like, see [29,43,49]. The Černý conjecture states that the length of a shortest synchronizing word for a deterministic complete automaton with n states has length at most $(n-1)^2$ [13,14]. The best bound up to now is cubic [44]. This conjecture is one of the most famous open problems in combinatorial automata theory [49]. More specifically, the following bounds have been established:

© IFIP International Federation for Information Processing 2021
Published by Springer International Publishing AG 2021. All Rights Reserved
Y.-S. Han and S.-K. Ko (Eds.): DCFS 2021, LNCS 13037, pp. 38–50, 2021.
https://doi.org/10.1007/978-3-030-93489-7_4

$2^n - n - 1$		(1964, Černý [13])
$\frac{1}{2}n^3 - \frac{3}{2}n^2 + n + 1$		(1966, Starke [45])
$\frac{1}{2}n^3 - n^2 + \frac{n}{2}$		(1970, Kohavi [29])
$\frac{1}{3}n^3 - n^2 - \frac{1}{3}n + 6$		(1970, Kfourny [28])
$\frac{1}{3}n^3 - \frac{3}{2}n^2 + \frac{25}{6}n - 4$		(1971, Černý et al. [14])
$\frac{7}{27}n^3 - \frac{17}{18}n^2 + \frac{17}{6}n - 3$	$n \equiv 0 \pmod{3}$	(1977, Pin [35])
$\left(\frac{1}{2} + \frac{\pi}{36}\right)n^3 + o(n^3)$		(1981, Pin [37])
$\frac{1}{6}n^3 - \frac{1}{6}n - 1$		(1983, Pin/Frankl [21,38])
$\alpha n^3 + o(n^3)$	$\alpha \approx 0.1664$	(2018, Szykuła [47])
$\alpha n^3 + o(n^3)$	$\alpha \leqslant 0.1654$	(2019, Shitov [44])

Furthermore, the Černý conjecture [13] has been confirmed for a variety of classes of automata, just to name a few (without further explanation): circular automata [16,17,36], oriented or (generalized) monotonic automata [2,3,18], automata with a sink state [39], solvable and commutative automata [20,39,40], Eulerian automata [27], automata preserving a chain of partial orders [50], automata whose transition monoid contains a QI-group [7,8], certain one-cluster automata [46], automata that cannot recognize $\{a,b\}^*ab\{a,b\}^*$ [1], aperiodic automata [48], certain aperiodically 1-contracting automata [15] and automata having letters of a certain rank [9].

Černý [13] gave an infinite family of synchronizing n-state automata with shortest synchronizing words of length $(n-1)^2$. Families of synchronizing automata with shortest synchronizing words close to $(n-1)^2$ are called *slowly synchronizing*. There are only a few families of slowly synchronizing automata known, see [49].

The set of synchronizing words of an n-state automaton is a regular language and can be recognized by an automaton of size $2^n - n$ [13,32,45]. A property shared by most families of slowly synchronizing automata is that for them, every automaton for the set of synchronizing words needs exponentially many states [25,32,33]. Note that, of course, by taking an automaton and adjoining a letter mapping every state to a single state, as the extremal property of the set of synchronizing words is preserved by adding letters, automata whose sets of synchronizing words have exponential state complexity in the number of states are not necessarily slowly synchronizing. However, the evidence supports the conjecture that slowly synchronizing automata have this extremal property.

Testing if an automaton is synchronizing is doable in polynomial time [13,49]. However, computing a shortest synchronizing word is hard, more precisely, the decision variant of this problem is NP-complete [18,42], even for automata over a fixed binary alphabet. Moreover, variants of the synchronization problem for partial automata, or when restricting the set of allowed reset words, could even be PSPACE-complete [19,31].

The size of a smallest automaton for the set of synchronizing words seems to be also related to the difficulty to compute a shortest synchronizing word, or a synchronizing word subject to certain constraints. A first result in this direction was the realization that for commutative automata, i.e., where each permutation of an input word leads to the same state, and a fixed alphabet, we do not have such an exponential blowup for the size of the minimal automaton for set of synchronizing words [23,24]. As a consequence, the constrained synchronization problem for commutative input automata and a fixed constraint is always solvable in polynomial time [23,24]. Note that for commutative input automata and a fixed alphabet, computing a shortest synchronizing can be done in polynomial time [30]

So, it is natural to focus on synchronizing automata such that the smallest automaton for the set of synchronizing words has maximal possible size.

After realizing that for certain special cases for which the Černý conjecture was established [8,16,17,36,41], this was due to the reason that certain permutation groups were contained in the transformation monoid of the automaton, the notion of synchronizing permutation groups was introduced [7,8]. These are permutation groups with the property that if we adjoin a non-permutation to it, the generated transformation monoid contains a constant map. It was shown that these groups are contained strictly between the 2-transitive and the primitive groups [7,34]. Meanwhile, a lot of related permutation groups have been introduced or linked to the synchronizing groups, for example: spreading, separating, QI-groups. See [7] for a good survey and definitions. Furthermore, permutation groups in general have been investigated with respect to the properties of resulting transformation monoids if non-permutations were added [4–7].

The completely reachable automata have been introduced by Volkov & Bondar [10,11]. This is a stronger notion than being synchronizing by stipulating that, starting from the whole state set, not only some singleton set is reachable, but every non-empty subset of states is reachable by some word. In fact, this property was also previously observed for many classes of synchronizing automata [15,25,32,33].

It has been proven in [22] that a permutation group of degree n is primitive if and only if in the transformation monoid generated by the group and an arbitrary non-permutation with an image of size $n - 1$, there exists, for every non-empty subset of the permutation domain, an element mapping the whole permutation domain to this subset, or said differently that an associated automaton is completely reachable. In the same paper [22] the sync-maximal permutation groups were introduced by stipulating that, for an associated n-state automaton, the smallest automaton for the set of synchronizing words has size $2^n - n$. It was shown that the sync-maximal permutation groups are contained between the 2-homogeneous and the primitive permutation groups, and it was posed as an open problem if they are properly contained between them, and if so, what the precise relation to other permutation groups is.

Here, we solve this open problem by showing that the sync-maximal permutation groups are precisely the primitive permutation groups, which also yields new characterizations of the primitive permutation groups.

2   Preliminaries

Let Σ be a finite set of symbols, called an *alphabet*. By Σ^*, we denote the *set of all finite sequences*, i.e., of all words or strings. The *empty word*, i.e., the finite sequence of length zero, is denoted by ε. The subsets of Σ^* are called *languages*. For $n > 0$, we set $[n] = \{0, 1, \ldots, n-1\}$ and $[0] = \varnothing$. For a set X, we denote the *power set* of X by $\mathcal{P}(X)$, i.e., the set of all subsets of X. Every function $f : X \rightarrow Y$ induces a function $\hat{f} : \mathcal{P}(X) \rightarrow \mathcal{P}(Y)$ by setting $\hat{f}(Z) := \{f(z) \mid z \in Z\}$. Here, we denote this extension also by f. Let $k \geqslant 1$. A *k-subset* $Y \subseteq X$ is a finite set of cardinality k. A 1-set is also called a *singleton set*. For functions $f : A \rightarrow B$ and $g : B \rightarrow C$, the *functional composition* $gf : A \rightarrow C$ is the function $(gf)(x) = g(f(x))$, i.e., the function on the right is applied first[1]. A function $f : X \rightarrow X$ is called *idempotent* if $f^2 = f$.

A *semi-automaton* is a triple $\mathcal{A} = (\Sigma, Q, \delta)$ where Σ is the *input alphabet*, Q the finite set of *states* and $\delta : Q \times \Sigma \rightarrow Q$ the *transition function*. The transition function $\delta : Q \times \Sigma \rightarrow Q$ extends to a transition function on words $\delta^* : Q \times \Sigma^* \rightarrow Q$ by setting $\delta^*(s, \varepsilon) := s$ and $\delta^*(s, wa) := \delta(\delta^*(s, w), a)$ for $s \in Q$, $a \in \Sigma$ and $w \in \Sigma^*$. In the remainder we drop the distinction between both functions and also denote this extension by δ. For $S \subseteq Q$ and $w \in \Sigma^*$, we write $\delta(S, w) = \{\delta(s, w) \mid s \in S\}$. A state $q \in Q$ is *reachable* from a state $p \in Q$, if there exists $w \in \Sigma^*$ such that $\delta(p, w) = q$. The *set of synchronizing words* is $\mathrm{Syn}(\mathcal{A}) = \{w \in \Sigma^* \mid |\delta(Q, w)| = 1\}$. A semi-automaton $\mathcal{A} = (\Sigma, Q, \delta)$ is called *synchronizing*, if $\mathrm{Syn}(\mathcal{A}) \neq \varnothing$. We call $\mathcal{A}$ *completely reachable*, if for each non-empty $S \subseteq Q$ there exists a word $w \in \Sigma^*$ such that $\delta(Q, w) = S$. Note that every completely reachable automaton is synchronizing.

A *(finite) automaton* is a quintuple $\mathcal{A} = (\Sigma, Q, \delta, q_0, F)$ where (Σ, Q, δ) is a semi-automaton, $q_0 \in Q$ is the *start state* and $F \subseteq Q$ the set of *final states*. The *languages recognized (by $\mathcal{A}$)* is $L(\mathcal{A}) = \{w \in \Sigma^* \mid \delta(q_0, w) \in F\}$. An automaton with a start state and a set of final states is used for the description of languages, whereas, when we consider a semi-automaton, we are only concerned with the transition structure of the automaton itself. When the context is clear, we also call semi-automata simply automata and concepts and notions that do not use the start state or the final state carry over from semi-automata to automata and vice versa.

A language recognized by a finite automaton is called *regular*. An automaton $\mathcal{A}$ has the least number of states to recognize a language [26], i.e., is a *minimal automaton*, if and only if every state is reachable from the start state and every two distinct states $p, q \in Q$ are *distinguishable*, i.e., there exists $w \in \Sigma^*$ such that precisely one of the states $\delta(p, w)$ and $\delta(q, w)$ is a final state, but not the other. A minimal automaton is unique up to isomorphism [26], where two automata are isomorphic if one can be obtained from the other by renaming of states. Hence, we can speak about the minimal automaton.

If $\mathcal{A} = (\Sigma, Q, \delta)$ is a semi-automaton with a non-empty state set, then define $\mathcal{P}_{\mathcal{A}} = (\Sigma, \mathcal{P}(Q) \backslash \{\varnothing\}, \hat{\delta}, Q, F)$ where $\hat{\delta} : \mathcal{P}(Q) \times \Sigma \rightarrow \mathcal{P}(Q)$ is the extension $\hat{\delta}(S, u) = \{\delta(s, u) \mid s \in S\}$, for $S \subseteq Q$ and $u \in \Sigma^*$, of δ to subsets of states and $F = \{\{q\} \mid q \in Q\}$. As for functions $f : X \rightarrow Y$ introduced above, we drop the distinction between δ and $\hat{\delta}$ and denote both functions by δ. We have,

---

[1] In group theory, usually the other convention is adopted, but we stick to the convention most often seen in formal language theory.

$\mathrm{Syn}(\mathcal{A}) = \{w \in \Sigma^* \mid \delta(Q, w) \in F\}$. The states in F can be merged to a single state to get a recognizing automaton for $\mathrm{Syn}(\mathcal{A})$. So, $\mathrm{Syn}(\mathcal{A})$ is recognizable by an automaton with $2^{|Q|} - |Q|$ states.

Let $n \geqslant 0$. Denote by $\mathcal{S}_n$ the *symmetric group on* $[n]$, i.e., the group of all permutations of $[n]$. A *permutation group (of degree n)* is a subgroup of $\mathcal{S}_n$. A permutation group G over $[n]$ is *primitive*, if it preserves no non-trivial equivalence relation[2] on $[n]$, i.e., for no non-trivial equivalence relation $\sim \subseteq [n] \times [n]$ we have $p \sim q$ if and only if $g(p) \sim g(q)$ for all $g \in G$ and $p, q \in [n]$ (recall that the elements of G are functions from $[n]$ to $[n]$). Equivalently, a permutation group is primitive if there does not exist a non-empty proper subset $\Delta \subseteq [n]$ with $|\Delta| > 1$ such that, for every $g \in G$, we have $g(\Delta) = \Delta$ or $g(\Delta) \cap \Delta = \emptyset$. A permutation group G over $[n]$ is called k-homogeneous for some $k \geqslant 1$, if for every two k-subsets S, T of $[n]$, there exists $g \in G$ such that $g(S) = T$. A *transitive* permutation group is the same as a 1-homogeneous permutation group. Note that here, all permutation groups with $n \leqslant 2$ are primitive, and for $n > 2$ every primitive group is transitive. Because of this, some authors exclude the trivial group for $n = 2$ from being primitive. A permutation group G over $[n]$ is called k-*transitive* for some $k \geqslant 1$, if for two k-tuples $(p_1, \ldots, p_k), (q_1, \ldots, q_k) \in [n]^k$, there exists $g \in G$ such that $(g(p_1), \ldots, g(p_k)) = (q_1, \ldots, q_k)$.

By $\mathcal{T}_n$, we denote the set of all maps on $[n]$. The elements of $[n]$ are also called *points* in this context. A submonoid of $\mathcal{T}_n$ for some n is called a *transformation monoid*. If the set U is a submonoid (or a subgroup) of $\mathcal{T}_n$ (or $\mathcal{S}_n$) we denote this by $U \leqslant \mathcal{T}_n$ (or $U \leqslant \mathcal{S}_n$). For a set $A \subseteq \mathcal{T}_n$ (or $A \subseteq \mathcal{S}_n$), we denote by $\langle A \rangle$ the submonoid (or the subgroup) generated by A. If $A = \{a_1, \ldots, a_m\}$ we also write $\langle a_1, \ldots, a_m \rangle = \langle A \rangle$. Let $\mathcal{A} = (\Sigma, Q, \delta)$ be a semi-automaton and for $w \in \Sigma^*$ define $\delta_w : Q \to Q$ by $\delta_w(q) = \delta(q, w)$ for all $q \in Q$. Then, we can associate with $\mathcal{A}$ the *transformation monoid of the automaton* $\mathcal{T}_\mathcal{A} = \{\delta_w \mid w \in \Sigma^*\}$, where we can identify Q with $[n]$ for $n = |Q|$. We have $\mathcal{T}_\mathcal{A} = \langle \{\delta_x \mid x \in \Sigma\} \rangle$. The *rank* of a map $f : [n] \to [n]$ is the cardinality of its image. For a given semi-automaton $\mathcal{A} = (\Sigma, Q, \delta)$, the *rank of a word* $w \in \Sigma^*$ is the rank of δ_w. We call two sets $S, T \subseteq [n]$ *distinguishable* in a transformation monoid $M \leqslant \mathcal{T}_n$ if there exists an element in M mapping precisely one of both sets to a singleton set and the other to a non-singleton set.

The following implies that we can check if a given semi-automaton is synchronizing by only looking at pairs of states [13,49]. The proof basically works by repeatedly collapsing pairs of states to construct a synchronizing word [49]. It implies a polynomial time procedure to check synchronizability [49].

Theorem 1 Černý [13,49]. *Let* $\mathcal{A} = (\Sigma, Q, \delta)$. *Then,* $\mathcal{A}$ *is synchronizing if and only if for each* $p, q \in Q$ *there exists* $w \in \Sigma^*$ *such that* $\delta(p, w) = \delta(q, w)$. *Hence, a transformation monoid* $M \leqslant \mathcal{T}_n$ *contains a constant map if and only if every two points can be mapped to a single point by elements in* M.

The next result appears in [6,7] and despite it was never clearly spelled out by Rystsov himself, it is implicitly present in arguments used in [41].

---

[2] The trivial equivalence relations on $[n]$ are $[n] \times [n]$ and $\{(x, x) \mid x \in [n]\}$.

Theorem 2 Rystsov [6,7,41]. *A permutation group G on $[n]$ is primitive if and only if, for every map $f : [n] \to [n]$ of rank $n-1$, the transformation monoid $\langle G \cup \{f\} \rangle$ contains a constant map.*

In [22], the following characterization of the primitive permutation groups, connecting them to completely reachable automata, was shown.

Theorem 3 Hoffmann [22]. *Let $G = \langle g_1, \ldots, g_k \rangle \leqslant S_n$. Then the following are equivalent:*

1. *G is primitive;*
2. *for every transformation $f : [n] \to [n]$ of rank $n-1$ and non-empty $S \subseteq [n]$, there exists $g \in \langle G \cup \{f\} \rangle$ such that $g([n]) = S$;*
3. *for every transformation $f : [n] \to [n]$ of rank $n-1$, the semi-automaton $\mathcal{A} = (\Sigma, Q, \delta)$, with $\Sigma = \{g_1, \ldots, g_k, f\}$, $Q = [n]$ and $\delta(m, g) = g(m)$ for all $m \in [n]$ and all $g \in \Sigma$, is completely reachable.*

In the same work [22], in analogy with Theorem 2 and 3, the *sync-maximal permutation groups* were introduced.

Definition 4. *A permutation group $G = \langle g_1, \ldots, g_k \rangle \leqslant S_n$ is called sync-maximal, if for every map $f \colon [n] \to [n]$ of rank $n-1$, for the automaton $\mathcal{A} = (\Sigma, [n], \delta)$ with $\Sigma = \{g_1, \ldots, g_k, f\}$ and $\delta(m, g) = g(m)$ for $m \in [n]$ and $g \in \Sigma$, the minimal automaton of $\mathrm{Syn}(\mathcal{A})$ has $2^n - n$ states.*

This definition is independent of the choice of generators for G. In purely combinatorial language, using the characterization of the minimal automaton, applied to $\mathcal{P}_A$, this means the following.

Theorem 5. *A permutation group $G \leqslant S_n$ is sync-maximal if and only if for every transformation $f : [n] \to [n]$ of rank $n-1$, we have that (1) for every non-empty subset $S \subseteq [n]$ of size at least two[3] there exists $h \in \langle G \cup \{f\} \rangle$ such that $S = h([n])$, and (2) for two distinct non-empty and non-singleton subsets of $[n]$, there exists a transformation in $\langle G \cup \{f\} \rangle$ mapping precisely one to a singleton but not the other.*

In [22] it was shown that every sync-maximal permutation groups is primitive. The main result of the present work is that the converse implication holds true.

Proposition 6 [22]. *Every sync-maximal permutation group is primitive.*

In [22, Lemma 3.1] it was shown that distinguishability of all sets reduces to distinguishablity of the 2-subsets. Formulated without reference to automata, this gives the next result.

---

[3] As f has rank $n-1$, this also implies that at least one singleton set is reachable. In fact, even more holds true, with [22, Lemma 4.1] we can deduce that G is transitive and so for every non-empty $S \subseteq [n]$ there exists $h \in \langle G \cup \{f\} \rangle$ with $S = h([n])$.

Theorem 7 [22]. *Let $M \leqslant \mathcal{T}_n$ be a transformation monoid. Then, for every two distinct non-empty and non-singleton $S, T \subseteq [n]$ there exists a transformation in M mapping precisely one to a singleton but not the other if and only if this condition holds true for every two distinct 2-subsets of $[n]$.*

The next lemma is obvious, as it basically states the definition of injectivity for the restriction of a function to a subset, and stated for reference.

Lemma 8. *Let $f : [n] \to [n]$ and $S \subseteq [n]$. Then, $|S \cap f^{-1}(x)| \leqslant 1$ for each $x \in [n]$ if and only if f acts injective on S, i.e., $|f(S)| = |S|$.*

3   Sync-Maximal Permutation Groups Equal Primitive Permutation Groups – The Proof

Here, we will prove the following theorem.

Theorem 9. *Let $G = \langle g_1, \ldots, g_k \rangle \leqslant S_n$. Then the following are equivalent:*

1. *G is primitive;*
2. *for every transformation $f : [n] \to [n]$ of rank $n - 1$ and $\{a, b\}, \{c, d\} \subseteq [n]$ with $\{a, b\} \neq \{c, d\}$, there exists $g \in \langle G \cup \{f\} \rangle$ such that precisely one of the subsets $g(\{a, b\})$ and $g(\{c, d\})$ is a singleton but not the other;*
3. *G is sync-maximal.*

At the heart of our result is the following statement.

Proposition 10. *Let $G \leqslant S_n$ be a permutation group and $f : [n] \to [n]$ be an idempotent map of rank $n - 1$. Suppose $\langle G \cup \{f\} \rangle$ contains a constant map. Then, for all $\{a, b\}, \{c, d\} \subseteq [n]$ with $\{a, b\} \neq \{c, d\}$ there exists a transformation in $\langle G \cup \{f\} \rangle$ mapping precisely one set to a singleton but not the other.*

Proof. Suppose $G = \langle g_1, \ldots, g_k \rangle$. Let $\{a, b\}, \{c, d\} \subseteq [n]$ be two distinct 2-sets and $f : [n] \to [n]$ being idempotent and of rank $n - 1$. Without loss of generality, we can suppose $f(0) = f(1) = 1$ and $f(i) = i$ for $i \in \{2, \ldots, n - 1\}$. As $\langle G \cup \{f\} \rangle$ contains a constant map, we can map $\{a, b\}$ to a singleton set. Choose a transformation $h \in \langle G \cup \{f\} \rangle$ represented by a shortest possible word in the generators of G and f such that $|h(\{a, b\})| = 1$. Then, we can write $h = f u_m f u_{m-1} f \cdots u_2 f u_1$ with $u_i \in G$, $m \geqslant 1$. Note that, by the minimal choice, the transformation f is applied at the end[4]. If $h(\{c, d\})$ is not a singleton set, we are done. So, suppose $h(\{c, d\})$ is also a singleton set. For $i \in \{1, \ldots, m\}$, set $h_i = f u_i f u_{i-1} f \cdots u_2 f u_1$. Then, $h = h_m$. By minimality of the representation in the generators of G and f, for all $i \in \{1, \ldots, m - 1\}$ we have $|h_i(\{a, b\})| = 2$. Hence, if there exists $i \in \{1, \ldots, m - 1\}$ such that $h_i(\{c, d\})$ is a singleton set, we are also done. So, suppose this is not the case.

---

[4] Recall that by our convention, the leftmost function is applied last.

Set $g_i = u_i f u_{i-1} f \cdots u_2 f u_1$. Then, $h_i = f g_i$. We must have $0 \in g_i(\{a, b\})$ for all i, for otherwise, as f acts as the identity on $\{1, \ldots, n-1\}$, we can leave f out, i.e., $g_i(\{a, b\}) = h_i(\{a, b\})$, in the expression for h and get a shorter representing word, contradicting the minimal choice of the expression representing h. Similarly, $0 \in g_i(\{c, d\})$ for all i, as otherwise we can leave a single instance of f out again and have a word that maps $\{c, d\}$ to a singleton, but not $\{a, b\}$ by the minimal choice of h in the length of a representing word.

Note that, as $|g_m(\{a, b\})| = |g_m(\{c, d\})| = 2$, $|h_m(\{a, b\})| = |h_m(\{c, d\})| = 1$ and $h_m = f g_m$, we must have $g_m(\{a, b\}) = g_m(\{c, d\}) = \{0, 1\}$.

Next, we will show by induction on $j \in \{1, \ldots, m\}$ that $g_j(\{a, b\}) = g_j(\{c, d\})$, where the base case is $j = m$. Then, $g_1(\{a, b\}) = g_1(\{c, d\})$ implies $\{a, b\} = \{c, d\}$ as $g_1 = u_1 \in G$ is a permutation. However, this is a contradiction as both 2-sets are assumed to be distinct. Hence, the case that h_m maps both to a singleton and h_i for all $i \neq m$ maps both to 2-sets is not possible. As noted, for the base case we have $g_m(\{a, b\}) = g_m(\{c, d\}) = \{0, 1\}$. Now suppose $j \in \{1, \ldots, m-1\}$ and $g_{j+1}(\{a, b\}) = g_{j+1}(\{c, d\})$. Then, as $g_{j+1} = u_{j+1} f g_j = u_{j+1} h_j$, we can deduce $h_j(\{a, b\}) = h_j(\{c, d\})$ as they only differ by the application of the permutation $u_{j+1} \in G$. As written above $0 \in g_j(\{a, b\}) \cap g_j(\{c, d\})$. This implies, as $|h_j(\{a, b\})| = |h_j(\{c, d\})| = 2$, that $1 \notin g_j(\{a, b\}) \cup g_j(\{c, d\})$. So, $|f^{-1}(x) \cap g_j(\{a, b\})| \leqslant 1$ and $|f^{-1}(x) \cap g_j(\{c, d\})| \leqslant 1$ for every $x \in [n]$. As $h_j = f g_j$, we can write $f(g_j(\{a, b\})) = f(g_j(\{c, d\}))$. Applying Lemma 8 then yields $g_j(\{a, b\}) = g_j(\{c, d\})$. □

The following lemma allows us to assume the transformation of rank $n - 1$ in Theorem 9 is idempotent.

Lemma 11. *Let $G \leqslant S_n$ be a transitive permutation group and $f : [n] \to [n]$ be a transformation of rank $n - 1$. Then, there exists an idempotent transformation $h : [n] \to [n]$ of rank $n - 1$ such that $\langle G \cup \{h\} \rangle \leqslant \langle G \cup \{f\} \rangle$.*

So, now we have everything together to prove Theorem 9.

Proof (Proof of Theorem 9). We can assume $n > 2$, as we have not included the assumption of transitivity in our definition of primitivity (which is implied for $n > 2$, see [12]) and so, for $n \leqslant 2$ every subgroup is primitive and also fulfills the second condition vacuously, as then we cannot find two distinct 2-sets. Also, for $n \leqslant 2$, every group is sync-maximal, as is easily seen by case analysis.

So first, let $G = \langle g_1, \ldots, g_k \rangle \leqslant S_n$ be primitive and suppose $f : [n] \to [n]$ is a transformation of rank $n - 1$. By Lemma 11, there exists an idempotent transformation $f' \in \langle G \cup \{f\} \rangle$. By Theorem 2 in $\langle G \cup \{f'\} \rangle$ we find a constant map. Then, by Proposition 10, for distinct 2-sets there exists an element in $\langle G \cup \{f'\} \rangle \subseteq \langle G \cup \{f\} \rangle$ mapping precisely one of both 2-sets to a singleton set.

Now, suppose the second condition holds true. First, note that the second condition implies for $n > 2$ and $\{a, b\} \subseteq [n]$ that there must exist $g \in G$ such that $g(\{a, b\}) \neq \{a, b\}$. Assume this is not the case. Then, for $c \notin \{a, b\}$, we have

$$\{g(\{a, c\}), g(\{b, c\})\} \cap \{\{a, b\}\} = \varnothing \tag{1}$$

for every $g \in G$ and, more generally, we have $\{g(\{d, e\}), g(\{d', e'\})\} \cap \{\{a, b\}\} = \varnothing$ for every $g \in G$ and $\{d, e\}, \{d', e'\}$ not equal to $\{a, b\}$. Choose $c \in [n] \backslash \{a, b\}$ and $f' : [n] \to [n]$ idempotent of rank $n - 1$ with $f'(a) = f'(b) = b$. Then, with Eq. (1) we can deduce $\{h(\{a, c\}), h(\{b, c\})\} \cap \{\{a, b\}\} = \varnothing$ for $h \in \langle G \cup \{f'\}\rangle$. So, it is not possible to map one of $\{a, c\}$ and $\{b, c\}$ to a singleton set. But this is excluded by assumption, so there must exist an element in G mapping $\{a, b\}$ to a different 2-subset.

So, now let $f : [n] \to [n]$ be an arbitrary transformation of rank $n - 1$ and $\mathcal{A} = (\Sigma, Q, \delta)$ be the automaton with $\Sigma = \{g_1, \ldots, g_k, f\}$, $Q = [n]$ and $\delta(i, x) = x(i)$ for $i \in [n]$ and $x \in \Sigma$. Then, the second condition precisely says that all non-empty 2-sets are distinguishable in $\mathcal{P}_\mathcal{A}$. With Theorem 7, then all non-empty subsets with at least two elements are distinguishable in $\mathcal{P}_\mathcal{A}$. So, we only need to show that all non-empty subsets with at least two elements are reachable and at least one singleton subset is reachable in $\mathcal{A}$. In fact, we will establish the stronger statement that $\mathcal{A}$ is completely reachable. Let $\{a, b\} \subseteq [n]$ be a 2-subset. As shown above, we can choose $g \in G$ with $g(\{a, b\}) \neq \{a, b\}$. Then, by assumption, there exists $h \in \langle G \cup \{f\}\rangle$ such that precisely one of $h(\{a, b\})$ or $(hg)(\{a, b\})$ is a singleton set. By Theorem 1, as $\{a, b\}$ was arbitrary, $\langle G \cup \{f\}\rangle$ contains a constant map. As $f : [n] \to [n]$ was arbitrary of rank $n - 1$, by Theorem 2 the group G is primitive and so, by Theorem 3, the automaton $\mathcal{A}$ is completely reachable.

Finally, suppose the last condition is fulfilled, i.e., G is sync-maximal. Then, by Proposition 6, G is primitive. □

Note that, by Lemma 11, in the statements of Theorem 3 and 9 it is enough if the mentioned conditions hold for idempotent transformations of rank $n - 1$ only.

With a little more work, we can show the following statement. By Lemma 11, we can always restrict to idempotent transformations for the mentioned characterizations[5], hence every statement entails two statements: one for all transformations of rank $n - 1$ and one for idempotent transformations of rank $n - 1$ only. Both formulations are put into a single statement by putting the word "idempotent" in square brackets in Theorem 12.

Theorem 12. *Let $G \leqslant S_n$ be a permutation group and $n \geqslant 5$. Then the following are equivalent:*

(1) G is primitive;

(2) for every [idempotent] transformation $f : [n] \to [n]$ of rank $n - 1$, in the transformation semigroup $\langle G \cup \{f\}\rangle$ we find, for each non-empty $S \subseteq [n]$, an element $g \in \langle G \cup \{f\}\rangle$ such that $g([n]) = S$;

(3) for every [idempotent] transformation $f : [n] \to [n]$ of rank $n - 1$ and 2-sets $\{a, b\}, \{c, d\} \subseteq [n]$ with $\{a, b\} \neq \{c, d\}$, there exists a transformation in $\langle G \cup \{f\}\rangle$ mapping precisely one to a singleton, but not the other;

---

[5] In case of Theorem 3, which was proven in the conference version [22], this was communicated to me, for which I am thankful, by an anonymous referee of [22].

(4) for every [idempotent] transformation $f: [n] \rightarrow [n]$ of rank $n - 1$ and two distinct non-empty and non-singleton subsets $S, T \subseteq [n]$, there exists a transformation in $\langle G \cup \{f\} \rangle$ mapping one to a singleton but not the other;

(5) for every [idempotent] transformation $f: [n] \rightarrow [n]$ of rank $n - 1$ and two distinct non-empty and non-singleton subsets $S, T \subseteq [n]$, there exists a transformation in $\langle G \cup \{f\} \rangle$ mapping both to subsets of different *cardinality;*

(6) for every [idempotent] transformation $f: [n] \rightarrow [n]$ of rank $n - 1$ and two disjoint non-empty 2-sets $\{a, b\}, \{c, d\} \subseteq [n]$, there exists a transformation in $\langle G \cup \{f\} \rangle$ mapping precisely one to a singleton, but not the other.

4 Strongly Sync-Maximal Permutation Groups

As the sync-maximal groups turned out to be precisely the primitive permutation groups, can we alter the definition to give us a new class of permutation groups related to the size of the minimal automata for the set of synchronizing words? One first approach might be to demand that, for each transformation of rank $n - k$, if we add this to the group, in the resulting transformation monoid every non-empty set of size at most $n - k$ is reachable and two distinct non-empty and non-singleton subsets S, T of states with $|S|, |T| \in \{m \mid m \leqslant n - k\} \cup \{n\}$ can be mapped to sets of different cardinality. However, it is easy to show that every such group is k-reachable as introduced in [22]. So, also with the results from [22], for $6 \leqslant k \leqslant n - 6$ this condition is only fulfilled by the symmetric or the alternating groups.

So, in the following definition, we only demand the distinguishability conditions, but not the reachability condition. Note that in the characterizations of primitive groups given above, both conditions – either distinguishability or reachability – are equivalent if we add a transformation of rank $n - 1$.

Definition 13. *A permutation group $G \leqslant S_n$ is called* strongly sync-maximal *if for each transformation $f : [n] \rightarrow [n]$ of rank r with $2 \leqslant r \leqslant n - 1$ in $\langle G \cup \{f\} \rangle$ all 2-subsets are distinguishable.*

Proposition 14. *Every 4-transitive group is strongly sync-maximal and every strongly sync-maximal group is primitive.*

Whether the strongly sync-maximal groups are properly contained between the above mentioned groups is an open problem. If so, the precise relation to the synchronizing groups and other classes of groups is an open problem and remains for future work.

Acknowledgement. I thank the anonymous referees for carefully reading through the present work and pointing out unclear formulations and typos. I am also grateful to the referee that pointed me to additional work I was not aware of. Unfortunately, due to space, I could not discuss all of them, in particular the connections to decoders and probabilistic investigations on the length of synchronizing words. The results of this submission will be incorporated into the extended version of [22].

References

1. Almeida, J., Steinberg, B.: Matrix mortality and the Černý-Pin conjecture. In: Diekert, V., Nowotka, D. (eds.) DLT 2009. LNCS, vol. 5583, pp. 67–80. Springer, Heidelberg (2009). https://doi.org/10.1007/978-3-642-02737-6_5

2. Ananichev, D.S., Volkov, M.V.: Synchronizing monotonic automata. In: Ésik, Z., Fülöp, Z. (eds.) DLT 2003. LNCS, vol. 2710, pp. 111–121. Springer, Heidelberg (2003). https://doi.org/10.1007/3-540-45007-6_8

3. Ananichev, D.S., Volkov, M.V.: Synchronizing generalized monotonic automata. Theor. Comput. Sci. **330**(1), 3–13 (2005)

4. Araújo, J., Bentz, W., Cameron, P.J.: Primitive permutation groups and strongly factorizable transformation semigroups. J. Algebra **565**, 513–530 (2021)

5. Araújo, J., Bentz, W., Cameron, P.J.: The existential transversal property: a generalization of homogeneity and its impact on semigroups. Trans. Am. Math. Soc. **371**, 105–136 (2019)

6. Araújo, J., Cameron, P.J.: Primitive groups synchronize non-uniform maps of extreme ranks. J. Comb. Theor. Ser. B **106**, 98–114 (2014)

7. Araújo, J., Cameron, P.J., Steinberg, B.: Between primitive and 2-transitive: synchronization and its friends. EMS Surv. Math. Sci. **4**(2), 101–184 (2017)

8. Arnold, F., Steinberg, B.: Synchronizing groups and automata. Theor. Comput. Sci. **359**(1–3), 101–110 (2006)

9. Berlinkov, M.V., Szykula, M.: Algebraic synchronization criterion and computing reset words. Inf. Sci. **369**, 718–730 (2016)

10. Bondar, E.A., Volkov, M.V.: Completely reachable automata. In: Câmpeanu, C., Manea, F., Shallit, J. (eds.) DCFS 2016. LNCS, vol. 9777, pp. 1–17. Springer, Cham (2016). https://doi.org/10.1007/978-3-319-41114-9_1

11. Bondar, E.A., Volkov, M.V.: A characterization of completely reachable automata. In: Hoshi, M., Seki, S. (eds.) DLT 2018. LNCS, vol. 11088, pp. 145–155. Springer, Cham (2018). https://doi.org/10.1007/978-3-319-98654-8_12

12. Cameron, P.J.: Permutation Groups. London Mathematical Society Student Texts, Cambridge University Press, Cambridge (1999)

13. Černý, J.: Poznámka k homogénnym experimentom s konečnými automatmi. Matematicko-fyzikálny časopis **14**(3), 208–216 (1964)

14. Černý, J., Pirická, A., Rosenauerova, B.: On directable automata. Kybernetica **7**, 289–298 (1971)

15. Don, H.: The černý conjecture and 1-contracting automata. Electron. J. Comb. **23**(3), P3.12 (2016)

16. Dubuc, L.: Les automates circulaires biaisés verifient la conjecture de Černý. Inform. Theor. Appl. **30**, 495–505 (1996)

17. Dubuc, L.: Les automates circulaires et la conjecture de Černý. Inform. Theor. Appl. **32**, 21–34 (1998)

18. Eppstein, D.: Reset sequences for monotonic automata. SIAM J. Comput. **19**(3), 500–510 (1990)

19. Fernau, H., Gusev, V.V., Hoffmann, S., Holzer, M., Volkov, M.V., Wolf, P.: Computational complexity of synchronization under regular constraints. In: Rossmanith, P., Heggernes, P., Katoen, J. (eds.) MFCS 2019. LIPIcs, vol. 138, pp. 63:1–63:14. Schloss Dagstuhl - Leibniz-Zentrum für Informatik (2019)

20. Fernau, H., Hoffmann, S.: Extensions to minimal synchronizing words. J. Autom. Lang. Comb. **24**(2–4), 287–307 (2019)

21. Frankl, P.: An extremal problem for two families of sets. Eur. J. Comb. **3**, 125–127 (1982)
22. Hoffmann, S.: Completely reachable automata, primitive groups and the state complexity of the set of synchronizing words. In: Leporati, A., Martín-Vide, C., Shapira, D., Zandron, C. (eds.) LATA 2021. LNCS, vol. 12638, pp. 305–317. Springer, Cham (2021). https://doi.org/10.1007/978-3-030-68195-1_24
23. Hoffmann, S.: Constrained synchronization and commutative languages. Theor. Comput. Sci. **890**, 147 170 (2021). https://doi.org/10.1016/j.tcs.2021.08.030
24. Hoffmann, S.: Constrained synchronization for commutative automata and automata with simple idempotents. CoRR (2021). https://arxiv.org/abs/2109.02743
25. Hoffmann, S.: State complexity of the set of synchronizing words for circular automata and automata over binary alphabets. In: Leporati, A., Martín-Vide, C., Shapira, D., Zandron, C. (eds.) LATA 2021. LNCS, vol. 12638, pp. 318–330. Springer, Cham (2021). https://doi.org/10.1007/978-3-030-68195-1_25
26. Hopcroft, J.E., Ullman, J.D.: Introduction to Automata Theory, Languages, and Computation. Addison-Wesley Publishing Company, Boston (1979)
27. Kari, J.: Synchronizing finite automata on Eulerian digraphs. In: Sgall, J., Pultr, A., Kolman, P. (eds.) MFCS 2001. LNCS, vol. 2136, pp. 432–438. Springer, Heidelberg (2001). https://doi.org/10.1007/3-540-44683-4_38
28. Kfoury, D.: Synchronizing sequences for probabilistic automata. Stud. Appl. Math. **49**, 101–103 (1970)
29. Kohavi, Z.: Switching and Finite Automata Theory. McGraw Hill, New-York (1970)
30. Martyugin, P.: Complexity of problems concerning reset words for some partial cases of automata. Acta Cybern. **19**(2), 517–536 (2009)
31. Martyugin, P.V.: Synchronization of automata with one undefined or ambiguous transition. In: Moreira, N., Reis, R. (eds.) CIAA 2012. LNCS, vol. 7381, pp. 278–288. Springer, Heidelberg (2012). https://doi.org/10.1007/978-3-642-31606-7_24
32. Maslennikova, M.I.: Reset complexity of ideal languages. CoRR abs/1404.2816 (2014)
33. Maslennikova, M.I.: Reset complexity of ideal languages over a binary alphabet. Int. J. Found. Comput. Sci. **30**(6–7), 1177–1196 (2019)
34. Neumann, P.M.: Primitive permutation groups and their section-regular partitions. Michigan Math. J. **58**, 309–322 (2009)
35. Pin, J.E.: Sur la longueur des mots de rang donné d'un automate fini. C. R. Acad. Sci. Paris Sér. A-B **284**, 1233–1235 (1977)
36. Pin, J.E.: Sur un cas particulier de la conjecture de Cerny. In: Ausiello, G., Böhm, C. (eds.) ICALP 1978. LNCS, vol. 62, pp. 345–352. Springer, Heidelberg (1978). https://doi.org/10.1007/3-540-08860-1_25
37. Pin, J.E.: Le problème de la synchronisation et la conjecture de černý. In: De luca, A. (ed.) Non-commutative Structures in Algebra and Geometric Combinatorics, Quaderni de la Ricerca Scientifica, vol. 109, pp. 37–48. CNR, Roma (1981)
38. Pin, J.E.: On two combinatorial problems arising from automata theory. Ann. Discrete Math. **17**, 535–548 (1983)
39. Rystsov, I.K.: Exact linear bound for the length of reset words in commutative automata. Publicationes Mathematicae Debrecen **48**(3–4), 405–409 (1996)
40. Rystsov, I.K.: Reset words for commutative and solvable automata. Theor. Comput. Sci. **172**, 273–279 (1997)
41. Rystsov, I.K.: Estimation of the length of reset words for automata with simple idempotents. Cybern. Syst. Anal. **36**(3), 339–344 (2000)

42. Rystsov, I.K.: On minimizing the length of synchronizing words for finite automata. In: Theory of Designing of Computing Systems, pp. 75–82. Institute of Cybernetics of Ukrainian Academy Science (1980). (in Russian)
43. Sandberg, S.: Homing and synchronizing sequences. In: Broy, M., Jonsson, B., Katoen, J.-P., Leucker, M., Pretschner, A. (eds.) Model-Based Testing of Reactive Systems. LNCS, vol. 3472, pp. 5–33. Springer, Heidelberg (2005). https://doi.org/10.1007/11498490_2
44. Shitov, Y.: An improvement to a recent upper bound for synchronizing words of finite automata. J. Automata Lang. Comb. **24**(2–4), 367–373 (2019)
45. Starke, P.H.: Eine Bemerkung über homogene Experimente. Elektronische Informationverarbeitung und Kybernetik (later J. Inf. Process. Cybern.) **2**, 61–82 (1966)
46. Steinberg, B.: The Černý conjecture for one-cluster automata with prime length cycle. Theor. Comput. Sci. **412**(39), 5487–5491 (2011)
47. Szykula, M.: Improving the upper bound on the length of the shortest reset word. In: Niedermeier, R., Vallée, B. (eds.) STACS 2018. LIPIcs, vol. 96, pp. 56:1–56:13. Schloss Dagstuhl-Leibniz-Zentrum fuer Informatik, Dagstuhl, Germany (2018)
48. Trahtman, A.N.: The Černý conjecture for aperiodic automata. Discrete Math. Theor. Comput. Sci. **9**(2), 3–10 (2007)
49. Volkov, M.V.: Synchronizing automata and the Černý conjecture. In: Martín-Vide, C., Otto, F., Fernau, H. (eds.) LATA 2008. LNCS, vol. 5196, pp. 11–27. Springer, Heidelberg (2008). https://doi.org/10.1007/978-3-540-88282-4_4
50. Volkov, M.V.: Synchronizing automata preserving a chain of partial orders. Theor. Comput. Sci. **410**(37), 3513–3519 (2009)

Commutative Regular Languages
with Product-Form Minimal Automata

Stefan Hoffmann[(✉)] [ID]

Informatikwissenschaften, FB IV, Universität Trier, Universitätsring 15,
54296 Trier, Germany
`hoffmanns@informatik.uni-trier.de`

Abstract. We introduce a subclass of the commutative regular languages
that is characterized by the property that the state set of the minimal
deterministic automaton can be written as a certain Cartesian product.
This class behaves much better with respect to the state complexity of
the shuffle, for which we find the bound $2nm$ if the input languages have
state complexities n and m, and the upward and downward closure and
interior operations, for which we find the bound n. In general, only the
bounds $(2nm)^{|\Sigma|}$ and $n^{|\Sigma|}$ are known for these operations in the commu-
tative case. We prove different characterizations of this class and present
results to construct languages from this class. Lastly, in a slightly more
general setting of partial commutativity, we introduce other, related, language classes and investigate the relations between them.

Keywords: Finite automaton · State complexity · Shuffle · Upward
closure · Downward closure · Commutative language · Product-form
minimal automaton · Partial commutation

1 Introduction

The state complexity, as used here, of a regular language L is the minimal number
of states needed in a complete deterministic automaton recognizing L. The state
complexity of an operation on regular languages is the greatest state complexity
of the result of this operation as a function of the (maximal) state complexities
of its arguments.

Investigating the state complexity of the result of a regularity-preserving
operation on regular languages, see [7] for a survey, was first initiated by Maslov
in [20] and systematically started by Yu, Zhuang and Salomaa in [27].

A language is called commutative, if for each word in the language, every
permutation of this word is also in the language. The class of commutative
automata, which recognize commutative regular languages, was introduced in [2].

The shuffle and iterated shuffle have been introduced and studied to understand the semantics of parallel programs. This was undertaken, as it appears
to be, independently by Campbell and Habermann [3], by Mazurkiewicz [22]
and by Shaw [25]. They introduced *flow expressions*, which allow for sequential

© IFIP International Federation for Information Processing 2021
Published by Springer International Publishing AG 2021. All Rights Reserved
Y.-S. Han and S.-K. Ko (Eds.): DCFS 2021, LNCS 13037, pp. 51–63, 2021.
https://doi.org/10.1007/978-3-030-93489-7_5

operators (catenation and iterated catenation) as well as for parallel operators (shuffle and iterated shuffle) to specify sequential and parallel execution traces.

The shuffle operation as a binary operation, but not the iterated shuffle, is regularity-preserving on all regular languages. The state complexity of the shuffle operation in the general cases was investigated in [1] for complete deterministic automata and in [4] for incomplete deterministic automata. The bound $2^{nm-1} + 2^{(m-1)(n-1)}(2^{m-1} - 1)(2^{n-1} - 1)$ was obtained in the former case, which is not known to be tight, and the tight bound $2^{nm} - 1$ in the latter case.

A word is a (scattered) subsequence of another word, if it can be obtained from the latter word by deleting letters. This gives a partial order, and the upward and downward closure and interior operations refer to this partial order. The upward closures are also known as shuffle ideals. The state complexity of these operations was investigated in [11–13, 19, 23]

The state complexity of the projection operation was investigated in [17, 18, 26]. In [26], the tight upper bound $3 \cdot 2^{n-2} - 1$ was shown, and in [18] the refined, and tight, bound $2^{n-1} + 2^{n-m} - 1$ was shown, where m is related to the number of unobservable transitions for the projection operator. Both results were established for incomplete deterministic automata.

In [14–17] the state complexity of these operations was investigated for commutative regular languages. The results are summarized in Table 1.

Table 1. Overview of results for commutative regular languages. The state complexities of the input languages are n and m. Also, $f(n, m) = 2^{nm-1} + 2^{(m-1)(n-1)}(2^{m-1} - 1)(2^{n-1} - 1)$ is the general bound for shuffle from [1] in case of complete automata.

Operation	Upper bound	Lower bound	References
$\pi_\Gamma(U), \Gamma \subseteq \Sigma$	n	n	[14, 17]
$U \shuffle V$	$\min\{(2nm)^{\mid\Sigma\mid}, f(n, m)\}$	$\Omega(nm)$	[1, 14, 15]
$\uparrow U$	$n^{\mid\Sigma\mid}$	$\Omega\left(\left(\frac{n}{\mid\Sigma\mid}\right)^{\mid\Sigma\mid}\right)$	[13, 14, 16]
$\downarrow U$	$n^{\mid\Sigma\mid}$	n	[14, 16]
$\Cap U$	$n^{\mid\Sigma\mid}$	$\Omega\left(\left(\frac{n}{\mid\Sigma\mid}\right)^{\mid\Sigma\mid}\right)$	[14, 16]
$\Cup U$	$n^{\mid\Sigma\mid}$	n	[14, 16]
$U \cup V, U \cap V$	nm	Tight for each Σ	[14, 15]

Table 2. State complexity results on the subclass of commutative languages with product-form minimal automaton for input languages with state complexities n and m.

Operation	Upper bound	Lower bound	Reference
$\pi_\Gamma(U), \Gamma \subseteq \Sigma$	n	n	Theorem 12
$U \shuffle V$	$2nm$	$\Omega(nm)$	Theorem 12
$\uparrow U, \downarrow U, \Cap U, \Cup U$	n	n	Theorem 12
$U \cap V, U \cup V$	nm	Tight for each Σ	Theorem 12

In [8] the minimal commutative automaton was introduced, which can be associated with every commutative regular language. This automaton played a crucial role in [14,15] to derive the bounds mentioned in Table 1. Here, we will investigate the subclass of those language for which the minimal commutative automaton is in fact the smallest automaton recognizing a given commutative language. For this language class, we will derive the following state complexity bounds summarized in Table 2. Additionally, we will prove other characterizations and properties of the subclass considered and relate it with other subclasses, in a more general setting, in the final chapter.

2   Preliminaries

In this section and Sect. 3, we assume that $k \geqslant 0$ denotes our alphabet size and $\Sigma = \{a_1, \ldots, a_k\}$ is our *alphabet*. We will also write a, b, c for a_1, a_2, a_3 in case of $|\Sigma| \leqslant 3$. The set Σ^* denotes the set of all finite sequences over Σ, i.e., of all *words*. The finite sequence of length zero, or the *empty word*, is denoted by ε. For a given word we denote by $|w|$ its *length*, and for $a \in \Sigma$ by $|w|_a$ the *number of occurrences* of the symbol a in w. For $a \in \Sigma$, we set $a^* = \{a\}^*$. A *language* is a subset of Σ^*. For $u \in \Sigma^*$, the *left quotient* is $u^{-1}L = \{v \in \Sigma^* \mid uv \in L\}$ and the *right quotient* is $Lu^{-1} = \{v \in \Sigma^* \mid vu \in L\}$.

The *shuffle operation*, denoted by $\shuffle$, is defined by

$$u \shuffle v = \{w \in \Sigma^* \mid w = x_1 y_1 x_2 y_2 \cdots x_n y_n \text{ for some words}$$

$$x_1, \ldots, x_n, y_1, \ldots, y_n \in \Sigma^* \text{ such that } u = x_1 x_2 \cdots x_n \text{ and } v = y_1 y_2 \cdots y_n\},$$

for $u, v \in \Sigma^*$ and $L_1 \shuffle L_2 := \bigcup_{x \in L_1, y \in L_2} (x \shuffle y)$ for $L_1, L_2 \subseteq \Sigma^*$. If $L_1, \ldots, L_n \subseteq \Sigma^*$, we set $\shuffle_{i=1}^n L_i = L_1 \shuffle \ldots \shuffle L_n$.

Let $\Gamma \subseteq \Sigma$. The *projection homomorphism* $\pi_\Gamma : \Sigma^* \to \Gamma^*$ is given by $\pi_\Gamma(x) = x$ for $x \in \Gamma$ and $\pi_\Gamma(x) = \varepsilon$ for $x \notin \Gamma$ and extended to Σ^* by $\pi_\Gamma(\varepsilon) = \varepsilon$ and $\pi_\Gamma(wx) = \pi_\Gamma(w)\pi_\Gamma(x)$ for $w \in \Sigma^*$ and $x \in \Sigma$. As a shorthand, we set, with respect to a given naming $\Sigma = \{a_1, \ldots, a_k\}$, $\pi_j = \pi_{\{a_j\}}$. Then $\pi_j(w) = a_j^{|w|_{a_j}}$.

A language $L \subseteq \Sigma^*$ is *commutative*, if, for $u, v \in \Sigma^*$ such that $|v|_x = |u|_x$ for every $x \in \Sigma$, we have $u \in L$ if and only if $v \in L$, i.e., L is closed under permutation of letters in words from L.

A quintuple $\mathcal{A} = (\Sigma, Q, \delta, q_0, F)$ is a *finite deterministic and complete automaton* (DFA), where Σ is the *input alphabet*, Q the *finite set of states*, $q_0 \in Q$ the *start state*, $F \subseteq Q$ the set of *final states* and $\delta : Q \times \Sigma \to Q$ is the *totally defined state transition function*. Here, we do not consider incomplete automata. The transition function $\delta : Q \times \Sigma \to Q$ extends to a transition function on words $\delta^* : Q \times \Sigma^* \to Q$ by setting $\delta^*(q, \varepsilon) := q$ and $\delta^*(q, wa) := \delta(\delta^*(q, w), a)$ for $q \in Q$, $a \in \Sigma$ and $w \in \Sigma^*$. In the remainder, we drop the distinction between both functions and also denote this extension by δ. The language *recognized* by an automaton $\mathcal{A} = (\Sigma, Q, \delta, q_0, F)$ is $L(\mathcal{A}) = \{w \in \Sigma^* \mid \delta(q_0, w) \in F\}$. A language $L \subseteq \Sigma^*$ is called *regular* if $L = L(\mathcal{A})$ for some finite automaton $\mathcal{A}$.

The *Nerode right-congruence* with respect to $L \subseteq \Sigma^*$ is defined, for $u, v \in \Sigma^*$, by $u \equiv_L v$ if and only if $\forall x \in \Sigma^* : ux \in L \Leftrightarrow vx \in L$. The equivalence class of $w \in \Sigma^*$ is denoted by $[w]_{\equiv_L} = \{x \in \Sigma^* \mid x \equiv_L w\}$. A language is regular if and only if the above right-congruence has finite index, and it can be used to define the *minimal deterministic automaton* $\mathcal{A}_L = (\Sigma, Q_L, \delta_L, [\varepsilon]_{\equiv_L}, F_L)$ with $Q_L = \{[u]_{\equiv_L} \mid u \in \Sigma^*\}$, $\delta_L([w]_{\equiv_L}, a) = [wa]_{\equiv_L}$ and $F_L = \{[u]_{\equiv_L} \mid u \in L\}$. Let $L \subseteq \Sigma^*$ be regular with minimal automaton $\mathcal{A}_L = (\Sigma, Q_L, \delta_L, [\varepsilon]_{\equiv_L}, F_L)$. The number $|Q_L|$ is called the *state complexity* of L and denoted by $sc(L)$. The *state complexity of a regularity-preserving operation* on a class of regular languages is the greatest state complexity of the result of this operation as a function of the (maximal) state complexities for argument languages from the class.

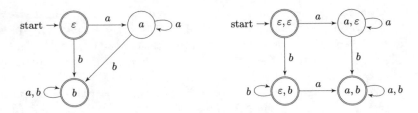

Fig. 1. The minimal deterministic automaton (left) and the minimal commutative automaton (right) of the language $\{w \in \Sigma^* \mid |w|_a = 0 \text{ or } |w|_b > 0\}$.

Given two automata $\mathcal{A} = (\Sigma, S, \delta, s_0, F)$ and $\mathcal{B} = (\Sigma, T, \mu, t_0, E)$, an *automaton homomorphism* $h : S \to T$ is a map between the state sets such that for each $a \in \Sigma$ and state $s \in S$ we have $h(\delta(s, a)) = \mu(h(s), a)$, $h(s_0) = t_0$ and $h^{-1}(E) = F$. If $h : S \to T$ is surjective, then $L(\mathcal{B}) = L(\mathcal{A})$. A bijective homomorphism between automata $\mathcal{A}$ and $\mathcal{B}$ is called an *isomorphism*, and the two automata are said to be isomorphic.

The *minimal commutative automaton* was introduced in [8] to investigate the learnability of commutative languages. In [14,15] this construction was used to define the index and period vector and in the derivation of the state complexity bounds mentioned in Table 1.

Definition 1 (minimal commutative aut.). *Let $L \subseteq \Sigma^*$ be regular. The minimal commutative automaton for L is $\mathcal{C}_L = (\Sigma, S_1 \times \ldots \times S_k, \delta, s_0, F)$ with*

$$S_j = \{[a_j^m]_{\equiv_L} : m \geqslant 0\}, \quad F = \{([\pi_1(w)]_{\equiv_L}, \ldots, [\pi_k(w)]_{\equiv_L}) : w \in L\}$$

and $\delta((s_1, \ldots, s_j, \ldots, s_k), a_j) = (s_1, \ldots, \delta_j(s_j, a_j), \ldots, s_k)$ with one-letter transitions $\delta_j([a_j^m]_{\equiv_L}, a_j) = [a_j^{m+1}]_{\equiv_L}$ for $j = 1, \ldots, k$ and $s_0 = ([\varepsilon]_{\equiv_L}, \ldots, [\varepsilon]_{\equiv_L})$.

In [8], the next result was shown.

Theorem 2 (Gómez and Alvarez [8]). *Let $L \subseteq \Sigma^*$ be a commutative regular language. Then, $L = L(\mathcal{C}_L)$.*

In general the minimal commutative automaton is not equal to the minimal deterministic and complete automaton for a regular commutative language L, see Example 1.

Example 1. For $L = \{w \in \Sigma^* \mid |w|_a = 0 \text{ or } |w|_b > 0\}$ with $\Sigma = \{a, b\}$ the minimal deterministic and complete automaton and the minimal commutative automaton are not the same, see Fig. 1. This language is from [8]. In fact, the difference can get quite large, as shown by $L_p = \{w \in \Sigma^* \mid \sum_{j=1}^{k} j \cdot |w|_{a_j} \equiv 0 \pmod{p}\}$ for a prime $p > k$. Here, $\mathrm{sc}(L_p) = p$, but $\mathcal{C}_{L_p}$ has p^k states.

The next definition from [14,15] generalizes the notion of a cyclic and non-cyclic part for unary automata [24], and the notion of periodic language [6,14,15].

Definition 3 (index and period vector). *The* index vector $(i_1, \ldots, i_k)$ *and* period vector $(p_1, \ldots, p_k)$ *for a commutative regular language* $L \subseteq \Sigma^*$ *with minimal commutative automaton* $\mathcal{C}_L = (\Sigma, S_1 \times \ldots \times S_k, \delta, s_0, F)$ *are the unique minimal numbers such that* $\delta(s_0, a_j^{i_j}) = \delta(s_0, a_j^{i_j + p_j})$ *for all* $j \in \{1, \ldots, k\}$.

Note that, in Definition 3, we have, for all $j \in \{1, \ldots, k\}$, $|S_j| = i_j + p_j$. Also note that for unary languages, i.e., if $|\Sigma| = 1$, $\mathcal{C}_L$ equals $\mathcal{A}_L$ and $i_1 + p_1$ equals the number of states of the minimal automaton.

Example 2. Let $L = (aa)^* \sqcup (bb)^* \cup (aaaa)^* \sqcup b^*$. Then $(i_1, i_2) = (0, 0)$, $(p_1, p_2) = (4, 2)$, $\pi_1(L) = (aa)^*$ and $\pi_2(L) = b^*$.

Let $u, v \in \Sigma^*$. Then, u is a *subsequence*[1] of v, denoted by $u \preccurlyeq v$, if and only if $v \in u \sqcup \Sigma^*$. The thereby given order is called the *subsequence order*. Let $L \subseteq \Sigma^*$. Then, we define (1) the *upward closure* $\uparrow L = L \sqcup \Sigma^* = \{u \in \Sigma^* : \exists v \in L : v \preccurlyeq u\}$; (2) the *downward closure* $\downarrow L = \{u \in \Sigma^* : u \sqcup \Sigma^* \cap L \neq \varnothing\} = \{u \in \Sigma^* : \exists v \in L : u \preccurlyeq v\}$; (3) the *upward interior*, denoted by ΥL, as the largest upward-closed set in L, i.e. the largest subset $U \subseteq L$ such that $\uparrow U = U$ and (4) the *downward interior*, denoted by ΩL, as the largest downward-closed set in L, i.e., the largest subset $U \subseteq L$ such that $\downarrow U = U$. We have $\Omega L = \Sigma^* \setminus \uparrow(\Sigma^* \setminus L)$ and $\Upsilon L = \Sigma^* \setminus \downarrow(\Sigma^* \setminus L)$.

The following two results, which will be needed later, are from [14,15].

Theorem 4. *Let* $U, V \subseteq \Sigma^*$ *be commutative regular languages with index and period vectors* $(i_1, \ldots, i_k), (j_1, \ldots, j_k)$ *and* $(p_1, \ldots, p_k), (q_1, \ldots, q_k)$. *Then, the index vector of* $U \sqcup V$ *is at most*

$$(i_1 + j_1 + \mathrm{lcm}(p_1, q_1) - 1, \ldots, i_k + j_k + \mathrm{lcm}(p_k, q_k) - 1)$$

and the period vector is at most $(\mathrm{lcm}(p_1, q_1), \ldots, \mathrm{lcm}(p_k, q_k))$. *So,* $\mathrm{sc}(U \sqcup V) \leqslant \prod_{l=1}^{k}(i_l + j_l + 2 \cdot \mathrm{lcm}(p_l, q_l) - 1)$.

Theorem 5. *Let* $\Sigma = \{a_1, \ldots, a_k\}$. *Suppose* $L \subseteq \Sigma^*$ *is commutative and regular with index vector* $(i_1, \ldots, i_k)$ *and period vector* $(p_1, \ldots, p_k)$. *Then,* $\max\{\mathrm{sc}(\uparrow L), \mathrm{sc}(\downarrow L), \mathrm{sc}(\Upsilon L), \mathrm{sc}(\Omega L)\} \leqslant \prod_{j=1}^{k}(i_j + p_j)$.

---

[1] Also called a *scattered subword* in the literature [11,19].

3 Product-Form Minimal Automata

As shown in Example 1, the minimal automaton, in general, does not equal the minimal commutative automaton. Here, we introduce the class of commutative regular languages for which both are isomorphic. The corresponding commutative languages are called *languages with a minimal automaton of product-form*, as the minimal commutative automaton is built with the Cartesian product.

Definition 6 (languages with product-form minimal automaton). *A commutative and regular language $L \subseteq \Sigma^*$ is said to have a* minimal automaton of product-form, *if C_L is isomorphic to A_L.*

If $|\Sigma| = 1$, we see easily that C_L is the minimal deterministic and complete automaton.

Proposition 7. *If $|\Sigma| = 1$, then each commutative and regular $L \subseteq \Sigma^*$ has a minimal automaton of product-form. More generally, if $L \subseteq \{a\}^*$, then $L \amalg (\Sigma \setminus \{a\})^*$ has a minimal automaton of product-form.*

Apart from the unary languages, we give another example of a language with minimal automaton of product-form next.

Example 3. Let $L = (aa)^* \amalg (bb)^* \cup (aaa)^* \amalg b(bb)^*$ over $\Sigma = \{a, b\}$. See Fig. 2 for the minimal commutative automaton. Here, the minimal commutative automaton equals the minimal automaton.

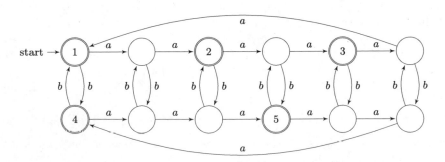

Fig. 2. C_L for $L = (aa)^* \amalg (bb)^* \cup (aaa)^* \amalg b(bb)^*$. Here C_L is isomorphic to A_L.

However, the next proposition gives a strong necessary criterion for a commutative language to have a minimal automaton of product-form.

Proposition 8. *If $L \subseteq \Sigma^*$ is commutative and regular with a minimal automaton of product-form, then $|\{x \in \Sigma \mid \pi_{\{x\}}(L) \text{ is finite }\}| \leqslant 1$. So, $\pi_\Gamma(L)$ is infinite for $|\Gamma| \geqslant 2$, in particular no finite language over an at least binary alphabet is in this class.*

For example, $L = \{\varepsilon\}$ over Σ does not have a minimal automaton of product-form if $|\Sigma| > 1$. Recall that the minimal automaton, as defined here, is always complete. Note that the converse of Proposition 8 is not true, as shown by aa^* over $\Sigma = \{a, b\}$.

In the following statement, we give alternative characterizations for commutative languages with minimal automata of product-form.

Theorem 9. *Let $L \subseteq \Sigma^*$ be a commutative regular language with index vector $(i_1, \ldots, i_k)$ and period vector $(p_1, \ldots, p_k)$. The following are equivalent:*

1. *the minimal automaton has product-form;*
2. $\mathrm{sc}(L) = \prod_{j=1}^{k}(i_j + p_j)$;
3. $u \equiv_L v$ *implies* $\forall a \in \Sigma : a^{|u|_a} \equiv_L a^{|v|_a}$;
4. $u \equiv_L v$ *if and only if* $\forall a \in \Sigma : a^{|u|_a} \equiv_L a^{|v|_a}$.

Next, we give a way to construct commutative regular languages with minimal automata of product-form.

Lemma 10. *Let $\Sigma = \{a_1, \ldots, a_k\}$ and, for $j \in \{1, \ldots, k\}$, $L_j \subseteq \{a_j\}^*$ be regular and infinite with index i_j and period p_j. Then,* $\mathrm{sc}\left(\underset{j=1}{\overset{k}{\sqcup\kern-0.3em\sqcup}} L_j\right) = \prod_{j=1}^{k} \mathrm{sc}(L_j) = \prod_{j=1}^{k}(i_j + p_j)$ *and* $\underset{j=1}{\overset{k}{\sqcup\kern-0.3em\sqcup}} L_j$ *has index vector $(i_1, \ldots, i_k)$ and period vector $(p_1, \ldots, p_k)$. With Theorem 9, $\underset{j=1}{\overset{k}{\sqcup\kern-0.3em\sqcup}} L_j$ has a product-form minimal automaton.*

In the next theorem and the following remark, we investigate closure properties of the class in question.

Theorem 11. *The class of commutative regular languages with minimal automata of product-form is closed under left and right quotients and complementation. It is not closed under union, intersection and projection.*

Remark 1. We have $a \sqcup\kern-0.3em\sqcup b^* \cap a^* \sqcup\kern-0.3em\sqcup b = a \sqcup\kern-0.3em\sqcup b$, showing, using Proposition 7 and 8, that this class is not closed under intersection and by DeMorgan's laws, as we have closure under complementation, we also cannot have closure under union. Also, $L = aa^* \sqcup\kern-0.3em\sqcup bb^* \sqcup\kern-0.3em\sqcup cc^* \cup bb^* \sqcup\kern-0.3em\sqcup a^* \cup b^*$ has a minimal automaton of product-form, but $\pi_{\{a,b\}}(L) = bb^* \sqcup\kern-0.3em\sqcup a^* \cup b^*$ is the language from Example 1. So, this class is also not closed under projection.

Theorem 12. *Let $U, V \subseteq \Sigma^*$ be commutative regular languages with product-form minimal automata with $\mathrm{sc}(U) = n$ and $\mathrm{sc}(V) = m$.*

1. *We have $\mathrm{sc}(U \sqcup\kern-0.3em\sqcup V) \leqslant 2nm$ if $|\Sigma| > 1$ and $\mathrm{sc}(U \sqcup\kern-0.3em\sqcup V) \leqslant nm$ if $|\Sigma| = 1$. Furthermore, for any Σ, there exist U, V as above such that $nm \leqslant \mathrm{sc}(U \sqcup\kern-0.3em\sqcup V)$.*
2. *In the worst case, n states are sufficient and necessary for a DFA to recognize $\uparrow U$. Similarly for the downward closure and interior operations.*
3. *In the worst case, n states are sufficient and necessary for a DFA to recognize the projection of U.*

4. *In the worst case, nm states are sufficient and necessary for a DFA to recognize $U \cap V$ or $U \cup V$.*

Remark 2. I do not know if the bound $2nm$ stated in Theorem 1 for the shuffle operation is tight, but the next example shows that if we have a binary alphabet, we can find commutative languages with state complexities n and m and product-form minimal automata whose shuffle needs an automaton with strictly more than nm states. A similar construction works for more than two letters. Let $p, q > 11$ be two coprime numbers. Set $U = a \shuffle b^{p-1}(b^p)^* \cup a^{p-1}(a^p)^* \shuffle bb^{p-1}(b^p)^*$ and $V = b^{q-1}(b^q)^* \cup a^{q-1}(a^q)^* \shuffle bbb^{q-1}(b^q)^*$. Then, using that shuffle distributes over union and a number-theoretical result from [27, Lemma 5.1], we find

$$U \shuffle V = a \shuffle W \cup a^{p-1}(a^p)^* \shuffle bW \cup$$
$$a^q(a^q)^* \shuffle bbW \cup a^{q-1+p-1}(a^p)^*(a^q)^* \shuffle bbbW,$$

where $a^{q-1+p-1}(a^p)^*(a^q)^* = F \cup a^{pq-1}a^*$ for some finite set $F \subseteq \{\varepsilon, a, \ldots, a^{pq-3}\}$ and $W = E \cup b^{pq-1}b^*$ for some $E \subseteq \{\varepsilon, b, \ldots, b^{pq-3}\}$. Note that by [27, Lemma 5.1] we have $a^{pq-2} \shuffle bbbW \cap U \shuffle V = \varnothing$. All languages involved have a product-form minimal automaton. The minimal automaton for U has $(2 + p) \cdot (1 + p)$ states, the minimal automaton for V has $(1 + q) \cdot (q + 2)$ states and that for $U \shuffle V$ has $2pq \cdot (pq + 3)$ states. As $(p - 11)(q - 11) > 0$ we can deduce $(1 + p)(2 + p)(1 + q)(2 + q) < 2(pq)^2 < 2pq(pq + 3)$.

4   Partial Commutativity and Other Subclasses

A *partial commutation* on Σ is a symmetric and irreflexive relation $I \subseteq \Sigma \times \Sigma$, often called the *independence relation*. Of interest is the *congruence* $\sim_I$ generated on Σ^* by the relation $\{(ab, ba) \mid (a, b) \in I\}$. A language $L \subseteq \Sigma^*$ is *closed under I-commutation* if $u \in L$ and $u \sim_I v$ implies $v \in L$. If $I = \{(a, b) \in \Sigma \times \Sigma \mid a \neq b\}$, then the languages closed under I-commutation are precisely the commutative languages.

Languages closed under some partial commutation relation have been extensively studied, see [10], also for further references, and in particular with relation to (Mazurkiewicz) trace theory [5, 10, 21], a formalism to describe the execution histories of concurrent programs.

Here, we will focus on the case that $(\Sigma \times \Sigma) \backslash I$ is transitive, i.e., if $u \not\sim_I v$ and $v \not\sim_I w$ implies $u \not\sim_I w$. In this case, $(\Sigma \times \Sigma) \backslash I$ is an equivalence relation and we will write $\Sigma_1, \ldots, \Sigma_k$ for the different equivalence classes.

The reason to focus on this particular generalization is, as we will see later, that the definition of the minimal commutative automaton transfers to this more general setting without much difficulty.

To ease the notation, if we have a partial commutation relation as above with a corresponding partition $\Sigma = \Sigma_1 \cup \ldots \Sigma_k$ of the alphabet, we also write $\mathcal{L}_{\Sigma_1, \ldots, \Sigma_k}$ for the *class of languages closed under this partial commutation*. Then, as is easily seen, we have $L \in \mathcal{L}_{\Sigma_1, \ldots, \Sigma_k}$ if and only if, for $x \in \Sigma_i$, $y \in \Sigma_j$

$(i \neq j)$ and each $u, v \in \Sigma^*$ we have $uxyv \in L \Leftrightarrow uyxv \in L$. For example, L is commutative if and only if $L \in \mathcal{L}_{\{a_1\},\dots,\{a_k\}}$ for $\Sigma = \{a_1, \dots, a_k\}$.

4.1   The Canonical Automaton

Here, we generalize our notion of commutative minimal automaton, Definition 1, to have uniform recognition devices for languages in $\mathcal{L}_{\Sigma_1,\dots,\Sigma_k}$.

Definition 13. *Let* $\Sigma = \Sigma_1 \cup \dots \cup \Sigma_k$ *be a partition and* $L \subseteq \Sigma^*$. *Set* $\mathcal{C}_{L,\Sigma_1,\dots,\Sigma_k} = (\Sigma, S_1 \times \dots \times S_k, \delta, s_0, F)$ *with, for* $i \in \{1,\dots,k\}$, $S_i = \{[u]_{\equiv_L} \mid u \in \Sigma_i^*\}$, $F = \{([\pi_{\Sigma_1}(u)]_{\equiv_L}, \dots, [\pi_{\Sigma_k}(u)]_{\equiv_L}) \mid u \in L\}$, $s_0 = ([\varepsilon]_{\equiv_L}, \dots, [\varepsilon]_{\equiv_L})$ *and, for* $x \in \Sigma_i$,

$$\delta(([u_1]_{\equiv_L}, \dots, [u_i]_{\equiv_L}, \dots, [u_k]_{\equiv_L}), x) = ([u_1]_{\equiv_L}, \dots, [u_i x]_{\equiv_L}, \dots, [u_k]_{\equiv_L})$$

with words $u_j \in \Sigma_j^*$, $j \in \{1,\dots,k\}$. *This is called the* canonical automaton *for the given* L *with respect to* $\Sigma = \Sigma_1 \cup \dots \cup \Sigma_k$.

Next, we show that the canonical automata recognize precisely the languages in $\mathcal{L}_{\Sigma_1,\dots,\Sigma_k}$. Note that we have dropped the assumption of regularity of L.

Theorem 14. *Let* $L \subseteq \Sigma^*$ *and* $\Sigma = \Sigma_1 \cup \dots \cup \Sigma_k$ *be a partition. Then,*

1. $L \subseteq L(\mathcal{C}_{L,\Sigma_1,\dots,\Sigma_k})$ *and* $L(\mathcal{C}_{L,\Sigma_1,\dots,\Sigma_k}) \in \mathcal{L}_{\Sigma_1,\dots,\Sigma_k}$.
2. $L = L(\mathcal{C}_{L,\Sigma_1,\dots,\Sigma_k}) \Leftrightarrow L \in \mathcal{L}_{\Sigma_1,\dots,\Sigma_k}$.
3. *Let* $L \in \mathcal{L}_{\Sigma_1,\dots,\Sigma_k}$. *Then* L *is regular if and only if* $\mathcal{C}_{L,\Sigma_1,\dots,\Sigma_k}$ *is finite.*

Also, used in defining a subclass in the next subsection, we will derive a canonical automaton for certain projected languages from $\mathcal{C}_{L,\Sigma_1,\dots,\Sigma_k}$. Essentially, the next definition and proposition mean that if we only use one "coordinate" of $\mathcal{C}_{L,\Sigma_1,\dots,\Sigma_k}$, then this recognizes a projection of L.

Definition 15. *Let* $i \in \{1,\dots,k\}$ *and* $L \in \mathcal{L}_{\Sigma_1,\dots,\Sigma_k}$. *The canonical projection automaton (for* Σ_i*) is* $\mathcal{C}_{L,\Sigma_i} = (\Sigma_i, S_i, \delta_i, [\varepsilon]_{\equiv_L}, F_i)$ *with* $S_i = \{[u]_{\equiv_L} \mid u \in \Sigma_i^*\}$, $\delta_i([u]_{\equiv_L}, x) = [ux]_{\equiv_L}$ *for* $x \in \Sigma_i$ *and* $F_i = \{[\pi_{\Sigma_i}(u)]_{\equiv_L} \mid u \in L\}$.

Proposition 16. *Let* $L \in \mathcal{L}_{\Sigma_1,\dots,\Sigma_k}$. *Then, for* $i \in \{1,\dots,k\}$, $\pi_{\Sigma_i}(L) = L(\mathcal{C}_{L,\Sigma_i})$.

4.2   Subclasses in $\mathcal{L}_{\Sigma_1,\dots,\Sigma_k}$

Here, we investigate several subclasses of $\mathcal{L}_{\Sigma_1,\dots,\Sigma_k}$. Recall that, for $L \subseteq \Sigma^*$, the minimal automaton of L is denoted by $\mathcal{A}_L$.

Definition 17. *Let* $\Sigma = \Sigma_1 \cup \dots \cup \Sigma_k$ *be a partition. Then, define the following classes of languages.*

$$\mathcal{L}_1 = \{L \mid \mathcal{C}_{L,\Sigma_1,\dots,\Sigma_k} \text{ has a single final state and } L = L(\mathcal{C}_{L,\Sigma_1,\dots,\Sigma_k}). \},$$

$$\mathcal{L}_2 = \left\{ L \mid L = \bigsqcup_{i=1}^{k} \pi_{\Sigma_i}(L) \right\},$$

$$\mathcal{L}_3 = \{L \mid L = L(\mathcal{C}_{L,\Sigma_1,\dots,\Sigma_k}), \forall i \in \{1,\dots,k\} : \mathcal{A}_{\pi_{\Sigma_i}(L)} \text{ is isomorphic to } \mathcal{C}_{L,\Sigma_i}\},$$

$$\mathcal{L}_4 = \{L \mid \mathcal{A}_L \text{ is isomorphic to } \mathcal{C}_{L,\Sigma_1,\dots,\Sigma_k}\}.$$

First, we show that these are in fact subclasses of $\mathcal{L}_{\Sigma_1,\ldots,\Sigma_k}$.

Proposition 18. *Let $\Sigma = \Sigma_1 \cup \ldots \cup \Sigma_k$ be a partition. For each $i \in \{1,2,3,4\}$ we have $\mathcal{L}_i \subseteq \mathcal{L}_{\Sigma_1,\ldots,\Sigma_k}$.*

Remark 3. Regarding $\mathcal{L}_1$, note that there exist languages $L = L(\mathcal{C}_{L,\Sigma_1,\ldots,\Sigma_k})$ such that the minimal automaton has a single final state, but $\mathcal{C}_{L,\Sigma_1,\ldots,\Sigma_k}$ has more than one final state. For example, $L = \{w \in \{a,b\}^* \mid |w|_a > 0 \text{ or } |w|_b > 0\}$. However, if $\mathcal{C}_{L,\Sigma_1,\ldots,\Sigma_k}$ has a single final state, then the minimal automata also has only a single final state.

Example 4. Let $\Sigma = \Sigma_1 \cup \Sigma_2$ with $\Sigma_1 = \{a\}$ and $\Sigma_2 = \{b\}$. Set $L = (aa(aaa)^* \sqcup bb(bbb)^*) \cup (a(aaa)^* \sqcup b(bbb)^*)$. Then $L \in (\mathcal{L}_3 \cap \mathcal{L}_4)\backslash\mathcal{L}_2$.

Example 5. Set $L = (a(aaa)^* \sqcup b) \cup aa(aaa)^*$. Then $L \in \mathcal{L}_3\backslash\mathcal{L}_4$.

The languages in $\mathcal{L}_1$ arise in connection with the canonical automaton.

Proposition 19. *Let $L \in \mathcal{L}_{\Sigma_1,\ldots,\Sigma_k}$ and $\mathcal{C}_{L,\Sigma_1,\ldots,\Sigma_k} = (\Sigma, S_1 \times \ldots \times S_k, \delta, s_0, F)$. Then, for all $s \in S_1 \times \ldots \times S_k$, $\{w \in \Sigma^* \mid \delta(s_0, w) = s\} \in \mathcal{L}_1$.*

Next, we give alternative characterization for $\mathcal{L}_2, \mathcal{L}_3$ and $\mathcal{L}_4$.

Theorem 20. *Let $L \in \mathcal{L}_{\Sigma_1,\ldots,\Sigma_k}$. Then,*

1. *$L \in \mathcal{L}_2$ if and only if, for each $w \in \Sigma^*$, the following is true:*

$$w \in L \Leftrightarrow \forall i \in \{1,\ldots,k\} : \pi_{\Sigma_i}(w) \in \pi_{\Sigma_i}(L);$$

2. *$L \in \mathcal{L}_3$ if and only if, for all $i \in \{1,\ldots,k\}$ and $u \in \Sigma_i^*$, we have*

$$[u]_{\equiv_L} \cap \Sigma_i^* = [u]_{\equiv_{\pi_{\Sigma_i}(L)}} \cap \Sigma_i^*;$$

3. *$L \in \mathcal{L}_4$ if and only if, for each $u, v \in \Sigma^*$,*

$$u \equiv_L v \Leftrightarrow \forall i \in \{1,\ldots,k\} : \pi_{\Sigma_i}(u) \equiv_L \pi_{\Sigma_i}(v).$$

Example 6. Let L_1 be the language from Example 3. Set $L_2 = a_1 \sqcup a_2 = \{a_1 a_2, a_2 a_1\}$. Both of their letters commute for the partition $\{a_1, a_2\} = \{a_1\} \cup \{a_2\}$. Then, $L_1 \in \mathcal{L}_4\backslash\mathcal{L}_3$ and $L_2 \in \mathcal{L}_1\backslash\mathcal{L}_4$.

Finally, in Theorem 21, we establish inclusion relations, which are all proper, between $\mathcal{L}_1, \mathcal{L}_2$ and $\mathcal{L}_3$, also see Fig. 3.

Theorem 21. *We have $\mathcal{L}_1 \subsetneq \mathcal{L}_2 \subsetneq \mathcal{L}_3$.*

Remark 4. Theorem 21 and Example 6 show that $\mathcal{L}_4$ is incomparable to each of the other language classes with respect to inclusion.

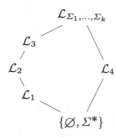

Fig. 3. Inclusion relations between the language classes.

5   Conclusion

The language class of commutative regular languages with minimal automata of product-form behaves well with respect to the descriptional complexity measure of state complexity for certain operations, see Table 2, and Lemma 10 allows us to construct infinitely many commutative regular languages with product-form minimal automaton. The investigation started could be carried out for other operations and measures of descriptional complexity as well. Likewise, as done in [8,9] for commutative and more general partial commutativity conditions, it might be interesting if the learning algorithms given there could be improved for the language class introduced.

Lastly, if the bound $2nm$ for shuffle is tight is an open problem. Remark 2 shows that the bound nm is not sufficient, however, giving an infinite family of commutative regular languages with minimal automata of product-form attaining the bound $2nm$ for shuffle is an open problem.

Acknowledgement. I thank the anonymous referees of [14] (the extended version of [15]), whose feedback also helped in the present work. I also sincerely thank the referees of the present submission, which helped me alot in identifying unclear or ungrammatical formulations and a missing definition.

References

1. Brzozowski, J., Jirásková, G., Liu, B., Rajasekaran, A., Szykuła, M.: On the state complexity of the shuffle of regular languages. In: Câmpeanu, C., Manea, F., Shallit, J. (eds.) DCFS 2016. LNCS, vol. 9777, pp. 73–86. Springer, Cham (2016). https://doi.org/10.1007/978-3-319-41114-9_6
2. Brzozowski, J.A., Simon, I.: Characterizations of locally testable events. Discret. Math. **4**(3), 243–271 (1973)
3. Campbell, R.H., Habermann, A.N.: The specification of process synchronization by path expressions. In: Gelenbe, E., Kaiser, C. (eds.) OS 1974. LNCS, vol. 16, pp. 89–102. Springer, Heidelberg (1974). https://doi.org/10.1007/BFb0029355
4. Câmpeanu, C., Salomaa, K., Yu, S.: Tight lower bound for the state complexity of shuffle of regular languages. J. Autom. Lang. Comb. **7**(3), 303–310 (2002)

5. Diekert, V., Rozenberg, G. (eds.): The Book of Traces. World Scientific, River Edge (1995)
6. Ehrenfeucht, A., Haussler, D., Rozenberg, G.: On regularity of context-free languages. Theor. Comput. Sci. **27**, 311–332 (1983)
7. Gao, Y., Moreira, N., Reis, R., Yu, S.: A survey on operational state complexity. J. Autom. Lang. Comb. **21**(4), 251–310 (2017)
8. Cano Gómez, A., Álvarez, G.I.: Learning commutative regular languages. In: Clark, A., Coste, F., Miclet, L. (eds.) ICGI 2008. LNCS (LNAI), vol. 5278, pp. 71–83. Springer, Heidelberg (2008). https://doi.org/10.1007/978-3-540-88009-7_6
9. Cano Gómez, A.: Inferring regular trace languages from positive and negative samples. In: Sempere, J.M., García, P. (eds.) ICGI 2010. LNCS (LNAI), vol. 6339, pp. 11–23. Springer, Heidelberg (2010). https://doi.org/10.1007/978-3-642-15488-1_3
10. Gómez, A.C., Guaiana, G., Pin, J.: Regular languages and partial commutations. Inf. Comput. **230**, 76–96 (2013)
11. Gruber, H., Holzer, M., Kutrib, M.: The size of Higman-Haines sets. Theor. Comput. Sci. **387**(2), 167–176 (2007)
12. Gruber, H., Holzer, M., Kutrib, M.: More on the size of Higman-Haines sets: effective constructions. Fundam. Informaticae **91**(1), 105–121 (2009)
13. Héam, P.: On shuffle ideals. RAIRO Theor. Inform. Appl. **36**(4), 359–384 (2002)
14. Hoffmann, S.: Commutative regular languages - properties and state complexity. Inf. Comput. (submitted)
15. Hoffmann, S.: Commutative regular languages – properties and state complexity. In: Ćirić, M., Droste, M., Pin, J.É. (eds.) CAI 2019. LNCS, vol. 11545, pp. 151–163. Springer, Cham (2019). https://doi.org/10.1007/978-3-030-21363-3_13
16. Hoffmann, S.: State complexity investigations on commutative languages - the upward and downward closure, commutative aperiodic and commutative group languages. In: Han, Y.-S., Ko, S.-K. (eds.) DCFS 2021, LNCS 13037, pp. 64–75. Springer, Cham (2021). https://doi.org/10.1007/978-3-030-93489-7_6
17. Hoffmann, S.: State complexity of projection on languages recognized by permutation automata and commuting letters. In: Moreira, N., Reis, R. (eds.) DLT 2021. LNCS, vol. 12811, pp. 192–203. Springer, Cham (2021). https://doi.org/10.1007/978-3-030-81508-0_16
18. Jirásková, G., Masopust, T.: On a structural property in the state complexity of projected regular languages. Theor. Comput. Sci. **449**, 93–105 (2012)
19. Karandikar, P., Niewerth, M., Schnoebelen, P.: On the state complexity of closures and interiors of regular languages with subwords and superwords. Theor. Comput. Sci. **610**, 91–107 (2016)
20. Maslov, A.N.: Estimates of the number of states of finite automata. Dokl. Akad. Nauk SSSR **194**(6), 1266–1268 (1970)
21. Mazurkiewicz, A.: Concurrent program schemes and their interpretations. Technical report, DAIMI Report Series 6(78) (1977)
22. Mazurkiewicz, A.: Parallel recursive program schemes. In: Bečvář, J. (ed.) MFCS 1975. LNCS, vol. 32, pp. 75–87. Springer, Heidelberg (1975). https://doi.org/10.1007/3-540-07389-2_183
23. Okhotin, A.: On the state complexity of scattered substrings and superstrings. Fundam. Informaticae **99**(3), 325–338 (2010)
24. Pighizzini, G., Shallit, J.: Unary language operations, state complexity and Jacobsthal's function. Int. J. Found. Comput. Sci. **13**(1), 145–159 (2002)
25. Shaw, A.C.: Software descriptions with flow expressions. IEEE Trans. Softw. Eng. **4**, 242–254 (1978)

26. Wong, K.: On the complexity of projections of discrete-event systems. In: Proceedings of WODES 1998, Cagliari, Italy, pp. 201–206 (1998)
27. Yu, S., Zhuang, Q., Salomaa, K.: The state complexities of some basic operations on regular languages. Theor. Comput. Sci. **125**(2), 315–328 (1994)

State Complexity Investigations on Commutative Languages – the Upward and Downward Closure, Commutative Aperiodic and Commutative Group Languages

Stefan Hoffmann$^{(\boxtimes)}$ [iD]

Informatikwissenschaften, FB IV, Universität Trier, Universitätsring 15, 54296 Trier, Germany
hoffmanns@informatik.uni-trier.de

Abstract. We investigate the state complexity of the upward and downward closure and interior operations on commutative regular languages. Then, we systematically study the state complexity of these operations and of the shuffle operation on commutative group languages and commutative aperiodic (or star-free) languages.

Keywords: Finite automata · State complexity · Shuffle · Upward and downward closure · Commutative languages · Group languages · Aperiodic languages · Star-free languages

1 Introduction

The state complexity, as used here, of a regular language L is the minimal number of states needed in a complete deterministic automaton recognizing L. The state complexity of an operation on regular languages is the greatest state complexity of the result of this operation as a function of the (maximal) state complexities of its arguments.

Investigating the state complexity of the result of a regularity-preserving operation on regular languages, see [7] for a survey, was first initiated by Maslov in [21] and systematically started by Yu, Zhuang and Salomaa in [31].

A language is called commutative, if for any word in the language, every permutation of this word is also in the language. The class of commutative automata, which recognize commutative regular languages, was introduced in [3].

The shuffle operation has been introduced to understand the semantics of parallel programs [4,22,28,30]. The shuffle operation is regularity-preserving on all regular languages. The state complexity of the shuffle operation in the general cases was investigated in [1] for complete deterministic automata and in [5] for incomplete deterministic automata. The bound $2^{nm-1} + 2^{(m-1)(n-1)}(2^{m-1} - 1)(2^{n-1} - 1)$ was obtained in the former case, which is not known to be tight in case of complete automata, and the tight bound $2^{nm} - 1$ in the latter case.

Y. S Han and S.-K. Ko (Eds.): DCFS 2021, LNCS 13037, pp. 64–75, 2021.
https://doi.org/10.1007/978-3-030-93489-7_6

A word is a (scattered) subsequence of another word, if it can be obtained from the latter word by deleting letters. This gives a partial order, and the upward and downward closure and interior operations, denoted by $\uparrow U$, $\downarrow U$, $\Diamond U$ and $\Diamond U$, refer to this partial order. Languages that result from upward closure operation are also known as shuffle ideals. The state complexity of these operations was investigated in [9, 10, 12, 19, 24]

In [14–17] the state complexity of these operations was investigated in the case of commutative regular languages. The results are summarized in Table 1.

Table 1. State complexity results on commutative regular languages, where n and m denote the state complexities of the input languages. Also, $f(n, m) = 2^{nm-1} + 2^{(m-1)(n-1)}(2^{m-1} - 1)(2^{n-1} - 1)$ is the general bound for shuffle from [1].

Operation	Upper bound	Lower bound	Reference
$\pi_\Gamma(U)$, $\Gamma \subseteq \Sigma$	n	n	[14, 17]
$U \sqcup V$	$\min\{(2nm)^{|\Sigma|}, f(n, m)\}$	nm	[1, 14, 15]
$\uparrow U$	$\min\{n^{|\Sigma|}, 2^{n-2} + 1\}$	$\Omega\left(\left(\frac{n}{|\Sigma|}\right)^{|\Sigma|}\right)$	Theorem 10 & [12, 17, 19]
$\downarrow U$	$\min\{n^{|\Sigma|}, 2^{n-1}\}$	n	Theorem 10 & [17, 19]
$\Diamond U$	$\min\{n^{|\Sigma|}, 2^{n-2} + 1\}$	$\Omega\left(\left(\frac{n}{|\Sigma|}\right)^{|\Sigma|}\right)$	Theorem 10 & [17, 19]
$\Diamond U$	$\min\{n^{|\Sigma|}, 2^{n-1}\}$	n	Theorem 10 & [17, 19]
$U \cup V$, $U \cap V$	nm	Sharp, for any Σ	[14, 17]

A *group language* is a language recognizable by an automaton where every letter induces a permutation of the state set. The investigation of the state complexity of these languages was started recently [18].

A *star-free language* is a language which can be written with an extended regular expression, i.e., an expression involving concatenation, the Boolean operations and Kleene star, without using the Kleene star [23]. The class of star-free languages coincides with the class of *aperiodic languages* [29], i.e., those languages recognizable by automata such that no subset of states is permuted by a word.

So, in this sense the aperiodic languages are as far away from the group languages as possible. In [14, 15] it has been shown that every commutative and regular language can be decomposed into commutative aperiodic and commutative group languages in the following way.

Theorem 1 ([14, 15]). *Suppose $L \subseteq \Sigma^*$ is commutative and regular. Then, L is a finite union of languages of the form $U \sqcup V$, where U is a commutative aperiodic language and V is a commutative group language over a subalphabet[1] of Σ.*

---

[1] Over the whole alphabet Σ, these languages are precisely the languages recognizable by automata whose transition monoids are 0-groups, i.e., groups with a zero element adjoined.

Here, we will investigate the state complexity of operations considered in [14,15] for general commutative regular languages for the commutative group and the commutative aperiodic languages separately. Additionally, we will investigate four new operations – the upward and downward closure and interior operations, denoted by $\uparrow U$, $\downarrow U$, $\bigcirc U$ and $\bigcirc U$ – for which we first state a bound on general commutative regular languages and then also bounds for commutative aperiodic and commutative group languages. See Table 1 and Table 2 for a summary of the results.

2 Preliminaries

In the present work, we assume that $k \geqslant 0$ denotes our *alphabet* size and $\Sigma = \{a_1, \ldots, a_k\}$. We will also write a, b, c for a_1, a_2, a_3 in case of $|\Sigma| \leqslant 3$. The set Σ^* denotes the set of all finite sequences, i.e., of all *words*. The finite sequence of length zero, or the *empty word*, is denoted by ε. For a given word we denote by $|w|$ its *length*, and for $a \in \Sigma$ by $|w|_a$ the *number of occurrences of the symbol* a in w. A *language* is a subset of Σ^*.

Table 2. The state complexity results for various operations for input languages of state complexities n and m. The upper bound ($\leqslant$) and the best known lower bound ($\geqslant$) are indicated for the group and the aperiodic commutative languages. Also, $f(n, m) = 2^{nm-1} + 2^{(m-1)(n-1)}(2^{m-1} - 1)(2^{n-1} - 1)$ is the general bound for shuffle from [1]. So, the bound for shuffle is actually the minimum of the bound stated and $f(n, m)$ as written in Table 1 (this is left out to save horizontal space). For the lower bound for projection, consider the group language $(a^n)^* \sqcup \Sigma \backslash \{a\}$ and the aperiodic language $\{a^{n-1}\} \sqcup \Sigma \backslash \{a\}$ and $\Gamma \subseteq \Sigma \backslash \{a\}$.

	Group case		Aperiodic case		
Op.	$\leqslant$	$\geqslant$	$\leqslant$	$\geqslant$	Reference
$\pi_\Gamma(U)$	n	n	n	n	[17]
$U \sqcup V$	$(nm)^{|\Sigma|}$	nm	$(n+m-1)^{|\Sigma|}$	$\begin{cases} \Omega\,(nm) & \text{if } \|\Sigma\| > 1 \\ n + m - 1 & \text{if } \|\Sigma\| = 1 \end{cases}$	Theorem 13, Proposition 14, [2, 14, 15] & Proposition 20
$\uparrow U$	$n^{|\Sigma|}$	n	$\min\{n^{|\Sigma|}, 2^{n-2} + 1\}$	$\Omega\left(\left(\frac{n}{|\Sigma|}\right)^{|\Sigma|}\right)$	Theorem 10, Proposition 16, Proposition 5 & [19]
$\downarrow U$	1	1	$\min\{n^{|\Sigma|}, 2^{n-1}\}$	n	Theorem 10, Proposition 15, Proposition 19 & [19]
$\bigcirc U$	$n^{|\Sigma|}$	n	$\min\{n^{|\Sigma|}, 2^{n-2} + 1\}$	$\Omega\left(\left(\frac{n}{|\Sigma|}\right)^{|\Sigma|}\right)$	Eq. (1)
$\bigcirc U$	1	1	$\min\{n^{|\Sigma|}, 2^{n-1}\}$	n	Eq. (1)
$U \cap V$ $U \cup V$	nm	nm	$\begin{cases} nm & \|\Sigma\| \geqslant 2 \\ \max\{n,m\} & \|\Sigma\| = 1 \end{cases}$	$\begin{cases} nm & \|\Sigma\| \geqslant 2 \\ \max\{n,m\} & \|\Sigma\| = 1 \end{cases}$	Theorem 17 & [2]

The *shuffle operation*, denoted by $\sqcup\!\sqcup$, is defined by

$$u \sqcup\!\sqcup v = \{w \in \Sigma^* \mid w = x_1 y_1 x_2 y_2 \cdots x_n y_n \text{ for some words}$$

$$x_1, \ldots, x_n, y_1, \ldots, y_n \in \Sigma^* \text{ such that } u = x_1 x_2 \cdots x_n \text{ and } v = y_1 y_2 \cdots y_n\},$$

for $u, v \in \Sigma^*$ and $L_1 \sqcup\!\sqcup L_2 := \bigcup_{x \in L_1, y \in L_2} (x \sqcup\!\sqcup y)$ for $L_1, L_2 \subseteq \Sigma^*$. If $L_1, \ldots, L_n \subseteq \Sigma^*$, we set $\sqcup\!\sqcup_{i=1}^n L_i = L_1 \sqcup\!\sqcup \ldots \sqcup\!\sqcup L_n$.

Let $\Gamma \subseteq \Sigma$. The *projection homomorphism* $\pi_\Gamma : \Sigma^* \to \Gamma^*$ is the homomorphism given by $\pi_\Gamma(x) = x$ for $x \in \Gamma$, $\pi_\Gamma(x) = \varepsilon$ otherwise and extended by $\pi_\Gamma(\varepsilon) = \varepsilon$ and $\pi_\Gamma(wx) = \pi_\Gamma(w)\pi_\Gamma(x)$ for $w \in \Sigma^*$ and $x \in \Sigma$. As a shorthand, we set, with respect to a given naming $\Sigma = \{a_1, \ldots, a_k\}$, $\pi_j = \pi_{\{a_j\}}$. Then $\pi_j(w) = a_j^{|w|_{a_j}}$. For $L \subseteq \Sigma^*$, we set $\pi_\Gamma(L) = \{\pi_\Gamma(u) \mid u \in L\}$.

A quintuple $\mathcal{A} = (\Sigma, Q, \delta, q_0, F)$ is a *finite deterministic and complete automaton*, where Σ is the *input alphabet*, Q the *finite set of states*, $q_0 \in Q$ the *start state*, $F \subseteq Q$ the set of *final states* and $\delta : Q \times \Sigma \to Q$ is the *totally defined state transition function*. The transition function $\delta : Q \times \Sigma \to Q$ extends to a transition function on words $\delta^* : Q \times \Sigma^* \to Q$ by setting $\delta^*(q, \varepsilon) := q$ and $\delta^*(q, wa) := \delta(\delta^*(q, w), a)$ for $q \in Q$, $a \in \Sigma$ and $w \in \Sigma^*$. In the remainder, we drop the distinction between both functions and will also denote this extension by δ. Here, we do not consider incomplete automata. The language *recognized* by an automaton $\mathcal{A} = (\Sigma, Q, \delta, q_0, F)$ is $L(\mathcal{A}) = \{w \in \Sigma^* \mid \delta(q_0, w) \in F\}$. A language $L \subseteq \Sigma^*$ is called *regular* if $L = L(\mathcal{A})$ for some finite automaton $\mathcal{A}$.

A language $L \subseteq \Sigma^*$ is a *group language*, if there exists a *permutation automaton* $\mathcal{A} = (\Sigma, Q, \delta, q_0, F)$, i.e., an automaton such that the map $q \mapsto \delta(q, a)$ is a permutation for each $a \in \Sigma$, recognizing L. A language $L \subseteq \Sigma^*$ is an *aperiodic language*, if there exists an automaton $\mathcal{A} = (\Sigma, Q, \delta, q_0, F)$ recognizing it such that, for each $w \in \Sigma^*$, $q \in Q$ and $n \geqslant 1$, if $\delta(q, w^n) = q$, then $\delta(q, w) = q$.

The *Nerode right-congruence* with respect to $L \subseteq \Sigma^*$ is defined, for $u, v \in \Sigma^*$, by $u \equiv_L v$ if and only if $\forall x \in \Sigma^* : ux \in L \leftrightarrow vx \in L$. The equivalence class of $w \in \Sigma^*$ is denoted by $[w]_{\equiv_L} = \{x \in \Sigma^* \mid x \equiv_L w\}$. A language is regular if and only if the above right-congruence has finite index, and it can be used to define the *minimal deterministic automaton* $\mathcal{A}_L = (\Sigma, Q_L, \delta_L, [\varepsilon]_{\equiv_L}, F_L)$ with $Q_L = \{[u]_{\equiv_L} \mid u \in \Sigma^*\}$, $\delta_L([w]_{\equiv_L}, a) = [wa]_{\equiv_L}$ and $F_L = \{[u]_{\equiv_L} \mid u \in L\}$. Let $L \subseteq \Sigma^*$ be regular with minimal automaton $\mathcal{A}_L = (\Sigma, Q_L, \delta_L, [\varepsilon]_{\equiv_L}, F_L)$. The number $|Q_L|$ is called the *state complexity* of L Two words are said to be *distinguishable*, if they denote different right-congruence classes for a given language.

A language $L \subseteq \Sigma^*$ is *commutative*, if, for $u, v \in \Sigma^*$ such that $|v|_x = |u|_x$ for every $x \in \Sigma$, we have $u \in L$ if and only if $v \in L$. For commutative regular languages we have the following normal form.

Theorem 2 ([14,15]). *Let $\Sigma = \{a_1, \ldots, a_k\}$ be our alphabet. A commutative language $L \subseteq \Sigma^*$ is regular if and only if it can be written in the form $L = \bigcup_{i=1}^n U_1^{(i)} \sqcup\!\sqcup \ldots \sqcup\!\sqcup U_k^{(i)}$ with non-empty unary regular languages $U_j^{(i)} \subseteq \{a_j\}^*$ for*

$i \in \{1,\ldots,n\}$ and $j \in \{1,\ldots k\}$ that can be recognized by unary automata with a single final state.

Let $L \subseteq \Sigma^*$ be a commutative regular language. For each $j \in \{1,\ldots,k\}$ let $i_j \geqslant 0$ and $p_j \geqslant 1$ be the smallest numbers such that $[a_j^{i_j}]_{\equiv_L} = [a_j^{i_j+p_j}]_{\equiv_L}$. The vectors $(i_1,\ldots,i_k)$ and $(p_1,\ldots,p_k)$ are then called the *index* and *period* vectors of L. These notions where introduced in [8,14,15] and it was shown that they can be used to bound the state complexity of L.

Theorem 3 ([8,14,15]). *Let $L \subseteq \Sigma^*$ be a commutative regular language with index vector $(i_1,\ldots,i_k)$ and period vector $(p_1,\ldots,p_k)$. Then, for any $j \in \{1,\ldots,k\}$, we have $i_j + p_j \leqslant \mathrm{sc}(L) \leqslant \prod_{r=1}^{k}(i_r + p_r)$.*

Example 1. Let $L = (aa)^* \sqcup (bb)^* \cup (aaaa)^* \sqcup b^*$. Then $(i_1,i_2) = (0,0)$, $(p_1,p_2) = (4,2)$, $\pi_1(L) = (aa)^*$ and $\pi_2(L) = b^*$.

The following result from [14,15] connects the index and period vector with the aperiodic and group languages.

Theorem 4. *A commutative regular language is:*

1. *aperiodic iff its period vector equals $(1,\ldots,1)$;*
2. *a group language iff its index vector equals $(0,\ldots,0)$.*

Let $u,v \in \Sigma^*$. Then, u is a *subsequence*[2] of v, denoted by $u \leqslant v$, if and only if $v \in u \sqcup \Sigma^*$. The thereby given order is called the *subsequence order*. Let $L \subseteq \Sigma^*$. Then, we define:

1. the *upward closure*, by $\uparrow L = L \sqcup \Sigma^* = \{u \in \Sigma^* : \exists v \in L : v \leqslant u\}$;
2. the *downward closure*, by $\downarrow L = \{u \in \Sigma^* : u \sqcup \Sigma^* \cap L \neq \varnothing\} = \{u \in \Sigma^* : \exists v \in L : u \leqslant v\}$;
3. the *upward interior*, denoted by $\circlearrowright L$, as the largest upward-closed set in L, i.e. the largest subset $U \subseteq L$ such that $\uparrow U = U$;
4. the *downward interior*, denoted by $\circlearrowleft L$, as the largest downward-closed set in L, i.e., the largest subset $U \subseteq L$ such that $\downarrow U = U$.

The following equations are valid [19]:

$$\circlearrowleft L = \Sigma^* \setminus \uparrow(\Sigma^* \setminus L) \quad \circlearrowright L = \Sigma^* \setminus \downarrow(\Sigma^* \setminus L). \tag{1}$$

A remarkable fact is that for *every* language, the above closure operators give regular languages. This is based on the fact that the subsequence order is a well-order, i.e., any upward-closed set is generated by a finite subset of words [11,13].

For general $L \subseteq \Sigma^*$, there is no way to compute a recognizing automaton for the upward and downward operations. This is seen by an easy argument, due to [9]. Let $L \subseteq \Sigma^*$ be a recursively enumerable language. Then, L is non-empty

---

[2] Also called a *scattered subword* in the literature [9,19].

if and only if $\uparrow L$ is non-empty. However, the former problem is undecidable for recursively enumerable languages, but decidable for regular languages. Hence, if we can compute a recognizing automaton for $\uparrow L$, we can decide non-emptiness for L, which is, in general, not possible. But for regular and context-free L, recognizing automata for these operations are computable [9,20].

In [12], a lower bound for the state complexity of the upward closure was established by using the language $L = \bigcup_{a \in \Sigma} \{a^N\}$, which is commutative and finite. As every finite language is aperiodic and we are interested in this class, let us highlight this fact with the next statement.

Proposition 5 (Héam [12]). *Set*

$$g(n) = \max\{\mathrm{sc}(\uparrow L) \mid \mathrm{sc}(L) \leqslant n \text{ and } L \text{ is finite and commutative}\}.$$

Then $g(n) \in \Omega\left(\left(\frac{n}{|\Sigma|}\right)^{|\Sigma|}\right)$.

The next is from [14,15].

Theorem 6. *Let* $U, V \subseteq \Sigma^*$ *be aperiodic commutative languages with index vectors* $(i_1, \ldots, i_k)$ *and* $(j_1, \ldots, j_k)$. *Then,* $U \uplus V$ *has index vector componentwise less than* $(i_1 + j_1, \ldots, i_k + j_k)$ *and period vector* $(1, \ldots, 1)$. *So,* $\mathrm{sc}(U \uplus V) \leqslant \prod_{l=1}^{k}(i_l + j_l + 1)$. *Hence, Theorem 3 yields* $\mathrm{sc}(U \uplus V) \leqslant (\mathrm{sc}(U) + \mathrm{sc}(V) - 1)^{|\Sigma|}$.

As a corollary of Theorem 6 and Theorem 4, we also get, as the star-free and aperiodic languages coincide [29], an old result by J.F. Perrot [6,25,27].

Corollary 7 (J.F. Perrot [25]). *The shuffle of two commutative star-free languages is star-free.*

3 The Upward and Downward Operations

In this section, we establish state complexity bounds for the upward and downward closure and interior operations. The constructions also yield polynomial time algorithms for computing those closures, if the alphabet is fixed and not allowed to vary with the input.

Theorem 8. *Let* $\Sigma = \{a_1, \ldots, a_k\}$. *Suppose* $L \subseteq \Sigma^*$ *is commutative and regular with index vector* $(i_1, \ldots, i_k)$ *and period vector* $(p_1, \ldots, p_k)$. *Then,*

$$\max\{\mathrm{sc}(\uparrow L), \mathrm{sc}(\downarrow L), \mathrm{sc}(\circlearrowleft L), \mathrm{sc}(\circlearrowright L)\} \leqslant \prod_{j=1}^{k}(i_j + p_j).$$

Proof (sketch). We only give a rough outline of the proof idea for the first operation. For L, as shown in [8,14,15], we can construct an automaton of size $\prod_{j=1}^{k}(i_j + p_j)$ for L whose states can be put in correspondence with the modulo and threshold counting for the different letters. More formally, it could be shown that there exists an automaton $\mathcal{C} = (\Sigma, S_1, \times \ldots \times S_k, \delta, s_0, F)$ with $S_j = \{0, \ldots, i_j + p_j - 1\}$ for $j \in \{1, \ldots, k\}$ recognizing L.

Construct automaton for $\uparrow L$: Set $\mathcal{A}_\uparrow = (\Sigma, S_1 \times \ldots \times S_k, \delta_\uparrow, s_0, F_\uparrow)$ with

$$F_\uparrow = \{(s_1, \ldots, s_k) \in S_1 \times \ldots \times S_k \mid$$
$$\exists (f_1, \ldots, f_k) \in F \ \forall j \in \{1, \ldots, k\} : f_j \leqslant s_j\};$$

$$\delta_\uparrow((s_1, \ldots, s_k), a_j) = \begin{cases} (s_1, \ldots, s_k) & \text{if } i_j + p_j - 1 = s_j; \\ \delta((s_1, \ldots, s_k), a_j) & \text{otherwise,} \end{cases}$$

for $j \in \{1, \ldots, k\}$ and $(s_1, \ldots, s_k) \in S_1 \times \ldots \times S_k$. With a similar idea, an automaton $\mathcal{A}_\downarrow$ such that $L(\mathcal{A}_\downarrow) = \downarrow L$ can be constructed. See Example 2 for concrete constructions.   □

Example 2. Let $L = bb(bb)^* \cup (b \sqcup a(aa)^*)$. Then, $\uparrow L = bbb^* \cup (bb^* \sqcup aa^*)$, $\downarrow L = b^* \cup (aa^* \sqcup \{\varepsilon, b\})$, $\circlearrowright L = \varnothing$ and $\circlearrowleft L = \varnothing$. The constructions of the automata $\mathcal{A}_\uparrow$ and $\mathcal{A}_\downarrow$ with $L(\mathcal{A}_\uparrow) = \uparrow L$ and $L(\mathcal{A}_\downarrow) = \downarrow L$ from the proof sketch of Theorem 8 are illustrated, for the example language L, in Fig. 1.

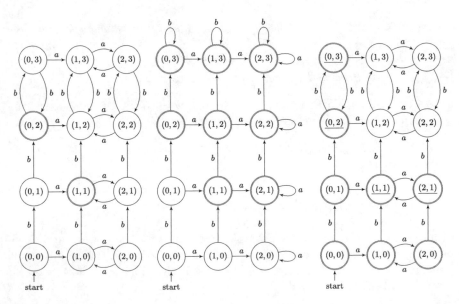

Fig. 1. Construction of automata for the upward and downward closure for the language $L = bb(bb)^* \cup (b \sqcup a(aa)^*)$ by starting from an automaton in a "rectangular" normal form for L. The left-most automaton recognizes L, the automaton in the middle recognized $\uparrow L$ and the right-most automaton recognized $\downarrow L$. See Example 2 for details.

The constructions done in the proof of Theorem 8 can actually be performed in polynomial time.

Corollary 9. *Fix the alphabet Σ. Let $L \subseteq \Sigma^*$ be commutative and regular, given by a finite recognizing automaton with n states. Then, recognizing automata for $\uparrow L$, $\downarrow L$, $\circlearrowright L$ and $\circlearrowleft L$ are computable in polynomial time in n.*

With Theorem 3, we can derive the next bound from Theorem 8.

Theorem 10. *Let $L \subseteq \Sigma^*$ be commutative and recognizable by an automaton with n states. Then, the upward and downward closures and interiors of L are recognizable by automata of size $n^{|\Sigma|}$.*

4 The Case of Commutative Group Languages

Before we investigate the state complexity of shuffle, union, intersection and the closure and interior operations for commutative group languages, we give a normal form theorem for commutative groups languages similar to Theorem 2.

Theorem 11. *Let $\Sigma = \{a_1, \ldots, a_k\}$ and $L \subseteq \Sigma^*$. Then, the following conditions are equivalent:*

1. *L is a commutative group language;*
2. *L is a finite union of languages of the form $U_1 ⧢ \ldots ⧢ U_k$ with $U_j \subseteq \{a_j\}^*$ a group language recognizable by an automaton with a single final state;*
3. *L is a finite union of languages of the form $U_1 ⧢ \ldots ⧢ U_k$ with $U_j \subseteq \{a_j\}^*$ being group languages.*

4.1 The Shuffle Operation

Here, we give a sharp bound for the state complexity of two commutative group languages. However, in this case, we do not express the bound in terms of the size of recognizing input automata, but in terms of the index and period vectors of the input languages. The result generalizes a corresponding result from [26] for unary group languages to commutative group languages.

Theorem 12. *Let $\Sigma = \{a_1, \ldots, a_k\}$. For commutative group languages $U, V \subseteq \Sigma^*$ with period vectors $(p_1, \ldots, p_k)$ and $(q_1, \ldots, q_k)$ their shuffle $U ⧢ V$ has index vector $(i_1, \ldots, i_k)$ with $i_j = \mathrm{lcm}(p_j, q_j) - 1$ for $j \in \{1, \ldots, k\}$ and period vector $(\gcd(p_1, q_1), \ldots, \gcd(p_k, q_k))$. Hence, by Theorem 3,*

$$\mathrm{sc}(U ⧢ V) \leqslant \prod_{j=1}^{k} (\gcd(p_j, q_j) + \mathrm{lcm}(p_j, q_j) - 1).$$

Furthermore, there exist commutative group languages such that a minimal automaton recognizing their shuffle reaches the bound.

As for any two numbers $n, m > 0$ we always have $\gcd(n, m) + \mathrm{lcm}(n, m) - 1 \leqslant nm$, we can deduce the next bound in terms of the size of recognizing automata. The result improves the general bound $(2nm)^{|\Sigma|}$ from [14,15].

Theorem 13. *Let $U, V \subseteq \Sigma^*$ be commutative group languages recognized by automata with n and m states. Then, $U ⧢ V$ is recognizable by an automaton with at most $(nm)^{|\Sigma|}$ states.*

We do not know if the last bound is sharp. The best lower bound we can give is the next one, which essentially follows by the lower bound for concatenation in case of unary languages, see [31, Theorem 5.4].

Proposition 14. *Let $n, m > 0$ be coprime numbers. Then, there exist commutative group languages of states complexities n and m such that their shuffle has state complexity nm.*

4.2   The Upward and Downward Closure and Interior Operations

First, we will show that every word is contained in the downward closure of a commutative group language.

Proposition 15. *Let $L \subseteq \Sigma^*$ be a commutative group language. Then the downward closure $\downarrow L$ equals Σ^*.*

This is not true for general commutative languages, see Proposition 19.

Proposition 16. *Let $n > 0$. There exists a commutative group language $L \subseteq \Sigma^*$ with period vector $(n, 1, \ldots, 1)$ such that $\mathrm{sc}(L) = n$ and its upward closure has state complexity n with index vector $(n-1, 1, \ldots, 1)$ and period vector $(1, \ldots, 1)$.*

Proof. Let $a \in \Sigma$ and $n > 0$. Set $L = \{w \in \Sigma^* \mid |w|_a \equiv n - 1 \ (\mathrm{mod}\ n)\} = a^{n-1}(a^n)^* \shuffle (\Sigma \backslash \{a\})^*$. Then, $\uparrow L = a^{n-1}a^* \shuffle (\Sigma \backslash \{a\})^*$ and $\mathrm{sc}(\uparrow L) = n$. $\square$

4.3   Union and Intersection

Theorem 17. *For any alphabet Σ and commutative group language of state complexities n and m, the intersection and union is recognizable by an automaton with nm states. Furthermore, there exists commutative group languages with state complexities n and m such that every automaton for their union (intersection) needs nm states.*

Proof. The upper bound holds for regular languages in general [31]. Let $a \in \Sigma$ and $n, m > 0$ two coprime numbers. The languages for the lower bound are similar to the ones given in [31], but also work for $\Sigma = \{a\}$ (in [31] $|\Sigma| \geqslant 2$ is assumed). Set $U = \{w \in \Sigma^* \mid |w|_a \equiv 0 \ (\mathrm{mod}\ n)\} = (a^n)^* \shuffle (\Sigma \backslash \{a\})^*$ and $V = \{w \in \Sigma^* \mid |w|_a \equiv 0 \ (\mathrm{mod}\ m)\}$. Then, $\mathrm{sc}(U \cap V) = \mathrm{sc}(U \cup V) = nm$. $\square$

5   The Case of Commutative Aperiodic Languages

For shuffle (Theorem 6), union and intersection (see [31, Theorem 4.3]), we already have upper bounds, see Table 2. Note that the lower bound construction for Boolean operations given in [2, Theorem 1 & 8] over an at least binary alphabet uses the commutative and aperiodic languages $\{w \in \Sigma^* \mid |w|_a = n-2\}$ and $\{w \in \Sigma^* \mid |w|_b = m-2\}$ for $n, m \geqslant 2$. For the upward closure, Proposition 5 gives a lower bound. So, here, we handle the missing cases of the downward closure and the shuffle operation.

But first, we give a similar normal form theorem for aperiodic commutative languages as for group languages. The proof is essentially the same as in the group case.

Theorem 18. *Let* $\Sigma = \{a_1, \ldots, a_k\}$ *and* $L \subseteq \Sigma^*$. *Then, the following conditions are equivalent:*

1. *L is a commutative and aperiodic language;*
2. *L is a finite union of languages of the form $U_1 \shuffle \ldots \shuffle U_k$ with $U_j \subseteq \{a_j\}^*$ aperiodic and recognizable by an automaton with a single final state;*
3. *L is a finite union of languages of the form $U_1 \shuffle \ldots \shuffle U_k$ with $U_j \subseteq \{a_j\}^*$ aperiodic.*

Next, we state a lower bound for the downward closure. By Eq. (1), using the complemented language, this implies the same lower bound for the upward interior.

Proposition 19. *Let $a \in \Sigma$ and $n > 0$. Set $L = \{a^n\}$. Then, $\downarrow L = \{\varepsilon, a, \ldots, a^n\}$ and so* $\mathrm{sc}(\downarrow L) = \mathrm{sc}(L) = n + 2$.

For concatenation it is known that the state complexity for unary languages is nm [31, Theorem 5.4 & Theorem 5.5]. In fact, the witness languages for the lower bound are group languages (see also Proposition 14). For unary aperiodic languages, concatenation has state complexity $n+m-1$ [2, Theorem 8]. By using these unary witness languages and introducing self-loops for additional letters, and as in the unary case (and for the mentioned extension to more letters) concatenation and shuffle coincide, this immediately gives lower bounds for the shuffle operation on commutative languages as well.

However, in the next result, we show that we can do better for aperiodic (even for finite) commutative languages.

Proposition 20. *Let Σ be an at least binary alphabet. Then for each even $n, m > 0$ there exist commutative and finite languages $U, V \subseteq \Sigma^*$ with $\mathrm{sc}(U) = n$, $\mathrm{sc}(V) = m$ such that $\mathrm{sc}(U \shuffle V) \geqslant \frac{nm}{4} + 1$.*

Proof. We give the construction for a binary alphabet, as for larger alphabets the lower bound is implied by adding self-loops to the automaton for each additional letter. Let $\Sigma = \{a, b\}$ and $N, M \geqslant 0$ with $n = |\Sigma|N + 2$ and $m = |\Sigma|M + 2$. Set $U = \{a^N, b^N\}$ and $V = \{a^M, b^M\}$. Then $\mathrm{sc}(U) = n$ and $\mathrm{sc}(V) = m$. Set

$$L = U \shuffle V = \{u \in \Sigma^* \mid (|u|_a = N + M, |u|_b = 0) \vee (|u|_a = N, |u|_b = M)$$
$$\vee (|u|_a = M, |u|_b = N) \vee (|u|_a = 0, |u|_b = N + M)\}.$$

We show that the words $a^i b^j$ for $i \in \{0, 1, \ldots, N\}$ and $j \in \{0, 1, \ldots, M\}$ are pairwise inequivalent for the Nerode right-congruence. Let $(n_1, n_2), (m_1, m_2) \in \{0, 1, \ldots, N\} \times \{0, 1, \ldots, M\}$ with $(n_1, n_2) \neq (m_1, m_2)$. First, suppose $n_i \neq 0$ for $i \in \{0, 1\}$ and $m_i \neq 0$ for $i \in \{0, 1\}$. Set $u = a^{N-n_1} b^{M-n_2}$. Then $a^{n_1} b^{n_2} u \in L$. By the assumptions, $a^{m_1} b^{m_2} u \in L$ if and only if $(m_1, m_2) + (N - n_1, M - n_2) = (M, N)$. So, if this is not the case, then u distinguishes both words. Otherwise, we must have $(n_1, n_2) + (N - m_1, M - m_2) \neq (M, N)$, for if not then $M - N = n_1 - m_1 = m_1 - n_1$. The last equality then gives $n_1 = m_1$ and similarly we find

$n_2 = m_2$. So, in that case with $v = a^{N-m_1}b^{M-m_2}$ we have $a^{m_1}b^{m_2}v \in L$ but $a^{n_1}b^{n_2}v \notin L$. Lastly, if at least one component is zero, we must distinguish more cases as $\{a^{N+M}, b^{N+M}\} \subseteq L$, which are left out here due to space.

So, we have $sc(L) \geqslant (N+1)(M+1)+1$ (the additional one accounts for a trap state necessary, as we measure the state complexity in terms of complete automata). Hence, $sc(L) \geqslant \frac{nm}{4}+1$.   □

6 Conclusion

As shown in Table 1 and Table 2, for shuffle and the upward and downward closure and interior operations, it is not known if the given upper bounds are tight. Hence, this is an open problem.

Acknowledgement. I thank the anonymous referees of [14] (the extended version of [15]) whose feedback also helped in the present work. I also thank the referees of the present work for critical and careful reading, and pointing out typos and parts that needed better explanation.

References

1. Brzozowski, J., Jirásková, G., Liu, B., Rajasekaran, A., Szykuła, M.: On the state complexity of the shuffle of regular languages. In: Câmpeanu, C., Manea, F., Shallit, J. (eds.) DCFS 2016. LNCS, vol. 9777, pp. 73–86. Springer, Cham (2016). https://doi.org/10.1007/978-3-319-41114-9_6
2. Brzozowski, J.A., Liu, B.: Quotient complexity of star-free languages. Int. J. Found. Comput. Sci. **23**(6), 1261–1276 (2012)
3. Brzozowski, J.A., Simon, I.: Characterizations of locally testable events. Discret. Math. **4**(3), 243–271 (1973)
4. Campbell, R.H., Habermann, A.N.: The specification of process synchronization by path expressions. In: Gelenbe, E., Kaiser, C. (eds.) OS 1974. LNCS, vol. 16, pp. 89–102. Springer, Heidelberg (1974). https://doi.org/10.1007/BFb0029355
5. Câmpeanu, C., Salomaa, K., Yu, S.: Tight lower bound for the state complexity of shuffle of regular languages. J. Autom. Lang. Comb. **7**(3), 303–310 (2002)
6. Castiglione, G., Restivo, A.: On the shuffle of star-free languages. Fundam. Informaticae **116**(1–4), 35–44 (2012)
7. Gao, Y., Moreira, N., Reis, R., Yu, S.: A survey on operational state complexity. J. Autom. Lang. Comb. **21**(4), 251–310 (2017)
8. Cano Gómez, A., Álvarez, G.I.: Learning commutative regular languages. In: Clark, A., Coste, F., Miclet, L. (eds.) ICGI 2008. LNCS (LNAI), vol. 5278, pp. 71–83. Springer, Heidelberg (2008). https://doi.org/10.1007/978-3-540-88009-7_6
9. Gruber, H., Holzer, M., Kutrib, M.: The size of Higman-Haines sets. Theor. Comput. Sci. **387**(2), 167–176 (2007)
10. Gruber, H., Holzer, M., Kutrib, M.: More on the size of Higman-Haines sets: effective constructions. Fundam. Informaticae **91**(1), 105–121 (2009)
11. Haines, L.H.: On free monoids partially ordered by embedding. J. Comb. Theory **6**, 94–98 (1969)
12. Héam, P.: On shuffle ideals. RAIRO Theor. Informatics Appl. **36**(4), 359–384 (2002)

13. Higman, G.: Ordering by divisibility in abstract algebras. Proc. London Math. Soc. (3) **2**(7), 326–336 (1952)
14. Hoffmann, S.: Commutative regular languages - properties and state complexity. Inf. Comput. (submitted)
15. Hoffmann, S.: Commutative regular languages – properties and state complexity. In: Ćirić, M., Droste, M., Pin, J.É. (eds.) CAI 2019. LNCS, vol. 11545, pp. 151–163. Springer, Cham (2019). https://doi.org/10.1007/978-3-030-21363-3_13
16. Hoffmann, S.: Commutative regular languages with product-form minimal automata. In: Han, Y.-S., Ko, S.-K. (eds.) DCFS 2021, LNCS 13037, pp. 51–63. Springer, Cham (2021). https://doi.org/10.1007/978-3-030-93489-7_5
17. Hoffmann, S.: State complexity of projection on languages recognized by permutation automata and commuting letters. In: Moreira, N., Reis, R. (eds.) DLT 2021. LNCS, vol. 12811, pp. 192–203. Springer, Cham (2021). https://doi.org/10.1007/978-3-030-81508-0_16
18. Hospodár, M., Mlynárčik, P.: Operations on permutation automata. In: Jonoska, N., Savchuk, D. (eds.) DLT 2020. LNCS, vol. 12086, pp. 122–136. Springer, Cham (2020). https://doi.org/10.1007/978-3-030-48516-0_10
19. Karandikar, P., Niewerth, M., Schnoebelen, P.: On the state complexity of closures and interiors of regular languages with subwords and superwords. Theoret. Comput. Sci. **610**, 91–107 (2016)
20. van Leeuwen, J.: Effective constructions in well-partially-ordered free monoids. Discret. Math. **21**(3), 237–252 (1978)
21. Maslov, A.N.: Estimates of the number of states of finite automata. Dokl. Akad. Nauk SSSR **194**(6), 1266–1268 (1970)
22. Mazurkiewicz, A.: Parallel recursive program schemes. In: Bečvář, J. (ed.) MFCS 1975. LNCS, vol. 32, pp. 75–87. Springer, Heidelberg (1975). https://doi.org/10.1007/3-540-07389-2_183
23. McNaughton, R.: The loop complexity of pure-group events. Inf. Control **11**(1/2), 167–176 (1967)
24. Okhotin, A.: On the state complexity of scattered substrings and superstrings. Fundam. Informaticae **99**(3), 325–338 (2010)
25. Perrot, J.: Varietes de langages et operations. Theor. Comput. Sci. **7**, 197–210 (1978)
26. Pighizzini, G., Shallit, J.: Unary language operations, state complexity and Jacobsthal's function. Int. J. Found. Comput. Sci. **13**(1), 145–159 (2002)
27. Restivo, A.: The shuffle product: new research directions. In: Dediu, A.-H., Formenti, E., Martín-Vide, C., Truthe, B. (eds.) LATA 2015. LNCS, vol. 8977, pp. 70–81. Springer, Cham (2015). https://doi.org/10.1007/978-3-319-15579-1_5
28. Riddle, W.E.: An approach to software system behavior description. Comput. Lang. **4**(1), 29–47 (1979)
29. Schützenberger, M.P.: On finite monoids having only trivial subgroups. Inf. Control **8**(2), 190–194 (1965)
30. Shaw, A.C.: Software descriptions with flow expressions. IEEE Trans. Softw. Eng. **4**, 242–254 (1978)
31. Yu, S., Zhuang, Q., Salomaa, K.: The state complexities of some basic operations on regular languages. Theoret. Comput. Sci. **125**(2), 315–328 (1994)

More on the Descriptional Complexity of Products of Finite Automata

Markus Holzer[✉] and Christian Rauch

Institut für Informatik, Universität Giessen, Arndtstr. 2, 35392 Giessen, Germany
{holzer,christian.rauch}@informatik.uni-giessen.de

Abstract. We investigate the descriptional complexity of the ν_i- and α_i-products with $0 \leq i \leq 2$ of two automata, for reset, permutation, permutation-reset, and finite automata in general. This is a continuation of the recent studies on the state complexity of the well-known cascade product undertaken in [7,8]. Here we show that in almost all cases, except for the direct product (ν_0) and the cascade product (α_0) for certain types of automata operands, the whole range of state complexities, namely the interval $[1, nm]$, where n is the state complexity of the left operand and m that of the right one, is attainable. To this end we prove a simulation result on products of automata that allows us to reduce the products and automata in question to the ν_0, α_0, and a double sided α_0-product.

1 Introduction

Recently the operational complexity of the cascade product on finite automata was investigated in [7,8], that is, the question which state complexities of languages resulting from the cascade product of two minimal deterministic finite automata with n and m states can be reached. It is obvious that nm is an upper bound on the state complexity. This upper bound can be reached by the cascade product of reset (RFA), permutation (PFA), permutation-reset (PRFA), and finite automata in general (DFAs) or combinations thereof. The subtle difference of these products is, that, except for the cascade product of two PFAs, the whole range $[1, nm]$ of state complexities can be reached if the input alphabet is at least binary. For the cascade product of two PFAs numbers in the interval $[1, nm]$ were identified that cannot be reached—following the work of [11] we call these numbers "magic." For unary automata the landscape of reachable state complexities is more diverse, see [7]; numerous magic numbers were identified there. These results are in line with research on other regularity preserving formal language operations such as, e.g., intersection and union [10], concatenation [12], square [4], star [3], reversal, and the cut operation [9].

   The direct and cascade product are two manifestations of products of finitely many component automata. The former one is well known from the intersection and union construction from automata theory, while the latter product is the main ingredient to the decomposition theorem of Krohn and Rhodes [2]. In general, a product of automata is obtained by series (cascading), parallel, and/or

Y.-S. Han and S.-K. Ko (Eds.): DCFS 2021, LNCS 13037, pp. 76–87, 2021.
https://doi.org/10.1007/978-3-030-93489-7_7

feedback composition of automata. In the direct product there is no communication between the component automata, while in the cascade product the
second automaton receives along with the input letter also the state of the first
automaton. In the terminology of automata networks [5] the direct and cascade
product are referred to as the ν_0- and α_0-product, respectively, and thus belong
to hierarchies of automata products of increasing feedback dependencies—for
the product of two automata this results in the products ν_0, α_0, ν_1, α_1, ν_2,
and α_2, where a product can be simulated by any other product that is to the
right of it. Moreover it is easy to see, since we are only interested in products
of *two* automata, that the ν_2- and α_2-product coincide. Thus, we are left with
five different products. This immediately raises the question on the operational
complexity of the ν_i- and α_i-products on finite state devices.

This is the starting point of this investigation. In the ν_i- and α_i-products all
the involved automata read at least the letter from the alphabet Σ. In addition
an automaton may get its own state as input and/or the state of the other
automaton Thus, any product of two automata can be encode by a three letter
word as described at the beginning of Sect. 3—observe, that there are $2 \cdot 4 \cdot
2 = 16$ different encodings for products. Studying the magic number problem
for all these products for RFAs, PFAs, PRFAs, and DFAs we are left with at
most $(2 \cdot 4 \cdot 2) \cdot (4 \cdot 4) = 256$ cases, where 16, namely all cases for the α_0-
product, were already investigated in [7,8] and one single case was studied for
the direct or ν_0-product [10]. Still, we are left with more than two hundred
cases. By a close inspection of the simulation capabilities of the various products
we are able to reduce these cases to a few ones on loop-free products, namely
the direct or ν_0-product, the cascade or α_0-product, and a special variant of
the α_1-product, where both automata transition functions depend crosswise on
the state sets, which we call α_{0}-product. This allows us to almost completely
classify the status of the magic number problem for all product types on the
various automata classes under investigation: There are no magic numbers, that
is, the whole range $[1, nm]$ of state complexities can be obtained, where n (m,
respectively) is the state size of the left (right, respectively) operand of the
considered product. Notable exceptions are direct product (ν_0) of two PFAs or
a PFA and a PRFA or two PRFAs and the cascade product (α_0) of two PFAs.
While for the latter case numerous magic numbers were shown to exist [7,8], we
only identify at least one magic number for the former cases already for very
small operand automata. Computer search indicates that the magic number
cases for the ν_0-product may be involved to be exactly solved, because it seems
that these cases heavily depend on the input alphabet size.

2   Preliminaries

We recall some definitions on finite automata as contained in [6]. A *deterministic
finite automaton* (DFA) is a quintuple $A = (Q, \Sigma, \cdot, q_0, F)$, where Q is the finite
set of *states*, Σ is the finite set of *input symbols*, $q_0 \in Q$ is the *initial state*, $F \subseteq Q$
is the set of *accepting states*, and the *transition function* $\cdot$ maps $Q \times \Sigma$ to Q.

The *language accepted* by the DFA A is defined as $L(A) = \{\, w \in \Sigma^* \mid q_0 {\cdot} w \in F \,\}$, where the transition function is recursively extended to a mapping $Q \times \Sigma^* \to Q$ in the usual way. Obviously, every letter $a \in \Sigma$ induces a mapping from the state set Q to Q by $q \mapsto q {\cdot} a$, for every $q \in Q$. A DFA is *unary* if the input alphabet Σ is a singleton set, that is, $\Sigma = \{a\}$, for some input symbol a. Moreover, a DFA is said to be a *permutation-reset* automaton (PRFA) if every input letter induces either a permutation or a constant mapping on the state set. If every letter of the automaton induces only permutations on the state set, then we simply speak of a *permutation* automaton (PFA). Finally, a DFA is said to be a *reset* automaton (RFA) if every letter induces either the identity or a constant mapping on the state set. The class of reset, permutation, permutation-reset, and deterministic automata in general are referred to as **RFA**, **PFA**, **PRFA**, and **FA**, respectively. It is obvious that the inclusions $X\textbf{FA} \subseteq \textbf{PRFA} \subseteq \textbf{FA}$, where $X \in \{\textbf{P}, \textbf{R}\}$, hold. Moreover, it is not hard to see that the classes **RFA** and **PFA** are incomparable.

The two most famous products of automata are the direct and cascade product [2], which are only special cases of the ν_i- and α_i-products of automata [5]. Originally, these products are introduced for semi-automata, which are automata with no initial nor final states. For our needs we enrich the product with initial and final states and follow for the definition of the final states the lines of [1]. For any product of two automata A and B, we say that A is the *first automaton* and B the *second automaton* in the product. The α_0-product, also known as the *cascade product*, of two DFAs $A = (Q_A, \Sigma, \cdot_A, q_{0,A}, F_A)$ and $B = (Q_B, Q_A \times \Sigma, \cdot_B, q_{0,B}, F_B)$, denoted by $A \circ_{\alpha_0} B$, is defined as the automaton

$$A \circ_{\alpha_0} B = (Q_A \times Q_B, \Sigma, \cdot, (q_{0,A}, q_{0,B}), F_A \times F_B),$$

where the transition function is given by

$$(q, p) \cdot a = (q \cdot_A a, p \cdot_B (q, a)),$$

for $q \in Q_A$, $p \in Q_B$, and $a \in \Sigma$. Observe, that the transitions of A depend only on Σ, while the transitions of B depend on Σ and additionally on Q_A. If we let the transitions of A also depend on Q_A and the transitions of B on both Q_A and Q_B, respectively, besides Σ, we obtain the α_1-product of two DFAs $A = (Q_A, Q_A \times \Sigma, \cdot_A, q_{0,A}, F_A)$ and $B = (Q_B, Q_A \times Q_B \times \Sigma, \cdot_B, q_{0,B}, F_B)$, denoted by $A \circ_{\alpha_1} B$, which is defined as the automaton

$$A \circ_{\alpha_1} B = (Q_A \times Q_B, \Sigma, \cdot, (q_{0,A}, q_{0,B}), F_A \times F_B),$$

where the transition function is given by

$$(q, p) \cdot a = (q \cdot_A (q, a), p \cdot_B (q, p, a)),$$

for $q \in Q_A$, $p \in Q_B$, and $a \in \Sigma$. Finally, the α_2-product of A and B all the transitions of A and of B depend on Q_A, Q_B and Σ. Roughly speaking the automaton A knows in which states A and B are and which input symbol has to be processed. The α_2-product is referred to as $\circ_{\alpha_2}$.

A product of automata is said to be a ν_i-product if all transition functions of the involved automata only depend on at most i state sets besides Σ. The ν_i-product is referred to as $\circ_{\nu_i}$. For instance, the α_0-product is also a ν_1-product, but not a ν_0-product. The only ν_0-product is the direct product. In the next section we develop a more abstract, refined, and general view on the products of (two) automata.

In order to explain the notation we give an example.

Example 1. Consider the PRFA $A = (\{q_0, q_1, q_2\}, \{a, b\}, \cdot_A, q_0, \{q_0, q_2\})$, where

$$q_0 \cdot_A a = q_1, \qquad\qquad q_1 \cdot_A a = q_0, \qquad\qquad q_2 \cdot_A a = q_2,$$
$$q_0 \cdot_A b = q_2, \qquad\qquad q_1 \cdot_A b = q_2, \qquad\qquad q_2 \cdot_A b = q_2.$$

Then assume that m is an arbitrary integer greater than or equal three and let

$$B = (\{p_0, p_1, \dots, p_{m-1}\}, \{q_0, q_1, q_2\} \times \{a, b\}, \cdot_B, p_0, \{p_1\}),$$

be the PFA, where

$$p_i \cdot_B (q_j, b) = p_{i+1 \bmod m}, \qquad \text{for } 0 \le j \le 1 \text{ and } 0 \le i \le m-1,$$
$$p_i \cdot_B (q_2, a) = p_{i+1 \bmod 3}, \qquad \text{for } 0 \le i \le 2,$$

and all other not explicitly stated transitions are self-loops. The automata A and B, for $m = 3$, are depicted in Fig. 1 on the top and lower right, respectively. It is easy to see that both automata are minimal.

By construction the α_0-product of A and B is given by

$$A \circ_{\alpha_0} B = (\{q_0, q_1, q_2\} \times \{p_0, p_1, \dots, p_{m-1}\}, \{a, b\}, \cdot, (q_0, p_0), \{q_0, q_2\} \times \{p_1\}),$$

where the transitions of the initially reachable states

$$(q_0, p_0), (q_1, p_0), (q_2, p_0), (q_2, p_1), (q_2, p_2),$$

can be deduced from Fig. 1, too, on the lower left. Although the drawing is only for automaton B with three states, the initially reachable part of $A \circ_{\alpha_0} B$ remains the same for larger B's as defined. Observe, that $A \circ_{\alpha_0} B$ is not a PRFA and it is not minimal. By inspection the only equivalent states in $A \circ_{\alpha_0} B$ are (q_0, p_0) and (q_1, p_0). Hence, the minimal DFA accepting $L(A \circ_{\alpha_0} B)$ has $\alpha = 4$ states.   □

When considering the descriptional complexity of the product of two automata, we limit ourselves to the case where the involved automata are non-trivial, i.e., they have more than one state. Thus, in the following we only consider non-trivial automata. It is easy to see that $n \cdot m$ states are sufficient for any product of an n-state and m-state automaton.

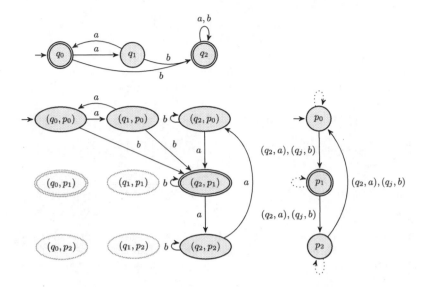

Fig. 1. The example automata A and B on the top and lower right, respectively. For a better representability not all transitions of an automaton are shown. In particular, this is the case for the automaton $A \circ_{\alpha_0} B$, where only the transitions of the initially reachable states are shown. The α_0-product $A \circ_{\alpha_0} B$ is depicted on the lower left. Additionally the index j is a placeholder for numbers 0 and 1. Note that self-loops will be only depicted by dotted loops without letters.

3   Results

A more abstract and refined view on the product of automata, regardless whether a ν_i- or α_i-product is considered, is given next. By the definitions, we have seen that the inputs, besides the letter, of the involved automata can be their own state and/or the states of the other device. Hence, every product of two automata can be characterized by an element from the set

$$\{\ell, -\} \times \{c, c^{-1}, b, -\} \times \{\ell, -\},$$

where ℓ refers to a loop, that is the automaton in addition to the letter also gets his own state as input, c refers to a cascade from left to right, that is the second automaton also gets the state of the first automaton as input besides the letter, c^{-1} refers to a cascade from right to left, that is the first automaton also gets the state of the second automaton as input in addition to the letter, and b refers to a bidirectional cascade, that is the first automaton also gets the state of the second automaton as input besides the letter and *vice versa*. The $-$ acts as a filler of a no-dependency in order to uniquely describe a certain product. For example, the direct product is referred to as $- - -$ and the ordinary cascade product by $-c-$. A complete list of all possible combinations and their classification as a ν_i- or α_i-product is given in Table 1. A special variant of the α_1-product is the $\alpha_{\wedge 0}$-product, where both automata transition functions depend crosswise

Table 1. A classification of the products of automata used throughout here. Encoding where c^{-1} appears are not listed, since they can be lead back to the case c. For instance, a product of the form $\ell c^{-1}-$ can be seen as a $(-c\ell)$-product, by switching the positions of the automata appropriately. A gray shaded entry indicates that for the corresponding product of automata magic numbers exist for certain cases.

Product of automata	α_0	α_1 / $\alpha_{\infty 0}$	α_2
ν_0	$-\!-\ -\!-\ -\!-$		
ν_1		$-c-$ $\quad$ $-b-$ $\quad$ $--\ell$ $\ell--$ $\ell-\ell$ $\ell c-$	
ν_2		$-c\ell$ $\qquad$ $-b\ell$ $\ell c\ell$ $\qquad$ $\ell b-$ $\ell b\ell$	

on the state sets. Hence the transition of A depends on Q_B and Σ and those of the device B on Q_A and Σ. Here Q_A (Q_B, respectively) refers to the state set of A (B, respectively). The $\alpha_{\infty 0}$-product together with the direct and cascade product are the only products under consideration that do not have an ℓ (loop) in their encodings. As we will see later, this is of significant importance. It is worth mentioning that the encodings also uniquely determine the input alphabets to both automata. For instance, a $(\ell c^{-1}-)$-product needs a left automaton A with input alphabet $Q_A \times Q_B \times \Sigma$, while the right automaton B has input alphabet Σ only—if this is the case, we speak of automata that are *compatible* with the product.

Whenever we speak of a product $\circ$ of automata of the form $u_0 u_1 u_2 \in \{\ell, -\} \times \{c, c^{-1}, b, -\} \times \{\ell, -\}$, we simply write $\circ_{u_0 u_1 u_2}$ for the product operation in question. This obviously refines the previously used notation on the α_i- and ν_i-products. For instance, the notation $\circ_{\alpha_0}$ and $\circ_{-c-}$ can be used interchangeably. Now we are ready for the next lemma, which describes a particular simulation of different products by each other.

Lemma 1. *Let $\circ$ be a product of automata of the form*

$$-u_1 u_2 \in \{-\} \times \{c, b, -\} \times \{\ell, -\}.$$

Let A and B two $\circ$-product compatible automata. Then there exists an RFA, PFA, or PRFA A' with the same number of states as A such that the initially reachable part of the product of A' and B w.r.t. the $(\ell u_1 u_2)$-product is equal to the initially reachable part of $A \circ B$. Additionally A' is minimal if it has at most two states or if it is a PFA or PRFA. A similar statement is valid for B if $\circ$ is a product of the form $u_0 u_1 - \in \{\ell, -\} \times \{c, b, -\} \times \{-\}$. Then the initially *reachable part of the product of A and B', for some RFA, PFA, or PRFA B', w.r.t. the $(u_0 u_1 \ell)$-product is equal to the initially reachable part of $A \circ B$.*

Proof. We show the lemma by constructing the automaton A'. Due to symmetry and because it is very easy to adapt the construction for all cases we prove the statement exemplary for the $(-c-)$-product. Let $A = (Q_A, \Sigma, \cdot_A, q_0, F_A)$ and let $B = (Q_B, Q_A \times \Sigma, \cdot_B, p_0, F_B)$. Let $A' = (Q_A, Q_A \times \Sigma, \cdot_{A'}, q_0, F_A)$, where we define

$$q \cdot_{A'} (q, a) = q',$$

for every state $q \in Q_A$ and every letter $a \in \Sigma$, if $q \cdot_A a = q'$; note that here the transition function is only partially defined. Because in the $(\ell c-)$-product the mapping a is given by

$$(q, p) \cdot_{A \circ_{\ell c-} B} a = (q \cdot_{A'} (q, a), p \cdot_B (q, a)) = (q \cdot_A a, p \cdot_B (q, a)) = (q, p) \cdot_{A \circ_{-c-} B} a$$

every image of the mapping (q, a) in A is irrelevant for the product automaton except the image of q. So we can choose the other images in any way we want. In particular we can choose them to let A' be a RFA, PFA, or PRFA. We can also make A' minimal in the last two cases for every number of states. Since all minimal RFAs have at most two states the minimality of A' can only be achieved if A' has at most two states. As shown above the automata $A' \circ_{\ell c-} B$ and $A \circ_{-c-} B$ have the same initially reachable part the statement follows.   □

Lemma 1 implies that for the automata products

$$\ell u_1 u_2 \in \{\ell\} \times \{c, c^{-1}, b, -\} \times \{\ell, -\}$$

and

$$u_0 u_1 \ell \in \{\ell, -\} \times \{c, c^{-1}, b, -\} \times \{\ell\}$$

at least the numbers are reachable which are reachable for the case the left (right, respectively) automaton is an arbitrary DFA of the product $-u_1 u_2$ ($u_0 u_1 -$, respectively). So the products without loops are given a particularly important role. These are the ν_0-, α_0-, and $\alpha\nu_0$-product. We investigate these products in the forthcoming subsections and then apply the previous lemma in order to obtain the main result of this paper, which reads as follows.

Theorem 1. *Let $\circ$ be a product of automata of the form $\{\ell, -\} \times \{c, b, -\} \times \{\ell, -\}$ and $X, Y \in \{\textbf{RFA}, \textbf{PFA}, \textbf{PRFA}, \textbf{FA}\}$ with $\{X, Y\} \neq \{\textbf{PFA}\}$ and $\{X, Y\} \neq \{\textbf{PFA}, \textbf{PRFA}\}$ and $\{X, Y\} \neq \{\textbf{PRFA}\}$, if $\circ$ is of type $- - -$, and $\{X, Y\} \neq \{\textbf{PFA}\}$, if $\circ$ is of type $-c-$. Moreover, let $n, m \geq 2$, where n (m, respectively) is restricted to 2 in case $X = \textbf{RFA}$ ($Y = \textbf{RFA}$, respectively). Then for every α with $1 \leq \alpha \leq nm$, there exists a minimal n-state automaton A of type X and a minimal m-state automaton B of type Y, both compatible to the $\circ$-product, such that the minimal DFA for the language $L(A \circ B)$ has α states.*

Roughly speaking, the theorem states that no magic numbers for the products of automata considered in the paper exists, except for the cases: (i) If both devices are permutation automata and the direct or cascade product is considered or (ii) one device is a permutation automaton and the other one is a permutation-reset device or both automata are permutation-reset devices and the direct product is considered.

3.1   The Direct- or ν_0-Product

The easiest product is the direct or ν_0-product. For the most general case, namely the product of two arbitrary DFAs, it was shown in [10] that for the ν_0-product no magic number exists. To our knowledge none of the other automata classes, namely reset, permutation, and permutation-rest automata were considered as inputs to the direct product. We close this gap in this subsection. Observe, that although the statements to come on the ν_0-product explicitly refer to left and right automata of certain types, these types can be obviously commuted, since in the direct product the order of the operand automata is not relevant to the product automaton (up to isomorphism). First we consider the cases where a RFA is involved in the direct product. Let us start with the direct product of two RFAs.

Theorem 2. *For every α with $1 \leq \alpha \leq 4$, there exists a binary minimal RFA A and a binary minimal RFA B such that the minimal DFA accepting the language $L(A \circ_{\nu_0} B)$ has α states.*

Proof. For $\alpha = 4$ let $A = (\{q_0, q_1\}, \{a, b\}, \cdot_A, q_0, \{q_1\})$ with

$$q_0 \cdot_A a = q_1, \qquad\qquad q_1 \cdot_A a = q_1,$$
$$q_0 \cdot_A b = q_0, \qquad\qquad q_1 \cdot_A b = q_1.$$

Additionally define $B = (\{p_0, p_1\}, \{a, b\}, \cdot_B, p_0, \{p_1\})$ with

$$p_0 \cdot_B a = p_0, \qquad\qquad p_1 \cdot_B a = p_0,$$
$$p_0 \cdot_B b = p_1, \qquad\qquad p_1 \cdot_B b = p_1.$$

Clearly the RFAs A and B are minimal and by applying the definition of the ν_0-product we obtain that the transitions of $A \circ_{\nu_0} B$ are

$$(q_0, p_0) \cdot a = (q_1, p_0), \qquad\qquad (q_1, p_0) \cdot a = (q_1, p_0),$$
$$(q_0, p_0) \cdot b = (q_0, p_1), \qquad\qquad (q_1, p_0) \cdot b = (q_1, p_1),$$
$$(q_0, p_1) \cdot a = (q_1, p_0), \qquad\qquad (q_1, p_1) \cdot a = (q_1, p_0),$$
$$(q_0, p_1) \cdot b = (q_0, p_1). \qquad\qquad (q_1, p_1) \cdot b = (q_1, p_1).$$

Therefore it is not hard to see that none of the four initially reachable states

$$(q_0, p_0), (q_1, p_0), (q_0, p_1), (q_1, p_1)$$

are equivalent.

In case $\alpha = 3$ we simply change the set of accepting states of A to be equal to $\{q_0\}$, which results in the equivalence of the states (q_1, p_0) and (q_1, p_1). Thus, exactly three states remain in the direct product. Finally, for $\alpha \in \{1, 2\}$, let A and B be two unary minimal non-trivial two-state RFAs. It is not hard to see that exactly two states are initially reachable in their product automaton. By choosing the sets of accepting states of A and B appropriately the product automaton has none or one accepting states which are initially reachable.

Thus, for all cases the minimal DFA accepting the language $L(A \circ_{\nu_0} B)$ has α states, which proves the stated claim.   □

We will now present a result from [8] since we will use it in the proofs of theorems to come several times.

Lemma 2. *Let A be a PFA with a sole accepting state with all states reachable from the initial state. Then A is minimal. Minimality is preserved even if the initial state is changed to any other state.*

Next we investigate the direct product of an RFA with a PFA.

Theorem 3. *Let $m \geq 2$. Then for every α with $1 \leq \alpha \leq 2m$, there exists a binary minimal RFA A and a binary minimal m-state PFA B such that the minimal DFA for the language $L(A \circ_{\nu_0} B)$ has α states.*

Clearly this theorem implies that the minimal DFA accepting $L(A \circ_{\nu_0} B)$ for an n-state RFA A and a m-state automaton B can have every number of states in the integer interval $[1, nm]$ in case B is a minimal PRFA or a minimal arbitrary DFA. This solves all cases of the direct product, where RFAs are involved.

Next we consider the direct products of PFAs, PRFAs and DFAs in general, where in the product at least one PFA is involved. Indeed, the ν_0-product of two PFAs contains magic numbers, which directly follows from the fact that for the α_0-product of two PFAs numerous magic numbers were identified in [8] and that the ν_0-product is a special α_0-product, which simulation does not change the automata types. Therefore, every magic number for the α_0-product of two PFAs is magic for the ν_0-product of two PFAs, too. When changing one of the automata to become a PRFA, one might think that we are back to the case that all numbers in the whole interval $[1, nm]$ can be reached, because for the α_0-product no magic numbers exist. In fact, this is not the case. By running a computer program we found out by exhaustive search that for $n = m = 3$ and an alphabet size of at most three the number $\alpha = 2$ is not attainable. Whether other magic numbers exist in this case has to be left open. Thus, let us summarize our findings in next theorem.

Theorem 4. *There exist $n, m \geq 2$ and α with $1 \leq \alpha \leq nm$ such that there does not exist a minimal n-state binary PFA A and a minimal m-state binary PFA or PRFA B such that the minimal DFA for the language $L(A \circ_{\nu_0} B)$ has α states.* □

Nevertheless, since magic numbers are related to the divisors of n and m in the case we deal with PFAs and PRFAs lead us to the following conjecture.

Conjecture 1. Let $n, m \geq 3$ and let them be odd. Then there exists no minimal n-state PFA A and no minimal PRFA B such that the minimal DFA for the language $L(A \circ_{\nu_0} B)$ has 2 states.

By allowing one of the two automata to be more powerful, in particular to be an arbitrary DFA, we obtain that no magic numbers exist anymore.

Theorem 5. *Let $n, m \geq 2$. Then for every α with $1 \leq \alpha \leq nm$, there exists a ternary minimal n-state PFA A and a ternary minimal DFA B such that the minimal DFA for the language $L(A \circ_{\nu_0} B)$ has α states.*

Since every PFA is also a PRFA we obtain directly that for the ν_0 product of a PRFA and an arbitrary DFA no magic numbers exist.

Corollary 1. *Let $n, m \geq 2$. Then for every α with $1 \leq \alpha \leq nm$, there exists a ternary minimal n-state PRFA A and a ternary minimal DFA B such that the minimal DFA for the language $L(A \circ_{\nu_0} B)$ has α states.*

The only case that remains is the direct product of two PRFAs. An exhaustive computer search on the direct product of small size PRFAs indicate that this case may be involved to solve since we found that, e.g., the number $\alpha = 8$ cannot be obtained by two PRFAs with $n = m = 3$ and an alphabet of size of at most three, but turns out to be attainable if the alphabet size is increased to at least four. There is further circumstantial evidence, that the exact solution to the magic number problem for the direct product of two PRFAs heavily depends on the input alphabet size. Thus, the statement of Theorem 4 can be strengthened to the case both operand automata are PRFAs. This completely exhausts all possible cases of direct products we are interested in.

3.2   The Cascade- or α_0-Product and the $\alpha\jmath_0$-Product

The descriptional complexity of the cascade- or α_0-product was recently studied in [7,8]. There it was shown that for the cascade product of RFAs, PFAs, PRFAs, and DFAs in general, where the left operand automaton has an alphabet of size at least two, in all cases, except for the cascade product of two PFAs, the whole range of state complexities, namely the interval $[1, nm]$, where n is the state complexity of the left operand and m that of the right one, is attainable. Moreover, for the cascade product of two PFAs numerous magic numbers were identified [7].

For the $\alpha\jmath_0$-product we can inherit all non-magic number cases from the cascade product by appropriately modifying the left automaton in the product. This is seen as follows: let $A = (Q_A, \Sigma, \cdot_A, q_{0,A}, F_A)$ and $B = (Q_B, Q_B \times \Sigma, \cdot_B, q_{0,B}, F_B)$ be the two automata from the cascade product. We define the automaton $A' = (Q_A, Q_B \times \Sigma, \cdot_{A'}, q_{0,A}, F_A)$, where the transition function is

$$q \cdot_{A'} (p, a) = q',$$

if $q \cdot_A a = q'$, for every state $q \in Q_A$ and letter $a \in \Sigma$. Then the initially reachable part of the $\alpha \wp_0$-product of A' and B is isomorphic to the initially reachable part of the cascade product of the automata A and B. By the construction it is easy to see that A' is from the same automata class under consideration as A, and that the minimality of A induces the minimality of A'.

Hence it only remains to consider the $\alpha \wp_0$-product for PFAs in detail.

Theorem 6. *Let $n, m \geq 2$. Then for every α with $1 \leq \alpha \leq nm$, there exists a minimal n-state PFA A and a minimal PFA B such that the minimal DFA for the language $L(A \circ_{\alpha \wp_0} B)$ has α states.*

The result on the $\alpha \wp_0$-product reads as follows:

Theorem 7. *Let $X, Y \in \{\mathbf{RFA}, \mathbf{PFA}, \mathbf{PRFA}, \mathbf{FA}\}$ and let $n, m \geq 2$, where n (m, respectively) is restricted to 2 in case $X = \mathbf{RFA}$ ($Y = \mathbf{RFA}$, respectively). Then for every α with $1 \leq \alpha \leq nm$, there exists a minimal n-state automaton A of type X and a minimal m-state automaton B of type Y, both compatible to the $\alpha \wp_0$-product, such that the minimal DFA for the language $L(A \circ_{\alpha \wp_0} B)$ has α states.* □

3.3   Proof of the Main Theorem

Now we are ready to prove the main theorem of this paper, by using the results on the descriptional complexity of the products of automata where no loops are involved together with the simulation result presented in Lemma 1.

Proof. For the loop-free products, namely ν_0, α_0, and $\alpha \wp_0$, the statement of the theorem follows for the

- ν_0-product by the Theorems 2, 3, 4, and 5, for the
- α_0-product by the results of [7], and for the
- $\alpha \wp_0$-product by Theorem 7.

Let $\circ$ by a product of automata of the form $\ell u_1 u_2 \in \{\ell\} \times \{c, b, -\} \times \{\ell, -\}$ and we assume that the left operand is an automaton of type X and the right one a finite state device of type Y, for $X, Y \in \{\mathbf{RFA}, \mathbf{PFA}, \mathbf{PRFA}, \mathbf{FA}\}$. By the theorems mentioned above for every $\alpha \in [1, nm]$ there is a DFA A and an automaton of type Y such that the minimal DFA accepting the language of their ν_0-product has α states. Lemma 1 gives a construction technique which can be used to build an automaton A' of type X such that the minimal DFA accepting their $(\ell - -)$-product has α states, too. Since the $(\ell - -)$-product is a special case of every product in $\{\ell\} \times \{c, b, -\} \times \{\ell, -\}$ the statement of the theorem under consideration follows for all the products in this set. Since the arguments from above can be used analogously for the products in $\{\ell, -\} \times \{c, b, -\} \times \{\ell\}$ this completes the proof. □

We summarize the results of the main theorem in Table 2. For all other products no magic numbers exist for the automata classes studied in this paper. Thus, besides a precise characterizations of the magic numbers that can be obtained for certain automata types, we have completely solved the magic number problem for products of automata.

Table 2. The magic number problem for the ν_0- and α_0-product of automata. The entry indicates whether magic numbers exist for the products of the appropriate automata classes. A line entry determines the left automaton, while the column entry specifies the right automaton of the automaton product. For other products of automata studied in this paper no magic numbers exist at all.

ν_0	RFA	PFA	PRFA	DFA
RFA	no	no	no	no
PFA	no	yes	yes	no
PRFA	no	yes	yes	no
DFA	no	no	no	no

α_0	RFA	PFA	PRFA	DFA
RFA	no	no	no	no
PFA	no	yes	no	no
PRFA	no	no	no	no
DFA	no	no	no	no

References

1. Ae, T.: Direct or cascade product of pushdown automata. J. Comput. Syst. Sci. **14**(2), 257–263 (1977)
2. Arbib, M.A.: Algebraic Theory of Machines, Languages, and Semigroups. Academic Press, New York (1968)
3. Jirásková, G., Masopust, T.: State complexity of projected languages. In: Holzer, M., Kutrib, M., Pighizzini, G. (eds.) DCFS 2011. LNCS, vol. 6808, pp. 198–211. Springer, Heidelberg (2011). https://doi.org/10.1007/978-3-642-22600-7_16
4. Čevorová, K., Jirásková, G., Krajňáková, I.: On the square of regular languages. In: Holzer, M., Kutrib, M. (eds.) CIAA 2014. LNCS, vol. 8587, pp. 136–147. Springer, Cham (2014). https://doi.org/10.1007/978-3-319-08846-4_10
5. Dömösi, P., Nehaniv, C.L.: Algebraic Theory of Automata Networks: An Introduction. SIAM, Philadelphia (2005)
6. Harrison, M.A.: Introduction to Formal Language Theory. Addison-Wesley, Boston (1978)
7. Holzer, M., Rauch, C.: The range of state complexities of languages resulting from the cascade product—the general case (extended abstract). In: Moreira, N., Reis, R. (eds.) DLT 2021. LNCS, vol. 12811, pp. 229–241. Springer, Cham (2021). https://doi.org/10.1007/978-3-030-81508-0_19
8. Holzer, M., Rauch, C.: The range of state complexities of languages resulting from the cascade product–the unary case. In: Maneth, S. (ed.) Proceedings of the CIAA, pp. 90–101, LNCS, Springer, Bremen (2021)
9. Holzer, M., Hospodár, M.: The range of state complexities of languages resulting from the cut operation. In: Martín-Vide, C., Okhotin, A., Shapira, D. (eds.) LATA 2019. LNCS, vol. 11417, pp. 190–202. Springer, Cham (2019). https://doi.org/10.1007/978-3-030-13435-8_14
10. Hricko, M., Jirásková, G., Szabari, A.: Union and intersection of regular languages and descriptional complexity. In: Mereghetti, C., Palano, B., Pighizzini, G., Wotschke, D. (eds.) Proceedings of the DCFS, pp. 170–181. Universita degli Studi di Milano, Como (2005)
11. Iwama, K., Kambayashi, Y., Takaki, K.: Tight bounds on the number of states of DFAs that are equivalent to n-state NFAs. Theoret. Comput. Sci. **237**(1–2), 485–494 (2000)
12. Jirásková, G.: Magic numbers and ternary alphabet. Internat. J. Found. Comput. Sci. **22**(2), 331–344 (2011)

Width Measures of Alternating Finite Automata

C. Keeler[⊠] and Kai Salomaa

School of Computing, Queen's University, Kingston, ONT K7L 2N8, Canada
{keeler,ksalomaa}@cs.queensu.ca

Abstract. We study the tree width, maximal existential width and maximal universal width of AFAs, which, roughly speaking, count the largest number of leaves, the largest number of existential choices, and the largest number of universal branches in a computation tree. We give polynomial-time algorithms deciding finiteness of an AFA's tree width and (under certain conditions) the finiteness of an AFA's maximal existential width. We also show that the language of any m-state AFA with finite maximal existential width can be recognized by $O(m^2)$ m-state AFAs with no existential branching. Additionally, we give polynomial-time algorithms deciding the growth rate of an AFA's tree width, and (under certain conditions) the growth rate of an AFA's maximal universal width. Finally, we establish necessary and sufficient conditions for an AFA to have exponential tree width, as well as sufficient conditions for an AFA to have exponential maximal existential width or exponential maximal universal width.

1 Introduction

Deterministic and nondeterministic automata (DFAs and NFAs) are well understood models of computation that recognize exactly the regular languages. *Alternating* finite automata (AFAs) also recognize exactly the regular languages, and were first introduced by Chandra et al. [1], and by Ladner et al. [8]. AFAs are an extension of NFAs, where states are denoted as *existential*, or *universal*, and a computation is allowed to *alternate* between the two types of states. Much like how NFAs can be exponentially more succinct than DFAs [10], AFAs can also be exponentially more succinct than NFAs [2,4]. We have previously shown that, for certain restricted classes of AFA, there is at most a polynomial blow-up in the number of states required by an equivalent NFA [7]. Here we further examine AFAs with restricted computations, and also study the growth rates for measures of parallelism and existentiality. This work is analogous to existing works on the growth rates for measures of nondeterminism [3,5,9,12], except in the context of AFAs instead of NFAs. For a number of these results, we are even able to reduce the problem on AFAs to the problem on NFAs.

The paper is organized as follows. Section 2 fixes the notation for AFAs, specifies how an AFA accepts or rejects strings, and defines the maximal universal

Y.-S. Han and S.-K. Ko (Eds.): DCFS 2021, LNCS 13037, pp. 88–99, 2021.
https://doi.org/10.1007/978-3-030-93489-7_8

width and the maximal existential width measures. Section 3 compares AFAs
having finite versus unbounded maximal existential width. Section 4 character-
izes the various possible growth rates for an AFA's maximal existential width or
maximal universal width, and relates the exponential tree width of AFAs to the
exponential tree width of NFAs.

2   Preliminaries

An AFA is a 6-tuple, $A = (Q_e, Q_u, \Sigma, \delta, q_0, F)$ where Q_e (the existential state set)
and Q_u (the universal state set) are finite sets of states such that $Q_e \cap Q_u = \emptyset$,
Σ is the input alphabet, $\delta : (Q_e \cup Q_u) \times \Sigma \to 2^{Q_e \cup Q_u}$ is the transition function,
$q_0 \in Q_e \cup Q_u$ is the initial state, and $F \subseteq Q_e \cup Q_u$ is the set of final states. We
use ε to mean the empty string, and $A_q = (Q_e, Q_u, \Sigma, \delta, q, F)$ (that is, A_q is A
with a different specified starting state $q \in Q_e \cup Q_u$).

We further define the *language* of an AFA, to account for the differences
caused by universal states. We do so by defining them bottom-up with respect
to their states.

Definition 1. *Let $A = (Q_e, Q_u, \Sigma, \delta, q_0, F)$ be an AFA, $q \in Q_e \cup Q_u$, and $a \in \Sigma$.
If $q \in F$, then $\varepsilon \in L(A_q)$. Consider $\delta(q, a) = \{p_1, \ldots, p_n\}$ for $n \geq 1$, then for
$w \in \Sigma^*$, define:*

- *If $q \in Q_u$, then $aw \in L(A_q)$ if and only if $w \in L(A_{p_i})$ for all $1 \leq i \leq n$.*
- *If $q \in Q_e$, then $aw \in L(A_q)$ if and only if $w \in L(A_{p_i})$ for some $1 \leq i \leq n$.*

If $\delta(q, a) = \emptyset$, then $aw \notin L(A_q)$. The language of A is defined as $L(A) = L(A_{q_0})$.

A *computation tree* of an AFA is a tree structure whose internal nodes are
labeled by a tuple (p, a), for $p \in Q_e \cup Q_u, a \in \Sigma$ (that is, each internal node
is labeled by a state and character), and whose leaves are labeled by (p, ε) or
the fail symbol $\perp$. We call a node of the computation tree T labeled by (p, a) a
p-node of T, and the leaves of T labeled by (p, ε) are called *state leaves*.

The computation tree of an AFA A on ε from $q \in Q_e \cup Q_u$, denoted $T_{A,q,\varepsilon}$
is the singleton node (q, ε). The computation tree of an AFA A on cv from q,
denoted $T_{A,q,cv}$, such that $q \in Q_e \cup Q_u, c \in \Sigma, v \in \Sigma^*$ is defined inductively as
the tree where:

- the root is labeled by (q, c), and
- the trees rooted at the children of (q, c) are
  - the computation trees $(T_{A,p_1,v}, \ldots, T_{A,p_n,v})$, if $\delta(q, c) = \{p_1, \ldots, p_n\}$
  - the failure node $\perp$ if $\delta(q, c) = \emptyset$

If a computation tree of an AFA A on a string w starts on the initial state of A,
then we omit the state label, and denote it as $T_{A,w}$. If A is an NFA, this yields
the computation trees as considered in [3], since an NFA can be seen as an AFA
with no universal states.

For an AFA $A = (Q_e, Q_u, \Sigma, \delta, q_0, F)$ and a state $q \in Q_e \cup Q_u$, a *pruned
computation tree* of $T_{A,q,\varepsilon}$ is the singleton node (q, ε). For a string cv, where
$c \in \Sigma$ and $v \in \Sigma^*$, a pruned computation tree of A on cv from $q \in Q_e \cup Q_u$ is
obtained recursively from $T_{A,q,cv}$, where $\delta(q, c) = \{p_1, \ldots, p_k\}$, as follows:

i) If q is an existential state, then replace $k - 1$ of the children by a singleton tree consisting of a node labeled by a new symbol ψ (representing a pruning of that branch), and the final child $T_{A,p_i,v}$ by a pruned computation tree of $T_{A,p_i,v}$, for some $1 \leq i \leq k$.

ii) If q is a universal state, then replace each child $T_{A,p_i,v}$ by a pruned computation tree of $T_{A,p_i,v}$, for all $1 \leq i \leq k$.

We note that each pruned computation tree represents one specific "run" in an AFA. However, considering the pruned computation trees allows us to examine the number of existential branches which are *not* followed in a particular run, rather than only examining those branches which are followed. For more information on the run-view versus the computation tree view, we point the reader to a recent survey paper by Kapoutsis and Zakzok [4].

For a tree T, we use stateLeaves(T) to denote the multiset of all of T's leaves labeled by a state-ε pair, and failLeaves(T) to denote the multiset of leaves of T labeled by the fail symbol $\perp$. We call leaves labeled by ψ *cut leaves*, and use cutLeaves(T) to denote the multiset of all cut leaves in a tree T.

The set of all pruned computation trees of a tree T is denoted $\gtrdot\!\!\!\!<(T)$. A pruned computation tree is *accepting* if all of its state-ε leaves are labeled by accepting states, and no leaves are labeled by the fail symbol $\perp$. We denote the set of all accepting pruned computations of a tree T as $\gtrdot\!\!\!\!<^{acc}(T)$. Directly from the definitions of an AFA's language and the structure of pruned computation trees, we get the following corollary.

Corollary 1. *Let $A = (Q_e, Q_u, \Sigma, \delta, q_0, F)$ be an AFA. For any string $w \in \Sigma^*$, $w \in L(A)$ if and only if $\gtrdot\!\!\!\!<^{acc}(T_{A,w}) \neq \emptyset$.*

For an AFA $A = (Q_e, Q_u, \Sigma, \delta, q_0, F)$, we define the *skeleton* of A as follows: $A' = (Q_e \cup Q_u, \emptyset, \Sigma, \delta, q_0, F)$. That is, the skeleton of an AFA has the same state set and transition structure, except all of the states are existential. Since the skeleton of an AFA has only existential states, then it is an NFA. We note that the language of an AFA's skeleton is not usually the same as the original AFA's language.

For an AFA $A = (Q_e, Q_u, \Sigma, \delta, q_0, F)$, a state's designation as existential or universal affects the recognized language only if there are at least two outgoing transitions on the same character. That is, if we have some $q_e \in Q_e$ such that $|\delta(q_e, a)| \leq 1$ for all $a \in \Sigma$, then $L(A) = L(A')$ for the AFA $A' = (Q_e \setminus \{q_e\}, Q_u \cup \{q_e\}, \Sigma, \delta, q_0, F)$. The same also holds for universal states with at most one outgoing transition on each character. For AFAs we use the term *existential branching* to refer to existential states which have multiple outgoing transitions on the same character. This can be seen as being like "nondeterminism in AFAs", as NFAs also have a form of existential branching. We use *universal branching* analogously for universal states with multiple outgoing transitions on the same character.

Let $f(\ell) : \mathbb{N} \to \mathbb{N}$ be some function for some $\ell \in \mathbb{N}$. If $f(\ell) \in \Theta(\ell^d)$ (for some $d \in \mathbb{N}$), then we say that $f(\ell)$ has *polynomial growth degree d*. If $f(\ell) \in 2^{\Theta(\ell)}$ then we say that $f(\ell)$ has *exponential growth*.

2.1   Width Measures of Alternating Automata

The *tree width* of an AFA A on a string w, denoted $\mathrm{tw}(A, w)$, is the number of state leaves and fail symbols in the computation tree $T_{A,w}$ [7]. If A is an NFA, then our definition of tree width coincides with the tree width of NFAs [3,11]. Since there may be many pruned computation trees for a single alternating computation tree, we define the notions of universal width and existential width for pruned computation trees.

Definition 2. *For an AFA A and a pruned computation tree T^p of A, the* universal width *of T^p, denoted $\mathrm{uw}(T^p)$, is the number of leaves in T^p labeled by a state or fail symbol. Formally, this is:*

$$\mathrm{uw}(T^p) = |\mathrm{stateLeaves}(T^p)| + |\mathrm{failLeaves}(T^p)|.$$

We extend the universal width for strings.

Definition 3. *For an AFA $A = (Q_e, Q_u, \Sigma, \delta, q_0, F)$ and a string $w \in \Sigma^*$, the* maximal universal width *of A on w, denoted $\mathrm{uw}^{\max}(A, w)$, is the greatest number of leaves in any pruned computation tree of $T_{A,w}$. Formally, this is:*

$$\mathrm{uw}^{\max}(A, w) = \max\{\mathrm{uw}(T^p) \mid T^p \in {\succ\!\!\prec}(T_{A,w})\}.$$

Intuitively, the maximal universal width of an AFA A on a string w measures the amount of parallelism in the "worst" alternating computation over w.

We can also measure the amount of existential choices present in an alternating computation.

Definition 4. *For an AFA A and a pruned computation tree T^p of A, the* existential width *of T^p, denoted $\mathrm{ew}(T^p)$, is the number of leaves labeled by the symbol ψ. More formally, $\mathrm{ew}(T^p) = |\mathrm{cutLeaves}(T^p)|$.*

Again, we extend the measure for strings.

Definition 5. *For an AFA $A = (Q_e, Q_u, \Sigma, \delta, q_0, F)$ and a string $w \in \Sigma^*$, the* maximal existential width *of A on w, denoted $\mathrm{ew}^{\max}(A, w)$, is the largest number of leaves labeled by the symbol ψ in any pruned computation tree of $T_{A,w}$. Formally, this is:*

$$\mathrm{ew}^{\max}(A, w) = \max\{\mathrm{ew}(T^p) \mid T^p \in {\succ\!\!\prec}(T_{A,w})\}.$$

The maximal existential width of an AFA on a string w measures, roughly speaking, the number of existential branches that are not followed by a particular alternating computation on w. Using this measure, we can quantify the amount of "redundancy" present in the existential transitions of an AFA.

We extend the tree width, maximal universal width, and maximal existential width functions onto functions over the natural numbers and AFAs in the normal manner. For $f \in \{\mathrm{tw}, \mathrm{uw}^{\max}, \mathrm{ew}^{\max}\}$:

$$f(A, \ell) = \max\{f(A, w) \mid w \in \Sigma^\ell\}, \text{ and } f(A) = \sup_{\ell \in \mathbb{N}}\{f(A, \ell)\}. \tag{1}$$

If an AFA does not have any existential branching, then no branches are removed during the pruning operation. This means that there will be exactly one pruned computation tree for any string, and the maximal universal width and tree width will coincide.

Lemma 1. *Let $A = (Q_e, Q_u, \Sigma, \delta, q_0, F)$ be an AFA such that $|\delta(q,a)| \leq 1$ for all $q \in Q_e$ and $a \in \Sigma$. Then for all $w \in \Sigma^*$, we have $\mathrm{uw}^{\max}(A, w) = \mathrm{tw}(A, w)$ and $\mathord{\rightarrowtail}(T_{A,w}) = \{T_{A,w}\}$.*

3   Finite Universal and Existential Width

Throughout this paper, we use the term *widget* to describe subgraphs of AFAs. More formally, an AFA $A = (Q_e, Q_u, \Sigma, \delta, q_0, F)$ has a widget $\mathcal{W} = (Q'_e, Q'_u, \Sigma', \delta', F')$ if $Q'_e \subseteq Q_e$, $Q'_u \subseteq Q_u$, $\Sigma' \subseteq \Sigma$, $\delta' \subseteq \delta$, and $F' \subseteq F$.

In our figures, if a state q is universal (respectively, existential) then it is labeled (q, u) (respectively, (q, e)). If a state is labeled e/u, then it does not matter whether it is universal or existential.

For an m-state AFA A, if the tree width of A is finite, then $\mathrm{tw}(A) \leq 2^{m-2}$ [6], and this follows from the corresponding upper bound for NFAs [11]. For any AFA A and its skeleton A', we have $\mathrm{tw}(A, w) = \mathrm{tw}(A', w)$ for any string w.

Since the tree width of an AFA is defined over *unpruned* computation trees, we get that $\mathrm{ew}^{\max}(A, w), \mathrm{uw}^{\max}(A, w) \leq \mathrm{tw}(A, w)$ for any string w. We know that an AFA can only have unbounded maximal universal width if there exists a widget (IUW), as shown in Fig. 1 [6]. For unbounded maximal existential width, however, the number of cut leaves can grow unboundedly due to certain structures on existential states *or* universal states.

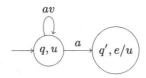

Fig. 1. Widget (IUW), for $a \in \Sigma, v \in \Sigma^*$ [6]

Lemma 2. *Let $A = (Q_e, Q_u, \Sigma, \delta, q_0, F)$ be an AFA where $\mathrm{ew}^{\max}(A) \notin O(1)$. Then either*

i) A has a cycle containing an existentially branching state, or
ii) For some strings $u, v, w \in \Sigma^*$, characters $a, b \in \Sigma$, and states $q \in Q_u$, $q_1, q_2 \in Q_e \cup Q_u$, and $p \in Q_e$, we have: $q \in \delta(q_0, u)$, $\{q_1, q_2\} \subseteq \delta(q, a)$, $q \in \delta(q_1, v)$, $p \in \delta(q_2, w)$, $|\delta(p, b)| \geq 2$, and $\mathrm{ew}(T_{A,u(av)^i wb}) < \mathrm{ew}(T_{A,u(av)^{i+1}wb})$ for some $k \geq 1$ and all $i \geq k$.

In the converse direction, we have a number of conditions sufficient to cause the maximal existential width to be unbounded.

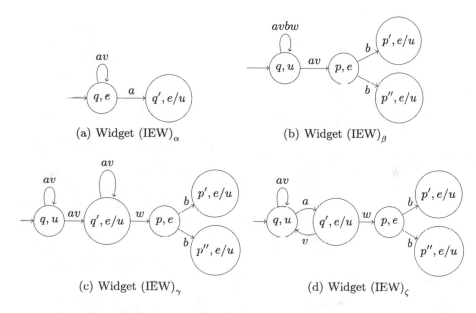

(a) Widget (IEW)$_\alpha$ (b) Widget (IEW)$_\beta$

(c) Widget (IEW)$_\gamma$ (d) Widget (IEW)$_\zeta$

Fig. 2. Widgets causing infinite $\mathrm{ew}^{\max}(A)$, where $a, b \in \Sigma, v, w \in \Sigma^*$

Theorem 1. *Let A be an AFA with at least one of the widgets from Fig. 2. Then* $\mathrm{ew}^{\max}(A) \notin O(1)$.

It is possible that there exist other structures involving cyclical universally branching states which can also cause unbounded maximal existential width.

Question 1. Do there exist any widgets causing unbounded maximal existential width not represented in Fig. 2?

3.1 Deciding Finiteness of Maximal Universal/Existential Width

The tree width of an NFA is unbounded if and only if there exists a state whose nondeterministic transition is involved in a cycle [3], and we can decide whether or not the tree width of an m-state NFA $A = (Q, \Sigma, \delta, q_0, F)$ is bounded in $O(m \cdot |\delta| \cdot |\Sigma|)$ time [5]. Since the tree width of an AFA and the tree width of its skeleton are the same, then deciding finiteness of an AFA's tree width can be reduced to the problem on NFAs.

Lemma 3. *Let A be an m-state AFA. Then we can decide whether or not* $\mathrm{tw}(A) \in O(1)$ *in* $O(m \cdot |\delta| \cdot |\Sigma|)$ *time.*

Since the structure of (IUW) widgets matches closely to the structure of the widgets causing unbounded tree width in NFAs, we can also decide finiteness of an AFA's maximal universal width using the same algorithm [7]. However, unbounded maximal existential width in AFAs can result from a number of different structures (cf. Fig. 2), and so we cannot use the same algorithm without modification. Since an AFA has unbounded tree width if and only if it has unbounded maximal existential width or maximal universal width [7], then we also get a polynomial time algorithm deciding finiteness of an AFA's maximal existential width, provided that the number of universal branches is guaranteed to be finite.

Theorem 2. *Let A be an m-state AFA such that* $\mathrm{uw}^{\max}(A) \in O(1)$. *Then we can decide whether or not* $\mathrm{ew}^{\max}(A) \in O(1)$ *in* $O(m \cdot |\delta| \cdot |\Sigma|)$ *time.*

With a more purpose-built algorithm, it is also possible that we can decide whether or not the maximal existential width of an AFA is bounded, even if the maximal universal width is unbounded. Since we can decide, in polynomial time, whether or not the tree width or the maximal universal width of an AFA are bounded, it seems reasonable to expect a polynomial-time algorithm deciding whether or not the maximal existential width of an AFA is bounded.

Conjecture 1. Let A be an AFA. Then there exists a polynomial-time algorithm deciding whether or not $\mathrm{ew}^{\max}(A) \in O(1)$.

We know that, if the maximal existential width of an m-state NFA is finite, then it is at most $\frac{(m-1)\cdot(m-2)}{2}$ [7]. However, in AFAs the addition of universal branches allows for the finite maximal existential width to be exponentially larger than the number of states. More specifically, for $m \geq 6$ there exist finite maximal existential width AFAs A_m such that $\mathrm{ew}^{\max}(A_m) = 5 \cdot 2^{m-5}$ [7]. We give an example of a 7-state AFA meeting this lower bound in Fig. 3. The general form requires at least 1 universal state at the beginning of the chain, followed by 5 existential states, where all states are maximally connected. We note that, strictly speaking, the final two states can be existential or universal, since they both have exactly one outgoing transition. We believe this to be the greatest finite maximal existential width among m-state AFAs.

Conjecture 2. Let A be an m-state AFA such that $\mathrm{ew}^{\max}(A) \in O(1)$. Then $\mathrm{ew}^{\max}(A) \leq 5 \cdot 2^{m-5}$.

3.2   Simulation of AFAs with Finite Maximal Existential Width

If an AFA has finite maximal existential width, then we can further bound the maximum number of existentially branching states.

Lemma 4. *Let A be an m-state AFA such that $\mathrm{ew}^{\max}(A) \in O(1)$. Then there are at most $m - 2$ existentially branching states.*

By Lemma 1, the tree width and the maximal universal width coincide for AFAs with no existential branching. If an AFA has finite maximal existential width, then we can simulate it with polynomially many AFAs where each simulating AFA has the same number of states as the original but *no* existential branching.

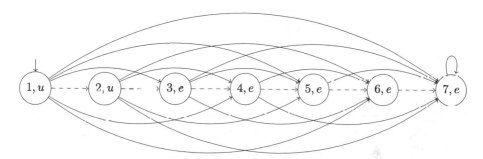

Fig. 3. An AFA with 2 universal states, 5 existential states, and a maximal existential width of $5 \cdot 2^2$. Dashed edges are labeled by a, b, and solid edges are labeled by a.

Theorem 3. *Let A be an m-state AFA such that $\mathrm{ew}^{\max}(A) \in O(1)$. Then there exist $O(m^2)$ AFAs, $B_1, \ldots, B_z$, each having m states, such that $L(A) = \bigcup_{i=1}^{z} L(B_i)$ and $\mathrm{ew}^{\max}(B_i) = 0$ for all $1 \le i \le z$.*

We note that the upper bound of the previous theorem is conservative and could be improved by a more detailed analysis. We can also relate the pruned computation trees of a finite maximal existential width AFA to the collection of AFAs simulating it.

Corollary 2. *Let $A = (Q_e, Q_u, \Sigma, \delta, q_0, F)$ be an m-state AFA such that $\mathrm{ew}^{\max}(A) \in O(1)$, and let $B_1, \ldots, B_z$ be the $O(m^2)$ m-state AFAs as in Theorem 3. Then for any $w \in \Sigma^*$, $\succ(T_{A,w}) = \bigcup_{i=1}^{z} \succ(T_{B_i, w})$.*

4   Infinite Maximal Universal/Existential Width

We know that either the tree width of an NFA is finite, or it has polynomial or exponential growth [3]. There exist widgets which cause polynomial or exponential growth for the tree width of an NFA, and if an NFA has none of these widgets, then the tree width will be finite [3,5].

Since an AFA and its skeleton have the same tree width, we can leverage existing algorithms which decide the growth rate of an NFA's tree width to decide the growth rate of an AFA's tree width.

Theorem 4. *Let $A = (Q_e, Q_u, \Sigma, \delta, q_0, F)$ be an m-state AFA. Then we can decide in $O(m^4 \cdot |\Sigma|)$ time whether $\mathrm{tw}(A)$ is finite, or if it has polynomial or exponential growth.*

For AFAs with finite maximal existential width, we can use the transformation of Theorem 3 to simulate the existential choices, and decide the tree width's growth rate for each simulating AFA. By doing so, we can decide the maximal universal width's growth rate for the original AFA.

Theorem 5. *Let $A = (Q_e, Q_u, \Sigma, \delta, q_0, F)$ be an m-state AFA such that $\mathrm{ew}^{\max}(A) \in O(1)$. Then we can decide whether $\mathrm{uw}^{\max}(A)$ is finite, polynomial, or exponential in $O(m^6 \cdot |\Sigma|)$ time.*

4.1   Exponential Growth

The tree width of an NFA will grow exponentially if and only if there is some widget (ECOMP) [5]. For an NFA, there is an (ECOMP) widget if, roughly speaking, there exists a state involved in two cycles over the same string. More formally, an NFA $A = (Q, \Sigma, \delta, q_0, F)$ has an (ECOMP) widget if there exists a state $q \in Q$, a character $a \in \Sigma$, and a string $w \in \Sigma^*$ such that $\{q_1, q_2\} \subseteq \delta(q, a)$, $q \in \delta(q_1, w)$, and $q \in \delta(q_2, w)$.

Recall that the structure of the widgets causing unbounded tree width for NFAs and unbounded maximal universal width for AFAs is the same, except that the latter requires the cyclical portion of the widget to be on a universal state. The same idea holds when extending the (ECOMP) structure to AFAs. By doing so, we get two new widgets, (EEW) and (EUW), as shown in Fig. 4. Since the structure of (EEW) and (EUW) widgets is derived from (ECOMP), we get necessary and sufficient conditions for an AFA to have exponential tree width.

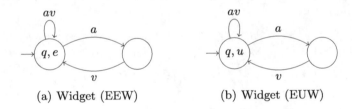

(a) Widget (EEW)   (b) Widget (EUW)

Fig. 4. Widgets for AFAs derived from (ECOMP), for $a \in \Sigma, v \in \Sigma^+$

Theorem 6. *Let A be an AFA. Then $\mathrm{tw}(A, \ell) \in 2^{\Theta(\ell)}$ if and only if A has an (EUW) widget or A has an (EEW) widget.*

Since the maximal universal width counts the number of parallel branches, the presence of an (EUW) widget is sufficient to cause exponential growth.

Lemma 5. *Let A be an AFA with an (EUW) widget. Then $\mathrm{uw}^{\max}(A, \ell) \in 2^{\Theta(\ell)}$.*

In addition to (EUW) widgets being sufficient to cause exponential maximal universal width, we also believe that they are necessary.

Conjecture 3. Let A be an AFA such that $\mathrm{uw}^{\max}(A, \ell) \in 2^{\Theta(\ell)}$. Then A has an (EUW) widget.

Even though (EEW) widgets are sufficient to cause exponential tree width, they do not necessarily cause exponential growth for the maximal existential width. We demonstrate this with the following example.

Example 1. Consider the AFA $A = (\{q_1, q_2\}, \emptyset, \{a\}, \delta, q_1, \{q_1\})$, where δ is defined as $\delta(q_1, a) = \{q_1, q_2\}$ and $\delta(q_2, a) = \{q_1\}$. Clearly, A is the smallest AFA having an (EEW) widget. In the tree T_{A,a^ℓ}, for any $\ell \in \mathbb{N}$, every non-leaf node labeled by q_1 will have two children, and every non-leaf node labeled by q_2 will have one child. Since there are no universal states in A, then any pruned tree $T^p \in \prec(T_{A,a^\ell})$ will have one branch. Since the branch consists of $\ell + 1$ nodes, and each node has at most 1 cut leaf attached to it, then $\text{ew}(T_{A,a^\ell}) \leq \ell + 1$. Since A is unary, then $\text{ew}^{\max}(A, a^\ell) = \text{ew}^{\max}(A, \ell)$, and therefore $\text{ew}^{\max}(A, \ell) \in O(\ell)$.

However, much like how (IUW) widgets are able to cause the maximal existential width to be unbounded (cf. Theorem 1), (EUW) widgets are also able to cause exponential growth for the maximal existential width. We recall the widgets of Fig. 2, and note that the (IEW)$_\zeta$ widget has an (EUW) widget as part of its structure, followed by an existentially branching state. We use this fact to strengthen our result for the maximal existential width's growth rate for AFAs with (IEW)$_\zeta$ widgets.

Lemma 6. *Let A be an AFA with an* (IEW)$_\zeta$ *widget. Then* $\text{ew}^{\max}(A, \ell) \subset 2^{\Theta(\ell)}$.

Since (EEW) widgets do not cause exponential growth for the maximal existential width, it seems plausible that any AFA having exponential maximal existential width must also have exponential maximal universal width.

Conjecture 4. Let A be an AFA. If $\text{ew}^{\max}(A, \ell) \in 2^{\Theta(\ell)}$, then $\text{uw}^{\max}(A, \ell) \in 2^{\Theta(\ell)}$.

4.2 Polynomial Growth

We know that the maximal universal width of an AFA grows unboundedly if and only if there exists an (IUW) widget [6]. The structure of (IUW) widgets is exactly the same as the widget which causes unbounded tree width for NFAs, except the former is over universal states and the latter is over existential states. Since the presence of an (IUW) widget forces at least linear growth, and any AFA with unbounded maximal universal width has an (IUW) widget, then there are no growth rates for an AFA's maximal universal width between finite and linear.

Corollary 3. *Let A be an AFA. If* $\text{uw}^{\max}(A) \notin O(1)$, *then* $\text{uw}^{\max}(A, \ell) \in \Omega(\ell)$.

If the tree width of an NFA is bounded by a polynomial, then we can decide what degree bounds that polynomial by, roughly speaking, determining how many successive (IEW)$_\alpha$ widgets over the same string can appear in any computation tree [5]. (Strictly speaking, it is the number of consecutive "(ITW)" widgets, since it is operating over NFAs.) However, for AFAs this process is not so simple, as an (IUW) widget appearing before an (IEW)$_\alpha$ widget will increase the growth rate of the maximal existential width, but an (IEW)$_\alpha$ widget appearing before an (IUW) widget will *not* increase the growth rate of the maximal universal width. We demonstrate this difference in the following example.

Example 2. In Fig. 5, there are two AFAs, B_1 and B_2, each of which have an (IUW) widget and an (IEW)$_\alpha$ widget; the only difference is which one comes first. Figure 5(a) has linear growth rate for both the maximal universal width and the maximal existential width, whereas Fig. 5(b)'s ordering of these widgets means that the number of pruned branches grows both because of the universally branching cyclical state *and* because of the existentially branching state.

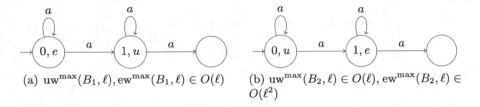

(a) $\mathrm{uw}^{\max}(B_1, \ell), \mathrm{ew}^{\max}(B_1, \ell) \in O(\ell)$ (b) $\mathrm{uw}^{\max}(B_2, \ell) \in O(\ell), \mathrm{ew}^{\max}(B_2, \ell) \in O(\ell^2)$

Fig. 5. Importance of widget ordering for polynomial growth

It seems plausible then that the maximal universal width of AFAs can have polynomial growth in a similar fashion to the polynomial tree width of NFAs. That is, an AFA with $1 \leq d \leq m$ consecutive universally branching cycles (and also no (EUW) widgets) would have at most $O(\ell^{d-1})$ universal branches in any pruned computation tree over strings of length ℓ.

Conjecture 5. Let A be an m-state AFA with no (EUW) widgets. Then $\mathrm{uw}^{\max}(A, \ell) \in O(\ell^{m-1})$.

Unfortunately, it is not exactly clear how to define the polynomial upper bound for maximal universal/existential width in AFAs with interleaved (IUW) and (IEW)$_\alpha$ widgets. However, since interleaved (IUW) and (IEW)$_\alpha$ widgets require that the computation *alternates* between existential and universal states, it seems likely that the polynomial growth rates of maximal universal/existential width are related to the number of alternations an AFA is allowed to make, as studied by Geffert [2].

5   Conclusion

We have characterized necessary and sufficient conditions for an AFA to have unbounded or exponential tree width by reducing the problem onto NFAs. For the maximal existential width of an AFA, we characterized necessary conditions for unbounded growth, and sufficient conditions for exponential growth, but the converse direction in each case remains open. Though we know that the finite maximal existential width of an AFA can be exponentially larger than the number of states, we were able to construct a transformation to simulate AFAs with finite maximal existential width by only polynomially many AFAs, each having the same number of states and no existential branching. The conditions causing polynomial growth for an AFA's tree width, maximal existential width, or maximal universal width remain unknown, though we have initiated their study by examining some of the nuance imposed by the ordering of existential and universal states.

Acknowledgements. Research supported by NSERC grant OGP0147224.

References

1. Chandra, A.K., Kozen, D.C., Stockmeyer, L.J.: Alternation. J. ACM **28**(1), 114–133 (1981)
2. Geffert, V.: An alternating hierarchy for finite automata. Theor. Comput. Sci. **445**, 1–24 (2012)
3. Hromkovič, J., Seibert, S., Karhumäki, J., Klauck, H., Schnitger, G.: Communication complexity method for measuring nondeterminism in finite automata. Inform. Comput **172**(2), 202–217 (2002)
4. Kapoutsis, C.A., Zakzok, M.: Alternation in two-way finite automata. Theor. Comput. Sci. **870**, 75–102 (2021)
5. Keeler, C., Salomaa, K.: Nondeterminism growth and state complexity. In: Hospodár, M., Jirásková, G., Konstantinidis, S. (eds.) DCFS 2019. LNCS, vol. 11612, pp. 210–222. Springer, Cham (2019). https://doi.org/10.1007/978-3-030-23247-4_16
6. Keeler, C., Salomaa, K.: Alternating finite automata with limited universal branching. In: Leporati, A., Martín-Vide, C., Shapira, D., Zandron, C. (eds.) LATA 2020. LNCS, vol. 12038, pp. 196–207. Springer, Cham (2020). https://doi.org/10.1007/978-3-030-40608-0_13
7. Keeler, C., Salomaa, K.: Combining limited parallelism and nondeterminism in alternating finite automata. In: Jirásková, G., Pighizzini, G. (eds.) DCFS 2020. LNCS, vol. 12442, pp. 91–103. Springer, Cham (2020). https://doi.org/10.1007/978-3-030-62536-8_8
8. Ladner, R.E., Lipton, R.J., Stockmeyer, L.J.: Alternating pushdown and stack automata. SIAM J. Comput. **13**(1), 135–155 (1984)
9. Leung, H.: Separating exponentially ambiguous finite automata from polynomially ambiguous finite automata. SIAM J. Comput **27**(4), 1073–1082 (1998)
10. Meyer, A.R., Fischer, M.J.: Economy of description by automata, grammars, and formal systems. In: SWAT (FOCS) 1971, pp. 188–191 (1971)
11. Palioudakis, A., Salomaa, K., Akl, S.G.: State complexity of finite tree width NFAs. J. Autom. Lang. Combin. **17**(2–4), 245–264 (2012)
12. Weber, A., Seidl, H.: On the degree of ambiguity of finite automata. Theor. Comput. Sci. **88**(2), 325–349 (1991)

Partial Derivative Automaton
by Compressing Regular Expressions

Stavros Konstantinidis[1], António Machiavelo[2], Nelma Moreira[2(✉)],
and Rogério Reis[2]

[1] Saint Mary's University, Halifax, NS, Canada
s.konstantinidis@smu.ca
[2] CMUP & DM, DCC, Faculdade de Ciências da Universidade do Porto,
Rua do Campo Alegre, 4169-007 Porto, Portugal
{antonio.machiavelo,nelma.moreira,rogerio.reis}@fc.up.pt

Abstract. The partial derivative automaton ($\mathcal{A}_{\mathsf{PD}}$) is an elegant simulation of a regular expression. Although it is, in general, smaller than the position automaton ($\mathcal{A}_{\mathsf{POS}}$), the algorithms that build $\mathcal{A}_{\mathsf{PD}}$ in quadratic worst-case time, first compute $\mathcal{A}_{\mathsf{POS}}$. Asymptotically, and on average for the uniform distribution, the size of $\mathcal{A}_{\mathsf{PD}}$ is half the size of $\mathcal{A}_{\mathsf{POS}}$, being both linear on the size of the expression. We address the construction of $\mathcal{A}_{\mathsf{PD}}$ efficiently, on average, avoiding the computation of $\mathcal{A}_{\mathsf{POS}}$. The expression and the set of its partial derivatives are represented by a directed acyclic graph with shared common subexpressions. We develop an algorithm for building $\mathcal{A}_{\mathsf{PD}}$'s from expressions in strong star normal form of size n that runs in time $O\big(n^{3/2}\sqrt[4]{\log(n)}\,\big)$ and space $O\big(n^{3/2}/(\log n)^{3/4}\big)$, on average. Empirical results corroborate its good practical performance.

1 Introduction

The partial derivative automaton ($\mathcal{A}_{\mathsf{PD}}$) is an elegant construction to obtain nondeterministic finite automata (without ε-transitions) from regular expressions. The use of derivatives has several advantages: they are easily extended to operations other than union, concatenation, and Kleene star; word membership can be evaluated without the need to build the automaton; and the $\mathcal{A}_{\mathsf{PD}}$ is a quotient of the position (or Glushkov) automaton ($\mathcal{A}_{\mathsf{POS}}$) [6,7]. In the worst-case, for a standard regular expression of size n, both automata can have $O(n)$ states, $O(n^2)$ transitions, and can be computed in time $O(n^2)$. However, the known algorithms to build $\mathcal{A}_{\mathsf{PD}}$ in quadratic time first compute $\mathcal{A}_{\mathsf{POS}}$ and then compute a right-invariant equivalence on the states of $\mathcal{A}_{\mathsf{POS}}$ [8,16]. For practical applications, the drawbacks of these methods are the need to build a larger automaton (which is not easy to generalize for nonstandard operations) and the computation of the equivalence relation on the set of $\mathcal{A}_{\mathsf{POS}}$ states. In particular, Khorsi et al. [16] base their algorithm on the construction and minimization of

Research supported by NSERC (Canada) and by CMUP through FCT project UIDB/00144/2020.

Y.-S. Han and S.-K. Ko (Eds.): DCFS 2021, LNCS 13037, pp. 100–112, 2021.
https://doi.org/10.1007/978-3-030-93489-7_9

two acyclic deterministic finite automata, which burdens the practical performance of the algorithm, despite their linear worst-case time.

Asymptotically, and on average for the uniform distribution, the size of $\mathcal{A}_{\text{PD}}$ (both in states and transitions) is half the size of $\mathcal{A}_{\text{POS}}$, being both linear on the size of the expression [3,19]. Being smaller, in general, it is interesting to know if the $\mathcal{A}_{\text{PD}}$ can be built efficiently without the computation of the $\mathcal{A}_{\text{POS}}$. In this paper we address this problem considering regular expressions in strong star normal form (ssnf). The star normal form was first defined to construct the position automaton in time $O(n^2)$, for expressions of size n [6]. The conversion of an expression to star normal form can be done in linear time (in both the worst and average cases). This form was extended to strong star normal form (ssnf) by Gruber and Gulan [14]. The average-case complexity of conversions from ssnf expressions to other models was studied by Broda et al. [4]. Then Konstantinidis et al. [17] considered the size of partial derivatives on the average case both for standard and ssnf expressions. For the latter, asymptotically and on average, the size of the largest partial derivative is $O(n/2)$, n being the size of the expression, while one has $O(n^{3/2})$ for the standard. Any partial derivative of an expression is a concatenation of some of its subexpressions. Thus, it is interesting to estimate the number of new concatenations obtained, on average, when partial derivatives are computed. By using a tree representation of a regular expression and its set of partial derivatives, those concatenations correspond to the new nodes that are added to the initial tree. Konstantinidis et al. showed that when computing a partial derivative w.r.t. one symbol that number is asymptotically constant.

In this paper we attain asymptotic estimates for the number of new concatenations when computing the set of all partial derivatives. To represent a regular expression and the set of its partial derivatives, instead of a tree, we consider a directed acyclic graph (DAG) with shared common subexpressions. Flajolet et al. [13] showed that a tree of size n has, in this compact form, an expected size of $O\left(n / \sqrt{\log n}\right)$. We present an algorithm that computes $\mathcal{A}_{\text{PD}}(\alpha)$ by constructing a DAG for α, and simultaneously builds the set of all partial derivatives by adding new concatenation nodes to the DAG. Using the asymptotic estimates mentioned above we show that for ssnf expressions the algorithm uses, on average, time $O\left(n^{3/2}\sqrt[4]{\log(n)}\right)$ and space $O\left(n^{3/2}/(\log n)^{3/4}\right)$. Experiments for uniformly randomly generated expressions, as well as for some extreme expressions, suggest that the algorithm has a good practical performance.

2 Preliminaries

A *nondeterministic finite automaton* (NFA) is a five-tuple $A = \langle Q, \Sigma, \delta, I, F \rangle$ where Q is a finite set of states, Σ is a finite alphabet, $I \subseteq Q$ is the set of initial states, $F \subseteq Q$ is the set of final states, and $\delta : Q \times \Sigma \to 2^Q$ is the transition function. The size of an NFA is its number of states plus its number of transitions. The transition function can be extended to words and to sets of states in the natural way. The *language accepted* by A is $\mathcal{L}(A) = \{w \in \Sigma^\star \mid \delta(I, w) \cap F \neq \emptyset\}$. Given an alphabet $\Sigma = \{\sigma_1, \sigma_2, \ldots, \sigma_k\}$ of size $k \geq 1$, the set $\mathcal{R}_k$ of (standard) *regular expressions* α over Σ consists of $\emptyset$ and the expressions defined by the following context-free grammar:

$$\alpha := \varepsilon \mid \sigma_1 \mid \cdots \mid \sigma_k \mid (\alpha + \alpha) \mid (\alpha \odot \alpha) \mid (\alpha^\star), \tag{1}$$

where the symbol $\odot$ is often omitted, and represents concatenation. The *language* associated with α is denoted by $\mathcal{L}(\alpha)$ and is defined as usual. If $S \subseteq \mathcal{R}_k$, then $\mathcal{L}(S) = \bigcup_{\alpha \in S} \mathcal{L}(\alpha)$. We say that α is *nullable* if $\varepsilon \in \mathcal{L}(\alpha)$ and, in this case, define $\varepsilon(\alpha) = \varepsilon$, with $\varepsilon(\alpha) = \emptyset$, otherwise. For the *size* of a regular expression α, denoted by $\|\alpha\|$, we will consider the size of its syntactic tree, i.e. the number of symbols in α, not counting parentheses. The *alphabetic size* of α, denoted by $|\alpha|_\Sigma$, is the number of letters in α. The notions of language, nullability and of the above measures extend in a natural way to sets of expressions. The set of letters that occur in α is denoted by Σ_α. The partial derivative automaton of a regular expression was introduced independently by Mirkin [18] and Antimirov [1]. For $\alpha \in \mathcal{R}_k$, let the *linear form* (LF) of α, $\varphi(\alpha) \subseteq \Sigma \times \mathcal{R}_k$, be inductively defined by

$$\begin{aligned}
\varphi(\emptyset) = \varphi(\varepsilon) = \emptyset, \qquad & \varphi(\alpha + \alpha') = \varphi(\alpha) \cup \varphi(\alpha'), \\
\varphi(\sigma) = \{(\sigma, \varepsilon)\}, \qquad & \varphi(\alpha\alpha') = \begin{cases} \varphi(\alpha)\alpha' \cup \varphi(\alpha'), & \text{if } \varepsilon(\alpha) = \varepsilon, \\ \varphi(\alpha)\alpha' & \text{otherwise,} \end{cases} \qquad (2) \\
\varphi(\alpha^\star) = \varphi(\alpha)\alpha^\star, \qquad &
\end{aligned}$$

where, for any $S \subseteq \Sigma \times \mathcal{R}_k$, we define $S\emptyset = \emptyset$, $S\varepsilon = S$, and $S\alpha' = \{(\sigma, \alpha\alpha') \mid (\sigma, \alpha) \in S \wedge \alpha \neq \varepsilon\} \cup \{(\sigma, \alpha') \mid (\sigma, \varepsilon) \in S\}$ for $\alpha' \neq \emptyset, \varepsilon$. For $\alpha \in \mathcal{R}_k$ and $\sigma \in \Sigma$, *the set of partial derivatives of* α *w.r.t.* σ is defined by $\partial_\sigma(\alpha) = \{\alpha' \mid (\sigma, \alpha') \in \varphi(\alpha)\}$. Partial derivatives (PD) can be extended w.r.t. words in a natural way, as well as w.r.t languages and, both, to sets of regular expressions. We have $\mathcal{L}(\partial_w(\alpha)) = \{w' \mid ww' \in \mathcal{L}(\alpha)\}$, for $w \in \Sigma^*$. The set of all partial derivatives of α w.r.t. nonnull words is denoted by $\partial^+(\alpha)$, and satisfies the following.

Proposition 1 ([18]).

$$\begin{aligned}
\partial^+(\emptyset) = \partial^+(\varepsilon) = \emptyset, \qquad & \partial^+(\alpha + \alpha') = \partial^+(\alpha) \cup \partial^+(\alpha'), \\
\partial^+(\sigma) = \{\varepsilon\}, \qquad & \partial^+(\alpha\alpha') = \partial^+(\alpha)\alpha' \cup \partial^+(\alpha'), \\
\partial^+(\alpha^\star) = \partial^+(\alpha)\alpha^\star, \qquad &
\end{aligned} \tag{3}$$

where, for any $S \subseteq \mathcal{R}_k$, *we define* $S\emptyset = \emptyset$, $S\varepsilon = S$, *and* $S\alpha' = \{\alpha\alpha' \mid \alpha \in S \wedge \alpha \neq \varepsilon\} \cup \{\alpha' \mid \varepsilon \in S\}$ *for* $\alpha' \neq \emptyset, \varepsilon$.

The set of all partial derivatives of α w.r.t. words is denoted by $\mathsf{PD}(\alpha) = \partial_{\Sigma^*}(\alpha) = \partial^+(\alpha) \cup \{\alpha\}$. The *partial derivative automaton* of α is

$$\mathcal{A}_{\mathsf{PD}}(\alpha) = \langle \mathsf{PD}(\alpha), \Sigma, \delta_{\mathsf{PD}}, \{\alpha\}, \{\alpha' \in \mathsf{PD}(\alpha) \mid \varepsilon(\alpha') = \varepsilon\}\rangle, \tag{4}$$

with $\delta_{\mathsf{PD}}(\alpha', \sigma) = \partial_\sigma(\alpha')$, for all $\alpha' \in \mathsf{PD}(\alpha)$ and $\sigma \in \Sigma$.

Proposition 2 ([1], **Theorem 3.4**). *For any regular expression* α, $|\partial^+(\alpha)| \leq |\alpha|_\Sigma$.

Proposition 3 ([1], Theorem 3.8). *Given $\alpha \in \mathcal{R}_k$, a partial derivative of α is either ε or a concatenation $\alpha_1\alpha_2 \cdots \alpha_n$ such that α_i is a subexpression of α and $n - 1$ is no greater than the number of occurrences of concatenations and stars in α.*

Corollary 1. *For $\beta \in \partial^+(\alpha)$, the size $\|\beta\|$ is $O(\|\alpha\|^2)$.*

Proposition 4 ([1,18]). *For $\alpha \in \mathcal{R}_k$, we have $|\varphi(\alpha)| \leq |\alpha|_\Sigma$ and for $(\sigma, \alpha') \in \varphi(\alpha)$, the size $\|\alpha'\|$ is $O(\|\alpha\|^2)$. Moreover, $|\delta_{\text{PD}}(\alpha)|$ is $O(|\alpha|_\Sigma^2)$. If α contains no subexpression of the form $\alpha_1^\star$, then the size $\|\alpha'\|$ is $O(\|\alpha\|)$.*

Example 1. Let $\alpha_n = a_1^\star \cdots a_n^\star$, with $|\alpha|_\Sigma = n$. Then $\partial^+(\alpha_n) = \{a_i^\star \cdots a_n^\star \mid 2 \leq i \leq n\}$, and $|\varphi(\alpha_n)| = |\alpha_n|_\Sigma = n$. The largest partial derivative has size $n - 1$, and $|\delta_{\text{PD}}(\alpha_n)| = \sum_{i=1}^{n-1} i = \frac{n(n+1)}{2}$.

Proposition 5 ([2,3,19]). *Asymptotically in the size of the expression, and as the alphabet size grows, the average sizes $|\alpha|_\Sigma$, $|\varphi(\alpha)|$, $|\partial^1(\alpha)|$, and $|\delta_{\text{PD}}(\alpha)|$ are $\frac{\|\alpha\|}{2}$, the constant 6, $\frac{\|\alpha\|}{4}$, and $\frac{\|\alpha\|}{2}$, respectively.*

3 Strong Star Normal Form and Partial Derivatives

A regular expression is in *strong star normal form* (ssnf) if for any subexpression of the form $\beta^\star$ or $\beta + \varepsilon$, β is not nullable. Introducing the operator *option*, $?$, with $\mathcal{L}(\beta^?) = \mathcal{L}(\beta) \cup \{\varepsilon\}$, one can define the set $\mathcal{S}_k$ of *regular expressions in* ssnf over some alphabet $\Sigma = \{\sigma_1, \ldots, \sigma_k\}$ by the following grammar:

$$\beta := \varepsilon \mid \emptyset \mid \beta_\varepsilon \mid \beta_{\overline{\varepsilon}},$$
$$\beta_\varepsilon := (\beta_\varepsilon \odot \beta_\varepsilon) \mid (\beta_\varepsilon + \beta_{\overline{\varepsilon}}) \mid (\beta_{\overline{\varepsilon}} + \beta_\varepsilon) \mid (\beta_\varepsilon + \beta_\varepsilon) \mid (\beta_{\overline{\varepsilon}}^\star) \mid (\beta_{\overline{\varepsilon}}^?), \qquad (5)$$
$$\beta_{\overline{\varepsilon}} := \sigma_1 \mid \cdots \mid \sigma_k \mid (\beta_{\overline{\varepsilon}} \odot \beta_{\overline{\varepsilon}}) \mid (\beta_{\overline{\varepsilon}} \odot \beta_\varepsilon) \mid (\beta_\varepsilon \odot \beta_{\overline{\varepsilon}}) \mid (\beta_{\overline{\varepsilon}} + \beta_{\overline{\varepsilon}}),$$

where β_ε is for (nontrivial) nullable regular expressions, while $\beta_{\overline{\varepsilon}}$ is for the others. In the remaining of the paper we will use β to denote either of β_ε and $\beta_{\overline{\varepsilon}}$. For $\beta \in \mathcal{S}_k$, the *linear form* $\varphi(\beta)$ is defined as in (2) for the base cases and for the union. For the remaining cases we define: $\varphi(\beta_\varepsilon\beta) = \varphi(\beta_\varepsilon)\beta \cup \varphi(\beta)$, $\varphi(\beta_{\overline{\varepsilon}}\beta) = \varphi(\beta_{\overline{\varepsilon}})\beta$, $\varphi(\beta_{\overline{\varepsilon}}^\star) = \varphi(\beta_{\overline{\varepsilon}})\beta_{\overline{\varepsilon}}^\star$, and $\varphi(\beta_{\overline{\varepsilon}}^?) = \varphi(\beta_{\overline{\varepsilon}})$. The set $\partial^+(\beta)$ of all partial derivatives of $\beta \in \mathcal{S}_k$ w.r.t. nonnull words satisfies Proposition 1 except for the following cases: $\partial^+(\beta_{\overline{\varepsilon}}^\star) = \partial^+(\beta_{\overline{\varepsilon}})\beta_{\overline{\varepsilon}}^\star$ and $\partial^+(\beta_{\overline{\varepsilon}}^?) = \partial^+(\beta_{\overline{\varepsilon}})$ [17]. In the next section, using the analytic combinatorics framework, we derive asymptotic estimates for the number of new concatenations obtained when computing $\partial^+(\beta)$ for $\beta \in \mathcal{S}_k$, and thus obtaining an average-case version of Proposition 3.

3.1 The Analytic Tools

Given some measure of the objects of a combinatorial class, $\mathcal{A}$, for each $n \in \mathbb{N}_0$, let a_n be the sum of the values of this measure for all objects of size n. Now, let $A(z) = \sum_n a_n z^n$ be the corresponding generating function (*cf.* [12]). We will use the notation $[z^n]A(z)$ for a_n. The generating function $A(z)$ can be seen as a complex analytic function, and when it has a unique dominant singularity ρ, the study of the behaviour of $A(z)$ around it gives us access to the asymptotic form of its coefficients. In particular, if $A(z)$ is analytic in some indented disc neighbourhood of ρ, then one can use the following [12, Corol. VI.1, p. 392]:

Theorem 1. *The coefficients of the series expansion of the complex function* $f(z) \underset{z \to \rho}{\sim} \lambda \left(1 - \frac{z}{\rho}\right)^{\nu}$, *where* $\nu \in \mathbb{C} \setminus \mathbb{N}_0$, $\lambda \in \mathbb{C}$, *have the asymptotic approximation* $[z^n]f(z) = \frac{\lambda}{\Gamma(-\nu)} n^{-\nu-1} \rho^{-n} + o\left(n^{-\nu-1} \rho^{-n}\right)$. *Here* Γ *is the Euler's gamma function and the notation* $f(z) \underset{z \to z_0}{\sim} g(z)$ *means that* $\lim_{z \to z_0} \frac{f(z)}{g(z)} = 1$.

To use this, one needs to have a way to obtain ρ, ν and λ. Here we only give a high level description of how this can be done, referring the reader to Broda et al. [4,5]. First, from an unambiguous generating grammar, one obtains a set of polynomial equations involving the generating functions for the objects corresponding to the variables of the grammar, in particular the one whose coefficients we want to asymptotically estimate. Then, either using Gröbner basis or by other means [5], one gets an algebraic equation for that generating function $w = w(z)$, i.e., an equation of the form $G(z, w) = 0$, where $G(z, w) \in \mathbb{Z}[z, w]$ of which $w(z)$ is a root. Analysing the form of the curve G, and using its partial derivatives, one can find an irreducible polynomial for the singularity ρ, and, when $\lim_{z \to \rho} w(z) = a \in \mathbb{R}^+$, an irreducible polynomial for a; when $\lim_{z \to \rho} w(z) = +\infty$, the irreducible polynomial for ρ is a factor of the leading coefficient of $G(z, w)$ when seen as a polynomial in w [15, Theorem 12.2.1]. After making the change of variable $s = 1 - z/\rho$, one knows that $w = w(s)$ has a Puiseux series expansion at the singularity $s = 0$, i.e., there exists a slit neighbourhood of that point in which $w(s)$ has a representation as a power series with fractional powers [15, Chap. 12],

Using the irreducible polynomial for ρ, and the one for a in the first case, while in the second case one changes variables in order to replace $+\infty$ with 0, one decides which partial derivatives of G are nonzero, and uses that information to draw a Newton polygon that yields the values of ν and λ. Then, Theorem 1 yields:

Theorem 2. *With the notations and in the conditions above described, one has*

$$[z^n]w(z) \underset{n \to \infty}{\sim} \begin{cases} \dfrac{-b_G}{\Gamma(-\nu)} \rho^{-n} n^{-\nu-1}, & \text{if } \lim_{z \to \rho} w(z) \in \mathbb{R}^+, \qquad (6) \\[2mm] \dfrac{1}{c_G \, \Gamma(\nu)} \rho^{-n} n^{\nu-1}, & \text{if } \lim_{z \to \rho} w(z) = +\infty, \qquad (7) \end{cases}$$

where ρ *and* ν *are as above, setting* $b_G = -\lambda$ *and* $c_G = \lambda^{-1}$.

Let the generating functions for β_ε and $\beta_{\overline{\varepsilon}}$ regular expressions be, respectively, $B_k = B_k(z) = \sum_{\beta_\varepsilon} z^{\|\beta_\varepsilon\|} = \sum_n b_n z^n$ and $\overline{B}_k = \overline{B}_k(z) = \sum_{\beta_{\overline{\varepsilon}}} z^{\|\beta_{\overline{\varepsilon}}\|} = \sum_n \overline{b}_n z^n$, where b_n and $\overline{b}_n$ are the corresponding numbers of expressions of size n.

From (5), one gets $B_k = 2zB_k^2 + 2zB_k\overline{B}_k + 2z\overline{B}_k$ and $\overline{B}_k = kz + 2zB_k\overline{B}_k + 2z\overline{B}_k^2$.
Using Theorem 2, Broda et al. [4] obtained that $[z^n]B_k(z) \underset{n \to \infty}{\sim} \frac{b_{B_k}}{2\sqrt{\pi}}\eta_k^{-n}n^{-\frac{3}{2}}$
and $[z^n]\overline{B}_k(z) \underset{n \to \infty}{\sim} \frac{b_{\overline{B}_k}}{2\sqrt{\pi}}\eta_k^{-n}n^{-\frac{3}{2}}$, where η_k is the unique dominant singularity of $B_k(z)$, which happens to be the same for $\overline{B}_k(z)$. It was also shown that $\eta_k \underset{k \to \infty}{\sim} \frac{1}{\sqrt{8k}}$, $b_{B_k} \underset{k \to \infty}{\sim} \sqrt{8}$ and $b_{\overline{B}_k} \underset{k \to \infty}{\sim} \sqrt{k}$, which yields the asymptotic behaviour of the size of β_ε and $\beta_{\overline{\varepsilon}}$.

3.2   Average Number of New Concatenations in Partial Derivatives

In this section we consider the quantities $|\partial^+(\beta)|$ and $|\partial^+(\beta)|_\odot = \sum_{\alpha \in \partial^+(\beta)}|\alpha|_\odot$ which is the number of new concatenations when computing $\partial^+(\beta)$, and we estimate the average value of $|\partial^+(\beta)|_\odot$. Let $\ell(\beta)$ be the function $|\partial^+(\beta)|$ and $h(\beta)$ be the function of $|\partial^+(\beta)|_\odot$, assuming that all computed partial derivatives are distinct. Thus, ℓ and h are upper bounds for those quantities in the general case. Using the definition of ∂^+ for $\beta \in \mathcal{S}_k$, we have that those cost functions (of the expressions) satisfy

$$
\begin{aligned}
h(\varepsilon) &= h(\sigma) = 0, & \ell(\varepsilon) &= 0, \; \ell(\sigma) = 1, \\
h(\beta + \beta') &= h(\beta) + h(\beta'), & \ell(\beta + \beta') &= \ell(\beta) + \ell(\beta'), \\
h(\beta\beta') &= h(\beta) + \ell(\beta) + h(\beta'), & \ell(\beta\beta') &= \ell(\beta) + \ell(\beta'), \\
h(\beta_{\overline{\varepsilon}}^\star) &= h(\beta_{\overline{\varepsilon}}) + \ell(\beta_{\overline{\varepsilon}}), & \ell(\beta_{\overline{\varepsilon}}^\star) &= \ell(\beta_{\overline{\varepsilon}}), \\
h(\beta_{\overline{\varepsilon}}^?) &= h(\beta_{\overline{\varepsilon}}), & \ell(\beta_{\overline{\varepsilon}}^?) &= \ell(\beta_{\overline{\varepsilon}}).
\end{aligned}
$$

In the computation of $h(\beta\beta')$, the summand $\ell(\beta)$ accounts for the number of partial derivatives of β. Similarly for $h(\beta_{\overline{\varepsilon}}^\star)$. For the special case of $\beta_{\overline{\varepsilon}}$ expressions, $h(\sigma) = 0$, $h(\beta_{\overline{\varepsilon}} + \beta_{\overline{\varepsilon}}') = h(\beta_{\overline{\varepsilon}}) + h(\beta_{\overline{\varepsilon}}')$, $h(\beta_{\overline{\varepsilon}}\beta_{\overline{\varepsilon}}) = h(\beta_{\overline{\varepsilon}}) + \ell(\beta_{\overline{\varepsilon}}) + h(\beta_{\overline{\varepsilon}})$, $h(\beta\beta_{\overline{\varepsilon}}) = h(\beta) + \ell(\beta) + h(\beta_{\overline{\varepsilon}})$ and $\ell(\sigma) = 1$, $\ell(\beta_{\overline{\varepsilon}} + \beta_{\overline{\varepsilon}}') = \ell(\beta_{\overline{\varepsilon}}) + \ell(\beta_{\overline{\varepsilon}}')$, $\ell(\beta_{\overline{\varepsilon}}\beta_{\overline{\varepsilon}}) = \ell(\beta_{\overline{\varepsilon}}) + \ell(\beta_{\overline{\varepsilon}})$, $\ell(\beta\beta_{\overline{\varepsilon}}) = \ell(\beta) + \ell(\beta_{\overline{\varepsilon}})$. Let $H_k = H_k(z)$ and $\overline{H}_k = \overline{H}_k(z)$ be the cost generating function for the measure h associated with the expressions β and $\beta_{\overline{\varepsilon}}$, respectively. Analogously, let $L_k = L_k(z)$ and $\overline{L}_k = \overline{L}_k(z)$ be the corresponding ones for ℓ. These coincide with the cost generating functions for the alphabetic size, and that was calculated in Broda et al. [4]. One has, where $T_k = B_k + \overline{B}_k$,

$$
\begin{aligned}
H_k &= 4zH_kT_k + zL_kT_k + 2z\overline{H}_k + z\overline{L}_k, \\
\overline{H}_k &= 2zH_k\overline{B}_k + 2z\overline{H}_kT_k + z\overline{L}_kB_k + zL_k\overline{B}_k. \\
B_k &= 2zB_k^2 + 2zB_k\overline{B}_k + 2\overline{B}_kz, \\
\overline{B}_k &= kz + 2zB_k\overline{B}_k + 2z\overline{B}_k^2, \\
L_k - \overline{L}_k &= 4zB_k(L_k - \overline{L}_k) + 2zB_k\overline{L}_k + 2z\overline{B}_k(L_k - \overline{L}_k) + 2z\overline{L}_k, \\
\overline{L}_k &= kz + 2zB_k\overline{L}_k + 2z\overline{B}_k(L_k - \overline{L}_k) + 4z\overline{B}_k\overline{L}_k.
\end{aligned}
$$

Using Gröbner basis for the equations of B_k and $\overline{B}_k$, and with the help of a symbolic manipulator, one can find a polynomial in $\mathbb{Q}(z, w)$ for which $w = H_k(z)$

is a zero, namely $16z^2\ell_k(z)^2\,w^3 + 4k\,\ell_k(z)p_4(z)\,w^2 + p_8(z)\,w + kz^2p_6(z)$, where the dominant singularity of H_k is only root in $]0,1[$ of

$$\ell_k(z) = z^3 + \frac{9}{2k+27}\,z^2 - \frac{1}{4(2k+27)}\,z - \frac{1}{k(2k+27)},$$

and p_i denotes a polynomial of degree i. Using the method described in [5], one sees that this falls in the case (7) of Theorem 2, and computing the respective constants, ρ, ν, c, one gets the following value for the asymptotic behaviour of the coefficients of $H_k(z)$:

$$[z^n]H_k(z) \underset{n \to \infty}{\sim} \frac{1}{c_{H_k}}\eta_k^{-n}, \tag{8}$$

where c_{H_k} is a function of k with an expression too cumbersome to write here, but that satisfies $c_{H_k} \underset{k \to \infty}{\sim} \frac{16\sqrt{2}}{\sqrt{k}}$. From this one now gets

Theorem 3. *The average value of the upper bound h considered above, for the number of new concatenations in all the partial derivatives of a regular expression in $\mathcal{S}_k$ is given by*

$$\frac{[z^n]H_k(z)}{[z^n](B_k(z) + \overline{B}_k(z))} \underset{n \to \infty}{\sim} \frac{2\sqrt{\pi}}{c_{G_k}(b_{B_k} + b_{\overline{B}_k})}\,n^{\frac{3}{2}} \underset{k \to \infty}{\sim} \sqrt{\frac{\pi}{128}}\,n^{\frac{3}{2}}. \tag{9}$$

And also, knowing that $[z^n]L_k(z) \sim \frac{\sqrt{k}}{4\sqrt{\pi}}\eta_k^{-n}n^{-1/2}$ (see [4]), one obtains

Theorem 4. *The average value of the upper bound h considered above, for the number of new concatenations per partial derivative of a regular expression in $\mathcal{S}_k$ is given by*

$$\frac{[z^n]H_k(z)}{[z^n]L_k(z)} \underset{n,\,k \to \infty}{\sim} \sqrt{\frac{\pi}{32}}\,n^{\frac{1}{2}}. \tag{10}$$

Note that in the worst case the number of new concatenations is $\Theta(\|\beta\|^2)$, as illustrated by the following example. Let $\beta_n = a_1a_2\cdots a_n$, for $n \geq 1$, with $\|\beta_n\| = 2n - 1$. We have $\partial^+(\beta_n) = \{\,a_i\cdots a_n \mid 2 \leq i \leq n\,\} \cup \{\varepsilon\}$ and the number of new concatenations is $|\partial^+(\beta_n)|_\odot = \sum_{i=2}^n (n - i) = (n^2 - 3n + 2)/2$.

4   DAG Representation and Partial Derivatives

Consider the (binary) tree representation of $\beta \in \mathcal{S}_k$. Each node v of the tree is labelled with an operator denoted by $\mathsf{lab}(v)$. Let β_v be the subexpression rooted at v. In what follows, we identify a node with its rooted subexpression. A node v is an op-node if $\mathsf{lab}(v) = op$, $op \in \{+, \star, ?, \odot\} \cup \Sigma$. Each node, except the root, has exactly one parent node and can have zero, one or two children. For $\beta_1 = (ab)^\star a + (ab)^\star$, its tree is depicted in Fig. 1(a). One can see that there are several identical subtrees (subexpressions). The identification of all common subexpressions of β leads to a directed acyclic graph (DAG) representation of

β. Let s be the number of distinct subexpressions of β. Each node of the DAG corresponds exactly to a distinct subexpression of β and can be identified by an index $i \in \{1, \ldots, s\}$. The node with index 0 corresponds to ε.

In Algorithm 1, we present an algorithm to build the DAG for a regular expression, as well as, to compute its $\mathcal{A}_{\text{PD}}$. In this section we focus on the construction of the DAG without constructing partial derivatives and thus $\mathcal{A}_{\text{PD}}$.

The function GETI constructs the DAG for an expression and for each type of operator calls a function that builds a node, if it does not exist, and returns its index. This function is inspired by Flajolet et al. [13], which is based on the more general algorithms presented in Downey et al. [11].

Let IND be a structure that associates each index i with a unique node (subexpression). Let last be the variable that counts the number of nodes already in the DAG. The function NODE(i, op, C) creates a node with index i, label op and children C, where C is a list of zero to two DAG indexes (which is omitted if $|C| = 0$). To construct the DAG one needs to determine if for a node i, the subtree β_i is already there. That can be decided by analysing the parents of node i and their labels, using the following functions. Let star(i) be the parent of i, in the case it is a $\star$-node, or Null, otherwise. Similarly define option(i). To uniquely identify a $\odot$-node one needs to know its left and right children. If dot(i, j) is not Null then a $\odot$-node with left child i and right child j exists. The same occurs for $+$-node and plus(i, j). Finally, leaves(σ) is not Null, if the node i is a σ-node.

Depending on the data structures used, the construction of the DAG can be achieved, in the worst-case, in quadratic time or, respectively, in linear time [11]. Using hash tables the running time is $O(n)$, on average [13, Prop. 1]. Using the result of Flajolet et al. [13], mentioned in Sect. 1, the expected size of the DAG of β is $O\left(\|\beta\| / \sqrt{\log \|\beta\|}\right)$. A DAG for β_1 is depicted in Fig. 1(b). When building the DAG, one can also compute for each node i, the functions $\varepsilon(i)$ and $\varphi(i)$. In Algorithm 1, the function ewp is a Boolean function such that ewp(i) = True if $\varepsilon(i) = \varepsilon$, and False otherwise. The computation of $\varphi(i)$ can lead to the creation of new $\odot$-nodes. For these nodes the computation of φ is delayed until the nodes of all subexpressions of a given expression are computed. The final DAG is shown in Fig. 1(c). Note that the indexes (numbers) given to nodes are different if one computes simultaneously the DAG for β_1 with or without the partial derivatives. In the latter case, the partial derivatives are computed after the DAG for β_1 is constructed (and that is what is assumed in Fig. 1). After constructing the DAG with all partial derivatives (LF), the $\mathcal{A}_{\text{PD}}(\beta)$ can be easily obtained. The automaton $\mathcal{A}_{\text{PD}}(\beta_1)$ is shown in Fig. 1(d). In the next section, we detail the algorithm to build the $\mathcal{A}_{\text{PD}}(\beta)$, as well as the overall complexity analysis.

5   Algorithm **PDDAG**

Given a regular expression β, we present an algorithm to compute the partial derivative automaton $\mathcal{A}_{\text{PD}}(\beta)$. Although the algorithm also applies to standard regular expressions, here, we assume expressions in ssnf. In Algorithm 1, the function PDDAG implements the main procedure that constructs a DAG not

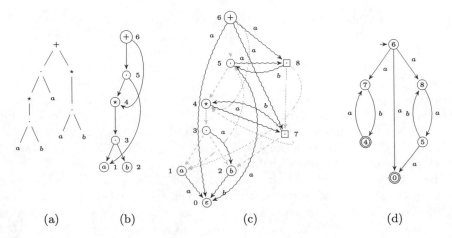

(a)   (b)   (c)   (d)

Fig. 1. For $\beta_1 = (ab)^\star a + (ab)^\star$ we show (a) a tree representation where the root corresponds to β_1, (b) the (minimal) DAG identifying common subexpressions of α_1, (c) DAG with partial derivative nodes (LF), and (d) the resulting $\mathcal{A}_{\text{PD}}$. In (c), new nodes created during the computation of $\partial^+(\beta_1)$ are presented by a square. The values of $\text{ewp}(i)$ are omitted. A (dark) zigzag directed edge between nodes i and j labelled by σ means that $j \in \partial_\sigma(i)$ (those accessible from the root correspond to the transitions in $\mathcal{A}_{\text{PD}}$).

only representing the expression but also all its partial derivatives. For each node, the corresponding linear form is computed and for $\star$-nodes or $\odot$-nodes special attention is needed. In both cases, the function CONCLF can add new $\odot$-nodes to the DAG. For those nodes the computation of their linear forms is delayed, as they can depend on the linear forms of the nodes that gave them origin. Hence, the function CONCI is called with the *delay* parameter as True (by default is False). When the computation of the linear form of the creator node is finished, the linear forms of the delayed nodes can safely be computed. Function DODELAYED computes the linear forms of the new $\odot$-nodes until no more delayed nodes exist. When all nodes of all partial derivatives have been created, the $\mathcal{A}_{\text{PD}}(\beta)$ can be constructed using definition (4), starting with the root node s corresponding to β. The function MAKENFA implements this construction (by space constraints, we omit its description). In the following, we discuss the complexity of the algorithm. We show that, *on average for $\beta \in \mathcal{S}_k$*, the algorithm PDDAG(β) works in time $O\left(\|\beta\|^{3/2} \sqrt[4]{\log \|\beta\|}\right)$. We make the ordinary assumption in formal language algorithms that an integer occupies space $O(1)$ and each basic integer arithmetic operation takes time $O(1)$ [10].

Lemma 1. *Given the DAG of β with partial derivatives, for every node v and $\sigma \in \Sigma$, $|\partial_\sigma(\beta_v)| \leq |\beta|_\Sigma$.*

Theorem 5. *Algorithm PDDAG(β) can be implemented such that*

(i) in the average case, it uses time $O\left(\|\beta\|^{3/2} \sqrt[4]{\log \|\beta\|}\right)$;

Algorithm 1. Partial Derivative Automaton with DAG

```
 1: function PDDAG(α)                          43:     else
 2:     IND[0] ←NODE(0, ε)                       44:         j ← option(i)
 3:     last ← 1;Delayed ← ∅                     45:     return i
 4:     s ← GETI(α)                              46: function PLUSI(i, j)
 5:     MAKENFA()                                47:     if plus(i, j) is Null then
 6: function GETI(α)                             48:         ℓ ← last; last ← last +1
 7:     if α = σ then                            49:         IND[ℓ] ← NODE(ℓ, +, i, j)
 8:         return ATOMI(σ)                      50:         ewp(ℓ) ← ewp(i) ∨ ewp(j)
 9:     else if α = α₁? then                     51:         φ(ℓ) ← φ(i) ∪ φ(j)
10:         return OPTIONI(GETI(α₁))             52:     else
11:     else if α = α₁* then                     53:         ℓ ← plus(i, j)
12:         return STARI(GETI(α₁))               54:     return ℓ
13:     else if α = α₁ + α₂ then                 55: function CONCI(i, j, delay = False)
14:         return PLUSI(GETI(α₁),GETI(α₂))      56:     if i = 0 then return j
15:     else if α = α₁ ⊙ α₂ then                 57:     if j = 0 then return i
16:         return CONCI(GETI(α₁),GETI(α₂))      58:     if dot(i, j) is Null then
17:     else return 0                            59:         ℓ ← last; last ← last +1
18: function ATOMI(σ)                            60:         IND[ℓ] ← NODE(ℓ, ⊙, i, j)
19:     if leaves(σ) is Null then                61:         ewp(ℓ) ← ewp(i) ∧ ewp(j)
20:         i ← last; last ← last +1             62:         if delay = True then
21:         IND[i] ← NODE(i, σ)                  63:             add ℓ to Delayed
22:         ewp(i) ← False                       64:         else
23:         φ(i) ← (σ, 0)                         65:             φ(ℓ) ← CONCLF(i, j)
24:     else                                     66:             if ewp(i) then
25:         i ← leaves(σ)                         67:                 φ(ℓ) ← φ(ℓ) ∪ φ(j)
26:     return i                                 68:             DODELAYED()
27: function STARI(i)                            69:     else
28:     if star(i) is Null then                  70:         ℓ ← dot(i, j)
29:         j ← last; last ← last +1             71:     return ℓ
30:         IND[j] ← NODE(j, ⋆, i)               72: function CONCLF(i, j)
31:         ewp(j) ← True                        73:     F ← ∅
32:         φ(j) ← CONCLF(i, j)                  74:     for all (σ, ℓ) ∈ φ(i) do
33:         DODELAYED()                          75:         add (σ,CONCI(ℓ, j, True)) to F
34:     else                                     76:     return F
35:         j ← star(i)                          77: function DODELAYED( )
36:     return j                                 78:     while Delayed ≠ ∅ do
37: function OPTIONI(i)                          79:         i ← Delayed.pop()
38:     if option(i) is Null then                80:         φ(i) ← CONCLF(left(i), right(i))
39:         j ← last; last ← last +1             81:         if ewp(left(i)) then
40:         IND[j] ← NODE(j, ?, i)               82:             φ(i) ← φ(i) ∪ φ(right(i))
41:         ewp(j) ← True
42:         φ(j) ← φ(i)
```

(ii) in the worst case, it uses time $O\left(|\Sigma_\beta||\beta|_\Sigma^2\|\beta\| \log \|\beta\|\right)$;

(iii) in the average case, it uses space $O\left(\|\beta\|^{3/2} / (\log \|\beta\|)^{3/4}\right)$;

(iv) in the worst case, it uses space $O\left(|\Sigma_\beta||\beta|_\Sigma^2\|\beta\|\right)$.

Proof. As seen in Sect. 4, making the DAG for β can take time $\Theta(\|\beta\|)$ and the number s of initial DAG nodes is $O(\|\beta\|/\sqrt{\log \|\beta\|})$ in the average case, and $\Theta(\|\beta\|)$ in the worst case. All finite sets in the algorithm are implemented using AVL-trees. The structure IND contains pairs (i, p) such that i is an index and p is the DAG node with index i. The structure DOT contains triples (i, j, ℓ) of integers such that ℓ is the index for a $\odot$-node with $i = \text{left}(\ell)$ and $j = \text{right}(\ell)$. The search is based on the pairs (i, j) and works as in single integer comparisons. Function $\text{dot}(i, j)$ returns ℓ when the triple (i, j, ℓ) is in DOT, and Null otherwise. When $\text{NODE}(\ell, \odot, i, j)$ is created the triple (i, j, ℓ) is added to DOT. The structure

PLUS is analogous to DOT for +-nodes and used by the function plus. The structure Δ contains pairs (ℓ, F) such that $F = \varphi(\ell)$. Specifically, F is an AVL-tree containing pairs (σ, S) such that $S = \partial_\sigma(\ell)$. To access the set $\partial_\sigma(\ell)$, Δ is searched on ℓ to get the pair (ℓ, F), and then F is searched on σ to get the set $S = \partial_\sigma(\ell)$. Let t be the number of new nodes created when computing the linear forms. Each such node is a partial derivative of β or of a subexpression of β. Let $\{\beta_\ell\}_{\ell=1}^{s}$ be the set of subexpressions of β, including $\beta = \beta_s$. Then $t \leq |\bigcup_{\ell=1}^{s} \partial^+(\ell)| \leq \sum_{\ell=1}^{s} |\beta_\ell|_\Sigma \leq s|\beta|_\Sigma$. By Theorem 3 we have that, on average, $t = O(s^{3/2})$. In the worst-case, $t = \Theta(s|\beta|_\Sigma)$. For each node ℓ, the set $\varphi(\ell)$ is computed and stored as $\Delta[\ell]$. Each $|\Delta[\ell]|$ is $O(|\Sigma_\beta||\beta|_\Sigma)$ in the worst case (by Lemma 1), and $O(1)$ in the average case [17, 19]. Based on the above observations, the algorithm's space complexity is $O(|\Sigma_\beta||\beta|_\Sigma s|\beta|_\Sigma) = O(|\Sigma_\beta||\beta|_\Sigma^2||\beta||)$ in the worst case, and $O(s^{3/2}) = O(||\beta||^{3/2} / (\log ||\beta||)^{3/4})$ in the average case. We turn now to the time complexity. The task to compute the set $\Delta[\ell]$, for each node ℓ, depends on $\mathsf{lab}(\ell)$ and the children of ℓ. We only examine the time for +-nodes and $\odot$-nodes, as the time for the others is not more significant. If ℓ is a +-node, then $\Delta[\ell] = \Delta[\mathsf{left}(\ell)] \cup \Delta[\mathsf{right}(\ell)]$. Thus, the cost for each +-node ℓ is $O(|\Delta[\ell]| \log |\Delta[\ell]|)$. If ℓ is a $\odot$-node with children i, j then the time of $\mathrm{CONCLF}(i,j)$ is $O(|\Delta[i]| \log t + |\Delta[\ell]| \log |\Delta[\ell]|)$, where $\log t$ accounts for the cost of accessing DOT and $|\Delta[\ell]| \log |\Delta[\ell]|$ for making the set F (line 75). As $|\Sigma_\beta|, |\beta|_\Sigma \leq ||\beta||$, we have that $\log t = O(\log ||\beta||)$.

Thus, the algorithm's time complexity is $O(|\Sigma_\beta||\beta|_\Sigma^2||\beta|| \log ||\beta||)$ in the worst case, and $O(||\beta||^{3/2} (\log ||\beta||)^{1/4})$ in the average case. $\square$

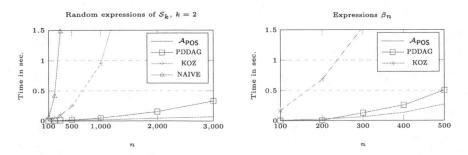

Fig. 2. Running times (per expression) of the simulation of expressions in ssnf by NFA using different algorithms: position ($\mathcal{A}_{\mathrm{POS}}$), partial derivatives ($\mathcal{A}_{\mathrm{PD}}$) using, respectively, PDDAG, KOZ, and a naive implementation, NAIVE.

6   Empirical Results and Conclusions

We implemented the algorithm PDDAG in Python within FAdo (https://pypi. org/project/FAdo/). Instead of AVL-trees we used hash tables, as those are Python's natural data structures. In the experiments we uniformly random generated expressions $\beta \in \mathcal{S}_k$, in prefix notation. For each expression size $n \in$

$\{100, 200, 300, 500, 1000, 2000, 3000, 4000\}$, and alphabet size $k \in \{2, 5, 10, 50\}$, samples of 10000 expressions were generated. This is sufficient to ensure a 95% confidence level within a 1% error margin [9, p. 75]. In FAdo there is a naive implementation of $\mathcal{A}_{PD}$ that recursively computes the linear forms with some memoization (NAIVE), as well as implementations of the position automaton $\mathcal{A}_{POS}$. The algorithm for $\mathcal{A}_{PD}$ by Khorsi et a. (KOZ) [16] was implemented using FAdo methods for acyclic finite automata. The tests were performed in Python 2.7 with a 2.5 GHz Quad-Core i7 CPU and 16 GB memory. In Fig. 2, on the left, we present the average running times of the algorithms per expression of size n, and $k = 2$. On the right, we present the running times for expressions $\beta_n = a_1^? \cdots a_n^?$, over a growing alphabet $\Sigma = \{a_1, \ldots, a_n\}$, that attain the worst-case size of $\mathcal{A}_{PD}$. Both results suggest that the algorithm PDDAG has a good practical performance.

Future research is the adaptation of the tools used here to the word membership problem without computing the automaton.

References

1. Antimirov, V.M.: Partial derivatives of regular expressions and finite automaton constructions. Theoret. Comput. Sci. **155**(2), 291–319 (1996)
2. Broda, S., Machiavelo, A., Moreira, N., Reis, R.: On the average state complexity of partial derivative automata: an analytic combinatorics approach. Int. J. Found. Comput. Sci. **22**(7), 1593–1606 (2011). https://doi.org/10.1142/S0129054111008908
3. Broda, S., Machiavelo, A., Moreira, N., Reis, R.: On the average size of Glushkov and partial derivative automata. Int. J. Found. Comput. Sci. **23**(5), 969–984 (2012). https://doi.org/10.1142/S0129054112400400
4. Broda, S., Machiavelo, A., Moreira, N., Reis, R.: On average behaviour of regular expressions in strong star normal form. Int. J. Found. Comput. Sci. **30**(6–7), 899–920 (2019). https://doi.org/10.1142/S0129054119400227
5. Broda, S., Machiavelo, A., Moreira, N., Reis, R.: Analytic combinatorics and descriptional complexity of regular languages on average. ACM SIGACT News **51**(1), 38–56 (2020). https://doi.org/10.1145/3388392.3388400
6. Brüggemann-Klein, A.: Regular expressions into finite automata. Theoret. Comput. Sci. **48**, 197–213 (1993)
7. Champarnaud, J.M., Ziadi, D.: Canonical derivatives, partial derivatives and finite automaton constructions. Theoret. Comput. Sci. **289**, 137–163 (2002)
8. Champarnaud, J., Ziadi, D.: From c-continuations to new quadratic algorithms for automaton synthesis. Int. J. Algor. Comput. **11**(6), 707–736 (2001)
9. Cochran, W.G.: Sampling Techniques, 3rd edn., John Wiley and Sons, New York (1977)
10. Crochemore, M., Hancart, C., Lecroq, T.: Algorithms on Strings. CUP, Cambridge (2007)
11. Downey, P.J., Sethi, R., Tarjan, R.E.: Variations on the common subexpression problem. J. ACM **27**(4), 758–771 (1980). https://doi.org/10.1145/322217.322228
12. Flajolet, P., Sedgewick, R.: Analytic Combinatorics. CUP, Cambridge (2008)
13. Flajolet, P., Sipala, P., Steyaert, J.-M.: Analytic variations on the common subexpression problem. In: Paterson, M.S. (ed.) ICALP 1990. LNCS, vol. 443, pp. 220–234. Springer, Heidelberg (1990). https://doi.org/10.1007/BFb0032034

14. Gruber, H., Gulan, S.: Simplifying regular expressions: a quantitative perspective. Tech. rep, IFIG Research Report (2009)
15. Hille, E.: Analytic Function Theory, vol. 2. Blaisdell Publishing Company, New York (1962)
16. Khorsi, A., Ouardi, F., Ziadi, D.: Fast equation automaton computation. J. Discrete Algor. **6**(3), 433–448 (2008). https://doi.org/10.1016/j.jda.2007.10.003
17. Konstantinidis, S., Machiavelo, A., Moreira, N., Reis, R.: On the size of partial derivatives and the word membership problem. Acta Inf. **58**(4), 357–375 (2021). https://doi.org/10.1007/s00236-021-00399-6
18. Mirkin, B.G.: An algorithm for constructing a base in a language of regular expressions. Eng. Cybernet. **5**, 51–57 (1966)
19. Nicaud, C.: On the average size of Glushkov's automata. In: Dediu, A.H., Ionescu, A.M., Martín-Vide, C. (eds.) LATA 2009. LNCS, vol. 5457, pp. 626–637. Springer, Heidelberg (2009). https://doi.org/10.1007/978-3-642-00982-2_53

State Complexity of Partial Word Finite Automata

Martin Kutrib$^{(\boxtimes)}$ and Matthias Wendlandt

Institut für Informatik, Universität Giessen, Arndtstr. 2, 35392 Giessen, Germany
{kutrib,matthias.wendlandt}@informatik.uni-giessen.de

Abstract. Partial word finite automata are deterministic finite automata that may have state transitions on a special symbol ◇ which represents an unknown symbol or a hole in the word. Together with a subset of the input alphabet that gives the symbols which may be substituted for the ◇, a partial word finite automaton represents a regular language. However, this substitution implies a certain form of limited nondeterminism in the computations when the ◇-transitions are replaced by ordinary transitions. In this paper we first reconsider the problem to prove the minimality of partial word finite automata and present a method to utilize minimal NFAs with certain properties for this purpose. Then we study the operational state complexity of partial word finite automata with respect to Boolean operations. It turns out that the upper and lower bounds for all these operations are exponential. Moreover, we establish a state complexity hierarchy on the number of productive ◇-transitions that may appear in partial word finite automata. The levels of the hierarchy are separated by exponential state costs.

1 Introduction

Partial words are strings where certain positions are not specified. These positions are often called holes or don't cares and printed by a diamond symbol ◇. Apart from theoretical reasons, the basic motivation for studying this mechanism comes from the study of biological operations in connection with DNA strands. In particular, DNA sequencing is a biological process to determine the base sequence of a given DNA strand. To this end, the two DNA strands are separated and cut into small pieces. Afterwards the small sequences are copied, multiplied, and then detected. Subsequently, the complete strand has to be derived out of the small pieces. This assembling can be done by aligning the fragments with the help of gaps (holes) which leads to the definition of partial words. The first time the idea of words with don't cares has been investigated goes back to [7], where they were considered in connection with string matching. The notation *partial word* has firstly been defined in [2].

Partial words were mainly investigated in connection with combinatorics on words. A survey can be found in [4]. An interesting motivation in theory for this model is that ordinary languages can be compressed by the usage of holes. Consider for example the language L over the ternary alphabet $\Sigma = \{a, b, c\}$,

Y.-S. Han and S.-K. Ko (Eds.): DCFS 2021, LNCS 13037, pp. 113–124, 2021.
https://doi.org/10.1007/978-3-030-93489-7_10

$L = \{aaa, aba, aca\}$. It can be compressed by using a hole into $L' = \{a \diamond a\}$. Simply by replacing the diamond by a, b, or c the original language L can be achieved.

In 2012, partial words were studied in connection with families of formal languages [6]. In particular, a regular language is represented by the image of a partial language under a substitution that only replaces the hole symbols. In connection with DFAs it turned out that the usage of holes can be somehow seen as a limited nondeterminism, since it allows to define DFAs with outgoing edges that are labeled with ordinary symbols and additionally with a diamond. If some of the ordinary symbols may be substituted for the hole symbol as well, the corresponding state allows a nondeterministic choice with respect to the target language. While in the original definition of partial words a hole represents a placeholder for all letters of the underlying alphabet, in investigations in connection with language families the substitution of the hole symbol can be an arbitrary subset of the alphabet (see for example [1,6,10]).

The applications of defining language families by partial words via partial word finite automata have also been investigated from a complexity point of view. Concerning the descriptional complexity, in [1] it has been shown that the state complexity for a DFA that simulates a partial word DFA is exponential in general. Moreover also the state complexity of the simulation of an NFA by a partial word DFA may become exponential. Concerning the computational complexity, different problems as, for example, minimization have been studied for partial word automata [5,10].

The main aim of this paper is to extend the investigations on the state complexity of partial word automata. In connection with lower bounds on the number of states necessary for an automaton to accept a given language, the problem arises to prove the minimality of a given automaton. In Sect. 3 we discuss this problem by referring to known results from the literature and provide methods to prove the minimality of partial word DFAs by utilizing minimal NFAs with certain properties. Section 4 considers the operational state complexity for Boolean operations. It turns out that upper and lower bounds are exponential. In the last section we consider the impact of the number of productive $\diamond$-transitions in a partial word finite automaton, where a transition is called productive, if it does not lead to the rejecting sink state. It comes out that even the reduction of one of these transitions may lead to an exponential state explosion, which leads to a state complexity hierarchy dependent on the number of $\diamond$-transitions.

2   Preliminaries

We denote the non-negative integers $\{0, 1, 2, \ldots\}$ by $\mathbb{N}$. Let Σ^* denote the set of all words over the finite alphabet Σ. A subset $L \subseteq \Sigma^*$ is said to be a *formal language* over Σ. We write $\overline{L}$ for the *complement* of L with respect to Σ, that is for $\Sigma^* \setminus L$. The *empty word* is denoted by λ and the *reversal* of a word w by w^R. For the *length* of w we write $|w|$. We use $\subseteq$ for *inclusions* and $\subset$ for *strict inclusions*.

Setting $\Sigma_\diamond = \Sigma \cup \{\diamond\}$, where $\diamond \notin \Sigma$ represents *undefined positions* or *holes*, a *partial word* over Σ is a sequence of symbols from $\Sigma_\diamond$. Denoting the set of all partial words over Σ by $\Sigma_\diamond^*$, a *partial language* over Σ is a subset of $\Sigma_\diamond^*$. Partial languages can be transformed to (ordinary) languages by using $\diamond$-substitutions over Σ. A $\diamond$-substitution $\sigma \colon \Sigma_\diamond^* \to 2^{\Sigma^*}$ satisfies $\sigma(a) = \{a\}$, for all $a \in \Sigma$, $\sigma(\diamond) \subseteq \Sigma$, and $\sigma(uv) = \sigma(u)\sigma(v)$, for $u, v \in \Sigma_\diamond^*$. As a result, σ is fully defined by $\sigma(\diamond)$, for example, if $\sigma(\diamond) = \{a, b\}$ and $L = \{\diamond b, \diamond c\}$ then $\sigma(L) = \{ab, bb, ac, bc\}$. So, applying σ to a partial language $L \subseteq \Sigma_\diamond^*$ results in a (ordinary) language $\sigma(L) \subseteq \Sigma^*$.

A *nondeterministic finite automaton* (NFA) is a system $M = \langle Q, \Sigma, \delta, q_0, F \rangle$, where Q is the finite set of *internal states*, Σ is the finite set of *input symbols*, $q_0 \in Q$ is the *initial state*, $F \subseteq Q$ is the set of *accepting states*, and $\delta \colon Q \times \Sigma \to 2^Q$ is the *transition function*. In the forthcoming, we sometimes refer to δ as a subset of $Q \times \Sigma \times Q$. A finite automaton M is *deterministic* (DFA) if and only if $|\delta(q, a)| = 1$, for all $q \in Q$ and $a \in \Sigma$. In this case, we simply write $\delta(q, a) = q'$ for $\delta(q, a) = \{q'\}$ assuming that the transition function is a total mapping $\delta \colon Q \times \Sigma \to Q$. Note that here any DFA is complete, that is, the transition function is total, whereas it may be a partial function for NFAs in the sense that the transition function of nondeterministic machines may map to the empty set. A finite automaton is said to be *minimal* if there is no finite automaton of the same type with fewer states, accepting the same language. Note that a rejecting sink state is counted for DFAs, since they are always complete, whereas it is not counted for NFAs, since their transition function may map to the empty set.

Generally speaking, a language L can be represented by a partial language L' together with a $\diamond$-substitution σ such that $\sigma(L') = L$. In particular, for regular languages, from the descriptional complexity point of view it is an interesting question to what extent there are regular languages L' such that the minimal DFA accepting L' has less states than the minimal DFA accepting L? In order to distinguish between finite automata accepting (ordinary) languages from those accepting partial languages, we refer to the latter as *partial word deterministic finite automata* ($\diamond$-DFA). Thus, $\diamond$-DFAs treat the hole symbol $\diamond$ as an ordinary input letter.

The number of states of the (complete) minimal DFA accepting a regular language L is denoted by $\min_{DFA}(L)$. Similarly, $\min_{NFA}(L)$ denotes the minimal number of states necessary for some NFA to accept L. For partial languages, we write $\min_{\diamond\text{-}DFA}(L)$ to denote the minimal number of states of a $\diamond$-DFA accepting a language L' such that there exists a $\diamond$-substitution σ with $\sigma(L') = L$.

3 Basic Constructions

In connection with lower bounds on the number of states necessary for an automaton to accept a given language, the problem arises to prove the minimality of a given automaton. While a couple of techniques exist to prove the minimality of DFAs, only a few techniques exist for NFAs. The situation is much worse for ◇-DFAs. Clearly, a ◇-DFA can be seen as a DFA over the alphabet $\Sigma_\diamond$. But, in general, the minimization of a ◇-DFA M changes the language that it represents, that is, $\sigma(L(M))$. It has been shown in [10] that the problem to find a minimal ◇-DFA M' (together with a ◇-substitution) for a given regular language is PSPACE-complete. The problem has been studied in more detail in [5], where algorithms are given for the construction of minimal partial languages, associated with some ◇-substitution, as well as approximation algorithms for the construction of minimal ◇-DFAs. However, for particular languages that witness certain lower bounds, their minimality has to be proved almost from scratch. Here we continue with some observations that can nevertheless be applied in lower bound proofs.

First, we briefly recall the so-called (extended) *fooling set* technique (see, for example, [3, 8, 12]) that is widely used for proving lower bounds on the number of states necessary for an NFA to accept a given language.

Theorem 1. *Let $L \subseteq \Sigma^*$ be a regular language and suppose there exists a set of pairs $P = \{ (x_i, y_i) \mid 1 \leq i \leq n \}$ such that (1) $x_i y_i \in L$, for $1 \leq i \leq n$, and (2) $i \neq j$ implies $x_i y_j \notin L$ or $x_j y_i \notin L$, for $1 \leq i, j \leq n$. Then any nondeterministic finite automaton accepting L has at least n states. Here P is called an (extended)* fooling set *for L.*

Let M be a ◇-DFA $= \langle Q, \Sigma_\diamond, \delta, q_0, F \rangle$ and σ be an associated ◇-substitution. Then a minimal DFA M' that accepts the language $\sigma(L(M))$ can be constructed as follows. First, modify M to the NFA $\hat{M} = \langle Q, \Sigma, \hat{\delta}, q_0, F \rangle$ by replacing any transition $\delta(p, \diamond) = q$ by the transitions $\{ \hat{\delta}(p, a) = q \mid a \in \sigma(\diamond) \}$ and keeping all other transitions from δ. Then determinize $\hat{M}$ and minimize the outcome. We call M' constructed in this way the *canonical* DFA for M and σ. This construction is presented as Algorithm 1 in [1].

The intermediate NFA in the construction exhibits the limited nondeterminism provided by ◇-DFAs. In fact, for each state of the NFA, there are at most two outgoing transitions for each input symbol. This is a valuable hint for the seek for suitable witness automata. For example, it is known that $2^n - 1$ is a tight bound on the number of states for a DFA that accepts the language $\sigma(L(M))$ of an n-state ◇-DFA M with associated ◇-substitution [1]. In order to find further witnesses for the lower bound it is sufficient to look for complete NFAs having (i) the required form of limited nondeterminism for just one input symbol and (ii) causing the maximal state blow-up of $2^n - 1$ when determinized. An example is depicted in Fig. 1.

In such an NFA M the nondeterminism can be removed by replacing one of the two nondeterministic outgoing transitions by a transition on ◇, respectively, and setting $\sigma(\diamond) = \{x\}$, where x is the sole input symbol for which the nondeterminism occurs. Since M is complete, for all states of the resulting automaton on which a ◇-transition is defined, transitions on all other input symbols are defined as well. So, in order to make the resulting automaton complete, it is sufficient to add a ◇-transition to the states for which no ◇-transition is defined so far. This can safely be done by copying the transition on x. The transition

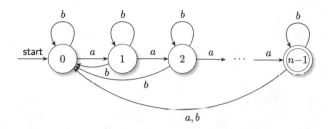

Fig. 1. A complete n-state NFA whose minimal equivalent DFA has $2^n - 1$ states.

on x must exist, since M is complete. Clearly, the resulting automaton M' is a $\diamond$-DFA with $\sigma(L(M')) = L(M)$ (see Fig. 2 for a possible $\diamond$-DFA obtained from the NFA of Fig. 1). Since $\min_{NFA}(L) \leq \min \diamond$-DFA$(L)$ [6] and M' has the same number of states as M has, the $\diamond$-DFA M' is minimal, that is, even for any other $\diamond$-substitution no smaller equivalent $\diamond$-DFA exists.

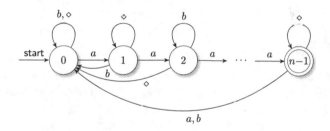

Fig. 2. A minimal $\diamond$-DFA obtained from the NFA depicted in Fig. 1, $\sigma(\diamond) = \{b\}$.

The example above dealt with the maximal state blow-up for "determinization". However, the method to prove the minimality of $\diamond$-DFAs by utilizing minimal NFAs with certain properties can be extended.

Lemma 1. *Let $M = \langle Q, \Sigma, \delta, q_0, F \rangle$ be a possibly incomplete DFA, $S \subseteq \Sigma$ be a fixed subset of input symbols, $P \subseteq Q$, and $\alpha \colon Q \to Q$ be a total mapping. Moreover, let $\hat{M} = \langle Q, \Sigma, \hat{\delta}, q_0, F \rangle$ be an NFA obtained from M by adding the transitions $\{\hat{\delta}(p, a) = \alpha(p) \mid p \in P, a \in S\}$ to δ. Then $\min_{\diamond\text{-}DFA}(L(\hat{M})) \leq |Q|$ if M is complete and $P = Q$, and $\min_{\diamond\text{-}DFA}(L(\hat{M})) \leq |Q| + 1$ otherwise.*

Proof. We set $\sigma(\diamond) = S$ and construct a $\diamond$-DFA $M' = \langle Q, \Sigma_\diamond, \delta', q_0, F \rangle$ from the given NFA $\hat{M}$. To this end, for any state $p \in P$, a set of transitions $\{\hat{\delta}(p, a) = \alpha(p) \mid a \in S\}$ is replaced by the transition $\hat{\delta}(p, \diamond) = \alpha(p)$. By the construction of $\hat{M}$ from the DFA M it follows that M' is deterministic. If M is complete and $P = Q$, that is, for all states there is an outgoing $\diamond$-transition in M', then M' is complete. Otherwise, it is completed by adding missing transitions to a new rejecting sink state. This gives the transition function δ'. Since the input alphabet of M' is $\Sigma_\diamond$, it is a $\diamond$-DFA. Moreover, the canonical DFA for M' and σ is equivalent to $\hat{M}$. Since apart from a possible new sink state the state set is the same for M' and $\hat{M}$, we conclude $\min_{\diamond\text{-}DFA}(L(\hat{M})) \leq |Q|$ if M is complete and $P = Q$. Otherwise, we have $\min_{\diamond\text{-}DFA}(L(\hat{M})) \leq |Q| + 1$. $\square$

Let $L = \{aa, aaa, aaaa, aca, aaca, baca, baa, baaa\} \subset \{a, b, c\}^*$ be a finite language. It has been shown in [5] that any $\diamond$-DFA accepting L has at least seven states if $\sigma(\diamond) = \{a, b\}$, and at least eight states if $\sigma(\diamond) = \{a, c\}$. In order to show that any minimal NFA accepting L has five states, we apply Theorem 1 by providing the set $P = \{(\lambda, a^4), (b, a^3), (ba, a^2), (bac, a), (baca, \lambda)\}$ whose fooling set property for L is easily verified. A minimal NFA M accepting L is shown in Fig. 3.

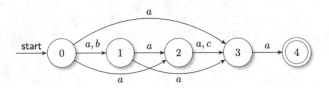

Fig. 3. A minimal NFA accepting a finite language.

This NFA M cannot serve as witness for the constructions from above because there are three transitions on input symbol a defined for state 0. Moreover, let α be the mapping of Lemma 1. Then, it can map state 0 to state 1 or to state 2 or to state 3 to remove the nondeterminism. However, in any case the nondeterminism is not removed entirely, when the transition $\delta(0, a) = \alpha(0)$ is deleted. It is not hard to show that *any* minimal NFA accepting L must have three a-transitions from the initial state. So, changing to a possibly different but equivalent minimal NFA does not help. Nevertheless, we can utilize M to show the minimality of a $\diamond$-DFA accepting the finite language L as follows.

By way of contradiction, assume that there is a 6-state $\diamond$-DFA M' and a $\diamond$-substitution σ such that $\sigma(L(M')) = L$. Since M' is complete and, for example, any input beginning with symbol c has to be rejected, M' has a rejecting sink state. We remove this sink state and all transitions to it, and obtain an equivalent incomplete 5-state $\diamond$-DFA M''. Next, we construct an NFA $\hat{M}$ from M'' as in the construction of the canonical DFA. That is, $\hat{M}$ is obtained from M'' by replacing any transition $\delta(p, \diamond) = q$ from M'' by the transitions $\{\hat{\delta}(p, a) = q \mid a \in \sigma(\diamond)\}$ and keeping all other transitions from δ. So, $\hat{M}$ has five states and is minimal. In particular, it has at most two transitions on input symbol a from the initial state. This is a contradiction, since any minimal NFA accepting L must have three a-transitions from the initial state. We conclude that, for *any* $\diamond$-substitution, a minimal $\diamond$-DFA accepting L has at least seven states.

In order to construct such a minimal ⬦-DFA with $\sigma(\diamond) = \{a\}$, we can resolve the nondeterminism by replacing two a-transitions from the initial state by a single a-transition to a new state $2, 3$ which, in turn, has the outgoing transitions of the states 2 and 3. The newly introduced nondeterminism for this state can be removed by a ⬦-transition as depicted in Fig. 4.

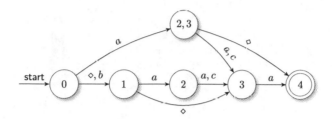

Fig. 4. A minimal ⬦-DFA accepting a finite language, where $\sigma(\diamond) = \{a\}$. The rejecting sink state is not depicted.

4   Operational State Complexity

Let ∘ be a fixed operation on languages that preserves regularity. Then the ∘-language operation problem for ⬦-DFAs is defined as follows:

- Given an n-state ⬦-DFA M_1 with ⬦-substitution σ_1 and an m-state ⬦-DFA M_2 with ⬦-substitution σ_2.
- How many states are sufficient and necessary in the worst case (in terms of n and m) for a ⬦-DFA M_3 with some ⬦-substitution σ_3 such that

$$\sigma_3(L(M_3)) = \sigma_1(L(M_1)) \circ \sigma_2(L(M_2))?$$

Obviously, this problem generalizes to unary language operations like, for example, complementation or reversal.

We first consider the operation of complementation and show an upper bound and a lower bound that is tight up to a constant factor. The result reveals that complementation is an expensive operation from the state complexity point of view.

Proposition 1. *Let $n \geq 1$ be an integer and M_1 be an n-state ⬦-DFA with ⬦-substitution σ_1. Then $2^n - 1$ states are sufficient for a ⬦-DFA M_2 with some ⬦-substitution σ_2 such that $\sigma_2(L(M_2))$ is the complement of $\sigma_1(L(M_1))$. Therefore, we have $\min_{\diamond\text{-}DFA}(\overline{L}) \leq 2^{\min_{\diamond\text{-}DFA}(L)} - 1$, for all regular languages L.*

Theorem 2. *Let $n > 2$ be an integer. There exists a minimal n-state ⬦-DFA M_1 with ⬦-substitution σ_1 such that any ⬦-DFA M_2 with any ⬦-substitution σ_2, where $\sigma_2(L(M_2))$ is the complement of $\sigma_1(L(M_1))$, has at least 2^{n-3} states. Therefore, we have $\min_{\diamond\text{-}DFA}(\overline{L}) \leq 2^{\min_{\diamond\text{-}DFA}(L)-3}$, for infinitely many regular languages L.*

Proof. We are going to utilize Lemma 1 to construct minimal witness automata. To this end, consider the incomplete DFA M depicted in Fig. 5. We set $S = \{a\}$,

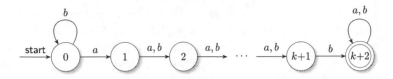

Fig. 5. An incomplete DFA.

$P = \{0\}$, and α to be the identity on the state set. After adding the required transitions to M, we obtain the NFA $\hat{M}$ depicted in Fig. 6.

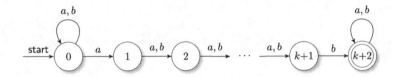

Fig. 6. The NFA obtained from the DFA of Fig. 5.

So, for $k \geq 0$, we consider the witness languages $L_k = \{a, b\}^* a\{a, b\}^k b\{a, b\}^*$. Now, by Lemma 1, we have $\min_{\diamond\text{-}DFA}(L_k) \leq k + 4$. On the other hand, it is not hard to see that the NFA of Fig. 6 is minimal. Therefore, by $\min_{NFA}(L_k) \leq \min_{\diamond\text{-}DFA}(L_k)$ we derive $k + 3 \leq \min_{\diamond\text{-}DFA}(L_k) \leq k + 4$. Since a minimal $\diamond$-DFA M' with $\diamond$-substitution σ' such that $\sigma'(L(M')) = L_k$ is complete and, thus, has a rejecting sink state which the NFA of Fig. 6 does not have, we conclude $\min_{\diamond\text{-}DFA}(L_k) = k + 4$.

Essentially, in order to accept the complement of L_k an NFA has to verify that the input has no substring $a\{a, b\}^k b$. Therefore, after reading a symbol a the NFA must be able to remember the next k input symbols. Altogether this needs 2^{k+1} states. In fact, it has been shown in [11] that any NFA that accepts the complement of L_k needs at least 2^{k+1} states. Again, by $\min_{NFA}(\overline{L_k}) \leq \min_{\diamond\text{-}DFA}(\overline{L_k})$, we derive that any $\diamond$-DFA M_2 with any $\diamond$-substitution σ_2 where $\sigma_2(L(M_2)) = \overline{L_k}$ has at least 2^{k+1} states. Setting $n = k + 4$ shows the theorem. $\qquad\square$

We continue with Boolean operations. In general, neither the union nor the intersection of partial languages gives a partial language whose substitution is the union or intersection of the substitutions of the given partial languages. So a simple cross-product construction does not help. The idea for the union is to take a $\diamond$-DFA for one of the given partial languages and the canonical DFA for the other one, and build their cross-product automaton to obtain a $\diamond$-DFA for the upper bound of the state costs. However, for the intersection, the idea does not apply. The reason is that a $\diamond$ in the input that can be substituted by at least two different symbols a_1 and a_2, must be treated by the canonical DFA as if the input were a_1 or a_2 and *both* symbols lead to accepting computations.

So, currently the best general upper bound for the intersection is the trivial one obtained by building the cross-product automaton of two canonical DFAs. In particular, let $m, n \geq 1$ be two integers, M_1 be an m-state $\diamond$-DFA with $\diamond$-substitution σ_1, and M_2 be an n-state $\diamond$-DFA with $\diamond$-substitution σ_2. Then $(2^m - 1) \cdot (2^n - 1)$ states are sufficient for a $\diamond$-DFA M_3 with some $\diamond$-substitution σ_3 such that $\sigma_3(L(M_3)) = \sigma_1(L(M_1)) \cap \sigma_2(L(M_2))$. In fact, M_3 is a DFA.

For the special case that one of the two involved $\diamond$-substitutions is a singleton, a much better upper bound can be shown, which turns out to be tight in the order of magnitude.

Theorem 3. *Let $m, n \geq 1$ be two integers, M_1 be an m-state $\diamond$-DFA with $\diamond$-substitution σ_1, where $|\sigma_1(\diamond)| = 1$, and M_2 be an n-state $\diamond$-DFA with $\diamond$-substitution σ_2. Then $m \cdot (2^n - 1)$ states are sufficient for a $\diamond$-DFA M_3 with some $\diamond$-substitution σ_3 such that $\sigma_3(L(M_3)) = \sigma_1(L(M_1)) \cap \sigma_2(L(M_2))$.*

Proof. To construct M_3, we take the $\diamond$-DFA M_1 with σ_1 as it is. Then we build the canonical DFA $M_2' = \langle Q, \Sigma, \delta, q_0, F \rangle$ for M_2 and σ_2. Let $\sigma_1(\diamond) = \{a\}$. We add a $\diamond$-transition to each state of M_2' by copying the a-transition. More precisely, for each state $q \in Q$, we define additionally $\delta(q, \diamond) = \delta(q, a)$. Finally, we construct the cross-product automaton from M_1 and M_2', call it M_3, and set $\sigma_3(\diamond) = \{a\}$.

Now let $w \in \sigma_1(L(M_1)) \cap \sigma_2(L(M_2))$. Then there is a word $w' \in \sigma_1^{-1}(w)$ accepted by M_1. Moreover, w is accepted by the canonical DFA for M_2 and σ_2. Since $\sigma_1(\diamond) = \{a\}$ and M_2' is this canonical DFA extended by a $\diamond$-transition in parallel to every a-transition, we derive that w' is accepted by M_2' as well. So, w' is accepted by M_3 and, thus, $w = \sigma_3(w') \in \sigma_3(L(M_3))$.

Conversely, let $w \in \sigma_3(L(M_3))$. Then there is a word $w' \in \sigma_3^{-1}(w)$ accepted by M_3. Therefore, w' is accepted by M_1 and by M_2'. Since $\sigma_1 = \sigma_3$, we have $w = \sigma_3(w') \in \sigma_1(L(M_1))$. Furthermore, by construction, $\sigma_2(L(M_2)) = \sigma_3(L(M_2'))$ and, hence, $w = \sigma_3(w') \in \sigma_2(L(M_2))$. We conclude $w \in \sigma_1(L(M_1)) \cap \sigma_2(L(M_2))$ and altogether have derived $\sigma_3(L(M_3)) = \sigma_1(L(M_1)) \cap \sigma_2(L(M_2))$.

For the construction of M_3 as cross-product automaton of M_1 and M_2', a number of states that is the product of the number of states of M_1 and M_2', that is $m \cdot (2^n - 1)$, is sufficient. $\qquad\square$

The proofs of the lower bounds are more involved, in a sense that the minimality of a $\diamond$-DFA accepting the intersection or union has to be shown.

Theorem 4. *Let $m \geq n \geq 1$ be two positive integers. There exist a $2m$-state $\diamond$-DFA M_1 with $\diamond$-substitution σ_1, and an n-state $\diamond$-DFA M_2 with $\diamond$-substitution σ_2, such that any $\diamond$-DFA M_3 with any $\diamond$-substitution σ_3 where $\sigma_3(L(M_3)) = \sigma_1(L(M_1)) \cap \sigma_2(L(M_2))$ has at least $(m + 1) \cdot (2^n - 1)$ states. Therefore, we have*

$$\min_{\diamond\text{-}DFA}(L_1 \cap L_2) \geq (\min_{\diamond\text{-}DFA}(L_1)/2 + 1) \cdot 2^{\min_{\diamond\text{-}DFA}(L_2)} - 1,$$

for infinitely many regular languages L_1 and infinitely many regular languages L_2.

The last Boolean operation we are looking at is the union. As mentioned above, the idea for the upper bound is to take a $\diamond$-DFA for one of the given partial languages and the canonical DFA for the other one, and build their cross-product automaton.

Theorem 5. *Let* $m \geq n \geq 1$ *be two integers,* M_1 *be an* m-*state* $\diamond$-DFA *with* $\diamond$-*substitution* σ_1, *and* M_2 *be an* n-*state* $\diamond$-DFA *with* $\diamond$-*substitution* σ_2. *Then* $m \cdot (2^n - 1)$ *states are sufficient for a* $\diamond$-DFA M_3 *with some* $\diamond$-*substitution* σ_3 *such that* $\sigma_3(L(M_3)) = \sigma_1(L(M_1)) \cup \sigma_2(L(M_2))$.

A lower bound for the union is shown in the next theorem. While it is exponential, it does not match the upper bound, since it consists of the sum of the number of states of the larger given automaton and two to the power of the number of states of the smaller given automaton. The upper bound was given by their product.

Theorem 6. *Let* $m \geq n \geq 0$ *be two positive integers. There exist a* $(m + 1)$-*state* $\diamond$-DFA M_1 *with* $\diamond$-*substitution* σ_1, *and an* $(n + 1)$-*state* $\diamond$-DFA M_2 *with* $\diamond$-*substitution* σ_2, *such that any* $\diamond$-DFA M_3 *with any* $\diamond$-*substitution* σ_3 *where* $\sigma_3(L(M_3)) = \sigma_1(L(M_1)) \cup \sigma_2(L(M_2))$ *has at least* $m + 2^n$ *states. Therefore, we have* $\min_{\diamond\text{-}DFA}(L_1 \cup L_2) \geq (\min_{\diamond\text{-}DFA}(L_1) - 1) + 2^{\min_{\diamond\text{-}DFA}(L_2)-1}$, *for infinitely many regular languages* L_1 *and infinitely many regular languages* L_2.

5   Hierarchy of $\diamond$-Transitions

Here we turn to considering the number of productive $\diamond$-transitions in a $\diamond$-DFA. Here a transition is called productive, if it does not lead to the rejecting sink state. By the tight bound of $2^n - 1$ states for the $\diamond$-DFA to DFA conversion, the state costs for removing all $\diamond$-transitions are already known. But this raises the question for the state costs when only some of the productive $\diamond$-transitions are removed. In other words, we consider the following (k_1, k_2)-$\diamond$-transition problem:

- Let $k_1 > k_2 \geq 0$ be two integers.
- Given an n-state $\diamond$-DFA M_1 with $\diamond$-substitution σ_1 having at most k_1 productive $\diamond$-transitions.
- How many states are sufficient and necessary in the worst case (in terms of n) for a $\diamond$-DFA M_2 with some $\diamond$-substitution σ_2 having at most k_2 productive $\diamond$-transitions such that $\sigma_2(L(M_2)) = \sigma_1(L(M_1))$?

Corollary 1. *For any* $k_1 > 0$, *the upper bound of the* $(k_1, 0)$-$\diamond$-*transition problem is* $2^n - 1$.

Next, we generalize the problem and derive exponential lower bounds. In particular, the lower bound for the $(k_1, k_1 - 1)$-$\diamond$-transition problem turns out to be exponential in the order of magnitude. Moreover, for every further productive $\diamond$-transition that is removed, an exponential number of states is additionally necessary in the worst case.

Theorem 7. *Let $k_1 > k_2 \geq 0$ be two constant integers. Then, for each $\ell \geq 2$, there exist a $(5k_1 + k_1\ell - 1)$-state $\diamond$-DFA M_1 with $\diamond$-substitution σ_1 having k_1 productive $\diamond$-transitions, such that any $\diamond$-DFA M_2 with any $\diamond$-substitution σ_2 having at most k_2 productive $\diamond$-transitions and $\sigma_2(L(M_2)) = \sigma_1(L(M_1))$ has at least $2k_1 + k_2(\ell + 1) + (k_1 - k_2)2^\ell - 1$ states.*

Proof. First, we construct a witness automaton. To this end, let $\ell \geq 2$ be an integer. We consider the $(\ell + 1)$-state $\diamond$-DFA $\hat{M}$ with $\sigma_1(\diamond) = \{a\}$ as depicted on the right-hand side of Fig. 7, where all transitions not depicted go into the rejecting sink-state that is not depicted as well. Clearly, $\hat{M}$ has exactly one productive $\diamond$-transition.

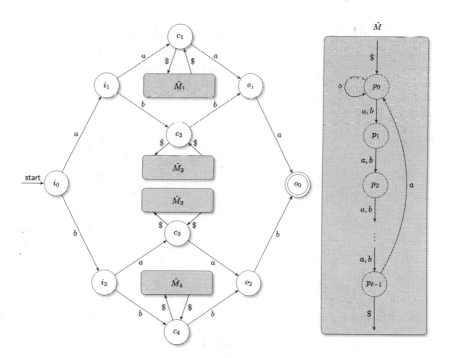

Fig. 7. A $\diamond$-DFA with $\sigma_1(\diamond) = \{a\}$ and 4 productive $\diamond$-transitions. Four copies of $\hat{M}$ are plugged in as $\hat{M}_i$, $1 \leq i \leq 4$. The common rejecting sink-state as well as the transitions to it are not depicted.

Next, we use k_1 copies $\hat{M}_i$, $1 \leq i \leq k_1$ of $\hat{M}$ that are distinct except for a common sink-state. Say the states are $p_{i,j}$, for $1 \leq i \leq k_1$ and $0 \leq j \leq \ell - 1$, and p_e, for the sink-state. Finally, these copies are assembled into one $\diamond$-DFA M_1 by selecting k_1 different words $z_1, z_2, \ldots, z_{k_1}$ of length $\lceil \log(k_1) \rceil$ from $\{a, b\}^*$. These words are processed from an initial state in a tree-like structure, where the initial state is the root and each of the k_1 leaves is connected to and from one copy by $\$$-transitions, where $\$$ is a new symbol (see the left-hand side of Fig. 7). In this way, each copy $\hat{M}_i$ is selected by an individual prefix z_i. Again, all missing transitions are directed to the common sink-state p_e. Let $L(\hat{M})$ denote the language of words accepted by $\hat{M}$ with initial state p_0 and sole accepting state $p_{\ell-1}$. Then a word w is accepted by M_1 if and only if it has the form $z(\$L(\hat{M})\$)^* z^R$, where $z \in \{z_1, z_2, \ldots, z_{k_1}\}$ (see Fig. 7 for an example with $k_1 = 4$). In total, the $\diamond$-DFA M_1 has k_1 productive $\diamond$-transitions and at most $(2 \cdot (2^{\lceil \log(k_1) \rceil} - 1)) + k_1 + k_1 \ell + 1 \le 5k_1 + k_1 \ell - 1$ states.

The rest of the proof is to show the claimed lower bound for the number of states necessary for any $\diamond$-DFA M_2 with any $\diamond$-substitution σ_2 having at most k_2 productive $\diamond$-transitions and $\sigma_2(L(M_2)) = \sigma_1(L(M_1))$. $\qquad\square$

References

1. Balkanski, E., Blanchet-Sadri, F., Kilgore, M., Wyatt, B.J.: On the state complexity of partial word DFAs. Theor. Comput. Sci. **578**, 2–12 (2015)
2. Berstel, J., Boasson, L.: Partial words and a theorem of Fine and Wilf. Theor. Comput. Sci. **218**, 135–141 (1999)
3. Birget, J.C.: Intersection and union of regular languages and state complexity. Inform. Process. Lett. **43**, 185–190 (1992)
4. Blanchet-Sadri, F.: Algorithmic Combinatorics on Partial Words. CRC Press, Boca Raton (2008)
5. Blanchet-Sadri, F., Goldner, K., Shackleton, A.: Minimal partial languages and automata. RAIRO Inform. Théor. **51**, 99–119 (2017)
6. Dassow, J., Manea, F., Mercaş, R.: Regular languages of partial words. Inf. Sci. **268**, 290–304 (2014)
7. Fischer, M.J., Paterson, M.S.: String-matching and other products. In: Karp, R.M. (ed.) Complexity of Computation. SIAM-AMS Proceedings, vol. 7, pp. 113–125. AMS, New Jersey (1974)
8. Glaister, I., Shallit, J.: A lower bound technique for the size of nondeterministic finite automata. Inform. Process. Lett. **59**, 75–77 (1996)
9. Goldstine, J., Kintala, C.M.R., Wotschke, D.: On measuring nondeterminism in regular languages. Inform. Comput. **86**, 179–194 (1990)
10. Holzer, M., Jakobi, S., Wendlandt, M.: On the computational complexity of partial word automata problems. Fund. Inform. **148**, 267–289 (2016)
11. Holzer, M., Kutrib, M.: Nondeterministic descriptional complexity of regular languages. Int. J. Found. Comput. Sci. **14**, 1087–1102 (2003)
12. Holzer, M., Kutrib, M.: Nondeterministic finite automata - recent results on the descriptional and computational complexity. Int. J. Found. Comput. Sci. **20**, 563–580 (2009)

State Complexity of Union
and Intersection on Graph-Walking
Automata

Olga Martynova[ID] and Alexander Okhotin[✉][ID]

Department of Mathematics and Computer Science, St. Petersburg State University,
14th Line V. O., 29, Saint Petersburg 199178, Russia
st062453@student.spbu.ru, alexander.okhotin@spbu.ru

Abstract. Finite automata traversing graphs by moving along their edges are known as graph-walking automata (GWA). This paper investigates the state complexity of union and intersection for this model. It is proved that the union of GWA with m and n states, with $m \leqslant n$, operating on graphs with k labels of edge end-points, is representable by a GWA with $2km + n + 1$ states, and at least $2(k-3)(m-1) + n - 1$ states are necessary in the worst case. For the intersection, the upper bound is $(2k+1)m + n$ and the lower bound is $2(k-3)(m-1) + n - 1$.

1 Introduction

Graph-walking automata (GWA) operate on undirected graphs with labelled nodes and edge end-points, moving along the edges using finitely many states. The labels of edge end-points are called *directions*. The basic examples of graph-walking automata are two-way finite automata (2DFA) and tree-walking automata (TWA). A graph-walking automaton models, e.g., a robot in a maze. There is a classical result by Budach [3] that for every GWA there exists a graph, which this automaton cannot fully traverse, see a succinct proof by Fraigniaud et al. [5]. Models with small but not finite memory, such as pebble automata, are studied as well, see a recent result by Disser et al. [4].

Kunc and Okhotin [11] studied transformations of graph-walking automata to several subclasses: to automata that halt on every input; to automata returning to the initial node before acceptance; to reversible automata. It was proved that every graph-walking automaton with n states operating on graphs with k directions can be transformed to these classes: to a halting automaton with $6kn + 1$ states, to a returning automaton with $3kn$ states, and to a reversible and returning automaton with $6kn + 1$ states. In a recent paper, the authors [12] have improved the constructions by Kunc and Okhotin, reducing the number of states to $2kn + 1$, $2kn + n$ and $4kn + 1$, respectively, and also established asymptotically close lower bounds that confirm that the constant factors 2, 2 and 4 are indeed optimal.

This work was supported by the Russian Science Foundation, project 18-11-00100.

Y.-S. Han and S.-K. Ko (Eds.): DCFS 2021, LNCS 13037, pp. 125–136, 2021.
https://doi.org/10.1007/978-3-030-93489-7_11

The new lower bound method for graph-walking automata opens the way to study the state complexity of operations for this model.

In this paper, Boolean operations on graph-walking automata are investigated. Union, intersection and complementation of languages defined by graph-walking automata can be recognized by a graph-walking automaton, for instance, by first transforming one of the given automata to reversible [15]. This yields some rough upper bounds on the number of states; but how many states are indeed necessary?

The state complexity of Boolean operations has been studied for many automaton models. For DFA, Maslov [13] showed that the state complexity for both union and intersection is mn, where m and n is the number of states in argument automata. For NFA, as shown by Holzer and Kutrib [9], the state complexity of union is $m + n + 1$, and mn for the intersection. Birget [1] proved that the state complexity of complementing an NFA is 2^n. Two-way finite automata turned out to be harder to study. Geffert et al. [7] obtained an upper bound of $4n + 3$ states for complementing 2DFA, but no lower bounds are known up to date. Kunc and Okhotin [11] proved that the union of 2DFA requires at least $m + n$ and at most $4m + n + 4$ states, while the state complexity of intersection is between $m + n$ and $m + n + 1$. Also Kunc and Okhotin [10] established the bounds for 2NFA: the precise state complexity $m + n$ for the union, and bounds between $m + n$ and $m + n + 1$ for the intersection. As proved by Geffert et al. [6], the complement of an 2AFA is representable by an automaton with $O(n^7)$ states, and there is a lower bound $\Omega(n \log n)$ [8]. Beyond finite automata, the complexity of union and intersection for input-driven pushdown automata, also known as visibly pushdown automata, was established as $\Theta(mn)$ by Piao and Salomaa [16]. For tree-walking automata, complementation was first investigated by Muscholl et al. [14], and the current upper bound of $4kn + 2k + 1$ states for k-ary trees was given by Kunc and Okhotin [11]. For nondeterministic tree-walking automata, their closure under complementation remains open [2].

This paper establishes asymptotically tight bounds on the state complexity of Boolean operations for graph-walking automata, using the recently introduced lower bound methods for this model [12]. For two graph-walking automata with m and n states, with $m \leqslant n$, operating on graphs with k directions, the bounds shown for the union are: lower bound $2(k - 3)(m - 1) + n - 1$ and upper bound $2km + 1 + n$. For the intersection, the bounds are between $2(k - 3)(m - 1) + n - 1$ and $2km + m + n$. For the complement of an n-state automaton, $2kn + 1$ states are enough, and at least $2(k - 3)(n - 1)$ are needed in the worst case.

2   Graph-Walking Automata and Their Subclasses

Formalizing the definition of graph-walking automata (GWA) requires a more elaborate notation than for 2DFA and TWA. It begins with a generalization of an alphabet to the case of graphs: a *signature*.

Definition 1 (Kunc and Okhotin [11]). A signature S *consists of*

- *A finite set D of directions, that is, labels attached to edge end-points;*
- *A bijection $-\colon D \to D$ providing an opposite direction, with $-(-d) = d$ for all $d \in D$;*
- *A finite set Σ of node labels;*
- *A non-empty subset $\Sigma_0 \subseteq \Sigma$ of possible labels of the initial node;*
- *A set of directions $D_a \subseteq D$ for every label $a \in \Sigma$. Every node labelled with a must be of degree $|D_a|$, with the incident edges corresponding to the elements of D_a.*

Like strings are defined over an alphabet, graphs are defined over a signature.

Definition 2. A graph over a signature $S = (D, -, \Sigma, \Sigma_0, (D_a)_{a \in \Sigma})$ *is a quadruple* $(V, v_0, +, \lambda)$, *where*

- *V is a finite set of nodes;*
- *$v_0 \in V$ is the initial node;*
- *$+\colon V \times D \to V$ is a partial function, such that if $v + d$ is defined, then $(v + d) + (-d)$ is defined and equals v; denote $v - d = v + (-d)$;*
- *a total mapping $\lambda\colon V \to \Sigma$, such that $v + d$ is defined if and only if $d \in D_{\lambda(v)}$, and $\lambda(v) \subset \Sigma_0$ if and only if $v = v_0$.*

A graph-walking automaton is defined similarly to a 2DFA, with an input graph instead of an input string.

Definition 3. A (deterministic) graph-walking automaton (GWA) over a signature $S = (D, -, \Sigma, \Sigma_0, (D_a)_{a \in \Sigma})$ *is a quadruple* $A = (Q, q_0, F, \delta)$, *where*

- *Q is a finite set of states;*
- *$q_0 \in Q$ is the initial state;*
- *$F \subseteq Q \times \Sigma$ is a set of acceptance conditions;*
- *$\delta\colon (Q \times \Sigma) \setminus F \to Q \times D$ is a partial transition function, with $\delta(q, a) \in Q \times D_a$ for all a and q where δ is defined.*

A computation of a GWA on a graph $(V, v_0, +, \lambda)$ is a uniquely defined sequence of configurations (q, v), with $q \in Q$ and $v \in V$. It begins with (q_0, v_0) and proceeds from (q, v) to $(q', v + d)$, where $\delta(q, \lambda(v)) = (q', d)$. The automaton accepts by reaching (q, v) with $(q, \lambda(v)) \in F$.

On each input graph, a GWA can accept, reject or loop. The language of GWA A is a set of graphs, which A accepts. It is denoted by $L(A)$.

There is a natural subclass of GWA that never loop.

Definition 4. *A graph-walking automaton is said to be halting, if its computation on every input graph is finite.*

Another property is getting back to the initial node before acceptance.

Definition 5. *A graph-walking automaton $A = (Q, q_0, F, \delta)$ over a signature $S = (D, -, \Sigma, \Sigma_0, (D_a)_{a \in \Sigma})$ is called returning, if $F \subseteq Q \times \Sigma_0$, which means that it can accept only in the initial node.*

A returning automaton is free to reject in any node, and it may also loop, that is, it need not be halting.

The next, more sophisticated property is *reversibility*, meaning that, for every configuration, the configuration at the previous step can be uniquely reconstructed. The first condition necessary for reversibility is that every state is reachable from only one direction.

Definition 6 (Kunc and Okhotin [11, Defn. 4]). *A graph-walking automaton $A = (Q, q_0, F, \delta)$ over a signature $S = (D, -, \Sigma, \Sigma_0, (D_a)_{a \in \Sigma})$ is called direction-determinate, if there is a function $d \colon Q \to D$, such that, for all $p \in Q$ and $a \in \Sigma$, if $\delta(p, a)$ is defined, then $\delta(p, a) = (q, d(q))$ for some $q \in Q$.*

Denote the transitions by each label a by a partial function $\delta_a \colon Q \to Q$.

Every automaton can be made direction-determinate by remembering the direction used in the last transition, using $Q \times D$ as the set of states [11, Lemma 1].

Definition 7. *A graph-walking automaton $A = (Q, q_0, F, \delta)$ over a signature $S = (D, -, \Sigma, \Sigma_0, (D_a)_{a \in \Sigma})$ is called reversible, if*

- *A is direction-determinate;*
- *for all $a \in \Sigma$ and $q \in Q$, there is at most one state p, such that $\delta(p, a) = (q, d(q))$; in other words, knowing a state and a previous label, one can determine the previous state.*

3   Upper Bounds

Now we will establish the upper bounds for Boolean operations with graph-walking automata. The construction for intersection of two given automata is obtained by making the smaller automaton returning.

Theorem 1. *Let $m \leqslant n$. For every signature with k directions and for every m-state automaton A and n-state automaton B over this signature, there exists a $(2km + m + n)$-state automaton, which accepts a graph if and only if both A and B accept this graph.*

Proof. As was proved by the authors in an earlier paper [12, Thm 9], the automaton A can be transformed to a returning automaton A' with $2km + m$ states (thus improving an earlier upper bound $3km$ by Kunc and Okhotin [11]).

Then the automata A' and B are joined into the automaton C, which works as A' at first. And if it reaches the accepting configuration at the initial node, then it continues as the automaton B.

If the automaton A rejects or loops, then A' rejects or loops as well, and so does C in its simulation of the automaton A'.

If A accepts, then A' returns to the initial node and accepts, and C simulates A' to the accepting configuration and then continues from this configuration as from the initial configuration of B, and proceeds with simulating B. If B accepts, then C accepts; if B rejects or loops, then C rejects or loops.

So the automaton C accepts the graph if and only if the graph is accepted by A and by B. The set of states of C is comprised of the states of A' and the states of B, so C is a $(2km + m + n)$-state automaton.   □

The upper bound for union is generally similar, but the smaller automaton is transformed so that it rejects at the initial node and accepts anywhere.

Theorem 2. *For every n-state direction-determinate automaton A, there exists a $(2n+1)$-state halting, direction-determinate and reversible (but not necessarily returning) automaton A' which recognizes the same set of graphs, and which can reject only at the initial node.*

The theorem is proved by adapting the construction of a reversible automaton by Kunc and Okhotin [11, Lemma 6], which implements Sipser's [17] idea of traversing the tree of accepting computations. The construction is omitted due to space constraints.

Theorem 3. *Let $m \leqslant n$. Let S be a signature with k directions. Then for every m-state automaton A and every n-state automaton B over the signature S, there exists a $(2km + 1 + n)$-state automaton, which accepts a graph if and only if the automaton A accepts this graph or B accepts it.*

Proof. The automaton A can be made direction-determinate with km states, and then, by Theorem 2, it can be transformed to a halting $(2km + 1)$-state automaton A', which rejects only at the initial node.

So it is possible to make a $(2km + 1 + n)$-state automaton C, which at first works as A', and accepts if A' accepts; and if A' rejects, this happens at the initial node, prompting C to start the simulation of B from the initial node.

This automaton C recognizes the union of languages of A and B.   □

The upper bound for the complement is given by a straightforward application of Theorem 2.

Theorem 4. *For every n-state automaton A over a signature with k directions there exists an $(2kn + 1)$-state automaton B, which recognizes the complement of the language $L(A)$. Furthermore, B is returning and halting.*

Proof. The automaton A can be made direction-determinate with nk states and then, by Theorem 2, it can be transformed into an $(2kn+1)$-state halting automaton A', which rejects only at the initial node.

Now let the automaton B work as A', but reject in accepting configurations of A' and accept in rejecting configurations. This automaton B is halting and returning, and it recognizes the complement of $L(A)$.   □

4   Graphs $H_{n,N}^{accept}$ and $H_{n,N}^{reject}$

Lower bounds for unions and intersections of languages recognized by GWA are proved using the method introduced by the authors [12] in a recent paper.

In particular, it was established that transforming an n-state graph-walking automaton to a returning automaton requires at least $2(n-1)(k-3)$ states in the worst case, where k is the number of directions in the signature. This method shall now be adapted for the new arguments.

According to the general method [12], the first to be defined are families of accepted and rejected graphs, parameterized by two integers n and N specifying the length of certain chains. The number n represents the minimal required number of states to reach a certain node, whereas N should be large enough to ensure periodic behaviour. In this paper, those graphs are denoted by $H_{n,N}^{accept}$ and $H_{n,N}^{reject}$. The graph $H_{n,N}^{accept}$ is introduced in Fig. 1; it is different from $H_{n,N}^{reject}$ only in the label of the node $v_{decisive}$.

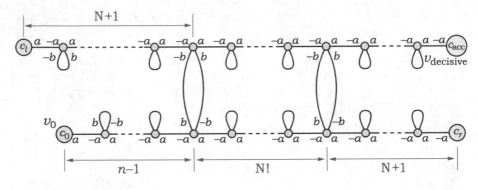

Fig. 1. The graph $H_{n,N}^{accept}$.

The distance from v_0 to the left $(b, -b)$ "bridge" is $n-1$, and this allows an n-state automaton to measure this distance and reach $v_{decisive}$ to check that the label of the node $v_{decisive}$ is c_{acc}.

Lemma 1 [12, Sect. 5]. *For each n, there is an automaton with n states that accepts $H_{n,N}^{accept}$ for all N, does not accept any graphs without the label c_{acc}, and never moves in the direction $-a$.*

The number N is chosen to be large enough, that is, larger than the lower bounds being proved. The original paper used the graphs $H_{n,4kn}^{accept}$ and $H_{n,4kn}^{reject}$, because the number $4kn$ was large enough to prove the lower bounds [12]. However, the proofs of the main properties of these graphs hold for every $N \geqslant 2$, and the earlier result remains true in the following form.

Lemma 2 [12, Lemma 17]. *If an automaton with at most N states starts on a graph $H_{n,N}^{accept}$ or $H_{n,N}^{reject}$ at the node $v_{decisive}$ and arrives to the node v_0, then the automaton must enter at least $n-1$ distinct states after a transition in the direction $-a$.*

The idea of the proof is presented for completeness.

The automaton leaves $v_{decisive}$ and moves towards the right bridge. Since there are more than N steps, and all nodes besides the ends of the chains have the same label, the automaton soon begins repeating some sequence of states and directions periodically. This sequence has more directions $-a$ than a, for otherwise it would not move far from $v_{decisive}$. The distance between the two bridges, $N!$, is divisible by the period length, and hence the automaton approaches both bridges in the same phase of the period. Therefore, it behaves identically in the vicinity of each bridge. If the automaton enters fewer than $n-1$ states after moving by $-a$, then, once it moves away from a bridge by $n-1$ edges, it does not return to that bridge anymore. This means that its trajectory near the left bridge does not include v_0. Then the result of passing by each of the bridges is the same, and the automaton either remains on the upper chain while passing by both bridges, or changes to the other chain each time. In either case, the automaton ultimately remains on the upper chain and reaches the upper left corner without visiting v_0.

When leaving the upper left corner, the automaton similarly cannot reach v_0 due to having too few states after a move by $-a$, and has to return to $v_{decisive}$.

The next lemma is generally symmetric to Lemma 2.

Lemma 3. *If an automaton with fewer than N states starts on $H_{n,N}^{accept}$ or on $H_{n,N}^{reject}$ at the node v_0, and comes to the node $v_{decisive}$, then it enters at least $n-1$ distinct states after a transition by a.*

The proof of this lemma is analogous to the proof of Lemma 2. If an automaton has fewer than $n-1$ different states after transitions by a, then it is bound to move between the two ends of the lower chain, without ever visiting either end of the upper chain, because the automaton's actions on the two bridges are identical.

5   Diodes and Their Properties

Lower bound arguments for graph-walking automata use special subgraphs called *diodes* [12], which are easy to pass in one direction and hard to pass in the other. They are also used in this paper, this section recalls their main properties and adapts them for the new arguments.

Diodes are defined over signatures S_k, for all $k \geq 4$; the signature S_k has k directions, including $a, -a$ and $b_1, -b_1$. For each $N \geq 2$, the diode $\Delta_{N,k}$ is a subgraph over S_k without an initial node. Most of the nodes have the same label, "black circle".

The diode has two *external edges* in directions a and $-a$, by which it is connected to the outside world. Then, one can define an edge-replacement homomorphism $h_{N,k}$, which replaces every $(a, -a)$-edge in a graph with the diode $\Delta_{N,k}$.

The following properties of the diodes are known. First, it easy to pass a diode forward, in the direction a, as if by a single $(a, -a)$-edge. Every automaton that never moves in the direction $-a$ can be reconstructed to pass through all diodes this way, without increasing the number of states.

Lemma 4 [12, Lemma 13]. *Let S be any signature containing directions $a, -a$, which has no node labels from the signature S_k. Let $A = (Q, q_0, F, \delta)$ be a GWA over the signature S, which never moves in the direction $-a$. Then, there exists a GWA $A' = (Q', q'_0, F', \delta')$ over a joint signature $S \cup S_k$, with $|Q'| = |Q|$, so that A accepts a graph G if and only if A' accepts the graph $h_{N,k}(G)$.*

Conversely, if there is an automaton that works on graphs with diodes, then it can be reconstructed to pass through $(a, -a)$-edges instead, again without any extra states.

Lemma 5 [12, Lemma 14]. *Let $k \geqslant 4$ and $N \geqslant 2$, denote $h(G) = h_{N,k}(G)$ for brevity. Let S be a signature containing the directions $a, -a$ and no node labels from the diode's signature S_k. Let A' be a GWA over the signature $S \cup S_k$. Then there exists an automaton A over the signature S, using the same set of states, with the following properties.*

- *For every graph G over S, the automaton A accepts G if and only if A' accepts $h(G)$.*
- *If A can enter a state q by a transition in the direction $-a$, then A' can enter the state q after traversing the diode backwards.*
- *If A can enter a state q by a transition in the direction a, then A' can enter the state q after traversing the diode forward.*

The third claim of this lemma was not stated in the original paper [12], but it can be proved similarly to the second claim.

The next lemma shows that moving through diodes in the reverse direction requires many states.

Lemma 6 [12, Lemma 15]. *Let $A' = (Q, q_0, F, \delta)$ be a GWA over a signature that includes the diode's signature S_k, with $|Q| \leqslant N$. Assume that A', after traversing the diode $\Delta_{N,k}$ backwards, can leave the diode in any of h distinct states. Then A' has at least $2h(k-3)$ states, in which, at the label "black circle", it moves in a direction other than $\pm a$.*

The next lemma is new. It gives a modest lower bound on the number of states after forward traversals; however, in this paper, those few states are necessary to reach tight bounds.

Lemma 7. *Let $A' = (Q, q_0, F, \delta)$ be a GWA over a signature that includes diode's signature S_k. Assume that A', after traversing the diode $\Delta_{N,k}$ forward, can leave the diode in any of h distinct states. Then A' has at least h distinct states, in which, at the label "black circle", it moves in the direction a or $-a$.*

Note that neither of these h states may coincide with any of the $2h(k-3)$ states in Lemma 6, because they have different transitions at "black circles".

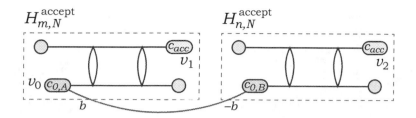

Fig. 2. Graph $(H_{m,N}^{accept}, H_{n,N}^{accept})$.

Proof. In the diode $\Delta_{N,k}$, there is a node v labelled with a "black circle", which the automaton must visit in every forward traversal of the diode, and which it leaves in the direction a or $-a$. Since there are h traversals ending in different states, these traversals must leave v in h distinct states. $\qquad\square$

6 Lower Bound for Intersection

Theorem 5. *For all $k \geqslant 4$, there exists a signature with k directions, such that, for all $n \geqslant m \geqslant 2$, there exist graph-walking automata A' and B' over this signature, with m and n states, such that every automaton recognizing the language $L(A') \cap L(B')$ must have at least $N = 2(k-3)(m-1) + n - 1$ states.*

It is useful to begin with the graphs, on which these automata operate. They are ultimately based on graphs of the form $H_{n,N}^{accept}$ and $H_{n,N}^{reject}$, given in Sect. 4. The latter graphs are defined over the signature $\widetilde{S}$, with four directions: $a, -a, b, -b$. A new signature S is obtained from $\widetilde{S}$ as follows: the initial label c_0 is replaced with two labels: an initial label $c_{0,A}$ with the set of directions $D_{c_{0,A}} = \{a, b\}$, and with a non-initial label $c_{0,B}$ with directions $D_{c_{0,B}} = \{a, -b\}$.

Every two graphs G_1 and G_2 over the signature $\widetilde{S}$ can be joined into a graph (G_1, G_2) over the signature S, defined as follows. The initial node of G_1, denoted by v_0 and originally labelled with c_0, is relabelled with $c_{0,A}$, and an extra edge in the direction b is sent to the former initial node of G_2, which is relabelled with $c_{0,B}$. The graphs are connected as in Fig. 2.

Now consider the graphs of the form $(H_{m,N}^{result_1}, H_{n,N}^{result_2})$, with $result_1$, $result_2 \in \{accept, reject\}$. The automaton A is defined to accept such a graph if $result_1 = accept$: this can be done using m states, by working as the automaton in Lemma 1 and ignoring the graph $H_{n,N}^{result_2}$. Similarly, B is defined to accept a graph if $result_2 = accept$: it uses n states and moves to $H_{n,N}^{result_2}$ at the first step, ignoring $H_{m,N}^{result_1}$.

The next lemma shows, what happens if the conditions on both graphs are to be checked simultaneously.

Lemma 8. *Let I be an automaton with at most N states, which recognizes the set of graphs accepted both by A and by B. Then **either** it enters at least $m-1$*

distinct states after moving by $-a$ *and at least* $n - 1$ *distinct states after moving by* a, **or** *it enters at least* $n - 1$ *distinct states after moving by* $-a$ *and at least* $m - 1$ *distinct states after moving by* a.

Proof. The automaton I accepts a graph $(H_{m,N}^{result_1}, H_{n,N}^{result_2})$ if and only if $result_1 = result_2 = accept$. Consider its computation on the graph $(H_{m,N}^{accept}, H_{n,N}^{accept})$, illustrated in Fig. 2. Denote the node $v_{decisive}$ in the graph $H_{m,N}^{accept}$ by v_1, and let v_2 be $v_{decisive}$ in $H_{n,N}^{accept}$. The automaton I must visit both nodes to check that each of them is labelled with c_{acc}.

If I first visits v_1, then, in order to make the decision, it has to visit v_2, and for that it needs to get back from v_1 to the initial node first. Then, by Lemma 2, the automaton I enters at least $m - 1$ distinct states after transitions by $-a$. Next, on the subgraph $H_{n,N}^{accept}$, it has to reach the node v_2 from the initial node, and hence, by Lemma 3, it enters at least $n - 1$ distinct states after transitions by a.

And if I visits the node v_2 first, then, similarly, it enters at least $n-1$ different states after moving in the direction $-a$ and at least $m - 1$ different states after moving by a.   □

Proof (of Theorem 5). The automata A and B over the signature S are constructed as above. The desired automata A' and B' shall work like A and B, but on the graphs with diodes substituted instead of $(a, -a)$-edges. Let $h_{N,k}$ be a graph homomorphism that replaces every edge $(a, -a)$ with the diode $\Delta_{N,k}$.

The automaton A' is obtained out of A by Lemma 4, this is possible because A never moves in the direction $-a$. The new automaton is defined over the signature $S \cup S_k$. The directions $\pm a$ are common for the signatures S and S_k, and $\pm b$ in S are identified with $\pm b_1$ in S_k. Overall, there are k directions in $S \cup S_k$. The automaton A' has m states, and it accepts a graph $h_{N,k}(G)$ if and only if A accepts G. The n-state automaton B' is defined analogously.

It remains to show that every automaton recognizing $L(A') \cap L(B')$, must have at least $N = 2(k-3)(m-1)+n-1$ states. Suppose that some automaton I' recognizes this language and has fewer than N states. Then, by Lemma 5, there exists an automaton I over the signature S with the same number of states as in I', which accepts a graph G if and only if I' accepts $h_{N,k}(G)$. Then I recognizes the intersection of $L(A)$ and $L(B)$. Therefore, by Lemma 8, the automaton I enters at least $m - 1$ distinct states after transitions by $-a$, and at least $n - 1$ distinct states after transitions by a, or vice versa.

Consider the case of $m-1$ states after transitions by $-a$ and $n-1$ states after transitions by a. Then Lemma 5 asserts that I' enters at least $m - 1$ distinct states after traversing a diode backwards, and at least $n - 1$ distinct states after traversing a diode forward. These two groups of states may potentially overlap.

Then, by Lemma 6, the automaton I' has at least $2(k - 3)(m - 1)$ distinct states, in which the transition at a "black circle" label is made not in the directions $\pm a$. On the other hand, according to Lemma 7, the automaton I' has $n-1$ distinct states with the transitions at a "black circle" label made in the directions a or $-a$. All these states are thus pairwise disjoint, and I' has at least $2(k - 3)(m - 1) + n - 1 = N$ states.

In the case of $n - 1$ states after moving by $-a$, and $m - 1$ states after moving by a, the automaton I' must have at least $2(k - 3)(n - 1) + m - 1 \geqslant N$ states. Overall, every automaton I' recognizing this intersection has at least N states. □

The lower bound for the union is established by a similar argument. The proof is different in replacing Lemma 8 with an analogous lemma for the union, which is proved using the graph $(H_{m,N}^{reject}, H_{n,N}^{reject})$, cf. $(H_{m,N}^{accept}, H_{n,N}^{accept})$ in Lemma 8.

Theorem 6. *For all $k \geqslant 4$ there is a signature with k directions, such that for all $n \geqslant m \geqslant 2$ there is an m-state automaton A' and an n-state automaton B' over that signature, such that every automaton recognizing the union $L(A') \cup L(B')$ has at least $N = 2(k - 3)(m - 1) + n - 1$ states.*

In addition, a lower bound on the state complexity of complementation can be proved by a direct application of the lower bound method for halting automata [12, Sect. 6].

Theorem 7. *For every $k \geqslant 4$ and $n \geqslant 2$ there exist a signature with k directions and an n-state automaton such that every automaton, which recognizes the complement of language of the original automaton, has at least $2(k - 3)(n - 1)$ states.*

The argument uses the same automaton A, and a graph obtained from $H_{n,N}^{reject}$ by merging both ends of the upper chain into a single node v_{joint} that is not specifically labelled. An automaton recognizing the complement must accept this graph, but unless it enters at least $n - 1$ distinct states after transitions by $-a$, it would end up looping through v_{joint}. The lower bound of $2(k - 3)(n - 1)$ states then follows after inserting the diodes, as in the proof of Theorem 5.

7   Conclusion

The new bounds on the state complexity of Boolean operations for graph-walking automata are asymptotically tight. Making them tighter would require more than a slight refinement of the lower bound method [12], and it would be interesting to achieve this improvement.

The authors' method is also inapplicable to showing lower bounds on the state complexity of union and complementation on tree-walking automata, because both the graphs $H_{n,N}^{result}$ and the diode essentially use cycles. Obtaining lower bounds using only trees is a challenging research problem. Proving tight bounds on the state complexity of these operations on 2DFA would be even harder.

References

1. Birget, J.-C.: Partial orders on words, minimal elements of regular languages, and state complexity. Theor. Comput. Sci. **119**, 267–291 (1993). http://dx.doi.org/10.1016/0304-3975(93)90160-U

2. Bojańczyk, M., Colcombet, T.: Tree-walking automata do not recognize all regular languages. SIAM J. Comput. **38**(2), 658–701 (2008). https://doi.org/10.1137/050645427
3. Budach, L.: Automata and labyrinths. Mathematische Nachrichten **86**(1), 195–282 (1978). http://dx.doi.org/10.1002/mana.19780860120
4. Disser, Y., Hackfeld, J., Klimm, M.: Tight bounds for undirected graph exploration with pebbles and multiple agents. J. ACM **66**(6), 40:1–40:41 (2019). https://doi.org/10.1145/3356883
5. Fraigniaud, P., Ilcinkas, D., Peer, G., Pelc, A., Peleg, D.: Graph exploration by a finite automaton. Theor. Comput. Sci. **345**(2–3), 331–344 (2005). http://dx.doi.org/10.1016/j.tcs.2005.07.014
6. Geffert, V., Kapoutsis, C.A., Zakzok, M.: Complement for two-way alternating automata. Acta Informatica **58**(5), 463–495 (2021). https://doi.org/10.1007/s00236-020-00373-8
7. Geffert, V., Mereghetti, C., Pighizzini, G.: Complementing two-way finite automata. Inf. Comput. **205**(8), 1173–1187 (2007). http://dx.doi.org/10.1016/j.ic.2007.01.008
8. Geffert, V., Okhotin, A.: Transforming two-way alternating finite automata to one-way nondeterministic automata. In: Csuhaj-Varjú, E., Dietzfelbinger, M., Ésik, Z. (eds.) MFCS 2014. LNCS, vol. 8634, pp. 291–302. Springer, Heidelberg (2014). https://doi.org/10.1007/978-3-662-44522-8_25
9. Holzer, M., Kutrib, M.: Nondeterministic descriptional complexity of regular languages. Int. J. Found. Comput. Sci. **14**, 1087–1102 (2003). http://dx.doi.org/10.1142/S0129054103002199
10. Kunc, M., Okhotin, A.: State complexity of union and intersection for two-way nondeterministic finite automata. Fundamenta Informaticae **110**(1–4), 231–239 (2011). http://dx.doi.org/10.3233/FI-2011-540
11. Kunc, M., Okhotin, A.: Reversibility of computations in graph-walking automata. Inf. Comput. 275, Article No. 104631 (2020). https://doi.org/10.1016/j.ic.2020.104631
12. Martynova, O., Okhotin, A.: Lower bounds for graph-walking automata. In: 38th Annual Symposium on Theoretical Aspects of Computer Science (STACS 2021, Saarbrücken, Germany, 16–19 March 2021), LIPIcs, vol. 187, pp. 52:1–52:13 (2020). https://doi.org/10.4230/LIPIcs.STACS.2021.52
13. Maslov, A.N.: Estimates of the number of states of finite automata. Sov. Math. Dokl. **11**, 1373–1375 (1970)
14. Muscholl, A., Samuelides, M., Segoufin, L.: Complementing deterministic tree-walking automata. Inf. Proces. Lett. **99**(1), 33–39 (2006). http://dx.doi.org/10.1016/j.ipl.2005.09.017
15. Okhotin, A.: Graph-Walking automata: from whence they come, and whither they are bound. In: Hospodár, M., Jirásková, G. (eds.) CIAA 2019. LNCS, vol. 11601, pp. 10–29. Springer, Cham (2019). https://doi.org/10.1007/978-3-030-23679-3_2
16. Piao, X., Salomaa, K.: Operational state complexity of nested word automata. Theor. Comput. Sci. **410**, 3290–3302 (2009). http://dx.doi.org/10.1016/j.tcs.2009.05.002
17. Sipser, M.: Halting space-bounded computations. Theor. Comput. Sci. **10**(3), 335–338 (1980). http://dx.doi.org/10.1016/0304-3975(80)90053-5

Gray Cycles of Maximum Length Related to k-Character Substitutions

Jean Néraud[(⊠)] [iD]

LITIS, University of Rouen-Normandy, Saint-Etienne-du-Rouvray, France
neraud.jean@gmail.com
http://neraud.jean.free.fr

Abstract. Given a word binary relation τ onto A^* we define a τ-Gray cycle over a finite language $X \subseteq A^*$ to be a permutation $\left(w_{[i]}\right)_{0 \le i \le |X|-1}$ of X such that each word w_i is an image of the previous word w_{i-1} by τ. We introduce the complexity measure $\lambda(n)$, equal to the largest cardinality of a language X having words of length at most n, and such that some τ-Gray cycle over X exists. The present paper is concerned with the relation $\tau = \sigma_k$, the so-called k-character substitution, such that (u, v) belongs to σ_k if, and only if, the Hamming distance of u and v is k. We compute the bound $\lambda(n)$ for all cases of the alphabet cardinality and the argument n.

Keywords: Character · Complexity · Cycle · Gray · Substitution · Relation · Word

1 Introduction

In the framework of combinatorial algorithms, one of the most documented questions consists in the development of methods in order to generate, exactly once, all the objects in some specific class [15]. Many topics are concerned by such a problem: suffice it to mention sequence counting [1], signal encoding [16], and data compression [18].

The so-called *binary Gray codes* first appeared in [10]: given a binary alphabet A and some positive integer n, they referred to sequences with maximum length of pairwise different n-tuples of characters (that is, words in A^n), provided that any pair of consecutive items differ by exactly one character. Shortly after, a similar study was drawn in the framework of non-binary alphabets [4,8]. With regard to other famous combinatorial classes of objects, the term of *combinatorial Gray code*, for its part, appeared in [11]: actually, the difference between successive items, although being fixed, need not to be small [20]. Generating all permutations of a given n-element set constitutes a noticeable example [7]. Subsets of fixed size are also concerned [6], as well as cross-bifix free words [2], Debruijn sequences [9], set partitions [13], necklaces [19]: the list is far to be exhaustive. Combinatorial Gray sequences are often needed to be *cyclic* [3], in

Y.-S. Han and S.-K. Ko (Eds.): DCFS 2021, LNCS 13037, pp. 137–149, 2021.
https://doi.org/10.1007/978-3-030-93489-7_12

the sense that the initial term itself can be retrieved as successor of the last one. Such a condition justifies the terminology of *Gray cycle* [14, Sect. 7.2.1.1].

In view of some formal framework, we notice that each of the sequences we mentioned above involves some word binary relation $\tau \subseteq A^* \times A^*$, where A stands for a finite alphabet, and A^* for the free monoid it generates. For its part, the combinatorial class of objects can be modelled by some finite language $X \subseteq A^*$. Given a sequence of words we denote in square brackets the corresponding indices: this will allow us to make a difference from w_i, the character in *position* i in a given word w. We define a *cyclic Gray sequence over X, with respect to τ* (for short: τ-*Gray cycle over X*) as every finite sequence of words $\left(w_{[i]}\right)_{i \in [0, |X|-1]}$ satisfying each of the three following conditions:

(G1) For every word $x \in X$, some $i \in [0, |X| - 1]$ exists such that we have $x = w_{[i]}$;

(G2) For every $i \in [1, |X| - 1]$, we have $w_{[i]} \in \tau\left(w_{[i-1]}\right)$; in addition, the condition $w_{[0]} \in \tau\left(w_{[|X|-1]}\right)$ holds;

(G3) For every pair $i, j \in [0, |X| - 1]$, $i \neq j$ implies $w_{[i]} \neq w_{[j]}$.

With this definition, the set X need not to be *uniform* that is, in the Gray cycle the terms may have a variable length. For instance, given the alphabet $A = \{0, 1\}$, take for τ the word binary relation Λ_1 which, with every word w associates all the strings located within a *Levenshtein distance* of 1 from w (see e.g. [17]); with such a relation, the sequence $(0, 00, 01, 11, 10, 1)$ is a Λ_1-Gray cycle over $X = A \cup A^2$. Actually, in addition to the topics we mentioned above, two other fields involved by those Gray cycles may be mentioned. Firstly, with regard to graph theory, a τ-Gray cycle over X exists if, and only if, there is some Hamiltonian circuit in the graph of the relation τ (see e.g. [20]). Secondly, given a binary word relation $\tau \subseteq A^* \times A^*$, and given $X \subseteq A^*$, if some τ-Gray cycle exists over X, then X is τ-*closed* [17] that is, the inclusion $\tau(X) \subseteq X$ holds, where $\tau(X)$ stands for the set of the images of the words in X under the relation τ. Such closed sets actually constitute a special subfamily in the famous *dependence systems* [5, 12]. Notice that, given a τ-*closed* set $X \subseteq A^*$, there do not necessarily exist non-empty τ-Gray cycles over X. A typical example is provided by τ being id_{A^*}, the identity over A^*, with respect to which every finite set $X \subseteq A^*$ is closed; however non-empty τ-Gray cycle can exist only over singletons.

In the present paper, given a positive integer n, and denoting by $A^{\leq n}$ the set of the words with length not greater than n, we consider the family of all sequences that can be a τ-Gray cycle over some subset X of $A^{\leq n}$. This is a natural question to study those sequences of maximum length which, of course, correspond to subsets X of maximum cardinality; such a length, which we denote by $\lambda_{A,\tau}(n)$, means introducing some complexity measure for the word binary relation τ. With regard to the preceding examples we have $\lambda_{\{0,1\},\Lambda_1}(2) = 6$; moreover, for every alphabet A and positive integer n, the identity $\lambda_{A,id_{A^*}}(n) = 1$ holds. We focus on the case where τ is σ_k, the so-called k-*character substitution*: with every word with length at least k, say w, this relation associates all the words w', with $|w'| = |w|$ and such that the character w'_i differs from w_i

in exactly k values of $i \in [1, |w|]$. As commented in [12,17], σ_k has noticeable inference in the famous framework of *error detection*. On the other hand, by definition, $w' \in \sigma_k(w)$ implies $|w'| = |w|$ therefore, if there is some σ_k-Gray cycle over X, then X is a uniform set. From this point of view, the classical Gray codes, which allow to generate all n-tuples over A, correspond to σ_1-Gray cycles over A^n, furthermore we have $\lambda_{A,\sigma_1}(n) = |A|^n$. In addition, in the case where A is a binary alphabet, it can be easily proved that, for every $n \geq 3$, we have $\lambda_{A,\sigma_2}(n) = 2^{n-1}$ [14, Exercise 8, p. 77]. However, in the most general case, although an exhaustive description of σ_k-closed variable-length codes has been provided in [17], the question of computing some σ_k-Gray cycle of maximum length has remained open. In our paper we establish the following result:

Theorem. *Let A be a finite alphabet, $k \geq 1$, and $n \geq k$. Then exactly one of the following conditions holds:*

(i) $|A| \geq 3$, $n \geq k$, and $\lambda_{A,\sigma_k}(n) = |A|^n$;
(ii) $|A| = 2$, $n = k$, and $\lambda_{A,\sigma_k}(n) = 2$;
(iii) $|A| = 2$, $n \geq k + 1$, k is odd and $\lambda_{A,\sigma_k}(n) = |A|^n$;
(iv) $|A| = 2$, $n \geq k + 1$, k is even, and $\lambda_{A,\sigma_k}(n) = |A|^{n-1}$.

In addition, in each case some σ_k-Gray cycle of maximum length can be explicitly computed.

We now shortly describe the contents of the paper. In Sect. 2, we recall the two famous examples of the *binary* (resp., $|A|$-ary) *reflected Gray code*. By applying some induction based methods, in Sect. 3 and Sect. 4, these sequences allow to compute special families of σ_k-Gray cycles with maximum length. In Sect. 5, in the case where A is a binary alphabet, and k an even positive integer, we also compute a family of Gray cycles with maximum length; in addition some further development is raised.

2   Preliminaries

Several definitions and notation have already been fixed. In the whole paper, A stands for some finite alphabet, with $|A| \geq 2$. Given a word $w \in A^*$, we denote by $|w|$ its length; in addition, for every $a \in A$, we denote by $|w|_a$ the number of occurrences of the character a in w.

The Reflected Binary Gray Cycle
Let $A = \{0, 1\}$, and $n \geq 1$. The most famous example of σ_1-Gray cycle over A^n is certainly the so-called *reflected binary Gray code* (see e.g. [10] or [14, p. 6]): in the present paper we denote it by $g^{n,1}$. It can be defined by the recurrent sequence initialized with $g_{[0]}^{n,1} = 0^n$, and satisfying the following property: for every $i \in [1, |A|^n - 1]$, a unique integer $j \in [1, n]$ exists such that, in both words $g_{[i]}^{n,1}$ and $g_{[i-1]}^{n,1}$ the corresponding characters in position j differ; in addition, the position j is chosen to be maximum in such a way that $g_{[i]}^{n,1} \notin \{g_{[0]}^{n,1}, \cdots, g_{[i-1]}^{n,1}\}$.

Example 1. In what follows we provide a column representation of $g^{2,1}$ and $g^{3,1}$:

$g^{2,1}$	$g^{3,1}$
00	000
01	001
11	011
10	010
	110
	111
	101
	100

By construction, for every $n \geq 1$, each of the following identities holds:

$$g^{n,1}_{[0]} = 0^n, \quad g^{n,1}_{[1]} = 0^{n-1}1, \quad g^{n,1}_{[2^n-2]} = 10^{n-2}1, \quad g^{n,1}_{[2^n-1]} = 10^{n-1} \tag{1}$$

The $|A|$-ary Reflected Gray Cycle
The preceding construction can be extended in order to obtain the so-called $|A|$-ary reflected Gray code [4,8], a σ_1-Gray cycle over A^n, which we denote by $h^{n,1}$. Set $A = \{0, \cdots, p-1\}$ and denote by θ the cyclic permutation $(0, 1, \ldots p-1)$. The sequence $h^{n,1}$ is initialized with $h^{n,1}_{[0]} = 0^n$. In addition, for every $i \in [1, |A|^n - 1]$, a unique integer j exists such that c and d, the characters respectively in position j in $h^{n,1}_{[i-1]}$ and $h^{n,1}_{[i]}$, satisfy both the following conditions: (i) $d = \theta(c)$; (ii) j is the greatest integer in $[1, n]$ such that $h^{n,1}_{[i]} \notin \{h^{n,1}_{[0]}, \cdots, h^{n,1}_{[i-1]}\}$.

Example 2. For $A = \{0, 1, 2\}$ the sequence $h^{3,1}$ is the concatenation in this order of the three following subsequences:

$h^{3,1}$		
000	120	210
001	121	211
002	122	212
012	102	222
010	100	220
011	101	221
021	111	201
022	112	202
020	110	200

3   The Case Where We Have $k \geq 1$ and $|A| \geq 3$

Let $n \geq k \geq 1$, $p \geq 3$, and $A = \{0, 1, \cdots, p-1\}$. We will indicate the construction of a peculiar σ_k-Gray cycle over A^n, namely $h^{n,k}$. This will be done by applying some induction over $k \geq 1$: in view of that we set $n_0 = n - k + 1$. The starting point corresponds to $h^{n_0,1}$, the p-ary reflected Gray code over A^{n_0} as reminded in Sect. 2. For the induction stage, starting with some σ_{k-1}-Gray cycle over A^{n-1}, namely $h^{n-1,k-1}$, we compute the sequence $h^{n,k}$ as indicated in what follows: let $i \in [0, p^n - 1]$, and let $q \in [0, p-1]$, $r \in [0, p^{n-1} - 1]$ be the unique pair of non-negative integers such that $i = qp^{n-1} + r$. We set:

$$h^{n,k}_{[i]} = h^{n,k}_{[qp^{n-1}+r]} = \theta^{q+r}(0)h^{n-1,k-1}_{[r]} \tag{2}$$

As illustrated by Example 3, the resulting sequence $h^{n,k}$ is actually the concatenation in this order of p subsequences namely $C_0, \ldots, C_{p-1}$, with $C_q = \left(h^{n,k}_{[qp^{n-1}+r]}\right)_{0 \le r \le p^{n-1}-1}$, for each $q \in [0, p-1]$. Since θ is one-to-one, given a pair of different integers $q, q' \in [0, p-1]$, for every $r \in [0, p^{n-1} - 1]$, in each of the subsequences C_q, $C_{q'}$, the words $h^{n,k}_{[qp^{n-1}+r]}$ and $h^{n,k}_{[q'p^{n-1}+r]}$ only differ in their initial characters, which respectively are $\theta^{q+r}(0)$ and $\theta^{q'+r}(0)$. In addition, since $h^{n-1,k-1}$ is a σ_{k-1}-Gray cycle over A^{n-1}, we have $|h^{n,k}| = p|h^{n-1,k-1}| = p^n$.

Example 3. Let $A = \{0, 1, 2\}$, $n = 3$, $k = 2$, thus $p = 3$, $n_0 = 2$. By starting with the sequence $h^{n-1,k-1} = h^{2,1}$, $h^{n,k}$ is the concatenation of C_0, C_1, and C_2 :

$h^{n-1,k-1}$	$h^{n,k}$		
00	000	100	200
01	101	201	001
02	202	002	102
12	012	112	212
10	110	210	010
11	211	011	111
21	021	121	221
22	122	222	022
20	220	020	120

Proposition 1. $h^{n,k}$ *is a* σ_k-*Gray cycle over* A^n.

Proof. We argue by induction over $k \ge 1$. With regard to the base case, as indicated above $h^{n_0,1}$ is the $|A|$-ary reflected Gray sequence. In view of the induction stage, we assume that the finite sequence $h^{n-1,k-1}$ is a σ_{k-1}-Gray cycle over A^{n-1}, for some $k \ge 2$.

(i) We start by proving that $h^{n,k}$ satisfies Condition (G2). This will be done through the three following steps:

(i.i) Firstly, we prove that, for each $q \in [0, p-1]$, in the subsequence C_q two consecutive terms are necessarily in correspondence under σ_k. Given $r \in [0, p^{n-1} - 1]$, by definition, we have $\theta^{r+q}(0) \in \sigma_1\left(\theta^{r+q-1}(0)\right)$. Since $h^{n-1,k-1}$ satisfies Condition (G2), we have $h^{n-1,k-1}_{[r]} \in \sigma_{k-1}\left(h^{n-1,k-1}_{[r-1]}\right)$. We obtain $\theta^{r+q}(0)h^{n-1,k-1}_{[r]} \in \sigma_k\left(\theta^{r+q-1}(0)h^{n-1,k-1}_{[r-1]}\right)$, thus according to (2): $h^{n,k}_{[qp^{n-1}+r]} \in \sigma_k\left(h^{n,k}_{[qp^{n-1}+r-1]}\right)$.

(i.ii) Secondly, we prove that, for each $q \in [1, p-1]$, the last term of C_{q-1} and the initial term of C_q are also connected by σ_k. Take $r = 0$ in Eq. (2): it follows from $\theta^{p^{n-1}} = id_A$ that we have $h_{[qp^{n-1}]}^{n,k} = \theta^q(0)h_{[0]}^{n-1,k-1} = \theta^{p^{n-1}+q}(0)h_{[0]}^{n-1,k-1}$. In (2) take $r = p^{n-1} - 1$, moreover substitute $q - 1 \in [0, p-2]$ to $q \in [1, p-1]$: we obtain $h_{[qp^{n-1}-1]}^{n,k} = \theta^{q+p^{n-1}-2}(0)h_{[p^{n-1}-1]}^{n-1,k-1}$. It follows from $p = |A| \geq 3$ that $\theta(0) \neq \theta^{-2}(0)$: since θ is one-to-one this implies $\theta^{q+p^{n-1}}(0) \neq \theta^{q+p^{n-1}-2}(0)$, thus $\theta^{q+p^{n-1}}(0) \in \sigma_1 \left(\theta^{q+p^{n-1}-2}(0) \right)$.

By induction we have $h_{[0]}^{n-1,k-1} = \sigma_{k-1} \left(h_{[p^{n-1}-1]}^{n-1,k-1} \right)$, thus $h_{[qp^{n-1}]}^{n,k} \in \sigma_k \left(\theta^{q+p^{n-1}-2}(0)h_{[qp^{n-1}-1]}^{n-1,k-1} \right)$ that is, $h_{[qp^{n-1}]}^{n,k} \in \sigma_k \left(h_{[qp^{n-1}-1]}^{n,k} \right)$.

(i.iii) At last, we prove that the first term of C_0 is an image under σ_k of the last term of C_{p-1}. In Eq. (2), take $q = 0$ and $r = 0$: we obtain $h_{[0]}^{n,k} = 0h_{[0]}^{n-1,k-1}$. Similarly, by setting $q = p - 1$ and $r = p^{n-1} - 1$, we obtain $h_{[(p-1)p^{n-1}+p^{n-1}-1]}^{n,k} = \theta^{p^{n-1}+p-2}(0)h_{[p^{n-1}-1]}^{n-1,k-1}$, thus $h_{[p^n-1]}^{n,k} = \theta^{-2}(0)h_{[p^{n-1}-1]}^{n-1,k-1}$. Since $h^{n-1,k-1}$ is a σ_{k-1}-Gray cycle over A^{n-1}, we have $h_{[0]}^{n-1,k-1} \in \sigma_{k-1} \left(h_{[p^{n-1}-1]}^{n-1,k-1} \right)$. In addition, it follows from $p \geq 3$, that $\theta^{-2}(0) \neq 0$, thus $0 \in \sigma_1 \left(\theta^{-2}(0) \right)$. We obtain $h_{[0]}^{n,k} \in \sigma_k \left(\theta^{-2}(0)h_{[p^{n-1}-1]}^{n-1,k-1} \right)$, thus $h_{[0]}^{n,k} \in \sigma_k \left(h_{[p^n-1]}^{n,k} \right)$ that is, the required property.

(ii) Now, we prove that, in the sequence $h^{n,k}$ all terms are pairwise different. Let $i, i' \in [0, p^n - 1]$ such that $h_{[i]}^{n,k} = h_{[i']}^{n,k}$ and consider the unique 4-tuple of integers $q, q' \in [0, p-1]$, $r, r' \in [0, p^{n-1} - 1]$ such that $i = qp^{n-1} + r$ and $i' = q'p^{n-1} + r'$. According to (2) we have $\theta^{q+r}(0)h_{[r]}^{n-1,k-1} = \theta^{q'+r'}(0)h_{[r']}^{n-1,k-1}$, thus $\theta^{q+r}(0) = \theta^{q'+r'}(0) \in A$ and $h_{[r]}^{n-1,k-1} = h_{[r']}^{n-1,k-1}$. Since $h^{n-1,k-1}$ satisfies (G3), the second equation implies $r = r'$, whence the first one implies $\theta^q(0) = \theta^{q'}(0)$, thus $q = q' \bmod p$. Since we have $q, q' \in [0, p-1]$ we obtain $q = q'$, thus $i = i'$.

(iii) Finally, since $h^{n,k}$ satisfies (G3), we have $\left| \bigcup_{0 \leq i \leq p^n - 1} \{h_{[i]}^{n,k}\} \right| = p^n$, hence $h^{n,k}$ satisfies Condition (G1). □

4   The Case Where A Is a Binary Alphabet, With k Odd

Let $A = \{0, 1\}$ and $n \geq k$. Classically, the cyclic permutation θ, which was introduced in Sect. 2, can be extended into a one-to-one monoid homomorphism onto A^*: in view of this, we set $\theta(\varepsilon) = \varepsilon$ and, for any non-empty n-tuple of characters $a_1, \cdots, a_n \in A$, $\theta(a_1 \cdots a_n) = \theta(a_1) \cdots \theta(a_n)$. Trivially, in the case where we have $n = k$, if a non-empty σ_k-Gray code exists over $X \subseteq A^n$, then we have $X = \{x, \theta(x)\}$, for some $x \in A^n$. In the sequel of the paper, we assume $n \geq k + 1$. In what follows, we indicate the construction of a peculiar pair of σ_k-Gray cycles over A^n, namely $\gamma^{n,k}$ and $\rho^{n,k}$. This will be done by induction over k', the unique non-negative integer such that $k = 2k' + 1$. Let $n_0 = n - 2k' = n - k + 1$.

– For the base case, $\gamma^{n_0,1}$ and $\rho^{n_0,1}$ are computed by applying some reversal (resp., shift) over the sequence $g^{n_0,1}$ from Sect. 2:

$$\gamma_{[0]}^{n_0,1} = g_{[0]}^{n_0,1} \quad \text{and} \quad \gamma_{[i]}^{n_0,1} = g_{[2^{n_0}-i]}^{n_0,1} \quad (1 \le i \le 2^{n_0} - 1); \tag{3}$$

$$\rho_{[0]}^{n_0,k} = g_{[2^{n_0}-1]}^{n_0,1} \quad \text{and} \quad \rho_{[i]}^{n_0,k} = g_{[i-1]}^{n_0,1} \quad (1 \le i \le 2^{n_0} - 1). \tag{4}$$

By construction, $\gamma^{n_0,1}$ and $\rho^{n_0,1}$ are σ_1-Gray cycles over A^{n_0}. Moreover we have:

$$\gamma_{[0]}^{n_0,1} = g_{[0]}^{n_0,1} = 0^{n_0} \quad \text{and} \quad \rho_{[0]}^{n_0,1} = g_{[2^{n_0}-1]}^{n_0,1} = 10^{n_0-1}; \tag{5}$$

$$\gamma_{[2^{n_0}-1]}^{n_0,1} = g_{[1]}^{n_0,1} = 0^{n_0-1}1 \quad \text{and} \quad \rho_{[2^{n_0}-1]}^{n_0,1} = g_{[2^{n_0}-2]}^{n_0,1} = 10^{n-2}1. \tag{6}$$

Example 4. For $n_0 = 3$ we obtain the following sequences:

$g^{3,1}$	$\gamma^{3,1}$	$\rho^{3,1}$
000	000	100
001	100	000
011	101	001
010	111	011
110	110	010
111	010	110
101	011	111
100	001	101

– In view of the induction step, we assume that we have computed the σ_k-Gray cycles $\gamma^{n,k}$ and $\rho^{n,k}$. Notice that we have $n+2 = n_0+2(k'+1) = n_0+(k+2)-1$: below we explain the construction of the two corresponding 2^{n+2}-term sequences $\gamma^{n+2,k+2}$ and $\rho^{n+2,k+2}$. Let $i \in [0, 2^{n+2} - 1]$, and let $q \in [0,3]$, $r \in [0, 2^n - 1]$ be the unique pair of integers such that $i = q2^n + r$. Since we have $r \in [0, 2^n - 1]$, taking for q the value $q = 0$ (resp., 1, 2, 3), we state the corresponding equation (7a) (resp., (7b),(7c),(7d)):

$$\gamma_{[r]}^{n+2,k+2} = \theta^r(00)\gamma_{[r]}^{n,k}; \tag{7a}$$

$$\gamma_{[2^n+r]}^{n+2,k+2} = \theta^r(01)\rho_{[r]}^{n,k}; \tag{7b}$$

$$\gamma_{[2.2^n+r]}^{n+2,k+2} = \theta^r(11)\gamma_{[r]}^{n,k}; \tag{7c}$$

$$\gamma_{[3.2^n+r]}^{n+2,k+2} = \theta^r(10)\rho_{[r]}^{n,k}. \tag{7d}$$

Similarly the sequence $\rho^{n+2,k+2}$ is computed by substituting, in the preceding equations, the 4-tuple $(10, 11, 01, 00)$ to $(00, 01, 11, 10)$:

$$\rho_{[r]}^{n+2,k+2} = \theta^r(10)\gamma_{[r]}^{n,k}; \tag{8a}$$

$$\rho_{[2^n+r]}^{n+2,k+2} = \theta^r(11)\rho_{[r]}^{n,k}; \tag{8b}$$

$$\rho_{[2.2^n+r]}^{n+2,k+2} = \theta^r(01)\gamma_{[r]}^{n,k}; \tag{8c}$$

$$\rho_{[3.2^n+r]}^{n+2,k+2} = \theta^r(00)\rho_{[r]}^{n,k}. \tag{8d}$$

Example 5. (Example 4 continued) $\gamma^{5,3}$ is the concatenation, in this order, of the 4 following subsequences:

$\gamma^{3,1}$	$\rho^{3,1}$	$\gamma^{3,1}$	$\rho^{3,1}$
00 000	01 100	11 000	10 100
11 100	10 000	00 100	01 000
00 101	01 001	11 101	10 001
11 111	10 011	00 111	01 011
00 110	01 010	11 110	10 010
11 010	10 110	00 010	01 110
00 011	01 111	11 011	10 111
11 001	10 101	00 001	01 101

Lemma 1. *$\gamma^{n,k}$ and $\rho^{n,k}$ satisfy both the conditions (G1) and (G3).*

Proof. We argue by induction over $k' \geq 0$, with $k = 2k' + 1$. the base case corresponds to $k' = 0$ that is, $k = 1$ and $n = n_0$: as indicated above, $\gamma^{n_0,1}$ and $\rho^{n_0,1}$ are σ_1-Gray cycles over A^n. In view of the induction step we assume that, for some $k' \geq 0$, both the sequences $\gamma^{n,k}$ and $\rho^{n,k}$ are σ_k-Gray cycles over A^n.

(i) In order to prove that $\gamma^{n+2,k+2}$ satisfies Condition (G3), let $i, i' \in [0, 2^{n+2} - 1]$ such that $\gamma_{[i]}^{n+2,k+2} = \gamma_{[i']}^{n+2,k+2}$, and $q, q' \in [0,3]$, $r, r' \in [0, 2^n - 1]$ such that $i = q2^n + r$, $i' = q'2^n + r'$. According to Eqs. (7a)–(7d), words $x, x' \in A^2$, $w, w' \in A^n$ exist such that $\gamma_{[i]}^{n+2,k+2} = \theta^r(x)w$ and $\gamma_{[i']}^{n+2,k+2} = \theta^{r'}(x')w'$ that is, $\theta^r(x) = \theta^{r'}(x') \in A^2$ and $w = w'$. By the definition of θ, this implies either $x, x' \in \{00, 11\}$ or $x, x' \in \{01, 10\}$ that is, by construction, either $q, q' \in \{0, 2\}$, $x, x' \in \{00, 11\}$, $w = \gamma_{[r]}^{n,k} = \gamma_{[r']}^{n,k}$, or $q, q' \in \{1, 3\}$, $x, x' \in \{01, 10\}$, $w = \rho_{[r]}^{n,k} = \rho_{[r']}^{n,k}$. Since $\gamma^{n,k}$ and $\rho^{n,k}$ satisfies (G3), in any case we have $r = r'$. This implies $\theta^r(x) = \theta^r(x')$, thus $x = x'$. With regard to Eqs. (7a)–(7d), this corresponds to $q = q'$, thus $i = q2^n + r = q'2^n + r = i'$, therefore $\gamma^{n+2,k+2}$ satisfies Condition (G3).

(ii) By substituting $(10, 11, 01, 00)$ to $(00, 01, 11, 10)$, according to (8a)–(8d), similar arguments prove that $\rho_{[i]}^{n+2,k+2} = \rho_{[i']}^{n+2,k+2}$ implies $i = i'$, thus $\rho^{n+2,k+2}$ also satisfies (G3).

(iii) Since $\gamma^{n+2,k+2}$ satisfies (G3), we have $\bigcup_{0 \leq i < 2^{n+2}-1} \{\gamma_i^{n+2,k+2}\} = A^{n+2}$, hence it satisfies (G1). Similarly, since $\rho^{n+2,k+2}$ satisfies (G3) it satisfies (G1). □

In order to prove that our sequences satisfy (G2), we prove the following property:

Lemma 2. *We have $\gamma_{[0]}^{n,k} \in \sigma_{k+1}\left(\rho_{[2^n-1]}^{n,k}\right)$ and $\rho_{[0]}^{n,k} \in \sigma_{k+1}\left(\gamma_{[2^n-1]}^{n,k}\right)$.*

Proof. We argue by induction over the integer $k' \geq 0$. The case $k' = 0$ corresponds to $k = 1$ and $n = n_0$: with such a condition, our property comes from the identities (5) and (6). For the induction step, we assume that, for some $k' \geq 0$, we have $\gamma_{[0]}^{n,k} \in \sigma_{k+1}\left(\rho_{[2^n-1]}^{n,k}\right)$ and $\rho_{[0]}^{n,k} \in \sigma_{k+1}\left(\gamma_{[2^n-1]}^{n,k}\right)$.

(i) In (7a), by taking $r = 0$ we obtain $\gamma_{[0]}^{n+2,k+2} = 00\gamma_{[0]}^{n,k}$, hence by induction: $\gamma_{[0]}^{n+2,k+2} \in 00\sigma_{k+1}\left(\rho_{[2^n-1]}^{n,k}\right) \subseteq \sigma_{k+3}\left(11\rho_{[2^n-1]}^{n,k}\right)$. By setting $r = 2^n - 1$ in (8d), we obtain $\rho_{[2^{n+2}-1]}^{n+2,k+2} = 11\rho_{[2^n-1]}^{n,k}$, thus $\gamma_{[0]}^{n+2,k+2} \in \sigma_{k+3}\left(\rho_{[2^{n+2}-1]}^{n+2,k+2}\right)$.

(ii) Similarly, by setting $r = 0$ in (8a), and by induction we have: $\rho_{[0]}^{n+2,k+2} = 10\gamma_{[0]}^{n,k} \in \sigma_{k+3}\left(01\rho_{[2^n-1]}^{n,k}\right)$. By taking $r = 2^n - 1$ in (7d) we obtain $\gamma_{[2^{n+2}-1]}^{n+2,k+2} = 01\rho_{[2^n-1]}^{n,k}$, thus $\rho_{[0]}^{n+2,k+2} \in \sigma_{k+3}\left(\gamma_{[2^{n+2}-1]}^{n+2,k+2}\right)$.

$\square$

Since Eqs. (7a)–(8d) look alike, one may be tempted to compress them thanks to some unique generic formula. Based on our tests, such a formula needs to introduce at least two additionnal technical parameters, which would make their handling tedious. In the proof of the following result, we have opted to report some case-by-case basis argumentation: this has the advantage of making use of arguments which, although being similar, actually are easy to read.

Proposition 2. *Both the sequences $\gamma^{n,k}$ and $\rho^{n,k}$ are σ_k-Gray cycles over A^n.*

Proof sketch Once more we argue by induction over $k' \geq 0$. Since $\gamma^{n_0,1}$ and $\rho^{n_0,1}$ are σ_1-Gray cycles over A^n, the property holds for $k' = 0$. In view of the induction stage, we assume that, for some $k' \geq 0$ both the sequences $\gamma^{n,k}$ and $\rho^{n,k}$ are σ_k-Gray cycles over A^n. According to Lemma 1, it remains to establish that $\gamma^{n+2,k+2}$ and $\rho^{n+2,k+2}$ satisfy Condition (G2) that is:

$$(\forall q \in \{0,1,2,3\})(\forall r \in [1, 2^n - 1]) \; \gamma_{[q2^n+r]}^{n+2,k+2} \in \sigma_{k+2}\left(\gamma_{[q2^n+r-1]}^{n+2,k+2}\right); \qquad (9)$$

$$(\forall q \in \{1,2,3\}) \; \gamma_{[q2^n]}^{n+2,k+2} \in \sigma_{k+2}\left(\gamma_{[q2^n-1]}^{n+2,k+2}\right); \qquad (10)$$

$$\gamma_{[0]}^{n+2,k+2} \in \sigma_{k+2}\left(\gamma_{[2^{n+2}-1]}^{n+2,k+2}\right). \qquad (11)$$

$$(\forall q \in \{0,1,2,3\})(\forall r \in [1, 2^n - 1]) \; \rho_{[q2^n+r]}^{n+2,k+2} \in \sigma_{k+2}\left(\rho_{[q2^n+r-1]}^{n+2,k+2}\right); \qquad (12)$$

$$(\forall q \in \{1,2,3\}) \; \rho_{[q2^n]}^{n+2,k+2} \in \sigma_{k+2}\left(\rho_{[q2^n-1]}^{n+2,k+2}\right); \qquad (13)$$

$$\rho_{[0]}^{n+2,k+2} \in \sigma_{k+2}\left(\rho_{[2^{n+2}-1]}^{n+2,k+2}\right). \qquad (14)$$

<u>*Condition* (9).</u> (i) At first assume $q = 0$. According to (7a), and since $\gamma^{n,k}$ satisfies (G2), we have $\gamma_{[r]}^{n+2,k+2} = \theta^r(00)\gamma_{[r]}^{n,k} \in \theta^r(00)\sigma_k\left(\gamma_{[r-1]}^{n,k}\right)$, thus $\gamma_{[r]}^{n+2,k+2} \in \sigma_{k+2}\left(\theta^{r-1}(00)\gamma_{[r-1]}^{n,k}\right)$. In (7a), substitute $r-1$ to r (we have $0 \leq r-1 \leq 2^n-2$): we obtain $\gamma_{[r-1]}^{n+2,k+2} = \theta^{r-1}(00)\gamma_{[r-1]}^{n,k}$, thus $\gamma_{[r]}^{n+2,k+2} \in \sigma_{k+2}\left(\gamma_{[r-1]}^{n+2,k+2}\right)$.

(ii) Now assume $q = 1$. According to (7b), and since $\rho^{n,k}$ satisfies (G2), we have $\gamma_{[2^n+r]}^{n+2,k+2} = \theta^r(01)\rho_{[r]}^{n,k} \in \sigma_{k+2}\left(\theta^{r-1}(01)\rho_{[r-1]}^{n,k}\right)$. In (7b), substitute $r-1$ to r: we obtain $\gamma_{[2^n+r-1]}^{n+2,k+2} = \theta^{r-1}(01)\rho_{[r-1]}^{n,k}$, thus $\gamma_{[2^n+r]}^{n+2,k+2} \in \sigma_{k+2}\left(\gamma_{[2^n+r-1]}^{n+2,k+2}\right)$.

(iii) For $q = 2$, the arguments are similar to those applied in (i) by substituting $\gamma_{[2\cdot 2^n+r]}^{n+2,k+2}$ to $\gamma_{[r]}^{n+2,k+2}$, Eq. (7c) to (7a), and 11 to 00.

(iv) Similarly, for $q = 3$ the proof is obtained by substituting in (ii) $\gamma_{[3\cdot 2^n+r]}^{n+2,k+2}$ to $\gamma_{[2^n+r]}^{n+2,k+2}$, (7d) to (7b), and 10 to 01.

Condition (10). (i) Assume $q = 1$ and take $r = 0$ in (7b). According to Lemma 2, we obtain $\gamma_{[2^n]}^{n+2,k+2} = 01\rho_{[0]}^{n,k} \in 01\sigma_{k+1}\left(\gamma_{[2^n-1]}^{n,k}\right) \subseteq \sigma_{k+2}\left(11\gamma_{[2^n-1]}^{n,k}\right)$. Take $r = 2^n-1$ in (7a): we obtain $\gamma_{[2^n-1]}^{n+2,k+2} = 11\gamma_{[2^n-1]}^{n,k}$, thus $\gamma_{[2^n]}^{n+2,k+2} \in \sigma_{k+2}\left(\gamma_{[2^n-1]}^{n+2,k+2}\right)$.

(ii) Now, assume $q = 2$, and set $r = 0$ in Eq. (7c). According to Lemma 2 we have $\gamma_{[2\cdot 2^n]}^{n+2,k+2} = 11\gamma_{[0]}^{n,k} \in 11\sigma_{k+1}\left(\rho_{[2^n-1]}^{n,k}\right) \subseteq \sigma_{k+2}\left(10\rho_{[2^n-1]}^{n,k}\right)$. By taking $r = 2^n-1$ in (7b), we obtain $\gamma_{[2\cdot 2^n-1)]}^{n+2,k+2} = 10\rho_{[2^n-1]}^{n,k}$, thus $\gamma_{[2\cdot 2^n]}^{n+2,k+2} \in \sigma_{k+2}\left(\gamma_{[2\cdot 2^n-1]}^{n+2,k+2}\right)$.

(iii) For $q = 3$, substitute in (i) $\gamma_{[3\cdot 2^n]}^{n+2,k+2}$ to $\gamma_{[2^n]}^{n+2,k+2}$, Eq. (7d) to Eq. (7b), (7c) to (7a), 10 to 01 and 00 to 11: similar arguments prove that $\gamma_{[3\cdot 2^n]}^{n+2,k+2} \in \sigma_{k+2}\left(\gamma_{[3\cdot 2^n-1]}^{n+2,k+2}\right)$.

Condition (11). Take $r = 0$ in (7a). According to Lemma 2, we have $\gamma_{[0]}^{n+2,k+2} = 00\gamma_{[0]}^{n,k} \in 00\sigma_{k+1}\left(\rho_{[2^n-1]}^{n,k}\right) \subseteq \sigma_{k+2}\left(01\rho_{[2^n-1]}^{n,k}\right)$. By taking $r = 2^n - 1$ in (7d) we obtain $\gamma_{[2^{n+2}-1]}^{n,k} = 01\rho_{[2^n-1]}^{n,k}$, thus $\gamma_{[0]}^{n+2,k+2} \in \sigma_{k+2}\left(\gamma_{[2^{n+2}-1]}^{n,k}\right)$.

According to the structures of Eqs. (8a)–(8d), for proving the conditions (12)–(13), the method consists in substituting the word $\rho_{[r]}^{n+2,k+2}$ to $\gamma_{[r]}^{n+2,k+2}$, the 4-uple $(10, 11, 01, 00)$ to $(00, 01, 11, 10)$, and Eq. (8a) $\big($resp., (8b), (8c), (8d)$\big)$ to Eq. (7a) $\big($resp., (7b), (7c), (7d)$\big)$. $\square$

5   The Case Where We Have $|A| = 2$ and k Even

Beforehand, we recall some classical algebraic interpretation of the substitution σ_k in the framework of the binary alphabet $A = \{0, 1\}$. Denote by $\oplus$ the addition in the group $\mathbb{Z}/2\mathbb{Z}$ with identity 0. Given a positive integer n, and $w, w' \in A^n$, define $w \oplus w'$ as the unique word of A^n such that, for each $i \in [1, n]$: $(w \oplus w')_i = w_i \oplus w'_i$. With this notation the sets A^n and $(\mathbb{Z}/2\mathbb{Z})^n$ are in one-to-one correspondence. Moreover we have $w' \in \sigma_k(w)$ if, and only if, some word $u \in A^n$ exists such that $|u|_1 = k$ and $w = w' \oplus u$, therefore if k is even we have $|w|_1 = |w'|_1 \bmod 2$. Consequently, given a σ_k-Gray cycle $(\alpha_{[i]})_{0 \le i \le m}$, for each $i \in [0, m]$ we have $|\alpha_{[i]}|_1 = |\alpha_{[0]}|_1 \bmod 2$. As a corollary, setting $\mathrm{Even}_1^n = \{w \in A^* : |w|_1 = 0 \bmod 2\}$ and $\mathrm{Odd}_1^n = \{w \in A^* : |w|_1 = 1 \bmod 2\}$:

Lemma 3. *With the condition of Sect. 5, given a σ_k-Gray cycle α over X, either we have $X \subseteq \mathrm{Even}_1^n$, or we have $X \subseteq \mathrm{Odd}_1^n$.*

Since $k - 1$ is an odd integer, according to Proposition 2, the sequence $\gamma^{n-1,k-1}$ is a σ_{k-1}-Gray cycle over A^{n-1}. We set:

$$(\forall i \in [0, 2^{n-1} - 1]) \quad \gamma_{[i]}^{n,k} = \theta^i(0)\gamma_{[i]}^{n-1,k-1} \quad \text{and} \quad \underline{\gamma}_{[i]}^{n,k} = \theta^i(1)\gamma_{[i]}^{n-1,k-1} \quad (15)$$

For instance, we have $\gamma_{[0]}^{6,4} = 000000$, $\underline{\gamma}_{[0]}^{6,4} = 100000$, $\gamma_{[1]}^{6,4} = 111100$.

Proposition 3. $\gamma^{n,k}$ *(resp., $\underline{\gamma}^{n,k}$) is a σ_k-Gray cycle over* Even_1^n *(resp., Odd_1^n).*

Proof. (i) According to Eq. (15), since $\gamma^{n-1,k-1}$ satisfies (G3), both the sequences $\gamma^{n,k}$ and $\underline{\gamma}^{n,k}$ also satisfy (G3).

(ii) By Lemma 3, we have $\bigcup_{0 \le i \le 2^n - 1}\{\gamma^{n,k}\} \subseteq \text{Even}_1^n$ and $\bigcup_{0 \le i \le 2^n - 1}\{\underline{\gamma}^{n,k}\} \subseteq \text{Odd}_1^n$. In addition, according to (15), we have $|\gamma^{n,k}| = |\underline{\gamma}^{n,k}| = |\gamma^{n-1,k-1}| = 2^{n-1}$. This implies $\bigcup_{0 \le i \le 2^n - 1}\{\gamma^{n,k}\} = \text{Even}_1^n$ and $\bigcup_{0 \le i \le 2^n - 1}\{\underline{\gamma}^{n,k}\} = \text{Odd}_1^n$ that is, $\gamma^{n,k}$ and $\underline{\gamma}^{n,k}$ satisfy (G1).

(iii) Let $i \in [1, 2^{n-1} - 1]$. Since $\gamma^{n-1,k-1}$ satisfies (G2), we have $\gamma_{[i]}^{n-1,k-1} \in \sigma_{k-1}\left(\gamma_{[i-1]}^{n-1,k-1}\right)$. According to (15), the initial characters of $\gamma_{[i]}^{n,k}$ and $\gamma_{[i-1]}^{n,k}$ (resp., $\underline{\gamma}_{[i]}^{n,k}$ and $\underline{\gamma}_{[i-1]}^{n,k}$) are different, hence we have $\gamma_{[i]}^{n,k} \in \sigma_k\left(\gamma_{[i-1]}^{n,k}\right)$ and $\underline{\gamma}_{[i]}^{n,k} \in \sigma_k\left(\underline{\gamma}_{[i-1]}^{n,k}\right)$. In addition, once more according to (15) it follows from $\gamma_{[0]}^{n-1,k-1} \in \sigma_{k-1}\left(\gamma_{[2^{n-1}-1]}^{n-1,k-1}\right)$ that $\gamma_{[0]}^{n,k} = 0\gamma_{[0]}^{n-1,k-1} \in \sigma_k\left(1\gamma_{[2^{n-1}-1]}^{n-1,k-1}\right) \subseteq \sigma_k\left(\gamma_{[2^{n-1}-1]}^{n,k}\right)$, hence $\gamma^{n,k}$ satisfies (G2). Similarly, $\underline{\gamma}_{[0]}^{n-1,k-1} \in \sigma_{k-1}\left(\underline{\gamma}_{[2^{n-1}-1]}^{n-1,k-1}\right)$ implies $\underline{\gamma}_{[0]}^{n,k} \in \sigma_k\left(\underline{\gamma}_{[2^{n-1}-1]}^{n,k}\right)$, hence $\underline{\gamma}^{n,k}$ satisfies (G2). $\qquad \square$

The following statement provides the description of the complexity $\lambda_{A,\tau}$:

Theorem 1. *Given a finite alphabet A and $n \ge k \ge 1$, exactly one of the four following properties holds:*

(i) $|A| \ge 3$, $n \ge k$, and $\lambda_{A,\sigma_k}(n) = |A|^n$;
(ii) $|A| = 2$, $n = k$, and $\lambda_{A,\sigma_k}(n) = 2$;
(iii) $|A| = 2$, $n \ge k + 1$, k is odd and $\lambda_{A,\sigma_k}(n) = 2^n$;
(iv) $|A| = 2$, $n \ge k + 1$, and k is even, and $\lambda_{A,\sigma_k}(n) = 2^{n-1}$.

In addition, in each case some σ_k-Gray cycle of maximum length can be explicitly computed.

Proof. Recall that if some σ_k-Gray cycle exists over $X \subseteq A^{\le n}$, necessarily X is a uniform set that is, $X \subseteq A^m$ holds for some $m \le n$; hence, in any case we have $\lambda_{A,\sigma_k}(n) \le |A|^n$. According to Proposition 1, if we have $|A| \ge 3$ and $n \ge k$, a σ_k-Gray cycle exists over A^n, hence Property (i) holds. Similarly, (iii) comes from Proposition 2. As indicated in the preamble of Sect. 3, Property (ii) trivially holds. Finally, according to Lemma 3, given a binary alphabet A, if k is even we have $\lambda_{A,\sigma_k}(n) \le 2^{n-1}$, hence (iv) comes from Proposition 3. $\qquad \square$

Further Development. Since our Gray cycles were constructed by applying recursive processes, it is legitimate to ask whether some method could exist for computing $\gamma_{[i]}^{n,k}$ by directly starting with $\gamma_{[i-1]}^{n,k}$, as in the case of the classical reflected Gray cycles. In view of some of our more recent studies, we strongly believe that such algorithms can actually be devised: we hope to develop this point in a further paper.

On the other hand, it could be of interest to study the behaviour of $\Lambda_{A,\tau}$ in the framework of other word binary relations τ, even in restraining to special families of sets $X \subseteq A^*$, such as variable-length codes.

References

1. Bartucci, E., Lungo, A.D., Pergola, E., Pinzani, R.: ECO: a methodology for the enumeration of combinatorial objects. J. Differ. Equ. Appl. **5**, 435–490 (2009). https://doi.org/10.1080/10236199908808200
2. Bernini, A., Bilotta, S., Pinzani, R., Sabri, A., Vajnovszki, V.: Prefix partitioned gray codes for particular cross-bifix-free sets. Cryptogr. Commun. **6**(4), 359–369 (2014). https://doi.org/10.1007/s12095-014-0105-6
3. Chung, F., Diaconis, P., Graham, R.: Universal cycles for combinatorial structures. Discrete Math. **110**, 43–59 (1992). https://doi.org/10.1016/0012-365X(92)90699-G
4. Cohn, M.: Affine m-ary gray codes. Inf. Control **6**(1), 70–78 (1963). https://doi.org/10.1016/S0019-9958(63)90119-0
5. Cohn, P.: Universal Algebra (Mathematics and Its Applications), vol. 6. Springer, Dordrecht (1981). https://doi.org/10.1007/978-94-009-8399-1
6. Eades, P., McKay, B.: An algorithm for generating subsets of fixed size with a strong minimal change property. Inf. Proc. Lett. **19**, 131–133 (1984). https://doi.org/10.1016/0020-0190(84)90091-7
7. Ehrlich, G.: Loopless algorithms for generating permutations, combinations, and other combinatorial configurations. J. ACM **20**, 500–513 (1973). https://doi.org/10.1145/321765.321781
8. Er, M.C.: On generating the N-ary reflected gray codes. IEEE Trans. Comput. **C-33**(8), 739–741 (1984). https://doi.org/10.1109/TC.1984.5009360
9. Fredricksen, H., Maiorana, J.: Necklaces of beads in k colors and k-ary de Bruijn sequences. Discrete Math. **23**(3), 207–210 (1978). https://doi.org/10.1016/0012-365X(78)90002-X
10. Gilbert, E.: Gray codes and paths on the N-cube. The Bell Syst. Tech. J. **37**, 815–826 (1958). https://doi.org/10.1002/j.1538-7305.1958.tb03887.x
11. Joichi, J.T., White, D.E., Williamson, S.G.: Combinatorial Gray codes. SIAM J. Comput. **9**, 130–141 (1980). https://doi.org/10.1137/0209013
12. Jürgensen, H., Konstantinidis, S.: Codes. In: Handbook of Formal Languages, vol. 1, chap. 8, pp. 511–607. Springer Verlag, Berlin (1997). https://doi.org/10.1007/978-3-642-59136-5_8
13. Kaye, R.: A gray code for set partitions. Inform. Process. Lett. **5**(6), 171–173 (1976). https://doi.org/10.1016/0020-0190(76)90014-4
14. Knuth, D.: The Art of Computer programming. In: Fascicle 2: Generating All Tuples and Permutations, vol. 4. Addison Wesley, Boston (2005). ISBN-10: 0-201-85393-0, ISBN 13: 978-0-201-85393-3

15. Lehmer, D.H.: The machine tools of combinatorics. In: Beckenbach, E. (ed.) Applied Combinatorial Mathematics. pp. 5–31. John Wiley and Sons, New York (1964). ISBN 10: 0-471-06125-5, ISBN 13: 978-0-471-06125-0

16. Ludman, J.: Gray code generation for MPSK signals. IEEE Trans. Commun. **COM-29**, 1519–1522 (1981). https://doi.org/10.1109/TCOM.1981.1094886

17. Néraud, J.: Variable-length codes independent or closed with respect to edit relations. Inf. Comput. arXiv:2104.14185 (2021, to appear). https://doi.org/10.1016/j.ic.2021.104747

18. Richard, D.: Data compression and gray-code sorting. Inform. Process. Lett. **22**, 201–205 (1986). https://doi.org/10.1016/0020-0190(86)90029-3

19. Ruskey, F., Savage, C., Wang, T.M.Y.: Generating necklaces. J. Algorithms **13**, 414–430 (1992). https://doi.org/10.1016/0196-6774(92)90047-G

20. Savage, C.: A survey of combinatorial Gray codes. SIAM Rev. **39**, 605–629 (1997). https://doi.org/10.1137/S0036144595295272

Automata Equipped with Auxiliary Data Structures and Regular Realizability Problems

Alexander Rubtsov$^{(\boxtimes)}$ [ID] and Mikhail Vyalyi [ID]

National Research University Higher School of Economics, Moscow, Russia

Abstract. We consider general computational models: one-way and two-way finite automata, and logarithmic space Turing machines, all equipped with an auxiliary data structure (ADS). The definition of an ADS is based on the language of protocols of work with the ADS. We describe the connection of automata-based models with "Balloon automata" that are another general formalization of automata equipped with an ADS presented by Hopcroft and Ullman in 1967. This definition establishes the connection between the non-emptiness problem for one-way automata with ADS, languages recognizable by nondeterministic log-space Turing machines equipped with the same ADS, and a regular realizability problem (NRR) for the language of ADS' protocols. The NRR problem is to verify whether the regular language on the input has a non-empty intersection with the language of protocols. The computational complexity of these problems (and languages) is the same up to log-space reductions.

1 Introduction

Many computational models are derived from (one-way) finite automata (FAs) via equipping them with an auxiliary data structure (ADS). The best-known model of this kind is pushdown automata (PDAs), the deterministic version of which is widely used in compilers. Other examples are k-counter automata, (k, r)-reversal-bounded counter automata (equipped with k counters each of which can switch between increasing and decreasing modes at most r times), stack automata, nested stack automata, bag automata [3], set automata (SAs) [5] and their another variant [6]; more examples can be found in [4].

During the investigation of balloon automata (BAs) [4], Hopcroft and Ullman connected the decidability of the membership and the emptiness problems for one-way and two-way models; we denote them as $M\text{-}xyBA$ and $E\text{-}xyBA$ respectively, where $x = 1$ denotes one-way and $x = 2$ denotes two-way models, and $y \in \{D, N\}$ stands for determinism or nondeterminism respectively. Equation (1) summarizes results on decidability questions from [4], where $\leqslant_T$ is a *Turing-reduction* and $\{A, B\}$ means that $A \leqslant_T B$ and $B \leqslant_T A$.

$$\{\text{M-1DBA, M-2DBA}\} \leqslant_T \{\text{E-1DBA, E-1NBA, M-1NBA, M-2NBA}\} \leqslant_T$$
$$\leqslant_T \text{E-2DBA} \leqslant_T \text{E-2NBA} \tag{1}$$

Supported by Russian Science Foundation grant 20–11–20203.

We remark that the relation E-1NBA $\leqslant_T$ E-1DBA was proved for the case of at least a two-letter input alphabet.

While a lot of models can be described as BA, it is hard to invent such a model with good computational properties. One of the reasons is that the equipment of finite automata with a complex data structure (or with several simple data structures) often leads to a universal computational model. For example, FAs equipped with two pushdown stores are equivalent to Turing machines (TMs), as well as FAs equipped with two non-restricted counters.

In this paper, we investigate the computational power of FAs equipped with an ADS. We describe the model using the language of correct protocols of work with the ADS. We provide a general approach to analyze the complexity of the emptiness problem and prove that languages recognizable by nondeterministic logarithmic space TMs (log-TMs, see the definition in [12]) equipped with the same ADS are of the same complexity that the non-emptiness problem for FAs with the ADS. Our key tool is a regular realizability problem (Definition 1).

1.1 Our Contribution

BAs were initially defined as automata with access to additional storage of unspecified structure—*the balloon*. A rather general axioms were imposed for the balloon and the interaction of the balloon and the automaton (see Definition 4 below). In this paper, we propose another definition based on a language of the ADS' protocols that we denote as P, so we refer to the ADS as B_P. We prove that languages recognizable by $1NB_PA$ form not just a rational cone as in the case of 1NBA [4], but a principal rational cone generated by P (we provide the definition in Sect. 2.2).

This reformulation guarantees good structural properties, some of them follow from the connection with BA (Sect. 4), and provides the relation between E-$1NB_PA$ and the *nondeterministic regular realizability problem*.

Definition 1. *Fix a formal language F called a* filter, *the parameter of* regular realizability problems *DRR(F) and NRR(F) that are the problems of verifying non-emptiness of the intersection of the filter F with a regular language $L(\mathcal{A})$ described via the DFA or NFA $\mathcal{A}$ respectively. Formally,*

$$\mathrm{NRR}(F) = \{\mathcal{A} \mid \mathcal{A} \text{ is an NFA and } L(\mathcal{A}) \cap F \neq \varnothing\}.$$

$$\mathrm{DRR}(F) = \{\mathcal{A} \mid \mathcal{A} \text{ is a DFA and } L(\mathcal{A}) \cap F \neq \varnothing\}.$$

RR problems have independently been studied under the name regular intersection emptiness problems [16,17].

In this paper we focus on the computational complexity, so we use the weakest reduction suitable for our needs, the deterministic log-space reduction that we denote as $\leqslant_{\log}$. If $A \leqslant_{\log} B$ and $B \leqslant_{\log} A$ we write $A \sim_{\log} B$ and say that A and B are *log-space equivalent*. Note that in our constructions, emptiness and membership problems are the sets of instances' descriptions with positive answers, i.e., E-$xyB_PA = \{\langle M \rangle \mid L(M) = \varnothing\}$, M-$xyB_PA = \{\langle M, w \rangle \mid w \in L(M)\}$, where M

is a $xy\mathsf{B_PA}$ and $\langle x \rangle$ is the description of x. So, $\overline{\mathrm{E}\text{-}xy\mathsf{B_PA}} = \{\langle M \rangle \mid L(M) \neq \varnothing\}$. We prove that $\overline{\mathrm{E}\text{-}1\mathsf{NB_PA}} \sim_{\log} \mathrm{NRR(P)}$.

We equip with ADS not only FAs but also log-TMs. We denote deterministic and nondeterministic log-TMs equipped with an ADS $\mathsf{B_P}$ as $\mathsf{DB_P}$log-TM and $\mathsf{NB_P}$log-TM respectively. We prove that

$$\mathrm{NRR(P)} \sim_{\log} \mathscr{L}(\mathsf{NB_P}\text{log-TM}) = \{L \mid L \leqslant_{\log} \mathrm{NRR(P)}\}, \tag{2}$$

hereinafter $\mathscr{L}(\text{model})$ is the class of languages recognizable by the model. If P is a problem (formal language) and S is a set of problems (class of formal languages) the reductions mean as follows. $P \leqslant S$ means that $\exists P' \in S : P \leqslant P'$ and $S \leqslant P$ means that $\forall P' \in S : P' \leqslant P$; $S \sim P$ means $(P \leqslant S) \wedge (S \leqslant P)$.

It is easy to verify that in the original proofs in [4], Turing reductions in (1) can be replaced by the log-space reductions provided we replace the emptiness problems with non-emptiness ones. So, we obtain

$$\{\text{M-1DB_PA}, \text{M-2DB_PA}\} \leqslant_{\log} \{\overline{\text{E-1DB_PA}}, \overline{\text{E-1NB_PA}}, \text{M-1NB_PA}, \text{M-2NB_PA},$$
$$\mathrm{NRR(P)}, \mathscr{L}(\mathsf{NB_P}\text{log-TM})\} \leqslant_{\log} \overline{\text{E-2DBA}} \leqslant_{\log} \overline{\text{E-2NBA}} \leqslant_{\log} \overline{\text{E-NB_Plog-TM}} \tag{3}$$

These results combined with known facts imply assertions (4–7), where S is the set data structure as in SA, $\mathrm{S_1}$ is the set data structure that supports the insertion of at most one word, that cannot be removed further but can be tested if a query-word in the set. In $\mathrm{S_{1,|\Gamma|=1}}$ the word in the set is over an unary alphabet, **PSPACE-c** and **NP-c** are subclasses of complete languages.

$\mathbf{P} = \mathscr{L}(\mathrm{NPDlog\text{-}TM})$, where PD is Pushdown store $\hspace{2cm}$ (4)

$\mathbf{PSPACE} \supseteq \mathscr{L}(\mathrm{NSlog\text{-}TM}), \exists L \in \mathscr{L}(\mathrm{NSlog\text{-}TM}) : L \in \mathbf{PSPACE\text{-}c}$ $\hspace{0.5cm}$ (5)

$\mathbf{PSPACE} \supseteq \mathscr{L}(\mathrm{NS_1log\text{-}TM}), \exists L \in \mathscr{L}(\mathrm{NS_1log\text{-}TM}) : L \in \mathbf{PSPACE\text{-}c}$ $\hspace{0.3cm}$ (6)

$\mathbf{NP} \supseteq \mathscr{L}(\mathrm{NS_{1,|\Gamma|=1}log\text{-}TM}), \exists L \in \mathscr{L}(\mathrm{NS_{1,|\Gamma|=1}log\text{-}TM}) : L \in \mathbf{NP\text{-}c}$ $\hspace{0.3cm}$ (7)

Assertion (4) is a well-known fact. Our technique here just shows a new connection: (4) directly follows from the fact that the emptiness problem for PDA is **P**-complete. Assertions (5–7) are new results to the best of our knowledge, we prove them in Sect. 6. Assertions (6–7) lead to (3) for the corresponding classes of automata. For (5), we have already obtained the result in [8] in the same way and present in this paper the generalized technique.

2 Definitions

2.1 Notation on Binary Relations

We associate with a binary relation $R \subseteq A \times B$ the corresponding mappings $A \to 2^B$ and $2^A \to 2^B$ that are denoted by the same letter R, so $R(a) = \{b : aRb\}$ and $R(S) = \cup_{a \in S} R(a)$. A relation R is the *composition* of the relations $P \subseteq A \times C$ and $Q \subseteq C \times B$ if $R = \{(a,b) \mid \exists c : aPc \wedge cQb\}$; we denote the composition as $Q \circ P$. In the case of a set $S \subseteq C$ we treat S as a binary relation $S \subseteq C \times \{0,1\}$ in the composition $S \circ P = S'$ that returns the set $S' \subseteq A$. We denote the reflexive and transitive closure of $R \subseteq A \times A$ by R^*; the symbol $*$ can also be placed above the relation, e.g., $\overset{*}{\vdash}$. We denote by $R^{-1} \subseteq B \times A$ the inverse relation, i.e., $aRb \iff bR^{-1}a$.

2.2   Rational Transductions

Our technique is based on the connection of NRR problems with rational cones. We recall the definitions borrowing them from the book [2]. A *finite state transducer* (FST) is a nondeterministic finite automaton with an output tape. Let T be an FST; we also denote by T the corresponding relation, i.e., uTv iff there exists a run of T on the input u from the initial state to a final state such that at the end of the run the word v is written on the output tape. The *rational dominance* relation $A \leqslant_{\mathrm{rat}} B$ holds if there exists an FST T such that $A = T(B)$, here A and B are languages. The relations computable by FSTs are known as *rational relations*. The following lemmata are algorithmic versions of well-known facts (see [2], Chapter III), the first one is the algorithmic version of the Elgot-Mezei theorem. The log-space algorithms follow from straight-forward constructions.

Lemma 2. *For FSTs T_1 and T_2 such that $T_1 \subseteq \Sigma^* \times \Delta^*$, $T_2 \subseteq \Delta^* \times \Gamma^*$, and FA $\mathcal{A}$ such that $L(\mathcal{A}) \subseteq \Delta^*$, there exists an FST T such that $T = T_2 \circ T_1 \subseteq \Sigma^* \times \Gamma^*$, and NFA $\mathcal{B}$ recognizing the language $T_1^{-1}L(\mathcal{A})$. So, the relation $\leqslant_{\mathrm{rat}}$ is transitive. Moreover, T and $\mathcal{B}$ are constructible in logarithmic space. We denote FST T and NFA $\mathcal{B}$ as $T_2 \circ T_1$ and $\mathcal{A} \circ T_1$ respectively.*

Lemma 3. *For each FST T there exists an FST T^{-1} that computes the inverse relation of the relation T. FST T^{-1} is log-space constructible by FST T.*

A *rational cone* is a family of languages $\mathbf{C}$ that is closed under the rational dominance relation: $A \leqslant_{\mathrm{rat}} B$ and $B \in \mathbf{C}$ imply $A \in \mathbf{C}$. If there exists a language $F \in \mathbf{C}$ such that $L \leqslant_{\mathrm{rat}} F$ for any $L \in \mathbf{C}$, then $\mathbf{C}$ is a *principal* rational cone generated by F; we denote it as $\mathbf{C} = \mathcal{T}(F)$.

Rational transductions for context-free languages were thoroughly investigated in the 1970s, particularly by the French school. The main results of this research were published in Berstel's book [2]. As described in [2], it follows from the Chomsky-Schützenberger theorem that CFL is a principal rational cone: $\mathsf{CFL} = \mathcal{T}(D_2)$, where D_2 is the Dyck language on two types of brackets.

2.3   Computational Models

Firstly, we define BA. We provide the definition that is equivalent to the original definition from [4] but has technical differences, for the sake of convenience. Then we provide the definitions of other models: the refined definition of Balloon automata in terms of protocols and computational models based on log-TM that are connected with NRR-problem as well as with $1\mathrm{NB_PA}$.

As it said, the balloon is a storage medium of unspecified structure. Thus its states are represented by (a subset of) positive integers. A BA can get limited information about the state of the balloon (the balloon information function in the definition below) and can modify the states of the balloon (the balloon control function). Here we need 1BAs only. So we give the definition for them. The definitions for 2BAs are similar, they are provided in [4].

Definition 4. *A 1-way balloon automaton* (1BA) *is defined by a tuple*

$$\langle S, \Sigma_{\triangleright\triangleleft}, B_S, B_I, \mathsf{get}_{B_I}, \mathsf{upd}_{B_S}, F, s_0, \delta \rangle$$

- *S is the finite set of automaton states.*
- *$\Sigma_{\triangleright\triangleleft} = \Sigma \cup \{\triangleright, \triangleleft\}$, where Σ is the finite input alphabet and $\triangleright, \triangleleft$ are the endmarkers. The input has the form $\triangleright w \triangleleft$, $w \in \Sigma$.*
- *$B_S \subseteq \mathbb{Z}_{>0}$ is the set of the balloon states.*
- *B_I is the finite set of the balloon information states.*
- *$\mathsf{get}_{B_I} : B_S \to B_I$ is a total computable function (balloon information function).*
- *upd_{B_S} is a partially computable function from $S \times B_S$ to B_S (balloon control function).*
- *$F \subsetneq S$ is the set of the final states.*
- *$s_0 \in S \setminus F$ is the initial state.*
- *δ is the transition relation (a partial function for deterministic automata) defined as $\delta \subseteq (S \times \Sigma_{\triangleright\triangleleft,\varepsilon} \times B_I) \times S$.*

Definition 5. *A configuration of a 1BA is a triple $(q, u, i) \in S \times \Sigma_{\triangleright\triangleleft}^* \times B_S$, where u is the unprocessed part of the input w so u is either $\triangleright w \triangleleft$ or a suffix of $w \triangleleft$. The* initial configuration *of 1BA is $(s_0, \triangleright w \triangleleft, 1)$, a* move *of 1BA is defined by the relation $\vdash$ on configurations as follows: $(q, \sigma u, i) \vdash (p, u, j)$, where $\sigma \in \Sigma_{\triangleright\triangleleft,\varepsilon}$ if $j = \mathsf{upd}_{B_S}(p, i)$, $p \in \delta(q, \sigma, \mathsf{get}_{B_I}(i))$. A 1BA accepts the input w if there exists a sequence of moves (computational path) such that after processing of $\triangleright w \triangleleft$ the final state is reached, i.e., $(s_0, \triangleright w \triangleleft, 1) \vdash^* (q_f, \varepsilon, i)$, where $q_f \in F$, $i \in B_S$.*

It is not easy to define classes of balloon automata (like PDAs or SAs) since one needs to define valid families of functions get_{B_I} and upd_{B_S}. One can see an example of PDAs definition in terms of BA in [4]. We suggest another approach for the definition of BA classes in Sect. 4. The approach simplifies the definitions since it is only needed to define a language of correct protocols to define an ADS.

We define a protocol as a sequence of triples $p_i = u_i q_i r_i$ of the query-word u_i, the query q_i and the response r_i on the query. Numerous extra conditions are listed in the following formal definition.

Definition 6. *Let $\Gamma_{\mathsf{write}}, \Gamma_{\mathsf{query}}, \Gamma_{\mathsf{resp}}$ be finite disjoint alphabets such that $\Gamma_{\mathsf{query}} \neq \varnothing, \Gamma_{\mathsf{resp}} \neq \varnothing$. Let $\mathsf{valid} \subseteq \Gamma_{\mathsf{query}} \times \Gamma_{\mathsf{resp}}$ be a relation that provides the correspondence between queries and possible responses. A protocol is a word p such that $p = p_1 \cdots p_n$, where $n \geqslant 0$, $p_i = u_i q_i r_i$, $u_i \in \Gamma_{\mathsf{write}}^*$, $q_i \in \Gamma_{\mathsf{query}}$, $r_i \in \Gamma_{\mathsf{resp}}$, and $r_i \in \mathsf{valid}(q_i)$. We call a word p_i a query block. We say that a language $\mathsf{P} \subseteq (\Gamma_{\mathsf{write}}^* \Gamma_{\mathsf{query}} \Gamma_{\mathsf{resp}})^*$ is a language of correct protocols if the axioms (i–v) hold:*

(i) $\varepsilon \in \mathsf{P}$

(ii) $\forall p \in \mathsf{P} : p$ is a protocol

(iii) $\forall p \in \mathsf{P}$: if $p = p_1 p_2$ and p_1 is a protocol, then $p_1 \in \mathsf{P}$

(iv) $\forall p \in \mathsf{P} \; \forall u \in \Gamma_{\text{write}}^* \; \forall q \in \Gamma_{\text{query}} \; \exists r \in \Gamma_{\text{resp}} : puqr \in \mathsf{P}$

(v) $\forall puqr \in \mathsf{P}$: if $p' \in \mathsf{P}$ and $p' = puqr's$, then $r' = r$

(vi) $\exists q \in \Gamma_{\text{query}}, r \in \Gamma_{\text{resp}} \; \forall p_1, p_2 \in \mathsf{P} : p_1 q r p_2 \subset \mathsf{P}$.

Axiom (vi) does not hold in the general case, e.g., for SAs and counter automata without zero tests. It is needed to describe the connection of automata with an ADS with BAs in Sect. 4.

A language of correct protocols P generates the corresponding class of languages, the principal rational cone $\mathcal{T}(\mathsf{P})$. All examples of BAs languages classes in [4] can be presented as $\mathcal{T}(\mathsf{P})$. We provide here only two examples.

Example 7. It is well-known [2] that $\mathsf{CFL} = \mathcal{T}(D_2)$, where D_2 is the Dyck language with two types of parenthesis. It is also well-known that balanced parenthesis is a protocol of the stack. We transform the language D_2 into a language of protocols D_2-PROT as follows.

We define the alphabets $\Gamma_{\text{write}} = \varnothing$, $\Gamma_{\text{query}} - \{\text{push}_(, \text{push}_[, \text{pop}\}$, $\Gamma_{\text{resp}} = \{(,),[,]\}$, valid $= \{(\text{push}_[, [), (\text{push}_(, (), (\text{pop},]), (\text{pop},))\}$. To define correct protocols we use an FST T that erases all symbols from Γ_{query} of the input. So, $D_2\text{-PROT} = \{p \mid T(p) \in D_2\}$.

By the definition $D_2 \leqslant_{\text{rat}} D_2$-PROT, so we have that $\mathcal{T}(D_2) \subseteq \mathcal{T}(D_2\text{-PROT})$. It is also easy to show that D_2-PROT $\leqslant_{\text{rat}} D_2$, so $\mathcal{T}(D_2\text{-PROT}) = \mathcal{T}(D_2) = \mathsf{CFL}$.

Note that we set here $\Gamma_{\text{write}} = \varnothing$ for the sake of simplicity. One can use another variant: $\Gamma_{\text{write}} = \{(, [\}, \Gamma_{\text{query}} = \{\text{multipush}, \text{pop}\}, \Gamma_{\text{resp}} = \{\text{pushed},),]\}$. □

The following example is a starting point for the generalization presented in this paper.

Example 8. The data structure Set consists of the set $\mathbb{S}$ which is initially empty. Set supports the following operations: $\text{in}(x) : \mathbb{S} \to \mathbb{S} \cup \{x\}$, $\text{out}(x) : \mathbb{S} \to \mathbb{S} \setminus \{x\}$, $\text{test}(x) : x \overset{?}{\in} \mathbb{S}$. We define the protocol language SA-PROT consistently with [7,8], so the elements of alphabets below are individual symbols while they are words in [7,8]. $\Gamma_{\text{write}} = \{a, b\}$, $\Gamma_{\text{query}} = \{\#\text{in}, \#\text{out}, \#\text{test}\}$, $\Gamma_{\text{resp}} = \{\#, +\#, -\#\}$, valid $= \{(\#\text{in}, \#), (\#\text{out}, \#), (\#\text{test}, +\#), (\#\text{test}, -\#)\}$.

It was proved in [7] that $\mathscr{L}(1\text{NSA}) = \mathcal{T}(\text{SA-PROT})$. □

Definition 9. *Fix a language of correct protocols* P. *An* automaton equipped with auxiliary data structure B_P *(defined by* P*) is defined by a tuple*

$$\langle S, \Sigma_{\triangleright\triangleleft}, \Gamma_{\text{write}}, \Gamma_{\text{query}}, \Gamma_{\text{resp}}, F, s_0, \delta \rangle, \quad \text{where}$$

- $S, \Sigma_{\triangleright\triangleleft}, F, s_0$ *are the same as in Definition 4, so as* $\Sigma_{\triangleright\triangleleft,\varepsilon}$.
- $S = S_{\text{write}} \cup S_{\text{query}}, S_{\text{write}} \cap S_{\text{query}} = \varnothing$.
- $\mathsf{P} \subseteq (\Gamma_{\text{write}}^* \Gamma_{\text{query}} \Gamma_{\text{resp}})^*$.
- δ *is the transition relation defined as*

$$\delta \subseteq ([S_{\mathsf{write}} \times \Sigma_{\triangleright\triangleleft,\varepsilon}] \times [\Gamma_{\mathsf{write}}^* \times S]) \cup (S_{\mathsf{query}} \times \Gamma_{\mathsf{query}} \times \Gamma_{\mathsf{resp}} \times S_{\mathsf{write}}).$$

The automaton has a one-way write-only query tape. During the processing of the input, it writes query-words $u_i \in \Gamma_{\mathsf{write}}^*$ on the query tape, performs queries q_i, and receives responses r_i such that $u_1\mathsf{q}_1\mathsf{r}_1 \cdots u_n\mathsf{q}_n\mathsf{r}_n \in \mathsf{P}$. After each query, the query tape is erased.

A configuration *of an ADS-automaton is a tuple*

$$(s, v, u, p) \in S \times \Sigma_{\triangleright\triangleleft}^* \times \Gamma_{\mathsf{write}}^* \times (\Gamma_{\mathsf{write}}^* \Gamma_{\mathsf{query}} \Gamma_{\mathsf{resp}})^*,$$

where v is the unprocessed part of the input w, i.e., v is the suffix of $\triangleright w \triangleleft$, u is the content of the work tape, and p is the protocol of the automaton operating with the data structure. A move of an automaton is defined via the relation $\vdash$ on configurations which is defined as follows:

$$(s, av, u, p) \vdash (s', v, ux, p) \qquad if \ s \in S_{\mathsf{write}}, \ (s, a, x, s') \in \delta \tag{8}$$

$$(s, v, u, p) \vdash (s', v, \varepsilon, pu\mathsf{qr}) \qquad if \ s \in S_{\mathsf{query}}, \ (s, \mathsf{q}, \mathsf{r}, s') \in \delta, \ pu\mathsf{qr} \in \mathsf{P} \tag{9}$$

A configuration is initial *if it has the form $(s_0, \triangleright w \triangleleft, \varepsilon, \varepsilon)$, a configuration is* accepting *if it has the form $(s_f, \varepsilon, \varepsilon, p)$, where $s_f \in F, p \in \mathsf{P}$. A word w is* accepted *by an automaton with ADS if $(s_0, \triangleright w \triangleleft, \varepsilon, \varepsilon) \overset{*}{\vdash} (s_f, \varepsilon, \varepsilon, p)$. An automaton is* deterministic *if for all configurations c, c_1, c_2 from $c \vdash c_1$ and $c \vdash c_2$ follows $c_1 = c_2$.*

For the next two models, we provide the definitions on the implementation level only.

Definition 10. *A DB$_{\mathsf{P}}$log-TM (NB$_{\mathsf{P}}$log-TM) is a deterministic (nondeterministic) log-TM M equipped with an ADS defined by the language of correct protocols P. I.e., M is equipped with an additional write-only one-way query tape that is used to write down a query word u_i and perform a query. After a query q_i is performed, the tape is erased and the finite state control of M receives the result r_i of the query q_i. The query results are consistent with P, i.e., $p_1 \cdots p_n \in \mathsf{P}$, $p_i = u_i\mathsf{q}_i\mathsf{r}_i$.*

A configuration of B$_{\mathsf{P}}$log-TM is a triple (c, u, p) where c is the configuration of log-TM-part, u is the word written on the query tape, and $p \in \mathsf{P}$ is the protocol that is the result of all the performed queries. A B$_{\mathsf{P}}$log-TM M accepts a word w if $(c_0(w), \varepsilon, \varepsilon) \overset{*}{\vdash} (c_f, \varepsilon, p)$, where $c_0(w)$ is the initial configuration of the log-TM-part of M, c_f is the accepting configuration of log-TM-part of M, and $p \in \mathsf{P}$, the relation $\vdash$ corresponds to the M's moves.

Definition 11. *Let F be an arbitrary formal language (filter). A DA$_F$log-TM (NA$_F$log-TM) is a deterministic (non-deterministic) log-space TM equipped with a read-only one-way infinite tape called advice tape. At the beginning of the computation, the advice tape contains a word $y\Lambda^\infty$, where $y \in F$ and Λ is a symbol that indicates empty cells.*

A configuration of an $A_F$log-TM M is a pair (c, u) where c is the configuration of the log-TM-part of M, u is the unprocessed part of y. M accepts a word x if there exists $y \in F$ such that $(c_0(x), y) \vdash^* (c_f, \varepsilon)$, where $c_0(x)$ is the initial configuration of the log-TM-part of M, c_f is the accepting configuration of the log-TM-part of M.

DA$_F$log-TMs appeared in [13] and its journal version [15] under the name "models of generalized nondeterminism (GNA)" and lead to the appearance of the DRR(Γ) problem. In this paper we repeat the steps of [13,15] to establish the connection between NA$_F$log-TM and NRR(F) problem in Sect. 5 to prove one of the main results of the paper (2).

3   Principle Rational Cones and the NRR-Problem

In this section, we provide the core of our technique. We prove that $\mathscr{L}(1\mathrm{NB_P}A)$ is a principle rational cone generated by the language of correct protocols P, i.e., $\mathscr{L}(1\mathrm{NB_P}A) = T(\mathsf{P})$; it is the first main result of the section. This fact yields structural results about the family $\mathscr{L}(1\mathrm{NB_P}A)$, as well as the results on the complexity of the emptiness problem. We focus in this section on the connection between the non-emptiness problem and the NRR(P) problem. We prove that these problems are equivalent under log-space reductions, it is the second main result of the section. It leads us to the main results of the paper in Sect. 5. We provide in this section structural results that naturally arise in the proofs. Other structural results are discussed in Sect. 4 since their relation to [4].

The results of this section directly generalize the results of [7, Section 3]; the proofs could be found in the preprint [10] and/or in the full journal version [11]. In most cases, to get a generalized result, one should substitute SA protocols (see Example 8) by general protocols as defined in Definition 6. So we omit the proofs of most of the lemmata, just indicating the corresponding proof in [10], and provide a few proofs of key lemmata and theorems to make the main constructions clear.

Lemma 12 (cf. Proposition 14 in [10]). *There exists a* 1NB$_P$A M_P *recognizing* P.

Lemma 13 (cf. Proposition 12(i) in [10]). *For each language of correct protocols* $\mathsf{P} \subseteq (\Gamma^*_{write}\Gamma_{query}\Gamma_{resp})^*$ *there exists a language of correct protocols* $\mathsf{P}_{\{a,b\}} \subseteq (\{a,b\}^*\Gamma_{query}\Gamma_{resp})^*$, *provided* $(\Gamma_{query} \cup \Gamma_{resp}) \cap \{a,b\} = \varnothing$ *such that* $\mathscr{L}(1\mathrm{NB_P}A) = \mathscr{L}(1\mathrm{NB}_{\mathsf{P}_{\{a,b\}}}A)$. *Moreover there exists an FST* T *such that* $T(\mathsf{P}) = \mathsf{P}_{\{a,b\}}$.

Lemma 14. *Let* T *be an FST with the input alphabet* Δ *and the output alphabet* Σ *and* M *be a* 1NB$_P$A *over the alphabet* Σ. *There exists a* 1NB$_P$A $M' = M \circ T$ *recognizing the language* $T^{-1}(L(M))$.

Lemma 14 follows immediately from Lemma 12 and the general construction of an inversed transducer (see [2]).

Lemma 15 (cf. Lemma 15 in [10]). *Let M be a* $1\mathrm{NB_P}A$*. There exists an FST* T_M *such that* $w \in L(M) \iff T_M(w) \cap \mathrm{P} \neq \varnothing$*. Moreover,* $p \in T_M(w)$ *iff M has a run on w such that* $(s_0, w, \varepsilon, \varepsilon) \vdash^* (s_f, \varepsilon, \varepsilon, p)$*.*

Definition 16. *An FST T_M from Lemma 15 called* extractor *(of protocols).*

Theorem 17 (cf. Theorem 16 in [10]). $\mathscr{L}(1\mathrm{NB_P}A) = T(\mathrm{P})$

Theorem 18. $\overline{\mathrm{E\text{-}1NB_P A}} \leqslant_{\log} \mathrm{NRR(P)} \leqslant_{\log} \overline{\mathrm{E\text{-}1NB_P A}}$

Proof. Let M be the input of the non-emptiness problem $\overline{\mathrm{E\text{-}1NB_P A}}$ and T_M be the corresponding extractor. By Lemma 15, $w \in L(M) \iff T_M(w) \cap \mathrm{P} \neq \varnothing$. So, $L(M) \neq \varnothing \iff T_M(\Sigma^*) \cap \mathrm{P} \neq \varnothing$. Construct an NFA $\mathcal{A}$ recognizing $T_M(\Sigma^*)$ by Lemma 2 in log space. So,

$$L(M) \neq \varnothing \iff L(\mathcal{A}) \cap \mathrm{P} \neq \varnothing \overset{\text{Def. 1}}{\iff} \mathcal{A} \in \mathrm{NRR(P)},$$

So we have proved $\overline{\mathrm{E\text{-}1NB_P A}} \leqslant_{\log} \mathrm{NRR(P)}$.

The reduction $\mathrm{NRR(P)} \leqslant_{\log} \overline{\mathrm{E\text{-}1NB_P A}}$ follows from Lemmata 12 and 14. We construct by $\mathcal{A}$ on the input of $\mathrm{NRR(P)}$ the automaton $M = M_\mathrm{P} \circ T$, where $xTy \iff (x = y) \wedge (x \in L(\mathcal{A}))$. $\square$

4   Connection with Balloon Automata

We provide the high-level description of classes $\mathscr{M}_B$ of BAs due to the space limitations. The definition in a more formal style could be found in [4].

Definition 19. *A class of BAs is defined by the classes of functions* $\mathscr{F}(\mathrm{get}_{B_i})$*,* $\mathscr{F}(\mathrm{upd}_{B_s})$ *that satisfy the following properties. (I.a)* $\mathscr{F}(\mathrm{get}_{B_i})$ *contains all constant functions, and (I.b)* $\mathscr{F}(\mathrm{upd}_{B_s})$ *contains functions $f(s, i)$ such that for each state s either $f(s,i) = i$ for all i or $f(s,i) = j$ for all i and some constant j. (II). If $\mathcal{A}, \mathcal{B} \in \mathscr{M}_B$, $f_\mathcal{A}, f_\mathcal{B} \in \mathscr{F}(\mathrm{upd}_{B_s})$, $g_\mathcal{A}, g_\mathcal{B} \in \mathscr{F}(\mathrm{upd}_{B_s})$ are the corresponding functions of $\mathcal{A}$ and $\mathcal{B}$, then $\mathscr{M}_B$ includes each automaton $\mathcal{C}$ such that $f_\mathcal{C}$ and $g_\mathcal{C}$ are the functions that are obtained from the functions of $\mathcal{A}$ and $\mathcal{B}$ via finite control, i.e., for each state $s \in S_\mathcal{C}$ $f_\mathcal{C}(s, i)$ equals to either $f_\mathcal{A}(s, i)$ or $f_\mathcal{B}(s, i)$ for all i, for each i, j if $g_\mathcal{C}(i) \neq g_\mathcal{C}(j)$ then either $g_\mathcal{A}(i) \neq g_\mathcal{A}(j)$ or $g_\mathcal{B}(i) \neq g_\mathcal{A}(j)$.*

The definition implies that $\mathscr{F}(\mathrm{upd}_{B_s})$ contains a function that resets any state i of the balloon to the initial state 1. This property does not hold for SAs, so there is no direct correspondence between classes of languages of BAs and automata with an ADS in the general case.

Theorem 20. *For each ADS* $\mathrm{B_P}$ *there exists a balloon B such that classes* $\mathscr{F}(\mathrm{get}_{B_i})$*,* $\mathscr{F}(\mathrm{upd}_{B_s})$ *satisfy properties (I.a) and (II). If P has the reset operation (vi), then (I.b) is also satisfied.*

Proof Idea. A state of the balloon is an integer that is the encoding of pairs of words (p, u), where p is the current protocol, i.e., the protocol of all previous operations before the upcoming move, and u is the word on the query-tape. So, the function $\mathsf{upd}_{\mathsf{B_S}}$ simulates write operations and queries, and the function $\mathsf{get}_{\mathsf{B_l}} : \mathbb{Z}_{>0} \to \varGamma_{\mathsf{resp}}$ returns responses.   □

So all the results from [4] that do not rely on (I.b) hold for B_{P}-automata. We are most interested in (1) and its complexity analogue (3). Many structural results from [4] follow from the fact that $\mathscr{L}(1\mathrm{NB_PA})$ is a principle cone (Theorem 17), namely, closure of $\mathscr{L}(1\mathrm{NB_PA})$ over union and rational transductions[1]. We shall also mention the closure over gsm inverse mappings proved in [4] for all $xy\mathrm{BA}$ that implies the same closure for all $xy\mathrm{B_PA}$.

Lemma 21. *If B_{P} contains the reset operation then $\mathscr{L}(1\mathrm{NB_PA})$ is closed over concatenation and iteration.*

The proof is omitted due to the space limitations.
The standard technique from [2] implies the following lemma.

Lemma 22. *If $\mathsf{P}\#\mathsf{P} \leqslant_{\mathrm{rat}} \mathsf{P}$, $\# \notin \varGamma$, then $\mathscr{L}(1\mathrm{NB_PA})$ is closed over concatenation. If $(\mathsf{P}\#)^* \leqslant_{\mathrm{rat}} \mathsf{P}$, $\# \notin \varGamma$, then $\mathscr{L}(1\mathrm{NB_PA})$ is closed over iteration.*

Remark 23. We leave open the question of the reduction in the opposite direction. I.e., does for each class of BAs exist a language of correct protocols P such that BAs recognize the same class of languages as B_{P} automata? The essence of the problem is as follows. If axioms (I–II) for the class of BAs are satisfied, does it imply that there exists a "universal" BA M_U such that $\mathscr{L}(1\mathrm{NBA}) = \mathcal{T}(L(M_U))$ and for each $M \in 1\mathrm{NBA}$ there exists an FST T such that $L(M) = L(M_U \circ T)$?

5   The NRR Problem and Log-TM Models

In this section, we establish the connection between log-TM models and the NRR problem. This connection and Theorem 18 imply one of the main results of the paper: Theorem 29.

Lemma 24 ([9]). $F_1 \leqslant_{\mathrm{rat}} F_2 \Rightarrow \mathrm{NRR}(F_1) \leqslant_{\mathrm{log}} \mathrm{NRR}(F_2)$.

In the proofs below we prove log-space reductions $\leqslant_{\mathrm{log}}$ via *log space transducers* that are log-TMs with one-way, write-only output tape, see [12] for the details.

Lemma 25. $\mathrm{NA}_F\mathrm{log}\text{-}\mathrm{TM} \leqslant_{\mathrm{log}} \mathrm{NRR}(F)$.

The proof repeats the arguments from [13,15].

---

[1] Intersection and quotient with regular languages, gsm forward mapping are the partial cases of rational transductions.

Lemma 26. $\mathrm{NRR}(F) \leqslant_{\log} \mathrm{NA}_F\log\text{-TM}$. *Moreover, there exists an* $\mathrm{NA}_F\log\text{-TM}$ M_{NRR} *that recognizes the problem* $\mathrm{NRR}(F)$.

Proof. The proof is straightforward. M_{NRR} gets on the input an NFA $\mathcal{A}$ and verifies whether $\mathcal{A}$ accepts the word $y \in F$ written on the advice tape. If $y \in L(\mathcal{A})$, M_{NRR} nondeterministically guesses the $\mathcal{A}$'s run on y. So, by Definition 11, $\mathcal{A} \in L(M_{\mathrm{NRR}})$ iff $\exists y \in F : y \in L(\mathcal{A}) \iff \mathcal{A} \in \mathrm{NRR}(F)$.   □

Theorem 27. $\mathscr{L}(\mathrm{NA}_F\log\text{-TM}) = \{L \mid L \leqslant_{\log} \mathrm{NRR}(F)\}$.

Proof. By the definition of $\leqslant_{\log}$, $L \leqslant_{\log} \mathrm{NRR}(F)$ iff there exists a log-TM transducer T that maps the input x of the problem $x \overset{?}{\in} L$ to the input $T(x)$ of the problem $\mathrm{NRR}(F)$. We construct an $\mathrm{NA}_F\log\text{-TM}$ M recognizing L via the composition of T and $\mathrm{NA}_F\log\text{-TM}$ M_{NRR} from Lemma 26.

So $\{L \mid L \leqslant_{\log} \mathrm{NRR}(F)\} \subseteq \mathscr{L}(\mathrm{NA}_F\log\text{-TM})$; the opposite inclusion follows from Lemma 25.   □

Lemma 28. $\mathrm{NA_P}\log\text{-TM} \sim_{\log} \mathrm{NB_P}\log\text{-TM}$.

We provide only the proof idea due to the space limitations. Let M_A be a $\mathrm{NA_P}\log\text{-TM}$, M_B be a $\mathrm{NB_P}\log\text{-TM}$, and x be an input word. Since both kinds of log-TMs are nondeterministic, M_A can guess and verify M_B's successful run on x provided that M_B's protocol is written on the advice tape; M_B can guess $y \in \mathsf{P}$ and a successful run of M_A on (x, y), and verify it: the transitions on configurations are simulated on log space and the fact $y \in \mathsf{P}$ is verified by performing subsequently the queries from the sequence y.

The above results yield the main theorem of the section.

Theorem 29. $\mathrm{NRR}(\mathsf{P}) \sim_{\log} \mathscr{L}(\mathrm{NB_P}\log\text{-TM}) = \{L \mid L \leqslant_{\log} \mathrm{NRR}(\mathsf{P})\}$.

6   Applications

In this section we prove the applications (4–7) described in Sect. 1.1.

Theorem 30. *Assertions (4–7) hold.*

Proof. SA-PROT was defined in Example 8. It was proved in [8] that the problems $\overline{\mathrm{E\text{-}1NSA}} \sim \log \mathrm{NRR}(\text{SA-PROT})$ are **PSPACE**-complete. So we obtain (5) by applying Theorem 29. We prove (4) in the same way by combining the facts $D_2\text{-PROT} \sim_{\mathrm{rat}} D_2$ (Example 7) and $\mathrm{NRR}(D_2)$ is P-complete [9], and apply Lemma 24 and Theorem 29.

To prove (6–7) we use facts about the filters $\mathrm{Per}_k = \{(w\#)^k \mid w \in \Sigma_k\}$, where Σ_k is a k-letter alphabet. The problem $\mathrm{NRR}(\mathrm{Per}_1)$ is **NP**-complete and $\mathrm{NRR}(\mathrm{Per}_k), k > 1$ is **PSPACE**-complete [1,14]. We construct set-protocols based on these languages as follows. $\Gamma_{\mathsf{write}} = \Sigma_k$, $\Gamma_{\mathsf{query}} = \{\mathsf{in}, \mathsf{test}\}$, $\Gamma_{\mathsf{resp}} = \{+, -\}$. The response to the in-query is positive only for the first query, test-queries are the same as in Example 8. We denote the language of correct protocols with $\Gamma_{\mathsf{write}} = \Sigma_k$ as $\mathsf{S_{1,k}PROT}$. It is easy to see that $\mathrm{Per}_k \leqslant_{\mathrm{rat}} \mathsf{S_{1,k}PROT}$:

an FST T maps words of the form $w$in $+ w$test $+ \cdots w$test$+$ to $w\#w\# \cdots w\#$ by replacing queries and responses by $\#$; the sequence of queries with responses in$+$, test$+$, ..., test$+$ is verifiable via a finite state control (the inputs with invalid sequence are rejected by the FST), so $\mathrm{NRR}(\mathrm{Per}_k) \leqslant_{\log} \mathrm{NRR}(\mathsf{S}_{1,k}\mathsf{PROT})$ by Lemma 24.

Now we prove that $\mathsf{S}_{1,k}\mathsf{PROT} \leqslant_{\mathrm{rat}} \mathrm{Per}_k$. The FST T takes on the input a word $(w\#)^n$ and acts as follows. In each block $w\#$ it has the following options: (i) change at least one letter, (ii) erase at least one letter and maybe change others, (iii) add at leas one letter and maybe change others, (iv) do not change w. Until T has not write in, it replaces $\#$ by test$-$ in the cases (i–iii), and either by test$-$ or by in$+$ in the case (iv). After T wrote in$+$, it replaces $\#$ by test$+$ in the case (iv) and either by test$-$ or by in$-$ in the cases (i–iii). It is easy to see that $T((w\#)^n)$ consists of all correct protocols with either w first in-query or without in-queries at all, and exactly n queries. So $T(\mathrm{Per}_k) = \mathsf{S}_{1,k}\mathsf{PROT}$ and assertions (6–7) follows from Lemma 24 and Theorem 29.   □

References

1. Anderson, T., Loftus, J., Rampersad, N., Santean, N., Shallit, J.: Special issue: LATA 2008 detecting palindromes, patterns and borders in regular languages. Inf. Comput. **207**(11), 1096–1118 (2009)

2. Berstel, J.: Transductions and Context-Free Languages. Teubner, Wiesbaden (1979). https://doi.org/10.1007/978-3-663-09367-1

3. Daley, M., Eramian, M., Mcquillan, I.: The bag automaton: a model of nondeterministic storage. J. Autom. Lang. Comb. **13**(3), 185–206 (2008)

4. Hopcroft, J.E., Ullman, J.D.: An approach to a unified theory of automata. In: SWAT 1967, pp. 140–147 (1967)

5. Kutrib, M., Malcher, A., Wendlandt, M.: Set automata. Int. J. Found. Comput. Sci. **27**(02), 187–214 (2016)

6. Lange, K.J., Reinhardt, K.: Set automata. In: Combinatorics, Complexity and Logic; Proceedings of the DMTCS 1996, pp. 321–329. Springer, Berlin (1996)

7. Rubtsov, A.A., Vyalyi, M.N.: On computational complexity of set automata. In: Charlier, É., Leroy, J., Rigo, M. (eds.) DLT 2017. LNCS, vol. 10396, pp. 332–344. Springer, Cham (2017). https://doi.org/10.1007/978-3-319-62809-7_25

8. Rubtsov, A., Vyalyi, M.: On emptiness and membership problems for set automata. In: Fomin, F.V., Podolskii, V.V. (eds.) CSR 2018. LNCS, vol. 10846, pp. 295–307. Springer, Cham (2018). https://doi.org/10.1007/978-3-319-90530-3_25

9. Rubtsov, A., Vyalyi, M.: Regular realizability problems and context-free languages. In: Shallit, J., Okhotin, A. (eds.) DCFS 2015. LNCS, vol. 9118, pp. 256–267. Springer, Cham (2015). https://doi.org/10.1007/978-3-319-19225-3_22

10. Rubtsov, A., Vyalyi, M.: On computational complexity of set automata. CoRR abs/1704.03730 (2017)

11. Rubtsov, A., Vyalyi, M.: On computational complexity of set automata. Inf. Comput. (to appear)

12. Sipser, M.: Introduction to the theory of computation. Cengage Learning (2013)

13. Vyalyi, M.N.: On models of a nondeterministic computation. In: Frid, A., Morozov, A., Rybalchenko, A., Wagner, K.W. (eds.) CSR 2009. LNCS, vol. 5675, pp. 334–345. Springer, Heidelberg (2009). https://doi.org/10.1007/978-3-642-03351-3_31

14. Vyalyi, M.: On the models of nondeterminism for two-way automata. In: Proceedings of VIII International Conference «Discrete Models in the Theory of Control Systems», pp. 54–60 (2009). (in Russian)
15. Vyalyi, M.N.: On regular realizability problems. Probl. Inf. Transm. **47**(4), 342–352 (2011)
16. Wolf, P.: On the decidability of finding a positive ILP-instance in a regular set of ILP-instances. In: Hospodár, M., Jirásková, G., Konstantinidis, S. (eds.) DCFS 2019. LNCS, vol. 11612, pp. 272–284. Springer, Cham (2019). https://doi.org/10.1007/978-3-030-23247-4_21
17. Wolf, P., Fernau, H.: Regular intersection emptiness of graph problems: finding a needle in a haystack of graphs with the help of automata. CoRR abs/2003.05826 (2020)

Disambiguation of Weighted Tree Automata

Kevin Stier[1]([⊠]) and Markus Ulbricht[2]

[1] Faculty of Mathematics and Computer Science,
Universität Leipzig, Leipzig, Germany
stier@informatik.uni-leipzig.de
[2] Institute of Logic and Computation, TU Wien, Vienna, Austria
mulbricht@informatik.uni-leipzig.de

Abstract. Recently a disambiguation construction for weighted automata has been presented by Mohri and Riley. In this paper we extend these results in two ways. First we generalize the underlying structure of the automata from words to trees and second we show that these results hold not only for the tropical semiring but also the arctic one.

Keywords: Weighted automata · Unambiguous automata · Tree automata · Twins property

1 Introduction

Quantitative extensions of finite-state automata, called weighted automata (WA) [20], as well as of finite-state tree automata, called weighted tree automata (WTA) [9], have been proposed and thoroughly investigated. The weights are usually taken from a semiring like the non-negative reals $\mathbb{R}^{\geq 0}$, the tropical semiring $\mathbb{T}$ [21,22], or the related arctic semiring $\mathbb{A}$.

Needless to say computational properties improve for deterministic devices. In the unweighted case of finite-state automata and finite-state tree automata the expressive power of their deterministic counterpart is equal [7,19]. For their quantitative extensions however this equivalence does not hold [3]. Indeed given that not every WTA can be determinised [4, Example 5.9], the research is headed towards finding sufficient conditions for determinization.

Notable results include approaches for WA with set semantics [2,6] dealing with sequentiality, a notion similar to determinism. Furthermore there are determinization approaches of WA over the tropical semiring by Mohri [16] and a maximal factorization approach that generalizes these results to extremal semirings for WA [13] and WTA [5]. In addition approximate variants of Mohri's result have been proposed [1,8]. A powerful tool utilized in all of these approaches is the so-called twins property, which ensures that similar loops have identical weights.

Research of the first author was supported by the DFG through the Research Training Group QuantLA (GRK 1763).

Y.-S. Han and S.-K. Ko (Eds.): DCFS 2021, LNCS 13037, pp. 163–175, 2021.
https://doi.org/10.1007/978-3-030-93489-7_14

Situated between deterministic and non-deterministic devices are devices with limited ambiguity. While determinism requires a unique choice in each configuration, limited ambiguity only requires a limited number of outputs for each input. Unambiguous, finitely ambiguous and polynomially ambiguous devices for instance, restrict the number of outputs per input by 1, by a uniform bound, and by a polynomial, respectively [14,15]. Therefore a natural generalization of determinism is unambiguity [14,18]. Unambiguous equivalents of WA and WTA have however not been investigated as thoroughly.

Recently a disambiguation algorithm has been proposed by Mohri and Riley [17] for weighted automata. They give a construction that with input of a WA, outputs an equivalent unambiguous WA. Furthermore they give sufficient conditions, most notably a weaker version of the twins property that only compares states that are in a certain relation. This condition ensures the finiteness of the construction for WA over the non-negative tropical semiring.

In the present paper we generalize the construction to WTA and give a sufficient condition for finiteness for the tropical, arctic and non-negative tropical semiring. We subsume the results of [17]. We will closely follow the results and proofs by [17], dealing with issues specific to the structure of trees along the way.

More specifically in Sect. 2 we introduce some elementary technical machinery, including the semiring properties we require. In Sect. 3 we present the uniformity construction that will, applied to a WTA $\mathcal{T}$, output a WTA $\mathcal{U}$ that has uniformity in the following sense. Each run on a tree t of $\mathcal{U}$ will have the behavior of $\mathcal{T}$ as its weight, i.e. $[\![\mathcal{T}]\!](t)$. We then give sufficient conditions for the finiteness of $\mathcal{U}$ for the tropical, arctic and non-negative tropical semiring in Theorem 13 and gather some straightforward conditions in Proposition 14. Finally in Sect. 4 we derive an unambiguous WTA $\mathcal{V}$ that is equivalent to $\mathcal{T}$ by removing redundant transitions from $\mathcal{U}$.

2   Preliminaries

Basic Notation. For every $k \in \mathbb{N}$ we use the subset $[k] = \{i \in \mathbb{N} \mid 1 \le i \le k\}$. For any set A the set of all finite words over A is $A^* = \bigcup_{k \in \mathbb{N}} A^k$, where we let $A^k = A \times \cdots \times A$ containing k factors of A and $A^0 = \{\varepsilon\}$ contains just the *empty word* ε. The *length* $|w|$ of a word $w = a_1 \cdots a_k \in A^*$ with $a_1, \ldots, a_k \in A$ is $|w| = k$; i.e. the number of occurrences of symbols in w. Given words $v, w \in A^*$, their concatenation is written $v.w$ or simply vw. For two sets M, N we denote the set of mappings from M to N by N^M.

Trees and Contexts. A *ranked alphabet* (Σ, rk) is a pair consisting of a finite set Σ and a mapping $\mathrm{rk} \colon \Sigma \to \mathbb{N}$ that assigns a rank to each symbol of Σ. If there is no risk of confusion, we denote a ranked alphabet (Σ, rk) by just Σ. Moreover, for every $k \in \mathbb{N}$ we let $\Sigma^{(k)} = \{\sigma \in \Sigma \mid \mathrm{rk}(\sigma) = k\}$. Given a ranked alphabet Σ and a set Z, the set $\mathrm{T}_\Sigma(Z)$ of Σ trees indexed by Z is the smallest set T such that $Z \subseteq \mathrm{T}$ and $\sigma(t_1, \ldots, t_k) \in \mathrm{T}$ for every $k \in \mathbb{N}$, $\sigma \in \Sigma^{(k)}$, and $t_1, \ldots, t_k \in \mathrm{T}$. We abbreviate $\mathrm{T}_\Sigma(\emptyset)$ by T_Σ; any $L \subseteq \mathrm{T}_\Sigma$ is called *tree language*.

Next, we recall some common notions for trees. Let $t \in T_\Sigma(Z)$ be a tree for a ranked alphabet Σ and a set Z. The set $\text{pos}(t)$ of *positions* of t is defined by $\text{pos}(z) = \{\varepsilon\}$, $z \in Z$, and $\text{pos}(\sigma(t_1, \ldots, t_k)) = \{\varepsilon\} \cup \{iw \mid i \in [k], w \in \text{pos}(t_i)\}$ for all $k \in \mathbb{N}$, $\sigma \in \Sigma^{(k)}$, and $t_1, \ldots, t_k \in T_\Sigma(Z)$. The *height* of t is given as $\text{height}(t) = \max_{w \in \text{pos}(t)} |w|$, and the *size* of t is $\text{size}(t) = |\text{pos}(t)|$. Given a position $w \in \text{pos}(t)$, the label $t(w)$ of t at w and the subtree $t|_w$ of t at w are given by $z(\varepsilon) = z|_\varepsilon = z$ for all $z \in Z$ and

$$\big(\sigma(t_1, \ldots, t_k)\big)(w) = \begin{cases} \sigma & \text{if } w = \varepsilon \\ t_i(w') & \text{if } w = iw' \text{ with } i \in \mathbb{N} \text{ and } w' \in \text{pos}(t_i) \end{cases}$$

$$\sigma(t_1, \ldots, t_k)|_w = \begin{cases} \sigma(t_1, \ldots, t_k) & \text{if } w = \varepsilon \\ t_i|_{w'} & \text{if } w - iw' \text{ with } i \in \mathbb{N} \text{ and } w' \in \text{pos}(t_i) \end{cases}$$

for all $k \in \mathbb{N}$, $\sigma \in \Sigma^{(k)}$, and $t_1, \ldots, t_k \in T_\Sigma(Z)$. Finally, the *replacement* $t[t']_w$ of the subtree at position $w \in \text{pos}(t)$ by a tree $t' \in T_\Sigma(Z)$ is given by $z[t']_\varepsilon = t'$ for all $z \in Z$ and

$$\sigma(t_1, \ldots, t_k)[t']_w = \begin{cases} t' & \text{if } w = \varepsilon \\ \sigma(t_1, \ldots, t_{i-1}, t_i[t']_{w'}, t_{i+1}, \ldots, t_k) & \text{if } w = iw' \text{ with } i \in \mathbb{N}, \\ & \hspace{2.5cm} w' \in \text{pos}(t_i) \end{cases}$$

for every $k \in \mathbb{N}$, $\sigma \in \Sigma^{(k)}$, and $t_1, \ldots, t_k \in T_\Sigma(Z)$. For a set Y, the set of *positions of t labeled by elements in Y*, is the set $\text{pos}_Y(t) = \{w \in \text{pos}(t) \mid t(w) \in Y\}$.

We reserve the use of the special symbol $\square$. A tree $t \in T_\Sigma(\{\square\})$ is a *context*, if there exists exactly one $w \in \text{pos}(t)$ with $t(w) = \square$; i.e. $|\text{pos}_\square(t)| = 1$. The set of all such contexts is denoted by C_Σ. Given a context $C \in C_\Sigma$ and a tree $t \in T_\Sigma(\{\square\})$, the substitution $C[t]$ of t into C yields the tree $C[t]_w$, where w is the unique position $w \in \text{pos}(C)$ with $C(w) = \square$.

Semirings. A *semiring* [11,12] is a tuple $(S, \oplus, \otimes, 0, 1)$ such that $(S, \oplus, 0)$ is a commutative monoid and $(S, \otimes, 1)$ is a monoid, $\otimes$ distributes over $\oplus$ and $0 \otimes s = s \otimes 0 = 0$ for all $s \in S$. We will refer to a semiring $(S, \oplus, \otimes, 0, 1)$ by its carrier set S. A semiring S is called *commutative* if $(S, \otimes, 1)$ is commutative. It is said to be *cancellative* if $s, s', s'' \in S$ with $s'' \neq 0$ and $s \otimes s'' = s' \otimes s''$ implies $s = s'$. We call it *left divisible* if for all $s \in S \setminus \{0\}$ there exists $s^{-1} \in S$ such that $s^{-1} \otimes s = 1$. It is said to be *weakly left divisible* if for $s, s' \in S$ with $s \oplus s' \neq 0$ there exists $s'' \in S$ such that $s = (s \oplus s') \otimes s''$. If S is cancellative, s'' is unique and has the form $s'' = (s \oplus s')^{-1} \otimes s$. Moreover, S is called *zero-sum free* if $s \oplus s' = 0$ implies $s - 0$ and $s' = 0$. *Throughout the rest of this paper each considered semiring is assumed to be commutative, zero-sum free, cancellative, and weakly left divisible.* Considered examples include

- the semiring of non-negative real numbers $(\mathbb{R}^{\geq 0}, +, \cdot, 0, 1)$,
- the tropical semiring $\mathbb{T} = (\mathbb{R} \cup \{\infty\}, \min, +, \infty, 0)$,
- the arctic semiring $\mathbb{A} = (\mathbb{R} \cup \{-\infty\}, \max, +, -\infty, 0)$, and
- the non-negative tropical semiring $\mathbb{T}^{\geq 0} = (\mathbb{R}^{\geq 0} \cup \{\infty\}, \min, +, \infty, 0)$.

Weighted Tree Automata. A *weighted tree automaton* (WTA) [10] over a semiring S is a tuple $\mathcal{T} = (Q, \Sigma, \mu, \nu)$, where Q is a finite set of *states*, Σ is a ranked alphabet, μ is a family $(\mu(\sigma) : Q^k \times Q \to S \mid k \geq 0, \sigma \in \Sigma^{(k)})$ of transition mappings and $\nu \in S^Q$ is a *root weight* vector. We call a tuple $(q_1, \ldots, q_k, \sigma, w, q) \in Q^k \times \Sigma \times S \times Q$ a *transition* whenever $\mathrm{rk}(\sigma) = k$ and $\mu(\sigma)(q_1, \ldots, q_k, q) = w$. We sometimes denote a transition by $\sigma(q_1, \ldots, q_k) \xrightarrow{w} q$. The set of all transitions with $w \neq 0$ is denoted by $\Delta_{\mathcal{T}}$. A state $q \in Q$ is called *final* if $\nu(q) \neq 0$.

For $t \in T_\Sigma$ and $q \in Q$ we define the set of runs of $\mathcal{T}$ on t, assigning to the root position the state $q \in Q$ by $\mathrm{Run}_{\mathcal{T}}(t, q) = \{r : \mathrm{pos}(t) \to Q \mid r(\varepsilon) = q\}$. For $C \in C_\Sigma$ and for $p, q \in Q$ we define the set of runs of $\mathcal{T}$ on C, assigning to the position of $\square$ the state $p \in Q$ and to the root position the state $q \in Q$ by

$$\mathrm{Run}_{\mathcal{T}}(p, C, q) = \{r : \mathrm{pos}(C) \to Q \mid r(\varepsilon) = q \ \wedge$$
$$\forall w \in \mathrm{pos}(C) : (C(w) = \square) \Rightarrow r(w) = p\}.$$

We set $\mathrm{Run}_{\mathcal{T}}(p, C) = \cup_{q \in Q} \mathrm{Run}_{\mathcal{T}}(p, C, q)$ and $\mathrm{Run}_{\mathcal{T}}(t) = \cup_{q \in Q} \mathrm{Run}_{\mathcal{T}}(t, q)$. In case $r(\varepsilon) = q$ for a run $r \in \mathrm{Run}_{\mathcal{T}}(t)$ we sometimes say t reaches q. Finally for $u \in T_\Sigma \cup C_\Sigma$ define the weight of $r \in \mathrm{Run}_{\mathcal{T}}(u)$ by $\mathrm{wt}_{\mathcal{T}}(r) = \bigotimes_{w \in \mathrm{pos}(u)} \mathrm{wt}(r, w)$ where $\mathrm{wt}(r, w) = \mu(\sigma)(r(w1), \ldots, r(wk), r(w))$ if $u(w) \in \Sigma^{(k)}$ for $k \geq 0$ and $\mathrm{wt}(r, w) = 1$ otherwise. We call a run r *successful* if $\mathrm{wt}_{\mathcal{T}}(r) \otimes \nu(r(\varepsilon)) \neq 0$. For a set U we let $\mathrm{wt}_{\mathcal{T}}(U) = \bigoplus_{r \in U} \mathrm{wt}_{\mathcal{T}}(r)$. The semantics of a WTA $\mathcal{T}$ is defined for a tree $t \in T_\Sigma$ by

$$[\![\mathcal{T}]\!](t) = \bigoplus_{r \in \mathrm{Run}_{\mathcal{T}}(t)} \mathrm{wt}_{\mathcal{T}}(r) \otimes \nu(r(\varepsilon))$$

and for each context $C \in C_\Sigma$ and state $q \in Q$ by

$$[\![\mathcal{T}]\!](q, C) = \bigoplus_{r \in \mathrm{Run}_{\mathcal{T}}(q, C)} \mathrm{wt}_{\mathcal{T}}(r) \otimes \nu(r(\varepsilon)).$$

A tree $t \in T_\Sigma$ is *accepted* if there is some successful run for t. For zero-sum free semirings this is equivalent to $[\![\mathcal{T}]\!](t) \neq 0$. We call a WTA *trim* if for all $q \in Q$ there exist $t \in T_\Sigma$, $w \in \mathrm{pos}(t)$ and $r \in \mathrm{Run}_{\mathcal{T}}(t)$ with $\mathrm{wt}_{\mathcal{T}}(r) \neq 0$ and $\nu(r(\varepsilon)) \neq 0$ such that $r(w) = q$. Note that we can always trim a WTA by removing states that do not satisfy this condition, without changing the semantics of it. A WTA is called *unambiguous* iff for each $t \in T_\Sigma$ there is at most one successful run. Finally we call two WTA $\mathcal{T}$ and $\mathcal{U}$ *equivalent* if $[\![\mathcal{T}]\!](t) = [\![\mathcal{U}]\!](t)$ for all $t \in T_\Sigma$. *If not stated otherwise we assume any WTA $\mathcal{T}$ to be trim, of the form $\mathcal{T} = (Q_{\mathcal{T}}, \Sigma, \mu_{\mathcal{T}}, \nu_{\mathcal{T}})$ and over a semiring S; similarly for WTA $\mathcal{U}$ and $\mathcal{V}$.*

Example 1 (running example). Consider the WTA $\mathcal{T}$ over $\mathbb{R}^{\geq 0}$ with state space $Q_{\mathcal{T}} = \{q_1, q_2, q_3\}$, the transitions

$$\alpha \xrightarrow{2} q_2, \qquad \alpha \xrightarrow{3} q_1, \qquad \sigma(q_1, q_1) \xrightarrow{5} q_3, \qquad \sigma(q_1, q_2) \xrightarrow{4} q_3,$$
$$\beta \xrightarrow{1} q_1, \qquad \sigma(q_2, q_2) \xrightarrow{5} q_3, \qquad \sigma(q_2, q_1) \xrightarrow{4} q_3,$$

and root weights $\nu_T(q_3) = 1$ and $\nu_T(q_1) = \nu_T(q_2) = 0$. Let us examine the semantics by considering runs of T on the tree $\sigma(\alpha, \alpha)$ as depicted in Fig. 1. There are 4 distinct runs $r_1, r_2, r_3, r_4 \in \mathrm{Run}_T(\sigma(\alpha, \alpha))$ with weights $\mathrm{wt}_T(r_1) = 45$, $\mathrm{wt}_T(r_2) = 24$, $\mathrm{wt}_T(r_3) = 24$ and $\mathrm{wt}_T(r_4) = 20$. Adding these weights up we get $[\![T]\!](\sigma(\alpha, \alpha)) = 113$. All trees accepted by T and their respective weights are depicted in Fig. 2.

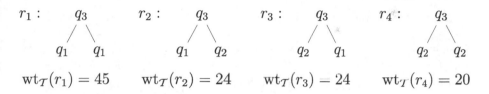

Fig. 1. Runs of T on the tree $\sigma(\alpha, \alpha)$ from Example 1

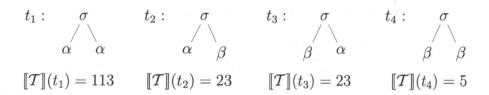

Fig. 2. Trees accepted by T and their weights from Example 1

3   Uniformity Construction

Let us introduce the uniformity construction, which Mohri and Riley refer to as pre-disambiguation algorithm. The construction will, applied to a WTA T over a semiring S, output a WTA U that has uniformity in the following sense. Each run on a tree t of U will have the behaviour of T as its weight, i.e. $[\![T]\!](t)$. More specifically for $t \in T_\Sigma$ and $r \in \mathrm{Run}_U(t)$ it will hold that $\mathrm{wt}_U(r) = \mathrm{wt}_T(\mathrm{Run}_T(t))$. The construction is similar to the factorization approach used for determinization [16] and closely follows [17]. Each state of U will be generated by a tree $t \in T_\Sigma$ and a pivot state p. The state itself, say $u(t, p)$, is a vector in S^{Q_T}.

The intuition is as follows. Each state $u(t, p)$ will be primed with 2 information. First, $u(t, p)$ knows which states $q \in Q_T$ are in the so-called common future relation R with p. Roughly speaking R checks whether a final state is reachable from both p and q with the same input tree. Evidently states that are in common future relation are threats to the unambiguity of the automaton. Second, adding up the entries of $u(t, p)$ will equal 1. This is due to the fact that its entries give some sort of proportion as will be described below. This way, the states in the constructed WTA $\mathcal{U}$ contain the required information about the semantics of T.

Let us now introduce the aforementioned common future relation R.

Definition 2 (common future relation). *For two states $q, q' \in Q_T$ define the common future relation R_T by setting qR_Tq' iff there exists a context $C \in C_\Sigma$ such that $[\![T]\!](q, C) \neq 0$ and $[\![T]\!](q', C) \neq 0$. We let $R_T(q) = \{p \in Q_T \mid qRp\}$ and will omit the subscript if the WTA is clear from context.*

Note that the relation R_T is reflexive, symmetric and not transitive. Let us now formally construct the WTA $\mathcal{U}$. Let $T = (Q_T, \Sigma, \mu_T, \nu_T)$ be a WTA over S. Define the WTA $\mathcal{U} = (Q_\mathcal{U}, \Sigma, \mu_\mathcal{U}, \nu_\mathcal{U})$ over S resulting from the uniformity-construction with input T as follows. Given a tree $t \in T_\Sigma$ and a state $p \in Q_T$, if $\mathrm{wt}_T(\mathrm{Run}_T(t, p)) \neq 0$ we define $u(t, p) \in S^{Q_T}$ via

$$u(t,p)_q = \begin{cases} \left(\bigoplus_{q' \in R(p)} \mathrm{wt}_T(\mathrm{Run}_T(t, q')) \right)^{-1} \otimes \mathrm{wt}_T(\mathrm{Run}_T(t, q)) & \text{if } q \in R(p), \\ 0 & \text{otherwise.} \end{cases}$$

We mention that $p \in R(p)$ implies that $\bigoplus_{q' \in R(p)} \mathrm{wt}_T(\mathrm{Run}_T(t, q')) \neq 0$ since our semiring is zero-sum free. The states of $\mathcal{U}$ are these vectors $u(t, p)$, i.e.

$$Q_\mathcal{U} = \{u(t, p) \in S^{Q_T} \mid t \in T_\Sigma, \ p \in Q_T\}.$$

Note that $Q_\mathcal{U}$ is not necessarily finite. Sufficient conditions will be discussed later; for now let us assume that it is. We refer to the designated state $p \in Q_T$ of $u(t, p)$ as its *pivot* and to the set $\{q \in Q_T \mid u(t, p)_q \neq 0\}$ as the *support* of the state $u(t, p)$ and denote it by $\mathrm{supp}(u(t, p))$.

As mentioned earlier entries of a state $u(t, p) \in Q_\mathcal{U}$ give proportions of weights. More specifically the entry $u(t, p)_q$ gives the sum of weights of all runs on t reaching q, relative to the sum over all runs reaching a state in $R(p)$.

Remark 3. Note that $q \in \mathrm{supp}(u(t, p))$ iff $\mathrm{wt}_T(\mathrm{Run}_T(t, q)) \neq 0$ and $q \in R(p)$.

For the definition of $\mu_\mathcal{U}$ let $u(t_1, p_1), \ldots, u(t_k, p_k), u(t, p) \in Q_\mathcal{U}$ with $\sigma \in \Sigma^{(k)}$ and $t = \sigma(t_1, \ldots, t_k)$. We set

$$w = \bigoplus_{(q_1, \ldots, q_k) \in Q_T^k} u(t_1, p_1)_{q_1} \otimes \cdots \otimes u(t_k, p_k)_{q_k} \otimes \bigoplus_{q \in \mathrm{supp}(u(t,p))} \mu_T(\sigma)(q_1, \ldots, q_k, q),$$

and consider for each $q \in \mathrm{supp}(u(t, p))$ the conditions

$$u(t,p)_q = w^{-1} \otimes \bigoplus_{(q_1, \ldots, q_k) \in Q_T^k} u(t_1, p_1)_{q_1} \otimes \cdots \otimes u(t_k, p_k)_{q_k} \otimes \mu_T(\sigma)(q_1, \ldots, q_k, q), \quad (1)$$

and

$$\mu_T(\sigma)(p_1, \ldots, p_k, p) \neq 0. \quad (2)$$

Define the transition mapping $\mu_{\mathcal{U}}$ by

$$\mu_{\mathcal{U}}(\sigma)(u(t_1,p_1),\ldots,u(t_k,p_k),u(t,p)) = \begin{cases} w & \text{if (1)for } q \in \operatorname{supp}(u(t,p)) \text{ and (2),} \\ 0 & \text{otherwise.} \end{cases}$$

Lastly, for each $u(t,p) \in Q_{\mathcal{U}}$. we let

$$\nu_{\mathcal{U}}(u(t,p)) = \begin{cases} \bigoplus_{q \in Q_T} u(t,p)_q \otimes \nu_T(q) & \text{if } \nu_T(p) \neq 0, \\ 0 & \text{otherwise.} \end{cases}$$

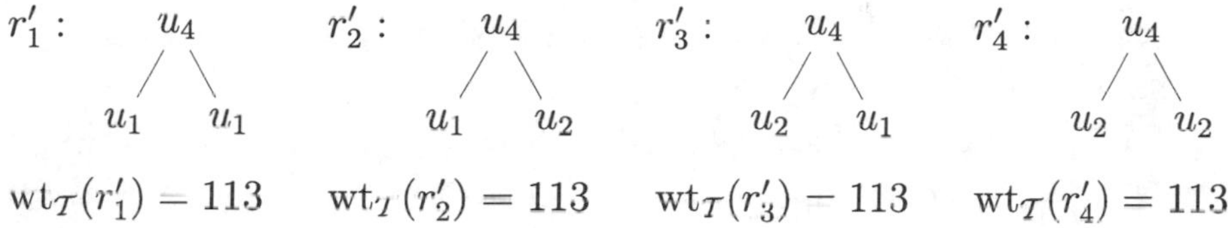

$r_1' :$ u_4 $r_2' :$ u_4 $r_3' :$ u_4 $r_4' :$ u_4
         / \\   / \\   / \\   / \\
    u_1 u_1 u_1 u_2 u_2 u_1 u_2 u_2

$\operatorname{wt}_T(r_1') = 113$ $\operatorname{wt}_T(r_2') = 113$ $\operatorname{wt}_T(r_3') - 113$ $\operatorname{wt}_T(r_4') = 113$

Fig. 3. Runs of $\mathcal{U}$ on the tree $\sigma(\alpha,\alpha)$ from Example 5

Remark 4. Given $u(t,p) \in Q_{\mathcal{U}}$, $t \in T_\Sigma$ is not necessarily the only tree reaching $u(t,p)$, i.e. there might exist $t' \in T_\Sigma$ with $t \neq t'$ and $\operatorname{wt}_{\mathcal{U}}(\operatorname{Run}_{\mathcal{U}}(t',u(t,p))) \neq 0$. On the other hand if for $u \in Q_{\mathcal{U}}$ we have $\operatorname{wt}_{\mathcal{U}}(\operatorname{Run}_{\mathcal{U}}(t,u)) \neq 0$ we can w.l.o.g. assume that $u = u(t,p)$ for some $p \in Q_T$.

Example 5 (running example). We return to Example 1 and consider the WTA $\mathcal{U}$ returned by the uniformity construction of the WTA T. Let $Q_{\mathcal{U}} = \{u_1,u_2,u_3,u_4\}$ with $u_1 := u(\alpha,q_1)$, $u_2 := u(\alpha,q_2)$, $u_3 := u(\beta,q_1)$ and $u_4 := u(\sigma(\alpha,\alpha),q_3)$ which coincides with $u(\sigma(\alpha,\beta),q_3)$, $u(\sigma(\beta,\alpha),q_3)$, and $u(\sigma(\beta,\beta),q_3)$. More specifically

$$u_1 = \begin{pmatrix} 3/5 \\ 2/5 \\ 0 \end{pmatrix}, \qquad u_2 = \begin{pmatrix} 3/5 \\ 2/5 \\ 0 \end{pmatrix}, \qquad u_3 = \begin{pmatrix} 1 \\ 0 \\ 0 \end{pmatrix}, \qquad u_4 = \begin{pmatrix} 0 \\ 0 \\ 1 \end{pmatrix}.$$

We have the transitions

$$\alpha \xrightarrow{5} u_1, \qquad \beta \xrightarrow{1} u_3, \qquad \sigma(u_3,x) \xrightarrow{23/5} u_4 \quad \text{for } x \in \{u_1,u_2\},$$

$$\alpha \xrightarrow{5} u_2, \qquad \sigma(u_3,u_3) \xrightarrow{5} u_4, \qquad \sigma(x,u_3) \xrightarrow{23/5} u_4 \quad \text{for } x \in \{u_1,u_2\},$$

$$\sigma(x,y) \xrightarrow{113/25} u_4 \quad \text{for } x,y \in \{u_1,u_2\},$$

and the root weight is $\nu_{\mathcal{U}}(u_4) = 1$ and $\nu_{\mathcal{U}}(u_1) = \nu_{\mathcal{U}}(u_2) = \nu_{\mathcal{U}}(u_3) = 0$. Let us reconsider the runs on the tree $\sigma(\alpha,\alpha)$ in order to understand the consequences of the construction. The depiction in Fig. 3 shows that the number of runs on $\sigma(\alpha,\alpha)$ remains 4 but the weights of the runs are uniform. In fact the weight of each run is equal to $[\![T]\!](\sigma(\alpha,\alpha))$. This is the case for every tree and run on it, as we will establish in Corollary 7. Note that the WTA T and $\mathcal{U}$ are not equivalent. Equivalence will only be achieved for idempotent semirings (Proposition 9).

The following theorem summarizes the properties of our uniformity construction. More precisely, it shows that the weight assigned to each tree is the sum of its weights in the processed WTA.

Theorem 6. *Let* $\mathcal{U}$ *be the* WTA *returned by the uniformity construction for the* WTA $\mathcal{T}$. *Given a run* $r \in \mathrm{Run}_{\mathcal{U}}(t, u(t,p))$ *with* $\mathrm{wt}_{\mathcal{U}}(r) \neq 0$ *where* $t \in \mathrm{T}_{\Sigma}$ *and* $u(t,p) \in Q_{\mathcal{U}}$ *we have*

1. $\mathrm{wt}_{\mathcal{U}}(r) = \bigoplus_{q \in \mathrm{supp}(u(t,p))} \mathrm{wt}_{\mathcal{T}}(\mathrm{Run}_{\mathcal{T}}(t,q)),$
2. $\mathrm{wt}_{\mathcal{U}}(r) \otimes u(t,p)_q = \mathrm{wt}_{\mathcal{T}}(\mathrm{Run}_{\mathcal{T}}(t,q)) \quad \forall q \in \mathrm{supp}(u(t,p)).$

As a simple corollary, we are now able to reconstruct $[\![\mathcal{T}]\!](t)$ for each tree $t \in \mathrm{T}_{\Sigma}$ in a straightforward way.

Corollary 7. *Let* $\mathcal{U}$ *be the* WTA *returned by the uniformity construction for the* WTA $\mathcal{T}$. *Given a successful run* $r \in \mathrm{Run}_{\mathcal{U}}(t, u(t,p))$ *where* $t \in \mathrm{T}_{\Sigma}$ *and* $u(t,p) \in Q_{\mathcal{U}}$ *we have*

$$\mathrm{wt}_{\mathcal{U}}(r) \otimes \nu_{\mathcal{U}}(r(\varepsilon)) = [\![\mathcal{T}]\!](t).$$

We have now established that the successful runs have the desired behavior. Let us continue by showing that the same set of trees is accepted by $\mathcal{T}$ and the WTA $\mathcal{U}$ returned by the uniformity construction.

Proposition 8. *Let* $\mathcal{U}$ *be the* WTA *returned by the uniformity construction for the* WTA $\mathcal{T}$. *If* $[\![\mathcal{T}]\!](t) \neq 0$ *for* $t \in \mathrm{T}_{\Sigma}$, *then there is a successful run on* t *for* $\mathcal{U}$.

As mentioned above the uniformity construction does in general not produce a WTA equivalent to $\mathcal{T}$. An exception is the case that the considered semiring S is idempotent, i. e. for any $s \in S$ it holds that $s + s = s$ as stated in the following result. Note that in particular the semirings $\mathbb{T}, \mathbb{A}$ and $\mathbb{T}^{\geq 0}$, for which we will later give a sufficient condition for finiteness, are idempotent.

Proposition 9. *Let* $\mathcal{T}$ *be a* WTA *over an idempotent semiring* S *and* $\mathcal{U}$ *the* WTA *returned by the uniformity construction. For any tree* $t \in \mathrm{T}_{\Sigma}$ *it holds that*

$$[\![\mathcal{T}]\!](t) = [\![\mathcal{U}]\!](t).$$

Having collected the basic properties of our uniformity construction, our goal is now to establish sufficient criteria for the finiteness of $\mathcal{U}$. Besides rather straightforward special cases, our most important result is based on ensuring that certain loops in our WTA $\mathcal{T}$ generate the same weights. This is similar to the so called twins property famously used for determinization of weighted finite automata [13, 16] and weighted tree automata [5]. We can however restrict it to cases where the involved states share a common future. Let us define both the twins property and our refined version.

Definition 10 (R-twins property). *A* WTA $\mathcal{T}$ *satisfies the* R-*twins property if for all* $p, q \in Q$ *s.t. i)* $p \mathrm{R} q$ *and ii) there is some* $t \in \mathrm{T}_{\Sigma}$ *which satisfies both*

$\mathrm{wt}_{\mathcal{T}}(\mathrm{Run}_{\mathcal{T}}(t,q)) \neq 0$ *and* $\mathrm{wt}_{\mathcal{T}}(\mathrm{Run}_{\mathcal{T}}(t,p)) \neq 0$, *the following statement holds. For each context* $C \in C_{\Sigma}$,

$$\mathrm{wt}_{\mathcal{T}}(\mathrm{Run}_{\mathcal{T}}(q,C,q)) \neq 0 \qquad and \qquad \mathrm{wt}_{\mathcal{T}}(\mathrm{Run}_{\mathcal{T}}(p,C,p)) \neq 0$$

implies $\mathrm{wt}_{\mathcal{T}}(\mathrm{Run}_{\mathcal{T}}(q,C,q)) = \mathrm{wt}_{\mathcal{T}}(\mathrm{Run}_{\mathcal{T}}(p,C,p))$. *If the above is true for the universal relation* $Q_{\mathcal{T}} \times Q_{\mathcal{T}}$ *instead of* R, *we say* $\mathcal{T}$ *satisfies the twins property.*

In contrast to the twins property our R-twins property additionally requires establishing sets of states that share a common future. This is however not a computational limitation.

Proposition 11. *Let* $\mathcal{T}$ *be a WTA over* $S \in \{\mathbb{T}, \mathbb{A}, \mathbb{T}^{\geq 0}\}$ *and* $q, p \in Q_{\mathcal{T}}$. *It is decidable whether* $p\mathrm{R}q$.

Let us now compare the twins property and the R-twins property.

Example 12. Consider the WTA $\mathcal{T}$ over $\mathbb{T}$ with state space $Q_{\mathcal{T}} = \{q_1, q_2, q_3, q_f\}$, the transitions

$$\alpha \xrightarrow{1} q_1, \qquad \beta \xrightarrow{0} q_3, \qquad \sigma(x,x) \xrightarrow{0} x \quad \text{for } x \in \{q_1, q_2\},$$

$$\alpha \xrightarrow{2} q_2, \qquad \sigma(q_2, q_3) \xrightarrow{0} q_f, \qquad \sigma(x, q_3) \xrightarrow{0} x \quad \text{for } x \in \{q_1, q_2\},$$

$$\sigma(q_3, q_1) \xrightarrow{0} q_f, \qquad \sigma(q_3, x) \xrightarrow{0} x \quad \text{for } x \in \{q_1, q_2\},$$

and root weight $\nu_{\mathcal{T}}(q_f) = 0$ and $\nu_{\mathcal{T}}(q_1) = \nu_{\mathcal{T}}(q_2) = \nu_{\mathcal{T}}(q_3) = \infty$. It is straightforward to see that $\mathrm{R}(q_1) = \{q_1, q_3\}$, $\mathrm{R}(q_2) = \{q_2, q_3\}$, $\mathrm{R}(q_3) = \{q_1, q_2, q_3\}$ and $\mathrm{R}(q_f) = \{q_f\}$. For any $C \in C_{\Sigma}$ we have

$$\mathrm{wt}_{\mathcal{T}}(\mathrm{Run}_{\mathcal{T}}(q_1, C, q_1)) = |\mathrm{pos}_{\alpha}(C)| \quad \text{and} \quad \mathrm{wt}_{\mathcal{T}}(\mathrm{Run}_{\mathcal{T}}(q_2, C, q_2)) = 2 \cdot |\mathrm{pos}_{\alpha}(C)|$$

in contrast to the twins property. If however we consider the R-twins property we may only compare states that have a common future. Particularly the states q_1 and q_2 do not have a common future, which is the reason why the argument from above does not hold for this case. In fact, one may easily verify that $\mathcal{T}$ does satisfy the R-twins property.

The following main result states that $\mathcal{U}$ is finite for our primary semirings.

Theorem 13. *Let* $\mathcal{T}$ *be a WTA over* $S \in \{\mathbb{T}, \mathbb{A}, \mathbb{T}^{\geq 0}\}$. *Let* $\mathcal{U}$ *be the WTA returned by the uniformity construction for* $\mathcal{T}$. *If* $\mathcal{T}$ *satisfies the R-twins property then* $Q_{\mathcal{U}}$ *is finite.*

Moreover, we also want to mention the following simple observations.

Proposition 14. *Let* $\mathcal{T}$ *be a WTA and* $\mathcal{U}$ *be the WTA returned by the uniformity construction. If one of the following conditions is satisfied* $Q_{\mathcal{U}}$ *is finite: i)* S *is finite. ii)* $\mathcal{T}$ *is acyclic. iii)* $S \in \{\mathbb{T}, \mathbb{A}, \mathbb{T}^{\geq 0}\}$, $\mathcal{T}$ *satisfies the twins property.*

4   Disambiguation

So far, we have seen that our uniformity construction $\mathcal{U}$ is capable of simulating $[\![\mathcal{T}]\!](t)$ in each single run on $t \in \mathrm{T}_\Sigma$ (Theorem 6) and we found criteria ensuring that the resulting WTA is finite (Theorem 13, Proposition 14). Recall however that our main goal is to transform $\mathcal{T}$ into an unambiguous WTA which is of course not yet achieved. Keeping Theorem 6 in mind, our strategy is as follows. Roughly speaking we inspect our WTA, successively looking for redundant transitions in the following sense. If there are two runs for some tree $t \in \mathrm{T}_\Sigma$, then at least one involved transition needs to be removed. We proceed in a specific order which will ensure that in each step, all accepted trees are still accepted even after the transition is removed. This is analogous to the approach in [17].

Let us come to the formal execution. For our WTA $\mathcal{T}$, a tree $t \in \mathrm{T}_\Sigma$ and a state $q \in Q_\mathcal{T}$ we will write $q \in \delta_\mathcal{T}(t)$ iff $\mathrm{wt}_\mathcal{T}(\mathrm{Run}_\mathcal{T}(t,q)) \neq 0$. We call two tuples of states $(q_1, \ldots, q_k), (q'_1, \ldots, q'_k) \in Q_\mathcal{T}^k$ co-reachable if there is a tuple of trees $(t_1, \ldots, t_k) \in \mathrm{T}_\Sigma^k$ such that $q_i \in \delta_\mathcal{T}(t_i)$ and $q'_i \in \delta_\mathcal{T}(t_i)$ for each $i \in [k]$. Let $Q_\mathcal{T} = \{p_1, \ldots, p_m\}$ and define the order of states by $p_1 < \cdots < p_m$. For $u(t,p) \in Q_\mathcal{U}$ and $\sigma \in \Sigma^{(k)}$ define the list of tuples of states that reach $u(t,p)$ via σ by

$$\mathcal{L}(u(t,p), \sigma) = \left((u(t_1^1, p_1^1), \ldots, u(t_k^1, p_k^1)), \ldots, (u(t_1^n, p_1^n), \ldots, u(t_k^n, p_k^n)) \right),$$

i.e. for each $i \in [n]$ we have that $(u(t_1^i, p_1^i), \ldots, u(t_k^i, p_k^i)) \in \mathcal{L}(u(t,p), \sigma)$ if and only if $(u(t_1^i, p_1^i), \ldots, u(t_k^i, p_k^i), \sigma, u(t,p)) \in \Delta_\mathcal{U}$. We assume the list to be lexicographically ordered with respect to its states, i.e. we assume that we have $(p_1^1, \ldots, p_k^1) < \cdots < (p_1^n, \ldots, p_k^n)$. We process such a list by removing the transition $(u(t_1^j, p_1^j), \ldots, u(t_k^j, p_k^j), \sigma, u(t,p)) \in \Delta_\mathcal{U}$ for $j \geq 2$ iff there exists a co-reachable tuple $(u(t_1^i, p_1^i), \ldots, u(t_k^i, p_k^i))$ in $\mathcal{L}(u(t,p), \sigma)$ with $1 \leq i < j$ that has not yet been removed. Afterwards we trim the WTA in order to remove unnecessary states and further transitions. In particular the first tuple of a list is not removed.

In a similar fashion we consider a list $\mathcal{L}(\mathcal{U}) = \{u_1, \ldots, u_m\}$ containing all states $u_j \in Q_\mathcal{U}$ with $\nu_\mathcal{U}(u_j) \neq 0$. We process this list analogously, by setting $\nu_\mathcal{U}(u_j) = 0$ whenever there is some $u_i < u_j$ which is co-reachable with u_j and still satisfies $\nu_\mathcal{U}(u_i) \neq 0$ after being processed.

The following result shows that processing the lists does not change the set of accepted trees.

Lemma 15. *Let $\mathcal{T}$ be a WTA, $\mathcal{U}$ the WTA resulting from the uniformity construction and $\mathcal{V}$ be the WTA after processing $\mathcal{L}(u(t,p), \sigma)$ for $u(t,p) \in Q_\mathcal{U}$ or $\mathcal{L}(\mathcal{U})$. Then the same set of trees is accepted by both $\mathcal{U}$ and $\mathcal{V}$.*

Hence, whenever $\mathcal{U}$ is finite we can process all lists $\mathcal{L}(u(t,p), \sigma)$ for $u(t,p) \in Q_\mathcal{U}$ and $\sigma \in \Sigma$ and $\mathcal{L}(\mathcal{U})$, obtaining the unambiguous WTA $\mathcal{V}$ equivalent to $\mathcal{T}$.

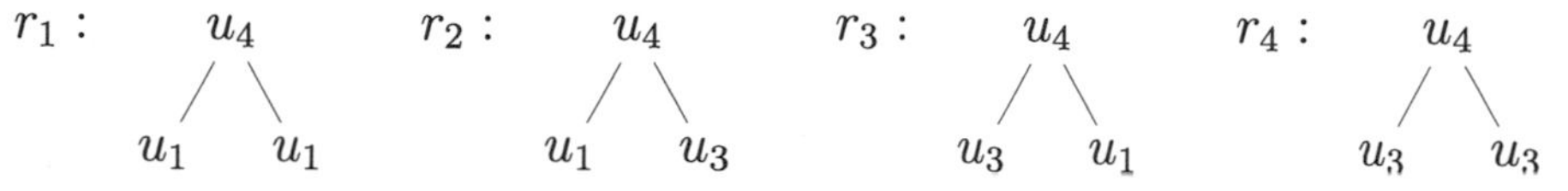

$r_1:$ u_4 $r_2:$ u_4 $r_3:$ u_4 $r_4:$ u_4

     u_1 u_1 u_1 u_3 u_3 u_1 u_3 u_3

$\mathrm{wt}_\mathcal{V}(r_1) = [\![\mathcal{V}]\!](t_1)$ $\mathrm{wt}_\mathcal{V}(r_2) = [\![\mathcal{V}]\!](t_2)$ $\mathrm{wt}_\mathcal{V}(r_3) = [\![\mathcal{V}]\!](t_3)$ $\mathrm{wt}_\mathcal{V}(r_4) = [\![\mathcal{V}]\!](t_4)$

      $= 113$ $= 69$ $= 69$ $= 5$

Fig. 4. Unique runs of $\mathcal{V}$ on the trees $t_1 = \sigma(\alpha, \alpha)$, $t_2 = \sigma(\alpha, \beta)$, $t_3 = \sigma(\beta, \alpha)$ and $t_4 = \sigma(\beta, \beta)$ from Example 16

Example 16 (running example). Recall the WTA $\mathcal{U}$ that resulted from the universality construction given in Example 5. We have $Q_\mathcal{U} = \{u_1, u_2, u_3, u_4\}$ and the following transitions for $x, y \in \{u_1, u_2\}$

$$\alpha \xrightarrow{5} u_1, \qquad \beta \xrightarrow{1} u_3, \qquad \sigma(u_3, x) \xrightarrow{23/5} u_4, \qquad \sigma(u_3, u_3) \xrightarrow{5} u_4,$$

$$\alpha \xrightarrow{5} u_2, \qquad\qquad\qquad\quad \sigma(x, u_3) \xrightarrow{23/5} u_4, \qquad \sigma(x, y) \xrightarrow{113/25} u_4,$$

as well as the root weight $\nu_\mathcal{U}(u_4) = 1$ and $\nu_\mathcal{U}(u_1) = \nu_\mathcal{U}(u_2) = \nu_\mathcal{U}(u_3) = 0$. Let us construct the WTA $\mathcal{V}$ resulting from processing

$$\mathcal{L}(u_4, \sigma) = \{(u_1, u_1), (u_1, u_2), (u_1, u_3),$$
$$(u_2, u_1), (u_2, u_2), (u_2, u_3), (u_3, u_1), (u_3, u_2), (u_3, u_3)\}.$$

In the following we will by abuse of notion talk about removing elements of $\mathcal{L}(u_4, \sigma)$, where in reality we are referring to the according transitions to u_4 via σ. As it has the first position in the list (u_1, u_1) is not removed by default. As $(u_1, u_2), (u_2, u_1), (u_2, u_2)$ are all respectively co-reachable with (u_1, u_1) via (α, α) we remove them. The tuple (u_1, u_3) is not removed because it is not co-reachable by (u_1, u_1); (u_2, u_3) is removed as it is co-reachable with (u_1, u_3) via (α, β); (u_3, u_1) is not removed because it is not co-reachable by neither (u_1, u_1) nor (u_1, u_3); (u_3, u_2) is removed as it is co-reachable with (u_3, u_1) via (β, α). Lastly (u_3, u_3) is not removed.

     Note that all transitions from u_2 to u_4, the only state with $\nu_\mathcal{U} \neq 0$ have been removed. This will result in u_2 being removed when trimming the WTA. The other lists $\mathcal{L}(u_1, \alpha) = \{(u_1)\}$, $\mathcal{L}(u_3, \beta) = \{(u_3)\}$ and $\mathcal{L}(\mathcal{U})$ contain only one element and will therefore not remove any more states. The WTA resulting from processing the list is unambiguous. Its unique runs are depicted in Fig. 4. One may verify that the weight for a given tree on $\mathcal{V}$ is equal to the weight on $\mathcal{T}$.

5   Conclusion

We have presented a uniformity construction that given a WTA $\mathcal{T}$ over a semiring S will output a WTA $\mathcal{U}$ that accepts the same trees and each of whose runs has the behaviour of $\mathcal{T}$ as its weight. We showed that the state space of $\mathcal{U}$ is finite in the cases where i) S is finite, ii) $\mathcal{T}$ is acyclic, or iii) S is the tropical or arctic semiring and $\mathcal{T}$ satisfies the twins property. Most notably though we attain finiteness in the case that S is the tropical or arctic semiring and $\mathcal{T}$ satisfies the weaker R-twins property. Furthermore we proved that by removing transitions from $\mathcal{U}$ in a specific manner we can derive an unambiguous WTA equivalent to $\mathcal{T}$, using arguments corresponding to those in [17].

We would like to conclude this paper by mentioning future research directions. Even though we did present sufficient conditions for the finiteness of the uniformity construction for all commonly used extremal semirings, we do believe a similar result can be shown for general extremal semirings. The proofs presented here will however not suffice for such an endeavour. Inspiration might be drawn from [13].

References

1. Aminof, B., Kupferman, O., Lampert, R.: Rigorous approximated determinization of weighted automata. Theoret. Comput. Sci. **480**, 104–117 (2013)
2. Béal, M.P., Carton, O.: Determinization of transducers over finite and infinite words. Theoret. Comput. Sci. **289**(1), 225–251 (2002)
3. Berstel, J., Reutenauer, C.: Rational Series and Their Languages. EATCS Monographs on Theoretical Computer Science, vol. 12. Springer, Heidelberg (1988)
4. Borchardt, B.: A pumping lemma and decidability problems for recognizable tree series. Acta Cybernet. **16**(4), 509–544 (2004)
5. Büchse, M., May, J., Vogler, H.: Determinization of weighted tree automata using factorizations. J. Autom. Lang. Comb. **15**(3/4), 229–254 (2010)
6. Choffrut, C.: Une Caracterisation des Fonctions Sequentielles et des Fonctions Sous-Sequentielles en tant que Relations Rationnelles. Theoret. Comput. Sci. **5**(3), 325–337 (1977). https://doi.org/10.1016/0304-3975(77)90049-4
7. Comon, H., et al.: Tree automata techniques and applications (2007)
8. Dörband, F., Feller, T., Stier, K.: Approximated determinisation of weighted tree automata. In: Leporati, A., Martín-Vide, C., Shapira, D., Zandron, C. (eds.) LATA 2021. LNCS, vol. 12638, pp. 255–266. Springer, Cham (2021). https://doi.org/10.1007/978-3-030-68195-1_20
9. Droste, M., Kuich, W., Vogler, H.: Handbook of Weighted Automata. Monographs in Theoretical Computer Science. An EATCS Series. Springer, Heidelberg (2009). https://doi.org/10.1007/978-3-642-01492-5
10. Fülöp, Z., Vogler, H.: Weighted tree automata and tree transducers. In: Handbook of Weighted Automata [9], chap. 9, pp. 313–403
11. Golan, J.S.: Semirings and Their Applications. Kluwer Academic, Dordrecht (1999)
12. Hebisch, U., Weinert, H.J.: Semirings-Algebraic Theory and Applications in Computer Science. World Scientific, Singapore (1998)
13. Kirsten, D., Mäurer, I.: On the determinization of weighted automata. J. Autom. Lang. Comb. **10**(2/3), 287–312 (2005)
14. Klimann, I., Lombardy, S., Mairesse, J., Prieur, C.: Deciding unambiguity and sequentiality from a finitely ambiguous max-plus automaton. Theoret. Comput. Sci. **327**(3), 349–373 (2004)
15. Krob, D.: The equality problem for rational series with multiplicities in the tropical semiring is undecidable. Internat. J. Algebra Comput. **4**(3), 405–425 (1994)
16. Mohri, M.: Finite-state transducers in language and speech processing. Comput. Linguist. **23**(2), 269–311 (1997)

17. Mohri, M., Riley, M.D.: A disambiguation algorithm for weighted automata. Theoret. Comput. Sci. **679**, 53–68 (2017)
18. Paul, E.: Expressiveness and decidability of weighted automata and weighted logics. Ph.D. thesis, University of Leipzig (2020)
19. Rabin, M.O., Scott, D.: Finite automata and their decision problems. IBM J. Res. Dev. **3**(2), 114–125 (1959)
20. Salomaa, A., Soittola, M.: Automata-Theoretic Aspects of Formal Power Series. Springer, New york (2012). https://doi.org/10.1007/978-1-4612-6264-0
21. Simon, I.: Limited subsets of a free monoid. In: Proceedings of the 19th Annual Symposium on Foundations of Computer Science, pp. 143–150. IEEE (1978)
22. Simon, I.: Recognizable sets with multiplicities in the tropical semiring. In: Chytil, M.P., Koubek, V., Janiga, L. (eds.) MFCS 1988. LNCS, vol. 324, pp. 107–120. Springer, Heidelberg (1988). https://doi.org/10.1007/BFb0017135

Image-Binary Automata

Stefan Kiefer and Cas Widdershoven[(✉)]

Department of Computer Science, University of Oxford, Oxford, UK
cas.widdershoven@seh.ox.ac.uk

Abstract. We introduce a certain restriction of weighted automata over the rationals, called *image-binary automata*. We show that such automata accept the regular languages, can be exponentially more succinct than corresponding NFAs, and allow for polynomial complementation, union, and intersection. This compares favourably with unambiguous automata whose complementation requires a superpolynomial state blowup. We also study an infinite-word version, *image-binary Büchi automata*. We show that such automata are amenable to probabilistic model checking, similarly to unambiguous Büchi automata. We provide algorithms to translate k-ambiguous Büchi automata to image-binary Büchi automata, leading to model-checking algorithms with optimal computational complexity.

1 Introduction

A weighted automaton assigns weights to words; i.e., it defines mappings of the form $f : \Sigma^* \to D$, where D is some domain of weights. Weighted automata are well-studied. Many variations have been discussed, such as max-plus automata [7] and probabilistic automata [21,22], both over finite words and over infinite words, in the latter case often combined with ω-valuation monoids [8]. However, it has been shown that many natural questions are undecidable for many kinds of weighted automata [1,9], including inclusion and equivalence. These problems become decidable for finitely ambiguous weighted automata [10].

In this paper we consider only numerical weights, where D is a subfield of the reals. A *language* $L \subseteq \Sigma^*$ can be identified with its characteristic function $\chi_L : \Sigma^* \to \{0,1\}$. We explore weighted automata that encode characteristic functions of languages, i.e., weighted automata that map each word either to 0 or to 1. We call such automata *image-binary finite automata (IFAs)* and view them as acceptors of languages $L \subseteq \Sigma^*$. We do not require, however, that individual transitions have weight 0 or 1. This makes IFAs a "semantic" class: it may not be obvious from the transition weights whether a given weighted automaton over, say, the rationals is image-binary. However, we will see that it can be checked efficiently whether a given $\mathbb{Q}$-weighted automaton is an IFA (Theorem 12).

An immediate question is on the expressive power of IFAs. Deterministic finite automata (DFAs) can be viewed as IFAs. On the other hand, in Sect. 2.2 we show that all languages accepted by IFAs are regular. It follows that IFAs accept exactly the regular languages. Moreover, IFAs are efficiently closed under

© IFIP International Federation for Information Processing 2021
Published by Springer International Publishing AG 2021. All Rights Reserved
Y.-S. Han and S.-K. Ko (Eds.): DCFS 2021, LNCS 13037, pp. 176–187, 2021.
https://doi.org/10.1007/978-3-030-93489-7_15

Boolean operations; i.e., given two IFAs that accept L_1, L_2, respectively, one can compute in polynomial time IFAs accepting $L_1 \cup L_2$, $L_1 \cap L_2$, and $\Sigma^* \setminus L_1$.

The latter feature, efficient closure under complement, might be viewed as a key advantage of IFAs over unambiguous finite automata (UFAs). UFAs are nondeterministic finite automata (NFAs) such that every word has either zero or one accepting runs. UFAs can be viewed as a special case of IFAs. Whereas we show that IFAs can be complemented in polynomial time, UFAs are known to be not polynomially closed under complement [23].

The next question is then on the succinctness of IFAs, and on the complexity of converting other types of finite automata to IFAs and vice versa. We study such questions in Sect. 2.4. In Sect. 2.5, we also study the relationship of IFAs to *mod-2 multiplicity automata*, which are weighted automata over $GF(2)$, the field $\{0, 1\}$ where $1 + 1 = 0$. Such automata [2] share various features with IFAs, in particular efficient closure under complement.

In the second part of the paper we put IFAs "to work". Specifically, we consider an infinite-word version, which we call *image-binary Büchi automata (IBAs)*. Following the theme that image-binary automata naturally generalise and relax unambiguous automata, we show that IBAs can be used for model checking Markov chains in essentially the same way as *unambiguous Büchi automata (UBAs)* [3]. Specifically, we show in Sect. 4 that given an IBA and a Markov chain, one can compute in NC (hence in polynomial time) the probability that a random word produced by the Markov chain is accepted by the IBA.

It was shown in [19] that a nondeterministic Büchi automaton (NBA) with n states can be converted to an NBA with at most 3^n states whose ambiguity is bounded by n. Known conversions from NBAs to UBAs have a state blowup of roughly n^n, see, e.g., [16]. We show in Sect. 3.2 that NBAs with logarithmic ambiguity (as produced by the construction from [19]) can be converted to IBAs in polylogarithmic space. This suggests that in order to translate NBAs into an automaton model suitable for probabilistic model checking (such as IBAs), it is reasonable to first employ the partial disambiguation procedure from [19] (which does most of the work). More specifically, by combining the partial disambiguation procedure from [19] with our translation to an IBA, we obtain a PSPACE transducer (i.e., a Turing machine whose work tape is polynomially bounded) that translates an NBA into an IBA. For example, combining that with the mentioned probabilistic model checking procedure for IBAs we obtain an (optimal) PSPACE procedure for model checking Markov chains against NBA specifications.

A full version of this paper including proofs and figures is available at [17].

2   Image-Binary Finite Automata

2.1   Definitions

Let $\mathbb{F}$ be one of the fields $\mathbb{Q}$ or $\mathbb{R}$ (with ordinary addition and multiplication). An $\mathbb{F}$-*weighted automaton* $\mathcal{A} = (Q, \Sigma, M, \alpha, \eta)$ consists of a set of states Q, a finite alphabet Σ, a map $M : \Sigma \to \mathbb{F}^{Q \times Q}$, an initial (row) vector $\alpha \in \mathbb{F}^Q$, and a final (column) vector $\eta \in \mathbb{F}^Q$. Extend M to Σ^* by setting $M(a_1 \cdots a_k) \overset{\text{def}}{=} M(a_1) \cdots M(a_k)$. The *language* L_A of an automaton A is the map $L_A : \Sigma^* \to \mathbb{F}$ with $L_A(w) = \alpha M(w) \eta$. Automata A, B over the same alphabet Σ are said to be *equivalent* if $L_A = L_B$.

Let $A = (Q, \Sigma, M, \alpha, \eta)$ be a $\mathbb{Q}$-weighted automaton. We call A an *image-binary (weighted) finite automaton (IFA)* if $L_A(\Sigma^*) \subseteq \{0,1\}$, i.e., $L_A(w) \in \{0,1\}$ holds for all $w \in \Sigma^*$. An $\mathbb{R}$-IFA is defined like an IFA, but with $\mathbb{Q}$ replaced by $\mathbb{R}$. An $(\mathbb{R})$-IFA A defines a language $L(A) := \{w \in \Sigma^* \mid L_A(w) = 1\}$. Note that we call both L_A and $L(A)$ the language of A; strictly speaking, the former is the characteristic function of the latter.

If an IFA $A = (Q, \Sigma, M, \alpha, \eta)$ is such that $\alpha \in \{0,1\}^Q$ and $\eta \in \{0,1\}^Q$ and $M(a) \in \{0,1\}^{Q \times Q}$ for all $a \in \Sigma$, then A is called an *unambiguous finite automaton (UFA)*. Note that this definition of a UFA is essentially equivalent to the classical one, which says that a UFA is an NFA (nondeterministic finite automaton) where each word has at most 1 accepting run. Similarly, a *deterministic finite automaton (DFA)* is essentially a special case of a UFA, and hence of an IFA.

Example 1. Figure 1 shows an IFA and a UFA in a graphical notation. Formally, the IFA on the left is $A = (Q_A, \Sigma, M_A, \alpha_A, \eta_A)$ with $Q = \{1, 2, 3\}$ and $\Sigma = \{a, b\}$ and

$$M_A(a) = \begin{pmatrix} -1 & 1 & 0 \\ 0 & 0 & 1 \\ 0 & 0 & 1 \end{pmatrix} \quad \text{and} \quad M_A(b) = \begin{pmatrix} 0 & 0 & 0 \\ 0 & 0 & 0 \\ 0 & 0 & 1 \end{pmatrix}$$

and $\alpha_A = \begin{pmatrix} 1 & 0 & 0 \end{pmatrix}$ and $\eta_A = \begin{pmatrix} 0 & 0 & 1 \end{pmatrix}^T$. Both automata recognise the language of words that start in an even (positive) number of as.

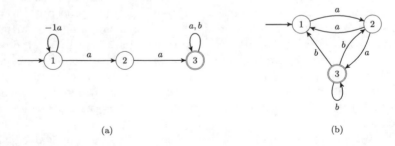

(a)   (b)

Fig. 1. The IFA in (a) is a forward conjugate of, and hence equivalent to, the UFA in (b). Unless indicated otherwise, edges in (a) have weight 1.

Let $A = (Q, \Sigma, M, \alpha, \eta)$ be an $\mathbb{R}$-weighted automaton. We call $\overrightarrow{A} := (\overrightarrow{Q}, \Sigma, \overrightarrow{M}, \overrightarrow{\alpha}, F\eta)$ a *forward conjugate* of A with base F if $F \in \mathbb{R}^{\overrightarrow{Q} \times Q}$ and

$FM(a) = \overrightarrow{M}(a)F$ for all $a \in \Sigma$ and $\alpha = \overrightarrow{\alpha}F$. Such $\mathcal{A}$ and $\overrightarrow{\mathcal{A}}$ are equivalent: indeed, let $w \in \Sigma^*$; by induction we have $FM(w) = \overrightarrow{M}(w)F$ and hence

$$L_{\mathcal{A}}(w) \;=\; \alpha M(w)\eta \;=\; \overrightarrow{\alpha}FM(w)\eta \;=\; \overrightarrow{\alpha}\,\overrightarrow{M}(w)F\eta \;=\; L_{\overrightarrow{\mathcal{A}}}(w).$$

A backward conjugate can be defined analogously.

Example 2. The IFA $\mathcal{A}$ on the left of Fig. 1 is a forward conjugate of the UFA on the right with base

$$F \;=\; \begin{pmatrix} 1 & 0 & 0 \\ 1 & 1 & 0 \\ 1 & 1 & 1 \end{pmatrix}.$$

Indeed, we have $\begin{pmatrix} 1 & 0 & 0 \end{pmatrix} F = \begin{pmatrix} 1 & 0 & 0 \end{pmatrix}$ and $\begin{pmatrix} 0 & 0 & 1 \end{pmatrix}^T = F \begin{pmatrix} 0 & 0 & 1 \end{pmatrix}^T$, where $\vec{v}^T$ denotes the transpose of a vector $\vec{v}$, and

$$F \begin{pmatrix} 0 & 1 & 0 \\ 1 & 0 & 1 \\ 0 & 0 & 0 \end{pmatrix} = \begin{pmatrix} 0 & 1 & 0 \\ 1 & 1 & 1 \\ 1 & 1 & 1 \end{pmatrix} = \begin{pmatrix} -1 & 1 & 0 \\ 0 & 0 & 1 \\ 0 & 0 & 1 \end{pmatrix} F \quad \text{and} \quad F \begin{pmatrix} 0 & 0 & 0 \\ 0 & 0 & 0 \\ 1 & 1 & 1 \end{pmatrix} = \begin{pmatrix} 0 & 0 & 0 \\ 0 & 0 & 0 \\ 0 & 0 & 1 \end{pmatrix} F.$$

For some proofs we need the following definition. Let $L : \Sigma^* \to \mathbb{F}$, where $\mathbb{F}$ is any field. Then the *Hankel matrix* of L is the infinite matrix $H_L \in \mathbb{F}^{\Sigma^* \times \Sigma^*}$ with $H_L[x, y] = L(xy)$. It was shown by Carlyle and Paz [5] and Fliess [11] that the rank of H_L is equal to the number of states of the minimal (in number of states) $\mathbb{F}$-weighted automaton $\mathcal{A}$ with $L_{\mathcal{A}} = L$.

Proposition 3 [5,11]. *Let L be an $\mathbb{F}$-weighted regular language, i.e. a function $L : \Sigma^* \to \mathbb{F}$ that can be represented by an $\mathbb{F}$-weighted automaton. Let $\mathcal{A} = (Q, \Sigma, M, \alpha, \eta)$ be a minimal $\mathbb{F}$-weighted automaton such that $L_{\mathcal{A}} = L$. Then $\operatorname{rank} H_L = |Q|$.*

2.2 Regularity

Since a DFA is an IFA, for each regular language there is an IFA that defines it. Conversely, we show that the language of an IFA is regular:

Theorem 4. *Let $\mathcal{A} = (Q, \Sigma, M, \alpha, \eta)$ be an $\mathbb{R}$-IFA. Then $L(\mathcal{A})$ is regular, and there is a DFA $\mathcal{B}$ with at most $2^{|Q|}$ states and $L(\mathcal{A}) = L(\mathcal{B})$.*

View $\mathbb{Z}_2 = \{0, 1\}$ as the field with two elements. In the proof of Theorem 4 we consider vector spaces *over* $\mathbb{Z}_2$, i.e., where the scalars are from $\mathbb{Z}_2$. In particular, we will argue with the vector space $\mathbb{Z}_2^{\mathbb{N}} \cong \mathbb{Z}_2^{\Sigma^*}$ over $\mathbb{Z}_2$. We first show:

Lemma 5. *Let V be a set of n vectors. Consider the vector space $\langle V \rangle$ spanned by V over $\mathbb{Z}_2$. Then $|\langle V \rangle| \le 2^n$.*

Proof. Let $V = \{v_1, \ldots, v_n\}$. Then $\langle V \rangle = \{\sum_{i=1}^n \lambda_i v_i \mid \lambda_i \in \mathbb{Z}_2\}$. □

Corollary 6. *Let V be a vector space over $\mathbb{Z}_2$. For any $n \in \mathbb{N}$, if $\dim V \le n$ then $|V| \le 2^n$.*

The following two lemmas show that if an $\mathbb{R}$-weighted automaton is image-binary, then the rank over $\mathbb{R}$ of its Hankel matrix H is at least the rank of H over $\mathbb{Z}_2$.

Lemma 7. *Let $V \subseteq \{0,1\}^{\mathbb{N}}$ be a set of vectors. If V is linearly dependent over $\mathbb{R}$ then V is linearly dependent over $\mathbb{Q}$. Hence $\dim\langle V \rangle_{\mathbb{Q}} \leq \dim\langle V \rangle_{\mathbb{R}}$.*

Lemma 8. *Let $V \subseteq \{0,1\}^{\mathbb{N}}$ be a set of vectors. If V is linearly dependent over $\mathbb{Q}$ then V is linearly dependent over $\mathbb{Z}_2$. Hence $\dim\langle V \rangle_{\mathbb{Z}_2} \leq \dim\langle V \rangle_{\mathbb{Q}}$.*

Hence we can prove Theorem 4:

Proof (Proof sketch of Theorem 4). By Proposition 3 and Lemma 7 and 8, the rank over $\mathbb{Z}_2$ of the Hankel matrix of $L_{\mathcal{A}}$ is at most $|Q|$. Hence, by Corollary 6 the Hankel matrix has at most $2^{|Q|}$ different rows and therefore there exists an equivalent DFA with $2^{|Q|}$ states. □

2.3   Boolean Operations and Checking Image-Binariness

IFAs are *polynomially closed* under all boolean operations, by which we mean:

Theorem 9. *Let $\mathcal{A}_1, \mathcal{A}_2$ be IFAs over Σ. One can compute in polynomial time IFAs $\mathcal{B}_{\neg}, \mathcal{B}_{\cap}, \mathcal{B}_{\cup}$ with $L(\mathcal{B}_{\neg}) = \Sigma^* \setminus L(\mathcal{A}_1)$ and $L(\mathcal{B}_{\cap}) = L(\mathcal{A}_1) \cap L(\mathcal{A}_2)$ and $L(\mathcal{B}_{\cup}) = L(\mathcal{A}_1) \cup L(\mathcal{A}_2)$.*

By De Morgan's laws it suffices to construct $\mathcal{B}_{\neg}$ and $\mathcal{B}_{\cap}$. Since $\mathcal{B}_{\neg}$ and $\mathcal{B}_{\cap}$ need to satisfy only $L_{\mathcal{B}_{\neg}} = 1 + (-L_{\mathcal{A}_1})$ (where $1 : \Sigma^* \to \{1\}$ denotes the constant 1 function) and $L_{\mathcal{B}_{\cap}} = L_{\mathcal{A}_1} \cdot L_{\mathcal{A}_2}$, it suffices to know that $\mathbb{Q}$-weighted automata are polynomially closed under negation and pointwise addition and multiplication:

Proposition 10 (see, e.g., [4, Chap. 1]). *Let $\mathcal{A}_1, \mathcal{A}_2$ be $\mathbb{Q}$-weighted automata. One can compute in polynomial time $\mathbb{Q}$-weighted automata $\mathcal{B}_{-}, \mathcal{B}_{+}, \mathcal{B}_{\times}$ with $L_{\mathcal{B}_{-}} = -L_{\mathcal{A}_1}$ and $L_{\mathcal{B}_{+}} = L_{\mathcal{A}_1} + L_{\mathcal{A}_2}$ and $L_{\mathcal{B}_{\times}} = L_{\mathcal{A}_1} \cdot L_{\mathcal{A}_2}$.*

While DFAs are also polynomially closed under complement (switch accepting and non-accepting states), NFAs and UFAs are not. For NFAs, it was shown in [13] that the (worst-case) blowup in the number n of states is $\Theta(2^n)$. For UFAs, it was shown recently:

Proposition 11 [23]. *For any $n \in \mathbb{N}$ there exists a unary (i.e., on an alphabet Σ with $|\Sigma| = 1$) UFA $\mathcal{A}_n$ with n states such that any NFA for the complement language has at least $n^{(\log\log\log n)^{\Theta(1)}}$ states.*

This super-polynomial blowup (even for unary alphabet and even if the output automaton is allowed to be ambiguous) refuted a conjecture that it may be possible to complement UFAs with a polynomial blowup [6]. An upper bound (for general alphabets and requiring the output to be a UFA) of $O(2^{0.79n})$ was shown in [15]; see also [14] for an (unpublished) improvement.

The authors believe Proposition 11 shows the strength of Theorem 9: while UFAs cannot be complemented efficiently, the more general IFAs are polynomially closed under all boolean operations.

Proposition 10 can be used to show:

Theorem 12. *Given a $\mathbb{Q}$-weighted automaton, one can check in polynomial time if it is an IFA.*

Proof. Let $\mathcal{A}$ be a $\mathbb{Q}$-weighted automaton. By Proposition 10 one can compute in polynomial time a $\mathbb{Q}$-weighted automaton $\mathcal{B}$ with $L_\mathcal{B} = L_\mathcal{A} \cdot L_\mathcal{A}$ (pointwise multiplication). Then $\mathcal{A}$ is an IFA if and only if $\mathcal{A}$ and $\mathcal{B}$ are equivalent. Equivalence of $\mathbb{Q}$-weighted automata can be checked in polynomial time, see [25, 26].   □

2.4 Succinctness

It is known that UFAs can be exponentially more succinct than DFAs: for each $n \in \mathbb{N}$ with $n \geq 3$ there is a UFA with n states such that the smallest equivalent DFA has 2^n states, see [18, Theorem 1]. Since UFAs are IFAs, Theorem 4 is optimal:

Corollary 13. *For converting IFAs to DFAs, a state blowup of 2^n is sufficient and necessary.*

It is also known from [18] that converting NFAs to UFAs can require $2^n - 1$ states. The argument carries over to IFAs:

Proposition 14. *For converting NFAs to IFAs, a state blowup of $\Theta(2^n)$ is sufficient and necessary.*

It follows from Theorem 9 and Proposition 11 that IFAs cannot be converted to NFAs in polynomial time:

Proposition 15. *Converting IFAs to NFAs requires a super-polynomial state blowup.*

2.5 Mod-2-Multiplicity Automata

We compare IFAs with the mod-2-multiplicity automata (mod-2-MAs) as introduced in [2], which are weighted automata over the field $\mathbb{Z}_2$. Given a mod-2-MA $\mathcal{A}$ and a word w, w is accepted iff $\mathcal{A}(w) = 1$. Like with IFAs, mod-2-MAs are exponentially more succinct than DFAs [2, Lemma 6]. Converting NFAs to mod-2-MAs requires a super-polynomial state blowup [2, Lemma 10] while (under the assumption that there are infinitely many Mersenne primes) converting mod-2-MAs to NFAs requires an exponential blowup [2, Lemma 11].

We can convert IFAs to mod-2-MAs without incurring a blowup:

Proposition 16. *For any IFA $\mathcal{A}$ with n states there exists a mod-2-MA $\mathcal{A}'$ of at most n states with $L_\mathcal{A} = L_{\mathcal{A}'}$.*

Proof. Let H be the Hankel matrix of $L_\mathcal{A}$. By Proposition 3, rank $H \leq n$, where the rank is taken over $\mathbb{R}$. Invoking Lemma 7 and Lemma 8 then shows that rank $H \leq n$ also when the rank is taken over $\mathbb{Z}_2$. Then by Proposition 3 there exists a mod-2-MA with rank $H \leq n$ (over $\mathbb{Z}_2$) states that accepts the same language as $\mathcal{A}$.   □

However, the converse requires an exponential blowup. Inspired by Angluin et al.'s [2] proof that mod-2 automata can be exponentially more succinct than NFAs, this proof makes use of shift register sequences. However, note that this proof does not require the assumption that there are infinitely many Mersenne primes. For further information on shift register sequences, see [12]. A *shift register sequence* of dimension d is an infinite periodic sequence $\{a_n\}$ of bits defined by initial conditions $a_i = b_i$ for $i = 0, \ldots, d-1$ and $b_i \in \{0,1\}$, and a linear recurrence

$$a_n = c_1 a_{n-1} + c_2 a_{n-2} + \ldots + c_d a_{n-d},$$

for all $n \geq d$, where each $c_i \in \{0,1\}$ and addition is done modulo 2. The *minimum period* of a periodic sequence $\{a_n\}$ is the lowest $p \in \mathbb{N}$ such that $a_n = a_{n \bmod p}$ for every n. The maximum possible minimum period of a shift register sequence is $2^d - 1$, and it is known that for each positive integer d there are shift register sequences of maximum period. These are known as *maximal length* or *pseudo-noise* sequences [12].

Given $d > 0$, let $a_n = c_1 a_{n-1} + c_2 a_{n-2} + \ldots + c_d a_{n-d}$ define a maximum period shift register sequence. Let L_d be the language over a unary alphabet $\{\#\}$ defined by $\#^n \in L_d$ if and only if $a_n = 1$. We have the following:

Proposition 17. *The language L_d is accepted by a mod-2-MA with d states, but not by any IFA with fewer than $2^d - 1$ states.*

3   Image-Binary Büchi Automata

3.1   Definitions

Let $\mathcal{A} = (Q, \Sigma, M, \alpha)$ be like in a weighted automaton over a field $\mathbb{F}$ and let F be a set of final states. We call $\mathcal{A}$ *ultimately stable* if for any $q, q' \in Q$ and $a \in \Sigma$ such that there exists a word w with $M(w)_{q',q} \neq 0$ (i.e., there is a path from q' to q over some word w), $M(a)_{q,q'} = 0$ or $M(a)_{q,q'} = 1$, meaning that any edges in a loop have weight 1. For any two sets A and B, let $A \cdot B$ denote the concatenation of elements in A and B, and let A^ω denote the set of infinite words over A. For any infinite word $w = w_0 w_1 \ldots$ we call $q_0 w_0 q_1 w_1 \ldots \in (Q \cdot \Sigma)^\omega$ a *path* over w if $\alpha(q_0) \neq 0$ and for all i, $M(w_i)_{q_i, q_{i+1}} \neq 0$. We call $q_0 w_0 q_1 w_1 \ldots$ a *final path* if $infinite(q_0 w_0 q_1 w_2 \ldots) \cap F \neq \emptyset$, where $infinite(q_0 w_0 q_1 w_2 \ldots)$ denotes the set of states in Q that occur infinitely often in the path. We will write $FinalPaths_{\mathcal{A}}(w)$ to denote the set of final paths of an automaton $\mathcal{A}$ over a word w.

It is clear that for any path $q_0 w_0 q_1 w_1 \ldots$ there exists an i such that for any $j \geq i$, q_j lies on a loop, and therefore we can define the weight of the path $q_0 w_0 q_1 w_1 \ldots$ to be $\lim_{i \to \infty} \prod_{n \leq i} M(w_n)_{q_n, q_{n+1}}$, denoted by $weight(q_0 w_0 q_1 w_1 \ldots)$. For any word w with finitely many final paths, we define the weight of w to be the sum of the weights of the final paths over w, denoted by $L_{\mathcal{A}}(w)$. We call $\mathcal{A} = (Q, \Sigma, M, \alpha, F)$ an *image-binary (weighted) Büchi automaton (IBA)* if it is ultimately stable, there exists a bound $N \in \mathbb{N}$ such that $|FinalPaths_{\mathcal{A}}(w)| \leq N$ for any word w, and $L_{\mathcal{A}}(\Sigma^\omega) \subseteq \{0,1\}$, i.e. for all $w \in \Sigma^\omega$, $L_{\mathcal{A}}(w) \in \{0,1\}$.

If an IBA $\mathcal{A}$ is such that $\alpha \in \{0,1\}^Q$ and $M(a) \in \{0,1\}^{Q \times Q}$ for all $a \in \Sigma$, then $\mathcal{A}$ is called an *unambiguous Büchi automaton (UBA)*. Similarly to the finite word case, we note that this definition of a UBA is essentially equivalent to the classical one, which says that a UBA is an NBA (nondeterministic Büchi automaton) where each word has at most 1 final path. We also see that a *deterministic Büchi automaton (DBA)* essentially is a special case of a UBA, and hence of an IBA.

We will use the following notation: given a finite sequence $a = a_1 a_2 \ldots a_n$, we will write $last(a)$ to denote a_n. Given a (possibly finite) sequence $a = a_1 a_2 \ldots$ and a character a_0 we will write $a_0 \cdot a$ to denote the concatenation $a_0 a_1 a_2 \ldots$. We will write $\mathbb{B}$ to denote the two element set $\{\bot, \top\}$ and for any set S we will write $\mathcal{P}^{\leq k}(S)$ to denote the set $\{S' \subseteq S \mid |S'| \leq k\}$.

3.2   IBAs and k-Ambiguous NBAs

In this section we introduce k-ambiguous NBAs (k-ABAs) and show that they can be exponentially more concise than IBAs. We give a procedure to translate a k-ABA into an equivalent IBA using a PSPACE transducer.

A non-deterministic Büchi automaton (NBA) is a tuple $(Q, \Sigma, \delta, Q_0, F)$ where Q is a state set, Σ is an alphabet, $\delta : Q \times \Sigma \to Q$ is a transition relation, $Q_0 \subseteq Q$ is a set of initial states, and F is a set of final states. For any infinite word $w = w_0 w_1 \ldots$ we call $q_0 w_0 q_1 w_1 \ldots \in (Q \cdot \Sigma)^\omega$ a *path* over w if $q_0 \in Q_0$ and for all i, $q_{i+1} \in \delta(q_i, w_i)$. We call $q_0 w_0 q_1 w_1 \ldots$ a *final path* if $infinite(q_0 w_0 q_1 w_2 \ldots) \cap F \neq \emptyset$, where $infinite(q_0 w_0 q_1 w_2 \ldots)$ denotes the set of states in Q that occur infinitely often in the path. We will write $FinalPaths_\mathcal{A}(w)$ to denote the set of final paths of an automaton $\mathcal{A}$ over a word w. The *language* of an NBA is the set of those words w such that $FinalPaths_\mathcal{A}(w) \neq \emptyset$. A k-ABA is an NBA such that for every word w, $|FinalPaths_\mathcal{A}(w)| \leq k$. For the rest of the section, fix a k-ambiguous NBA $\mathcal{A}_k = (Q, \Sigma, \delta, Q_0, F)$.

We have that k-ABAs can be exponentially more succinct than equivalent IBAs:

Lemma 18. *Let $\mathcal{A}$ be a k-ABA with n states. The minimal IBA accepting the same language as $\mathcal{A}$ may require at least 2^n states, even if $k = n$.*

The rest of this section will be dedicated to converting k-ABAs to equivalent IBAs, resulting in an IBA with at most a singly exponential state set size blowup.

Let R be the set of final runs of $\mathcal{A}_k$ over a word w. By the binomial theorem, $(1 + x)^n = \sum_{i=0}^n \binom{n}{i} x^i$, and hence, setting $x = -1$, $1 = 1 - \sum_{i=0}^n (-1)^i \binom{n}{i} = 1 - (-1)^0 \binom{n}{0} - \sum_{i=1}^n (-1)^i \binom{n}{i} = \sum_{i=1}^n (-1)^{i-1} \binom{n}{i}$. Hence, for any set S, $\sum_{S' \in \mathcal{P}(S) \setminus \{\emptyset\}} (-1)^{|S'|-1} = \sum_{i=1}^{|S|} (-1)^{i-1} \binom{|S|}{i} = 1$. We can design an (infinite state) IBA $\mathcal{A}'_k = (Q', \Sigma, \Delta', \alpha, F')$ where final paths correspond to subsets of R, and where for each $R' \subseteq R$, the final path corresponding to R' has weight $(-1)^{|R'|-1}$. This IBA is given as follows:

– $Q' = \mathcal{P}^{\leq k}(Q^* \times \mathbb{B}) \setminus \{\emptyset\}$,
– $\alpha_P = (-1)^{|P|-1}$ for each $P \in \mathcal{P}(Q_0 \times \{\bot\}) \setminus \{\emptyset\}$ and $\alpha_P = 0$ otherwise,
– $F' = \mathcal{P}(Q^* \times \{\top\})$, and
– for any $P \in Q'$, let $b'' = \bot$ if for all $(r,b) \in P$, $b = \top$, and let $b'' = \top$ otherwise. Let P' be such that:
  • For any $(r,b) \in P$, there exists $(r',b') \in P'$ and $q \in \delta(last(r),a)$ such that $r' = r \cdot q$ and $b' = ((last(r) \in F) \vee b) \wedge b''$, and
  • For any $(r',b') \in P'$, there exists $(r,b) \in P$ and $q \in \delta(last(r),a)$ such that $r' = r \cdot q$ and $b' = ((last(r) \in F) \vee b) \wedge b''$.
  Then $\Delta(a)_{P,P'} = (-1)^{|P'|-|P|}$. For any other P', $\Delta(a)_{P,P'} = 0$.

Intuitively, the bit b in a (r,b)-tuple flips to true every time r reaches a final state, and back to false every time all the prefixes have reached a final state. This ensures that every sequence of prefixes in a final path of $\mathcal{A}'_k$ visits final states infinitely often. This technique mirrors for instance Safra's construction [24].

Lemma 19. $\mathcal{A}'_k$ *is an infinite-state IBA equivalent to* $\mathcal{A}_k$.

We will construct a finite IBA called the k-disambiguation of $\mathcal{A}_k$ based on $\mathcal{A}'_k$ that accepts the same language as $\mathcal{A}_k$.

Let $\pi_{last} : Q' \to [k]^{Q \times \mathbb{B}}$ be defined as $\pi_{last}(P)_{q,b} = |\{(r,b) \in P \mid last(r) = q\}|$. We extend π_{last} over finite and infinite sequences of elements of Q' in the natural way, $\pi_{last}(P_1 P_2 \ldots) = \pi_{last}(P_1) \cdot \pi_{last}(P_2 \ldots)$.

Lemma 20. *Let* $\rho = \rho_1 \rho_2 \ldots \in (Q')^{\omega}$ *be a path of* $\mathcal{A}'_k$ *over a word* w *and let* $\rho'_1 \rho'_2 \ldots = \pi_{last}(\rho)$. *Then* $\rho_1 \rho_2 \ldots$ *is final if and only if for infinitely* i, $(\rho'_i)_{q,\bot} = 0$ *for all* $q \in Q$.

Runs in our k-disambiguation will be sequences in $([k]^{Q \times \mathbb{B}})^{\omega}$ such that there exist runs in $\mathcal{A}'_k$ that map to that sequence. However, there is generally not a one-to-one correspondence between sequences over $[k]^{Q \times \mathbb{B}}$ and runs in $\mathcal{A}'_k$.

Fix any $\vec{r}, \vec{r'} \in [k]^{Q \times \mathbb{B}}$ and $a \in \Sigma$. Let P be any state in Q' such that $\pi_{last}(P) = \vec{r}$. As it turns out, the number of states P' with $\pi_{last}(P') = \vec{r'}$ where P' is an a-successor of P does not depend on P. We call this number $w(\vec{r}, a, \vec{r'})$.

Lemma 21. *The number* $w(\vec{r}, a, \vec{r'})$ *is unique and at most exponential in* k.

We define the IBA k-dis$'(\mathcal{A}_k) = (Q'', \Sigma, \Delta'', \alpha', F'')$ where:

– $Q'' = ([k]^{Q \times \mathbb{B}}) \setminus \{\vec{0}\}$,
– $\Delta''(a)_{\vec{r},\vec{r'}} = (-1)^{\left(\sum_i (\vec{r'})_i - (\vec{r})_i\right)} w(\vec{r}, a, \vec{r'})$
– $\alpha'_{\vec{r}} = (-1)^{\left(\sum_i v_i\right)-1}$ for every $\vec{r}$ with:
  • $\vec{r}_{q,b} = 0$ if $q \notin Q_0$ or $b = \top$, and
  • $\vec{r}_{q,b} \leq 1$ otherwise.
  $\alpha'_{\vec{r}} = 0$ otherwise.
– $F'' = \{\vec{r} \in Q'' \mid \forall (q, \bot) \in Q'' : \vec{r}_{q,\bot} = 0\}$.

The IBA k-dis$(\mathcal{A}_k)$ (the k-disambiguation of $\mathcal{A}_k$) is then defined as k-dis$'(\mathcal{A}_k)$ restricted to those reachable states in Q'' that can reach a loop over a final state. This trimness condition helps the proofs later on, but could be omitted.

For a state $\vec{r} \in Q''$ we will write $size(\vec{r}) = \sum_{(q,b)} \vec{r}_{q,b}$ to denote the size of $\vec{r}$. The weights in k-dis$(\mathcal{A}_k)$ count the number of equivalent runs in $\mathcal{A}'_k$, where two runs $\rho, \rho' \in (Q')^\omega$ are equivalent if $\pi_{last}(\rho) = \pi_{last}(\rho')$:

Lemma 22. *Let $\rho \in (Q'')^\omega$ be a run in k-dis$(\mathcal{A}_k)$ over a word w. Let R be the set of those runs ρ' in $\mathcal{A}'_k$ over w such that $\pi_{last}(\rho') = \rho$, and let $n = \max_i \sum_{(q,b)} (\rho_i)_{q,b}$ be the maximum size of states of ρ. Then $weight(\rho) = (-1)^{n-1}|R|$.*

Since by Lemma 20, a run ρ in k-dis$(\mathcal{A}_k)$ is final whenever any run ρ' in $\mathcal{A}'_k$ with $\pi_{last}(\rho') - \rho$ is, this means $L_{k\text{-dis}(\mathcal{A}_k)} = L_{\mathcal{A}'_k}$. This proves the final result:

Theorem 23. k-dis$(\mathcal{A}_k)$ *is an IBA that accepts the same language as $\mathcal{A}_k$.*

Theorem 24. *Given a k-ambiguous automaton $\mathcal{A}_k$ with n states, the disambiguation k-dis$(\mathcal{A}_k)$ has at most k^{2n} states. Moreover, k-dis$(\mathcal{A}_k)$ can be calculated using a PSPACE transducer.*

Proof (sketch). The size of k-dis$(\mathcal{A}_k)$ follows from its definition. Note that k is at most singly exponential in $|Q|$, which follows from for instance [27, Theorem 2.1]. Hence, we only incur a single exponential blowup. Apart from $w(\vec{r}, a, \vec{r'})$ it is therefore obvious k-dis$(\mathcal{A}_k)$ can be calculated using a PSPACE transducer. Calculating $w(\vec{r}, a, \vec{r'})$ in PSPACE requires a combinatorial argument presented in the full version of this paper [17]. □

By Lemma 18, we have an $O(2^n)$ lower bound even if $k = n$. From Theorem 24 we already have a $2^{O(n \log n)}$ upper bound, leaving only a small gap.

When the ambiguity is comparatively low, we can do even better:

Theorem 25. *Given a k-ambiguous automaton $\mathcal{A}_k$ with n states where $k = O(\log n)$, the disambiguation k-dis$(\mathcal{A}_k)$ has at most $(2n)^{O(\log n)}$ states. Moreover, k-dis$(\mathcal{A}_k)$ can be calculated using a POLYLOGSPACE transducer.*

4   Model Checking IBA

In this section we will consider the problem of model checking IBAs against Markov chains. A *Markov chain* (MC) is a pair (S, M) where S is the finite state set, and $M \in [0, 1]^{S \times S}$ is a stochastic matrix specifying transition probabilities. Given an initial distribution ι, an MC $\mathcal{M}$ induces a probability measure $\Pr_\iota^\mathcal{M}$ over infinite words. The model checking question asks, what is the probability of the language accepted by an IBA?

We show that model checking IBAs against MCs can be done in NC using a modified procedure for model checking UBAs from [3]. The algorithm is described in the full version of this paper [17], in this section we discuss its implications. This is the main theorem:

Theorem 26. *Let $\mathcal{M}$ be an MC and let $\mathcal{A}$ be an IBA. The probability that a random word sampled from $\mathcal{M}$ is in $L_\mathcal{A}$ can be computed in NC.*

Corollary 27. *Let $\mathcal{M}$ be an MC and let $\mathcal{A}_k$ be a k-ABA with n states, where $k = O(\log n)$. The probability that a random word sampled from $\mathcal{M}$ is in $L_\mathcal{A}$ can be computed in POLYLOGSPACE.*

Proof. This combines Theorem 25 and 26. Since NC is contained in POLY-LOGSPACE [20], this proves the corollary.   □

Model checking k-ABAs is PSPACE-hard [17], we get PSPACE-completeness by converting k-ABAs into IBAs and model checking.

Theorem 28. *The model checking problem for k-ABAs is PSPACE-complete.*

Corollary 29. *Let $\mathcal{M}$ be an MC and let $\mathcal{A}$ be an NBA with n states. The probability that a word in $L_\mathcal{A}$ is accepted by $\mathcal{M}$ can be computed in PSPACE.*

Proof. By Löding et al. [19], $\mathcal{A}$ can be converted in a k-ABA $\mathcal{A}_k$ with at most 3^n states where $k = n$. Hence, using Corollary 27, we can calculate $\Pr(L_{\mathcal{A}_k}) = \Pr(L_\mathcal{A})$ in POLYLOG(2^n) = POLY(n) space.   □

Acknowledgements. Mathieu Kubik, Tomasz Ponitka, and Joao Paulo Costalonga contributed ideas to the proofs of Lemmas 8, 7, and [17, Lemma 25], respectively.

References

1. Almagor, S., Boker, U., Kupferman, O.: What's decidable about weighted automata? In: Bultan, T., Hsiung, P.-A. (eds.) ATVA 2011. LNCS, vol. 6996, pp. 482–491. Springer, Heidelberg (2011). https://doi.org/10.1007/978-3-642-24372-1_37
2. Angluin, D., Antonopoulos, T., Fisman, D.: Strongly unambiguous Büchi automata are polynomially predictable with membership queries. In: 28th EACSL Annual Conference on Computer Science Logic (CSL 2020) (2020)
3. Baier, C., Kiefer, S., Klein, J., Klüppelholz, S., Müller, D., Worrell, J.: Markov chains and unambiguous Büchi automata (extended version of a CAV'16 paper). arXiv:1605.00950 (2016), http://arxiv.org/abs/1605.00950
4. Berstel, J., Reutenauer, C.: Rational Series and Their Languages. Springer, Heidelberg (1988)
5. Carlyle, J.W., Paz, A.: Realizations by stochastic finite automata. J. Comput. Syst. Sci. 5(1), 26–40 (1971)
6. Colcombet, T.: Unambiguity in automata theory. In: 17th International Workshop on Descriptional Complexity of Formal Systems (DCFS) (2015)
7. Droste, M., Kuich, W., Vogler, H.: Handbook of Weighted Automata, 1st edn. Springer, Berlin (2009). https://doi.org/10.1007/978-3-642-01492-5
8. Droste, M., Meinecke, I.: Weighted automata and regular expressions over valuation monoids. Int. J. Found. Comput. Sci. 22(08), 1829–1844 (2011)
9. Fijalkow, N.: Undecidability results for probabilistic automata. ACM SIGLOG News 4(4), 10–17 (2017)

10. Filiot, E., Gentilini, R., Raskin, J.F.: Finite-valued weighted automata. In: 34th International Conference on Foundation of Software Technology and Theoretical Computer Science (FSTTCS 2014) (2014)
11. Fliess, M.: Matrices de Hankel. J. Math. Pures Appl. **53**, 197–222 (1974)
12. Golomb, S.W., Goldstein, R.M., Hales, A.W., Welch, L.R.: Shift Register Sequences. Holden-Day Series in Information Systems, Holden-Day, San Francisco (1967)
13. Holzer, M., Kutrib, M.: Nondeterministic descriptional complexity of regular languages. Int. J. Found. Comput. Sci. **14**, 1087–1102 (2003)
14. Indzhev, E., Kiefer, S.: On complementing unambiguous automata and graphs with many cliques and cocliques. arXiv preprint arXiv:2105.07470 (2021)
15. Jirásek, J., Jirásková, G., Sebej, J.: Operations on unambiguous finite automata. Int. J. Found. Comput. Sci. **29**(5), 861–876 (2018)
16. Karmarkar, H., Joglekar, M., Chakraborty, S.: Improved upper and lower bounds for Büchi disambiguation. In: Proceedings of the Automated Technology for Verification and Analysis - 11th International Symposium, ATVA 2013 (2013)
17. Kiefer, S., Widdershoven, C.: Image-binary automata (extended version of a DCFS'21 paper). arXiv:2109.01049 (2021), http://arxiv.org/abs/2109.01049
18. Leung, H.: Descriptional complexity of NFA of different ambiguity. Int. J. Found. Comput. Sci. **16**(5), 975–984 (2005)
19. Löding, C., Pirogov, A.: On finitely ambiguous Büchi automata. In: International Conference on Developments in Language Theory, LNCS, pp. 503–515. Springer, Cham (2018). https://doi.org/10.1007/978-3-319-09698-8
20. Papadimitriou, C.M.: Computational Complexity. Addison-Wesley, Reading (1994)
21. Paz, A.: Introduction to Probabilistic Automata. Academic Press, New York (2014)
22. Rabin, M.O.: Probabilistic automata. Inf. Control **6**(3), 230–245 (1963)
23. Raskin, M.: A superpolynomial lower bound for the size of non-deterministic complement of an unambiguous automaton. In: 45th International Colloquium on Automata, Languages, and Programming (ICALP 2018) (2018)
24. Safra, S.: On the complexity of omega-automata. In: Proceedings of the 27th Annual IEEE Symposium on Logic in Computer Science, pp. 319–327 (1988)
25. Schützenberger, M.: On the definition of a family of automata. Inf. Control **4**(2), 245–270 (1961)
26. Tzeng, W.G.: On path equivalence of nondeterministic finite automata. Inf. Process. Lett. **58**(1), 43–46 (1996)
27. Weber, A., Seidl, H.: On the degree of ambiguity of finite automata. Theoret. Comput. Sci. **88**(2), 325–349 (1991)

Improved Constructions for Succinct Affine Automata

Abuzer Yakaryılmaz[1,2,3(✉)] (iD)

[1] Center for Quantum Computer Science, University of Latvia, Rīga, Latvia
abuzer@lu.lv
[2] QWorld Association, Tallinn, Estonia
https://qworld.net
[3] Department of Mathematics and Statistics, University of Turku, Turku, Finland

Abstract. Affine finite automata (AfAs) can be more succinct than probabilistic and quantum finite automata when recognizing some regular languages with bounded error. In this paper, we improve previously known succinct AFA constructions in three ways. First, we replace some of the fixed error bounds with arbitrarily small error bounds. Second, we present new constructions by using fewer states than the previous constructions. Third, we show that any language recognized by a nondeterministic finite automaton (NFA) is also recognized by bounded-error AfAs having one more state, and so, AfAs inherit all succinct results by NFAs. As a special case, we also show that any language recognized by an NFA is recognized by AfAs with zero error if the number of accepting path(s) for each member is the same number.

Keywords: Succinctness · State complexity · Affine automata · Quantum automata · Probabilistic automata · Linear systems · Bounded error · One-sided error · Zero error

1 Introduction

Probabilistic finite automaton (PFA) [19,20] is a linear system implementing non-negative transitions by preserving ℓ_1-norm where a probabilistic state is represented as a non-negative real-valued column vector with entry summation 1. Similarly, quantum finite automaton (QFA) [4,21] is also a linear system but it implements complex-valued transitions by preserving ℓ_2-norm where a (pure) quantum state is represented as a complex-valued vector with length 1. Implementing both positive and negative valued transitions creates interference and so some transitions may disappear, which brings certain computational advantages to QFAs over PFAs, e.g., bounded-error QFAs can be exponentially more succinct than bounded-error PFAs [1], or nondeterministic QFAs are more powerful than nondeterministic finite automata (NFAs) [25].

One may ask whether it is possible to use interference[1] classically. The idea of using negative transition values for classical systems dates back to sixties.

---

[1] We refer the reader to [8] for certain discussions about interference with historical remarks.

ⓒ IFIP International Federation for Information Processing 2021
Published by Springer International Publishing AG 2021. All Rights Reserved
Y.-S. Han and S.-K. Ko (Eds.): DCFS 2021, LNCS 13037, pp. 188–199, 2021.
https://doi.org/10.1007/978-3-030-93489-7_16

Turakainen [22] defined generalized automaton (GA) as a linear system implementing real-valued transitions without any restrictions. The language recognition by GAs are defined based on cutpoints (and they were shown to be equivalent to PFAs), and bounded-error language recognition has never been considered.

After reading the whole input, the final state of a GA is represented as a column vector with real-valued entries. To calculate the accepting value, this vector is multiplied with a pre-defined real-valued row vector (with the same dimension). In other words, each state contributes to the accepting value by a real-valued weight:

$$f_G(x) = w \cdot v_f = (w_1 \quad w_2 \quad \cdots \quad w_n) \cdot \begin{pmatrix} \alpha_1 \\ \alpha_2 \\ \vdots \\ \alpha_n \end{pmatrix} = \sum_{i=1}^{n} w_i \cdot \alpha_i,$$

where G is the GA, x is the input, $f_G(x)$ is the accepting value of G on x, w is the pre-defined weights, and v_f is the final state. Remark that for PFAs, w contains only 0s and 1s, where 1s are corresponding to the accepting states.

In the above, $f_G(x)$ is in $\mathbb{R}$. On the other hand, an accepting probability is in $[0, 1]$. One way to observe each state with some probabilities when in v_f (similar to PFAs and QFAs) is making a normalization with respect to ℓ_1-norm. For QFAs, some measurement operators are applied to the quantum state, and then, the different outcomes are observed with some probabilities. In the classical case, we define an operator called weighting [6], which produces the outcomes with probabilities based on their normalized values in ℓ_1. Here we should remark that, contrary to quantum measurement operators, weighting is a non-linear operator.

Affine finite automaton (AfA) is a new and quantum-like generalization of PFA which evolves linearly followed by a non-linear weighting operator [6]. An affine state can have arbitrary real numbers but the summation of them must be 1 similar to the probabilistic state. The computational power of AfAs and their generalizations have been examined and compared with their probabilistic and quantum counterparts in a series of papers [5,9–14,18,23,24].

The classes of languages recognized by PFAs and QFAs with bounded error (resp., cutpoints) are identical: regular languages (resp., stochastic languages) [16,17,20,27]. AfAs with bounded error (resp., cutpoints) can recognize some nonregular (resp., non-stochastic) languages [6]. In the nondeterministic language recognition mode (a member (resp., non-member) string is accepted with nonzero (resp., zero) probability), QFAs and AfAs have the same computational power [6], and PFAs are weaker, i.e., PFAs can be seen as nondeterministic finite automata (NFAs), and so they recognize exactly regular languages; and, the class of languages recognized by nondeterministic QFAs (or AfAs) is a superset of regular languages called exclusive stochastic languages [19,25].

Regarding the state complexity, the gap between deterministic finite automata (DFAs) and bounded-error PFAs or between bounded-error PFAs and bounded-error QFAs can be at most exponential [1,2,4]. On the other hand, the gap between bounded-error QFAs and bounded-error AfAs is super-exponential

[5,13,24]. A super-exponential gap is possible between DFAs and bounded-error PFAs or between bounded-error PFAs and bounded-error QFAs but on promise problems [3,7].

In this paper, we improve previously known succinct AFA constructions in three ways. In the next section, we give the definitions and notations used throughout the paper. In Sect. 3, we quickly review the simulations by AfAs that we use in our proofs. In Sect. 4, we give our constructions for three-state AfAs. In Sect. 5, we present our results on NFAs.

2   Preliminaries

We assume the reader familiar with the basics of automata theory. Throughout the paper, we use the following notations. For a given matrix A, $A[i,j]$ is its entry at the i-th row and j-th column; and, for a given vector v, $v[i]$ is its i-th entry and $\zeta(v)$ is the summation of all entries. We denote the input alphabet as Σ not including ¢ (the left end-marker) and \$ (the right end-marker), and we denote $\Sigma \cup \{$¢$, $\$$\}$ as $\tilde{\Sigma}$. For a given input $x \in \Sigma$, $\tilde{x}$ denotes ¢x\$. For a given string x, $|x|$ is its length; for a numeric value α, $|\alpha|$ is the absolute value of α; and, for an n-dimensional vector v, $|v|$ is ℓ_1-norm of v, which is $|v| = v[1] + \cdots + v[n]$. For a non-empty string x, $x[i]$ denotes its i-th symbol, where $1 \leq i \leq |x|$. For an automaton M and input string x, $f_M(x)$ is the accepting probability of M on x.

An affine state is a real-valued column vector with entry summation 1. An affine operator is a real-valued square matrix where each column is an affine state. If we use only non-negative values, then an affine state is a probabilistic state (also called stochastic vector) and an affine operator is a probabilistic operator (also called stochastic matrix).

An n-state affine finite automaton (AfA)[2] M is a 5-tuple

$$M = (S, \Sigma, \{A_\sigma \mid \sigma \in \tilde{\Sigma}\}, s_I, S_a),$$

where

- $S = \{s_1, \ldots, s_n\}$ is the set of states,
- A_σ is the affine operator when reading symbol $\sigma \in \tilde{\Sigma}$,
- $s_I \in S$ is the initial state, and
- $S_a \subseteq S$ is the set of accepting state(s).

Let $x \in \Sigma^*$ be the input with length m. The automaton M starts in affine state v_0, which is the elementary basis e_I in $\mathbb{R}^n$. It uses the end-markers for pre- and post-processing.[3] If x is the empty string, then the final state is $v_f = A_\$ A_¢ v_0$. Otherwise, the final state is calculated as

$$v_f = A_\$ A_{x[m]} A_{x[m-1]} \cdots A_{x[1]} A_¢ v_0.$$

---

[2] We use lowercase "f" to differentiate AfAs from PFAs or QFAs due to its non-linear behavior.

[3] See [11] for the details about using end-markers and generalized versions of AfAs.

The input is accept with probability $f_M(x) = \frac{\sum_{s_i \in S_a} |v_f[i]|}{|v_f|}$.

If we use only non-negative transition values, then we obtain a probabilistic finite automaton (PFA). If we use only 0s and 1s, then we obtain a deterministic finite automaton (DFA).

A language $L \subseteq \Sigma^*$ is said to be recognized by an automaton M with error bound $\epsilon < \frac{1}{2}$ if (i) for each $x \in L$, $f_M(x) \geq 1 - \epsilon$ and (ii) for each $x \notin L$, $f_M(x) \leq \epsilon$.

A language $L \subseteq \Sigma^*$ is said to be recognized by an automaton M with positive one-sided error bound $\epsilon < 1$ if (i) for each $x \in L$, $f_M(x) \geq 1 - \epsilon$ and (ii) for each $x \notin L$, $f_M(x) = 0$.

A language $L \subseteq \Sigma^*$ is said to be recognized by an automaton M with negative one-sided error bound $\epsilon < 1$ if (i) for each $x \in L$, $f_M(x) = 1$ and (ii) for each $x \notin L$, $f_M(x) < \epsilon$.

When $\epsilon = 0$, then it is called zero error.

We call an automaton ((positive/negative) one-sided) bounded-error if it recognizes its language in the specified error mode for some error bounds.

3   Simulations

We review the basic simulations by AfAs. We start with a generic case.

3.1   A Sequence of Matrix-Vector Multiplication

Let v_0 be a real-valued n-dimensional column vector and let $A_1, \ldots, A_k$ be some $(n \times n)$-dimensional real-valued linear operators. We define affine vector v_0' and affine operator A_i' $(1 \leq i \leq k)$ as

$$v_0' = \left(\begin{array}{c} v_0[1] \\ \vdots \\ v_0[n] \\ \hline 1 - \zeta(v_0) \end{array} \right) \quad \text{and} \quad A_i' = \left(\begin{array}{ccc|c} c_1[0] & \cdots & c_n[0] & 0 \\ \vdots & \ddots & \vdots & \vdots \\ c_1[n] & \cdots & c_n[n] & 0 \\ \hline 1 - \zeta(c_1) & \cdots & 1 - \zeta(c_n) & 1 \end{array} \right),$$

where c_j is the j-th column of A_i $(1 \leq j \leq n)$. Then, for $v_f = A_k A_{k-1} \cdots A_1 v_0$, we have

$$v_f' = A_k' A_{k-1}' \cdots A_1' v_0' = \left(\begin{array}{c} v_f[1] \\ \vdots \\ v_f[n] \\ \hline 1 - \zeta(v_f) \end{array} \right).$$

3.2   Trivial Case for PFAs

It is trivial that any n-state PFA is an n-state AfA. So, PFAs and DFAs cannot be more succinct than bounded-error AfAs.

3.3   Rational Exclusive Stochastic Languages

Let L be a language defined by an n-state rational-valued PFA P with an exclusive cutpoint $\lambda \in [0,1]$, i.e.,

$$L = \{w \mid f_P(w) \neq \lambda\}.$$

Based on the simulation given in Sect. 3.1, it was shown [24] that L is recognized by an $(n+1)$-state integer-valued AfA as follows:

- each $x \in L$ is accepted by the AfA with probability no less than $\frac{1}{3}$, and,
- each $x \notin L$ is accepted by the AfA with zero probability.

3.4   Exact Simulation of QFAs

The computation of any given n-state QFA can be simulated by an (n^2+1)-state AfA [24]. The computation of a QFA on any input is linear. By tensoring the state vector and transition matrices with themselves, the probabilities can be directly accessed on the state vectors. Each complex number can be represented by two real numbers, but the tensoring vectors have some redundancy and so n^2-dimensional real-valued vectors can be obtained from n-dimensional quantum state. The rest of the proof is due to Sect. 3.1. If the QFA is real-valued, we still do not know any better bound.

Bounded-error QFAs may be quadratically more succinct than bounded-error AfAs, but it is open whether QFAs can be more succinct than AfAs or whether any n-state QFA can be simulated by an $\Theta(n)$-state or $o(n)$-state AfAs.

4   Three-State AfAs

In this section, we give our improved constructions of 3-state AfAs for some unary languages.

We start with the well-known counting problem: $\text{COUNT}_{\text{m}} = \{a^m\}$ for $m \geq 0$. It was shown [24] that the language COUNT_{m} is recognized by a 2-state AfA with (negative) one-sided error bound $\frac{1}{3}$. We decrease the error bound arbitrarily by using one more state.

Theorem 1. *The language* COUNT_{m} *is recognized by a 3-state AfA with (negative) one-sided error bound* $\frac{1}{2t+1}$ *for every* $t \in \mathbb{Z}^+$.

Proof. The affine states are s_1, s_2, and s_3, where s_1 is the initial and only accepting state. The initial affine state is $v_0 = (1 \ \ 0 \ \ 0)^T$. After reading ¢, the affine state is set to

$$v_1 = \begin{pmatrix} 1 \\ m \\ -m \end{pmatrix} = \begin{pmatrix} 1 & 0 & 0 \\ m & 1 & 0 \\ -m & 0 & 1 \end{pmatrix} \begin{pmatrix} 1 \\ 0 \\ 0 \end{pmatrix}.$$

For each symbol a, the value of e_2 (resp., e_3) is decreased (resp., increased) by 1 by using the following operator

$$A_a = \begin{pmatrix} 1 & 0 & 0 \\ -1 & 1 & 0 \\ 1 & 0 & 1 \end{pmatrix}, \text{ i.e., } \begin{pmatrix} 1 \\ i-1 \\ 1-i \end{pmatrix} = \begin{pmatrix} 1 & 0 & 0 \\ -1 & 1 & 0 \\ 1 & 0 & 1 \end{pmatrix} \begin{pmatrix} 1 \\ i \\ -i \end{pmatrix}.$$

Let l be the length of the input. Then, the affine state before reading \$ is

$$v_{l+1} = \begin{pmatrix} 1 \\ m-l \\ l-m \end{pmatrix}.$$

After reading \$ symbol, the values of e_2 and e_3 are multiplied by t:

$$v_f = \begin{pmatrix} 1 \\ t(m-l) \\ t(l-m) \end{pmatrix} = \begin{pmatrix} 1 & 1-t & 1-t \\ 0 & t & 0 \\ 0 & 0 & t \end{pmatrix} \begin{pmatrix} 1 \\ m-l \\ l-m \end{pmatrix}.$$

If $l = m$, then $v_f = v_0$ and the input is accepted with probability 1. Otherwise, $|m - l| \geq 1$, and so, the accepting probability is at most $\dfrac{1}{2t+1}$.   □

The number of states required by bounded-error PFAs and QFAs recognizing $\mathtt{COUNT_m}$ increases with m as the state gap between DFAs and PFAs (or QFAs) can be at most exponential [4,20] and DFAs require at least $m + 2$ states to recognize it. Similar to AfAs, two-way QFAs can recognize $\mathtt{COUNT_m}$ with a few states but in polynomial expected time in m [26].

We will continue with the language $\mathtt{MOD}_p = \{a^{j \cdot p} \mid j \in \mathbb{N}\}$ for every prime number p. This language is recognized by QFAs with $O(\log p)$ states and bounded-error PFAs require at least p states [1]. Previously, the bound for AfA was given by using the simulation given in Sect. 3.4 [24]. Here, we show that we can indeed use only 3 states.

Theorem 2. *The language* $\mathtt{MOD}_p$ *is recognized by a 3-state AfA with (negative) one-sided error bound* $\dfrac{\cot(\pi/p)}{t}$ *for every* $t > 1$.

Proof. We use the single qubit algorithm given for this problem [1]. By help of one more state, we will trace the computation by affine states, which also helps us to decrease the accepting probability arbitrarily for the non-members.

Let $\{s_1, s_2, s_3\}$ be our states and s_1 be the only accepting state. Let $\theta = \frac{2\pi}{p}$ be our rotation angle. We start in affine state $v_0 = (1 \ 0 \ 0)^T$ and we apply the identity operator when reading symbol ¢. Then, for each symbol a, we apply the following operator that implements the counter-clockwise rotation with angle θ on the unit circle by using $s1$ and s_2:

$$A_a = \begin{pmatrix} \cos\theta & -\sin\theta & 0 \\ \sin\theta & \cos\theta & 0 \\ \hline \alpha_1 & \alpha_2 & 1 \end{pmatrix},$$

where $\alpha_1 = 1 - \cos\theta - \sin\theta$ and $\alpha_2 = 1 + \sin\theta - \cos\theta$.

Let l be the length of input. Before reading $\$$ symbol, the affine state is

$$v_{l+1} = \begin{pmatrix} \cos(l\theta) \\ \sin(l\theta) \\ 1 - \cos(l\theta) - \sin(l\theta) \end{pmatrix}$$

After reading $\$$ symbol, the final affine state is set to

$$v_f = \begin{pmatrix} \cos(l\theta) \\ t\sin(l\theta) \\ 1 - \cos(l\theta) - t\sin(l\theta) \end{pmatrix} = \begin{pmatrix} 1 & 0 & 0 \\ 0 & t & 0 \\ 0 & 1-t & 1 \end{pmatrix} \begin{pmatrix} \cos(l\theta) \\ \sin(l\theta) \\ 1 - \cos(l\theta) - \sin(l\theta) \end{pmatrix}.$$

For members, $v_f = v_0$ and so the input is accepted with probability 1. For non-members, the ratio

$$\frac{|\cos(l\theta)|}{|\sin(l\theta)|} \geq \frac{\cos(\frac{\pi}{p})}{\sin(\frac{\pi}{p})} = \cot(\frac{\pi}{p}),$$

where the bound is obtained when

$$l \equiv \frac{p-1}{2} \mod p \quad \text{or} \quad l \equiv \frac{p+1}{2} \mod p,$$

i.e., the rotating vector is at its closest points to the x-axis. Thus, the accepting probability is less than $\dfrac{\cot(\pi/p)}{t}$. □

We close this section with a promise problem given in [3]: For any $k \in \mathbb{Z}^+$,

$$\text{MOD2}^k = (\text{OMOD2}^k, \text{1MOD2}^k),$$

where $\text{OMOD2}^k = \{a^{j \cdot 2^k} \mid j \equiv 0 \mod 2\}$ and $\text{1MOD2}^k = \{a^{j \cdot 2^k} \mid j \equiv 1 \mod 2\}$. This promise problem is solved by 2-state QFAs with zero error [3], and different types of classical automata require 2^{k+1} states to solve it [7].

By using the simulation in Sect. 3.4, it was given in [24] that 5-state AfA can solve this problem with zero error. We believe that 2-state AfAs cannot solve this problem with zero/bounded error, i.e., preserving the summation of affine states may require one extra auxiliary state. Here we give a 3-state AfAs with zero error.

Theorem 3. *For a given* $k \in \mathbb{Z}^+$, *the promise problem* MOD2^k *is solved by a 3-state AfA with zero error.*

Proof. The 2-state QFA algorithm uses a rotation with angle $\dfrac{\pi}{2^{k+1}}$ on the unit circle [3]:

$$\begin{pmatrix} 1 \\ 0 \end{pmatrix} \xrightarrow{2^k \ symbols} \begin{pmatrix} 0 \\ 1 \end{pmatrix} \xrightarrow{2^k \ symbols} \begin{pmatrix} -1 \\ 0 \end{pmatrix} \xrightarrow{2^k \ symbols} \begin{pmatrix} 0 \\ -1 \end{pmatrix} \xrightarrow{2^k \ symbols} \begin{pmatrix} 1 \\ 0 \end{pmatrix}.$$

Thus, the outcomes alternates between the states "0" or "1" for each block of 2^k symbols. Remark that the measurement results for $\begin{pmatrix} 1 \\ 0 \end{pmatrix}$ and $\begin{pmatrix} -1 \\ 0 \end{pmatrix}$ are the same. But, if we use the simulation given in Sect. 3.1, the affine states for members of $\texttt{0MOD2}^k$ will be

$$\begin{pmatrix} 1 \\ 0 \\ 0 \end{pmatrix} \quad \text{and} \quad \begin{pmatrix} -1 \\ 0 \\ 2 \end{pmatrix},$$

which are different from each other.

Instead of the rotating with angle $\dfrac{\pi}{2^{k+1}}$, we use a rotation with angle $\dfrac{\pi}{2^k}$. Then, we will have the following cycle:

$$\begin{pmatrix} 1 \\ 0 \end{pmatrix} \xrightarrow{\; 2^k \; symbols \;} \begin{pmatrix} -1 \\ 0 \end{pmatrix} \xrightarrow{\; 2^k \; symbols \;} \begin{pmatrix} 1 \\ 0 \end{pmatrix} \xrightarrow{\; 2^k \; symbols \;} \begin{pmatrix} -1 \\ 0 \end{pmatrix}.$$

Quantumly, we visit two states having the same statistics (i.e., they are identical and no measurement can separate them.). But, they are different vectors. Now, we use the simulation given in Sect. 3.1, and so we have the following affine states before reading \$ symbol for the members of $\texttt{0MOD2}^k$ and for the members of $\texttt{1MOD2}^k$

$$\begin{pmatrix} 1 \\ 0 \\ 0 \end{pmatrix} \quad \text{and} \quad \begin{pmatrix} -1 \\ 0 \\ 2 \end{pmatrix},$$

respectively. After reading \$ symbol, we half the value of s_3 and add the other half to the value of s_1 (such trick was used before in [18]). Then, these two affine states becomes

$$\begin{pmatrix} 1 \\ 0 \\ 0 \end{pmatrix} \quad \text{and} \quad \begin{pmatrix} 0 \\ 0 \\ 1 \end{pmatrix},$$

respectively. We make s_1 the only the accepting state, and so two different cases can be separated with zero error. $\square$

5   Simulating NFAs

When the cutpoint is picked as 0, then the given PFA in Sect. 3.3 turns out to be a NFA, where each non-zero probabilistic transition corresponds to a non-deterministic choice (transition). Thus, any succinctness result for NFAs can be obtained for AfAs having one more state with one-sided error bound $\frac{2}{3}$. (To obtain a better error bound, we can tensor a few copies of the same automaton, which increases the number of states polynomially.)

Here, we present a pedagogically easier construction and more importantly with arbitrarily small error bounds without increasing the previous state bound. We also show that if the number of accepting path(s) are the same (e.g., one) for each member, then the error is zero.

An NFA does not use end-markers but use ε-transition(s). By using the left end-marker, all ε-transition(s) without reading any symbol at the beginning of computation can be replaced with the transitions defined for the left end-marker. All other ε-transition(s) can also be removed by defining new transitions (without using any extra states). When using the right end-marker, NFAs may save at most one state, since any NFA using the right end-marker can be simulated by a NFA without using the right end-marker by using one extra state: each transition going to an accepting state when reading the right end-marker goes to this new state, which will be the single accepting state.

We represent the computation of an n-state NFA, say N, on a given input $x \in \Sigma^*$ linearly, where $|x| = l$ and $n > 1$. We assume that N does not have any ε-transitions and it uses the left end-marker. We use integer-valued vectors to represent the states of N and zero-one matrices to represent the transitions of N.

We assume that the set of states of N is $S = \{s_1, \ldots, s_n\}$ and s_1 is the initial state. Let $S_a \subseteq S$ be the set of accepting state(s). The vector $v_0 = (1 \ 0 \ \cdots \ 0)^T$ represents the initial "nondeterministic" state. For each symbol $\sigma \in \Sigma \cup \{¢\}$, we define the "nondeterministic" operator A_σ where $A_\sigma[j, i]$ is 1 if there is a transition from s_i to s_j when reading symbol σ, and it is 0, otherwise. Thus, the final nondeterministic state of N on x can be calculated as

$$v_{l+1} = A_{x[l]} \cdots A_{x[1]} A_¢ v_0.$$

Here v_{l+1} contains non-negative integers. A nice property of this presentation is that the value for s_i represents the number of nondeterministic path(s) ending in s_i at the end. Remark that some paths may be terminated before, which will not be counted on v_{l+1}.

By using the construction in Sect. 3.1, we can design an $(n+1)$-state AfA M such that its affine state before reading the right end-marker is

$$v'_{l+1} = \begin{pmatrix} v_l[1] \\ \vdots \\ v_l[n] \\ \hline 1 - \zeta(v_l) \end{pmatrix}.$$

Let $\alpha = \sum_{s_i \in S_a} v_l[i]$, i.e., the summation of all entries corresponding to the accepting state(s) of N. The AfA M maps v'_{l+1} to

$$v'_f = \begin{pmatrix} t\alpha \\ -t\alpha \\ 1 \\ 0 \\ \vdots \\ 0 \end{pmatrix}$$

after reading the right end-marker for $t \in \mathbb{Z}^+$. The operator for $ has zeros everywhere except the following entries: the third row is full of 1s and, for each $s_i \in S_a$, the $(1, i)$-th entry is t and the $(2, i)$-th entry is $-t$.

The accepting states of M are $\{s_1, s_2\}$. If $x \in L$, then α is a positive integer and so x is accepted with probability no less than $\dfrac{2t}{2t+1}$, which means that the error can be at most $\dfrac{1}{2t+1}$. If $x \notin L$, then $\alpha = 0$ and so it is accepted with probability 0.

Theorem 4. *Let L be a language recognized by an n-state NFA, where $n > 1$. Then, L is also recognized by an $(n+1)$-state AfA with arbitrarily small (positive) one-sided error bound.*

Suppose that the NFA has a single accepting path for each member. Then, α is 1 for the members and it is 0 for the non-members. Thus, we can design a zero-error AfA by setting the final affine state as

$$v_f' = \begin{pmatrix} \alpha \\ 0 \\ 1 - \alpha \\ 0 \\ \vdots \\ 0 \end{pmatrix}$$

after reading the right end-marker. The operator for $ has zeros everywhere except the following entries: for the single accepting state, say s_i, the $(1, i)$-th entry is 1 and the third row is full of 1s except the i-th column, which is 0. It is easy to see that the accepting probability is 1 (resp., 0) for each member (resp., non-member).

Theorem 5. *Let L be a language recognized by an n-state NFA such that each member is accepted on exactly one nondeterministic path, where $n > 1$. Then, L is also recognized by an $(n + 1)$-state AfA with zero error.*

Corollary 1. *Let L be a language recognized by an n-state NFA such that each member is accepted on exactly $k > 1$ nondeterministic paths, where $n > 1$. Then, L is also recognized by an $(n + 1)$-state AfA with zero error.*

Proof. The only modification in the above proof is on the final state as

$$v_f' = \begin{pmatrix} \dfrac{\alpha}{k} \\ 0 \\ 1 - \dfrac{\alpha}{k} \\ 0 \\ \vdots \\ 0 \end{pmatrix}$$

since $\dfrac{\alpha}{k}$ is 1 for the members, and 0, otherwise. The operator for $ has zeros everywhere except the following entries: the first row has $\frac{1}{k}$ in the entries for the accepting states, and the third row has respectively 1 and $1 - \frac{1}{k}$ in the entries for non-accepting and accepting states.   □

Remark that zero-error PFAs and QFAs cannot be more succinct than DFAs [15]. Thus, zero-error AfAs can be exponentially more succinct than zero-error PFAs and QFAs due to the following witness languages.

The language MODXOR_k [13] is formed by the strings

$$\{0,1\}^t x_1 \{0,1\}^{2k-1} x_2 \{0,1\}^{2k-1} \cdots x_m \{0,1\}^{2k-1},$$

where $t < 2k, m > 0$, each $x_i \in \{0,1\}$ for $1 \le i \le m$, and $\bigoplus_{i=1}^m x_i = 1$. It was shown [13] that MODXOR_k for $k > 0$ is recognized by a $(2k+1)$-state AfA with zero error. Due to Theorem 5, the same results can also be obtained by designing a $2k$-state NFA, which accepts each member on a single path.

Compared to MODXOR_k, the language $\text{END}_n = \{0,1\}^* 1 \{0,1\}^{n-1}$ is much simpler, and we know that it is recognized by an $(n+1)$-state NFA, which accepts each member on a single path, and any DFA (and so any zero-error QFA) requires at least 2^n states.

Corollary 2. *The language* END_n *is recognized by an* $(n+2)$-*state AfA with zero error.*

Acknowledgements. Yakaryılmaz was partially supported by the ERDF project Nr. 1.1.1.5/19/A/005 "Quantum computers with constant memory".

We thank anonymous reviewers for their helpful corrections and suggestions.

References

1. Ambainis, A., Freivalds, R.: 1-way quantum finite automata: strengths, weaknesses and generalizations. In: FOCS'98, pp. 332–341. IEEE (1998)
2. Ambainis, A.: The complexity of probabilistic versus deterministic finite automata. In: Asano, T., Igarashi, Y., Nagamochi, H., Miyano, S., Suri, S. (eds.) ISAAC 1996. LNCS, vol. 1178, pp. 233–238. Springer, Heidelberg (1996). https://doi.org/10.1007/BFb0009499
3. Ambainis, A., Yakaryılmaz, A.: Superiority of exact quantum automata for promise problems. Inf. Process. Lett. **112**(7), 289–291 (2012)
4. Ambainis, A., Yakaryılmaz, A.: Automata and quantum computing. In: Éric Pin, J. (ed.) Handbook of Automata Theory, vol. 2, chap. 39, pp. 1457–1493. European Mathematical Society Publishing House (2021)
5. Belovs, A., Montoya, J.A., Yakaryılmaz, A.: On a conjecture by Christian Choffrut. Int. J. Found. Comput. Sci. **28**(5), 483–502 (2017)
6. Díaz-Caro, A., Yakaryılmaz, A.: Affine Computation and Affine Automaton. In: Kulikov, A.S., Woeginger, G.J. (eds.) CSR 2016. LNCS, vol. 9691, pp. 146–160. Springer, Cham (2016). https://doi.org/10.1007/978-3-319-34171-2_11
7. Geffert, V., Yakaryılmaz, A.: Classical automata on promise problems. Discrete Math. Theoret. Comput. Sci. **17**(2), 157–180 (2015)
8. Hirvensalo, M.: Interference as a computational resource: a tutorial. Nat. Comput. **17**(1), 201–219 (2017). https://doi.org/10.1007/s11047-017-9654-x

9. Hirvensalo, M., Moutot, E., Yakaryılmaz, A.: On the Computational power of affine automata. In: Drewes, F., Martín-Vide, C., Truthe, B. (eds.) LATA 2017. LNCS, vol. 10168, pp. 405–417. Springer, Cham (2017). https://doi.org/10.1007/978-3-319-53733-7_30

10. Hirvensalo, M., Moutot, E., Yakaryılmaz, A.: Computational Limitations of Affine Automata. In: McQuillan, I., Seki, S. (eds.) UCNC 2019. LNCS, vol. 11493, pp. 108–121. Springer, Cham (2019). https://doi.org/10.1007/978-3-030-19311-9_10

11. Hirvensalo, M., Moutot, E., Yakaryılmaz, A.: computational limitations of affine automata and generalized affine automata. Nat. Comput. **20**(1), 1–12 (2021). https://doi.org/10.1007/s11047-020-09815-1

12. Ibrahimov, R., Khadiev, K., Prūsis, K., Yakaryılmaz, A.: Error-Free Affine, Unitary, and Probabilistic OBDDs. In: Konstantinidis, S., Pighizzini, G. (eds.) DCFS 2018. LNCS, vol. 10952, pp. 175–187. Springer, Cham (2018). https://doi.org/10.1007/978-3-319-94631-3_15

13. Ibrahimov, R., Khadiev, K., Prūsis, K., Yakaryılmaz, A.: Error-free affine, unitary, and probabilistic OBDDs. Int. J. Found. Comput. Sci. (2021). https://doi.org/10.1142/S0129054121500246

14. Khadieva, A., Yakaryılmaz, A.: Affine automata verifiers. In: Kostitsyna, I., Orponen, P. (eds.) UCNC 2021. LNCS, vol. 12984, pp. 84–100. Springer, Cham (2021)

15. Klauck, H.: On quantum and probabilistic communication: Las Vegas and one-way protocols. In: STOC'00: Proceedings of the Thirty-Second Annual ACM Symposium on Theory of Computing, pp. 644–651 (2000)

16. Kondacs, A., Watrous, J.: On the power of quantum finite state automata. In: FOCS 1997, pp. 66–75 (1997)

17. Li, L., Qiu, D., Zou, X., Li, L., Wu, L., Mateus, P.: Characterizations of one-way general quantum finite automata. Theoret. Comput. Sci. **419**, 73–91 (2012)

18. Nakanishi, M., Khadiev, K., Prūsis, K., Vihrovs, J., Yakaryılmaz, A.: Exact affine counter automata. In: 15th International Conference on Automata and Formal Languages. EPTCS, vol. 252, pp. 205–218 (2017). arXiv:1703.04281

19. Paz, A.: Introduction to Probabilistic Automata. Academic Press, New York (1971)

20. Rabin, M.O.: Probabilistic automata. Inf. Control **6**, 230–243 (1963)

21. Say, A.C.C., Yakaryılmaz, A.: Quantum finite automata: a modern introduction. In: Calude, C.S., Freivalds, R., Kazuo, I. (eds.) Computing with New Resources. LNCS, vol. 8808, pp. 208–222. Springer, Cham (2014). https://doi.org/10.1007/978-3-319-13350-8_16

22. Turakainen, P.: Generalized automata and stochastic languages. Proc. Am. Math. Soc. **21**, 303–309 (1969)

23. Villagra, M., Yakaryılmaz, A.: Language recognition power and succinctness of affine automata. In: Amos, M., Condon, A. (eds.) UCNC 2016. LNCS, vol. 9726, pp. 116–129. Springer, Cham (2016). https://doi.org/10.1007/978-3-319-41312-9_10

24. Villagra, M., Yakaryılmaz, A.: Language recognition power and succinctness of affine automata. Nat. Comput. **17**(2), 283–293 (2017). https://doi.org/10.1007/s11047-017-9652-z

25. Yakaryılmaz, A., Say, A.C.C.: Languages recognized by nondeterministic quantum finite automata. Quant. Inf. Comput. **10**(9 & 10), 747–770 (2010)

26. Yakaryılmaz, A., Say, A.C.C.: Succinctness of two-way probabilistic and quantum finite automata. Discrete Math. Theoret. Comput. Sci. **12**(2), 19–40 (2010)

27. Yakaryılmaz, A., Say, A.C.C.: Unbounded-error quantum computation with small space bounds. Inf. Comput. **279**(6), 873–892 (2011)

Author Index

Printed in the United States
by Baker & Taylor Publisher Services